A HISTORY OF THE WORLD

Toward Modernity

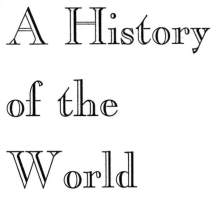

A History
of the
World

Volume II
TOWARD MODERNITY

EDITORS:
JOHN A. GARRATY
PETER GAY

 HARPER & ROW, PUBLISHERS

NEW YORK, EVANSTON, SAN FRANCISCO, LONDON

Cover map is Gerardus Mercator's Double Cordiform Map of the World, 1538. From original in Lenox Collection, Rare Book Division, The New York Public Library, Astor, Lenox and Tilden Foundation.

Maps by Harry Scott

A HISTORY OF THE WORLD: TOWARD MODERNITY. Copyright © 1972 by Harper & Row, Publishers, Inc. All rights reserved. Printed in the United States of America. No part of this book may be used or reproduced in any manner whatsoever without written permission except in the case of brief quotations embodied in critical articles and reviews. This book first appeared as a portion of THE COLUMBIA HISTORY OF THE WORLD, copyright © 1972 by Harper & Row, Publishers, Inc., published simultaneously in Canada by Fitzhenry & Whiteside Limited, Toronto. For information address Harper & Row, Publishers, Inc., 49 East 33rd Street, New York, N.Y. 10016.

FIRST EDITION

STANDARD BOOK NUMBER: 06-042255-6

LIBRARY OF CONGRESS CATALOG CARD NUMBER: 72-75674

Contents

The Enlightenment

Europe: The Great Powers

Revolution in the Western World

Maps

Introduction

We live in the Age of World History, and as ages go, ours is relatively young. Until the fifteenth century, the many cultures of this earth developed in comparative isolation, their boundaries breached only by occasional traders, by border warfare, and by spectacular mass migrations, such as the "barbarian" invasion of the Roman Empire in the early centuries of the Christian Era. But after Columbus and Cortez had awakened the people of Western Europe to the possibilities, their appetite for converts, profits, and fame was thoroughly aroused and Western civilization was introduced, mainly by force, over nearly all the globe. Equipped with an unappeasable urge to expand and with superior weapons, conquerors made the rest of the world into an unwilling appendage of the great European powers; Africa, Asia, and the Americas became sources of raw materials, markets, objects of scientific curiosity, and places for the permanent settlement of Europeans. The peoples of these continents were, in short, the victims of a ruthless, unrelenting exploitation.

But then came the scientific and technological revolutions of modern times, which, in transforming the Western world, also transformed its non-Western dependencies. We are now witnessing two simultaneous, only apparently contradictory developments. World civilization is becoming more uniform, as the West imposes its techniques and its ideas. And the dependent nations are breaking away from the domination of the West, using these very Western techniques and ideas to establish their separate identities, and find their places in the councils of power. Isolation has become impossible; ancient empires like China and the newly self-conscious nations of Africa alike involve the whole world in their activities. Thus both the traditional division between Western and non-Western history and the patronizing assumption that non-Western is a kind of footnote to Western history have become obsolete. This, as we have said, is the Age of World History. It is therefore supremely the age *for* world history.

The difficulty with most currently available world history textbooks is that they look at this enormous, multifaceted subject from the present backward and from the perspective of Western society. Recognizing that the world is no longer a congeries of unrelated nations and civilizations, the authors of such books pay lip service to a global conception of history, but more often than not they actually write about the development of Western civilization and discuss other civilizations only as and when they influenced or were influenced by "the West." Typically they trace history from its "roots" in Mesopotamia and Egypt through Greece and Rome and medieval Europe and on to the present, and only begin to pay serious attention to Asia, Africa, and other regions when Western civilization came "in contact" with the cultures of these areas. When they do treat non-Western civilizations as separate entities, they usually attach the material to the main narrative without either relating it to the rest or concerning themselves with the continuity of the histories of these "exotic" societies.

Our approach has been quite different. We have tried to examine human development as it might be studied by a visitor from outer space and also to write our history in a truly chronological way—looking at the whole globe and all its civilizations at each stage of development. Of course we devote far more space to human history than to the remote eons during which the universe and our planet evolved, and more to recent centuries than to ancient times. Generally speaking, the closer our account approaches the present, the more detailed and extensive it becomes. Similarly we devote more space to the history of the West than to other civilizations. We do so partly because more is known about recent times and about the West, and partly because we (and our readers) are modern Westerners. To take an obvious example, we use throughout the Western calendar, dating events backward and forward from the birth of Christ. No other system would be intelligible. Nevertheless, we are writing world history, not merely a history of how the rest of the world has affected us, or we it. Our book is meant to be equally relevant to anyone who can read English, without regard for "race, creed, or national origin." And while it is also designed to be read as a whole, the separate histories of all major civilizations can be followed from their origins on without loss of continuity. Volume I commences with the still-unsolved mystery of the origin of the universe and proceeds through the evolution of the earth and of life and of the human animal to the earliest civilizations. It carries the story down to about 1500 A.D. Volume II treats the emergence of the modern world in the 16th, 17th, and 18th centuries. Volume III attempts (the task becomes increasingly difficult!) to describe the development and interactions of the societies of the world in the last 200-odd years.

World history conceived of in this manner is difficult to write under any circumstances. Surely no individual possesses the factual knowledge or has the "feel" that comes only from deep and prolonged study of a period or culture that are necessary if one is to describe and evaluate all history and all cultures authoritatively. We have dealt with this problem by assembling a group of experts (forty in number), thus bringing together their special knowledge and insights in a collaborative enterprise. Naturally a history of the world written by forty specialists presents other problems that would not arise in a work by a single author; it runs the risk of becoming a mere collection of encyclopedia articles, held together only by the covers in which the parts are bound. Aware from the beginning of this danger, we sought to surmount it in several ways. First our historians and other experts all know one another personally. Throughout the writing, we were in frequent contact and could repeatedly consult, debate, compare, and criticize in order to fuse our several efforts into a unified intellectual construct. This process went on at each stage of the book's development, over a period of more than five years.

Consider our first and most crucial tasks: the preparation of an outline and the allocation of space to various regions and periods of time. How should the history of the early civilization of India be related to that of Egypt and China or, for that matter, of Mexico and Peru? How many chapters should the history of Africa occupy as compared with that of South America or Eastern Europe? As editors—one a historian of the United States, the other of Western Europe—we knew that any answer we could devise for such questions would be inadequate and surely distorted. We therefore asked our specialists to tell us how they proposed to organize their material and how much space they needed, bearing in mind the ultimate limitation imposed by our decision to produce a work of roughly half a million words. Using draft outlines prepared by the contributors, and consulting with them at every stage, we eventually worked out the structure of our history.

The collaborative effort did not, however, end at this point. Whenever appropriate our authors consulted with one another in order to avoid repetition and omission, and they read and criticized their colleagues' manuscripts in all cases where they had special knowledge, and in many—out of friendship or curiosity—where they did not. Many of the following chapters bring together the writing of two and even three authorities, yet it is our belief that the parts of such chapters fit together as smoothly and as logically as those produced by a single mind.

Finally, our contributors have generously allowed us a remarkable latitude in organizing and editing their manuscripts. Given our common commitment to the production of an integrated synthesis of world history, all conceded that a more-than-ordinary editorial license was essential. Our object as editors has been to try to impose a basic uniformity of approach, to supply connecting passages and cross-references, and to alter the individual prose styles of the authors (without too great artistic loss, we hope) in the interest of creating the illusion not that we two have written what follows, but that all of us have written it all. It goes without saying, however, that each author has remained the ultimate arbiter of the facts and opinions in his own sections. Each has carefully read and corrected our "final" version.

Our original thought in planning and writing this book was that it was to be aimed at the so-called general reader. Only when the project was well under way did we realize that it might also serve as a text in world history courses. In retrospect, we believe that our original "oversight" was a fortunate one. If we had planned to write a conventional textbook we might have crowded our pages with too many dates, with the names of too many kings and battles and the like, and thus have lost the forest in the trees. Our assumption that our "general reader" would be impatient with enormous masses of detail led us to focus instead on the meaning of events and their broad influences, upon whole civilizations and their patterns of development, upon the shape of world history rather than the billions of discrete facts from which that shape emerges. And of course this is exactly what a world history textbook should also do. Perhaps students can be compelled to learn the names and dates of all the kings of England, and the terms of every major treaty that the many nations of the world have negotiated with one another over the centuries—although we doubt it. More important, they should not be asked to do so. Such matters are part of the history of the world it is true, but they do not help much in making *world history* meaningful. Our book is crowded with facts, but our facts have been chosen to explicate the whole, not simply as ends in themselves.

Consider the matter this way. To answer the question "What is man?" one does not put a slice of human tissue under a microscope, however necessary microscopic study may be in seeking the answer to many questions about man. Similarly, to answer our question, which essentially is "How has mankind fared on this earth?" one must view the history of mankind in its widest outlines. On the other hand, the reader's understanding of world history can and should be greatly increased by the study of selected parts of the whole in greater detail. We assume that instructors will want their students to delve more deeply at many points as they proceed with the subject. Thus, at the end of each chapter we have listed the best available special works on the topics covered. In addition, the instructors' manual designed to accompany this text contains extensive annotated bibliographies, again organized by chapters.

Much of whatever merit this volume possesses it owes to Cass Canfield of Harper & Row. His faith in our idea encouraged us to work out the details, and his generosity enabled us to enlist the services of the many busy scholars whose brains and energies produced this book. He has guided and supported our efforts through countless drafts and around a hundred unforeseen difficulties. Beulah Hagen of Harper & Row has laboriously, patiently, and with a fine intelligence supervised the design of the book and seen our complicated manuscript through the press. Cass Canfield, John Ryden, Mary Lou Mosher, Mel Arnold, and John Gordon, also of Harper & Row, have made important contributions to our project. We are deeply grateful. To thank individually all those who have helped our authors would be impractical in the space at our disposal; we leave that happy task to our colleagues. But we, as editors, wish to extend our loving thanks and appreciation to our wives, Gail Garraty and Ruth Gay, whose critical reading of the manuscript has been of great help and whose support at every stage has been truly invaluable.

JOHN A. GARRATY
PETER GAY

Contributors

René Albrecht-Carrié Professor Emeritus of History, Barnard College and the School of International Affairs, Columbia University

Herman Ausubel Professor of History at Columbia University

A. Doak Barnett Senior Fellow in the Foreign Policy Studies Division of Brookings Institution

Jacques Barzun University Professor at Columbia University

Elias J. Bickerman Professor Emeritus of History at Columbia University and Professor of Jewish History at the Jewish Theological Seminary

Hans H. A. Bielenstein Professor of Chinese History at Columbia University

Shepard B. Clough Professor Emeritus of European History at Columbia University

Gerson D. Cohen Jacob H. Schiff Professor of Jewish History at The Jewish Theological Seminary of America

Robert D. Cross President of Swarthmore College and Professor of American Social History

Ainslie T. Embree Professor of History at Duke University

Rhodes W. Fairbridge Professor of Geology at Columbia University

John A. Garraty Professor of History at Columbia University

Nina G. Garsoïan Professor of Armenian Studies and Professor of History at Columbia University

Peter Gay Professor of History at Yale University

J. Mason Gentzler Professor of History at Sarah Lawrence College

Henry F. Graff Professor of History at Columbia University

Lewis Hanke Clarence and Helen Haring Professor of History at the University of Massachusetts, Amherst

Richard Hofstadter De Witt Clinton Professor of American History at Columbia University (d. 1970)

Graham W. Irwin   Professor of African History at Columbia University

Charles Issawi   Ragnar Nurske Professor of Economics at Columbia University

Edward P. Lanning   Professor of Anthropology at Columbia University

William E. Leuchtenburg   De Witt Clinton Professor of History at Columbia University

Maan Z. Madina   Associate Professor of Arabic at Columbia University

John A. Moore   Professor of Biology at the University of California

Richard B. Morris   Gouverneur Morris Professor of History at Columbia University

John H. Mundy   Professor of European History at Columbia University

Ernest Nagel   University Professor Emeritus at Columbia University

Peter A. Pardue   Associate Professor of Religion at Indiana University (Bloomington)

Orest Ranum   Professor of History at the Johns Hopkins University

Eugene F. Rice, Jr.   Professor of History at Columbia University

Henry L. Roberts   Professor of History at Dartmouth College

James P. Shenton   Professor of History at Columbia University

Jacob W. Smit   Queen Wilhelmina Professor of History at Columbia University

Morton Smith   Professor of History at Columbia University

Fritz Stern   Seth Low Professor of History at Columbia University Visiting Professor at the University of Konstanz in Germany

Alden T. Vaughan   Professor of History at Columbia University

Immanuel Wallerstein   Professor of Sociology at McGill University

Hershel Webb   Associate Professor of Japanese History at Columbia University

Robert K. Webb   Managing Editor of the American Historical Review

Lodewyk Woltjer   Rutherford Professor of Astronomy at Columbia University and Editor of the Astronomical Journal

A HISTORY OF THE WORLD

Toward Modernity

The Renaissance and Reformation in Europe

1 The State System of the Italian Renaissance

No historical period has a name at once so plausible and so contested as the Renaissance. Fifteenth- and sixteenth-century intellectuals coined the term to assert the superiority of their own age over the "middle," or "dark," ages. (They coined those terms too.) So from the beginning "Renaissance" was a polemical word, even a bullying one. By calling the age between their own day and antiquity "dark," they stamped it for centuries as an age of cultural squalor. By giving their own period a name pregnant with images and metaphors of light, awakening, spring, youth, vigor, and innovation, they demanded that everyone admire it.

Consider how a fifteenth-century Florentine scholar sketched the history of poetry from the Augustan age to his own time: poetry, he wrote, flourished in Rome until Claudian, a contemporary of St. Augustine:

> After Claudian, who was well nigh the last of the poets whom ancient times brought forth, almost all poetry decayed, because of the weakness and avarice of the emperors, and also perhaps because art was no longer prized, since the Catholic faith began to abhor the figments of poetic imagination as pernicious and a vain thing. Poetry, therefore, lying prostrate without honor or dignity, that great man Petrarch recalled it as from an abyss of shadows into the light, and giving it his hand, set the fallen art upon its feet.

In the sixteenth century, Giorgio Vasari, the author of the great series of lives of the Renaissance painters, gave a similar picture of the history of painting, sculpture, and architecture. Art, he insisted, had reached perfection in the classical world. But after Constantine, like poetry, it began to decline, first slowly, then rapidly under the pressure of the barbarian invasions and the iconoclastic zeal of the Christians. Vasari's dismal picture of medieval art shaped European taste for centuries and underlies the use of the word "Gothic" as a term of stylistic abuse by fifteenth-century men

A.D.
1250	Death of Frederick II and beginning of the imperial interregnum
1308	Removal of the papacy from Rome to Avignon
1321	Death of Dante
c. 1325	Beginning of regular sea traffic between Italy and northern Europe via the open Atlantic
1327	Earliest mention of an artillery piece in the documents
1342	Petrarch's *Italia mia*
1347	Outbreak of the Black Death
1378	Beginning of the Great Schism
1385–1402	Reign of Gian Galeazzo Visconti, Duke of Milan
1404–1414	Reign of Ladislas of Durazzo, King of Naples
1414	Opening of the Council of Constance
1434	Accession to power in Florence of Cosimo de' Medici
1450	Francesco Sforza becomes Duke of Milan
1457	Publication of the first surviving dated printed book
1469	Succession to power in Florence of Lorenzo the Magnificent
1494	First French invasion of Italy; fall of the Medici and reestablishment of the Florentine Republic
1497	Vasco da Gama reaches India by sea
1502	The Spanish conquer Naples
1513	Machiavelli's *Prince*
1530	Fall of the last Florentine Republic; return of the Medici
1535	Charles V occupies Milan as an imperial fief

of letters. At last appeared Cimabue and Giotto, artists "able to distinguish the good from the bad." They abandoned the old style and "began to copy the ancients with all ardor and industry," thus initiating what Raphael and Michelangelo consummated—the expression is Vasari's own—a renaissance of the arts.

Fifteenth-century intellectuals imposed a similar periodization on the history of religion, for they complemented their admiration for pagan antiquity with a corresponding veneration for Christian antiquity. They studied St. Jerome as well as Cicero, the Greek fathers as well as Greek philosophers, believing that true religion and literature had flourished together during the early centuries of the Roman Empire. Both had been gradually barbarized after the fifth century, and true gospel piety had been almost extinguished during the middle age by the barren subtleties, logic chopping, and arid and arrogant elaboration of scholastic theologians. And just as now, in their own age, good letters were being raised as from the grave, painting and sculpture and music reborn, so also religion was sharing in the same *renovatio* or renewal, the same *reformatio* or reformation (a usage that was to form one link between the revival of letters and the Protestant Reformation), as a reviving knowledge of the early church showed how Christianity could be stripped of the vain accretions of centuries and restored to its ancient purity and simplicity.

There are sound reasons for not withholding our admiration from the cultural achievements of the Renaissance. The cities of Italy and the museums and libraries of the world preserve an inheritance of unparalleled richness and variety: paintings and frescoes by Masaccio, Botticelli, Raphael, and Titian; statues by Donatello and Michelangelo; churches and palaces by Brunelleschi, Bramante, and Palladio; masses, operas, madrigals, and instrumental music by Palestrina, Gabrielli, and Monteverdi; love poems, epics, and tales by Petrarch, Boccaccio, and Ariosto; moral and educational treatises; influential works of history (like Machiavelli's *History of Florence* or Guicciardini's *History of Italy*), of philosophy (like Marsilio Ficino's *Platonic Theology* and Pietro Pomponazzi's *On the Immortality of the Soul*), of political theory, scholarship, and science. For centuries Italy was the school of Europe as Athens had been the school of Hellas.

So we can give our admiration legitimately enough. The difficulty with "Renaissance" lies elsewhere: in a tendency to accept the vernal metaphors contemporary intellectuals built into the word as adequate descriptions of the period itself. No one need take the idea of rebirth literally, of course, and argue that fifteenth-century Italy was Roman Italy reborn. On the other hand a great many people, influenced as much by images of youth and spring as by the reading of texts and documents, believe that innova-

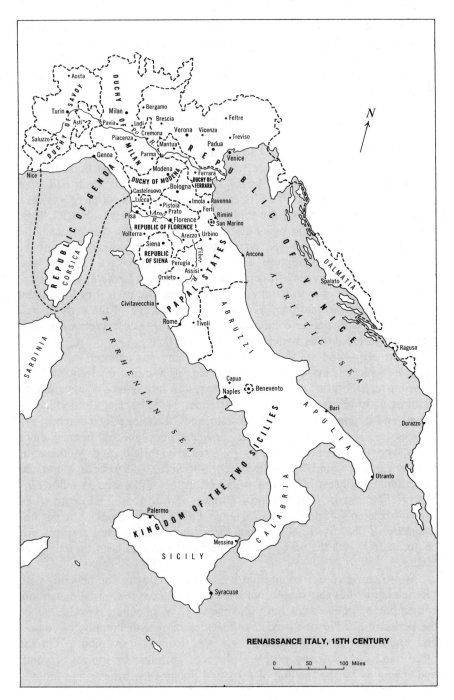

RENAISSANCE ITALY, 15TH CENTURY

0   50   100 Miles

tion, prosperity, and modernity were as central to the period as cultural brilliance. To what extent is this true?

Certainly the hundred years before and after 1450 were enormously fertile in innovation. But the great discoveries and historical mutations of the age were not confined to Italy; while even in Italy continuity and tradition mark the age as deeply as change and innovation. The history of discovery and novelty must be balanced by the equally interesting and important story of the survival and adaptation of traditional institutions, social distinctions, professional disciplines, and modes of thought.

The fact that innovation during the fourteenth and fifteenth centuries was a European-wide phenomenon is well illustrated by the history of technology. The most remarkable technological innovations of the Renaissance were printing with movable metal type, the use of gunpowder to propel cannonballs and bullets, and important advances in shipbuilding and navigation. In none of these was the contribution of Italy indisputably central. The complex prehistory of printing involved China and every region of Western Europe. Johann Gutenberg perfected the process in the little ecclesiastical city of Mainz, and in 1457 his son-in-law, Johann Fust, printed the first surviving dated book, an edition of the Psalms in Latin. The first mention of gunpowder in the sources is by the English Franciscan scientist and theologian Roger Bacon in the late thirteenth century. The first mention of a gun occurs in 1327 in the records of the Florentine republic, and the first illustration in an English manuscript of the same year, a crude fire pot designed to shoot arrows. Innovation in navigation and shipbuilding was similarly international. Regular traffic between northern and southern Europe via the open Atlantic began about 1325. In the next century and a half bigger ships, improvements in steering and propulsion like the stern rudder and new kinds of sails and rigging, the use of the compass and astrolabe to estimate course and position more reliably—all of these steps to the great discoveries and to the "Atlantic Revolution" of early modern times—were taken by Europeans of every nation. By the early fifteenth century Portuguese and Spaniards, rather than Italians, were in the vanguard of exploration and discovery of new trade routes and new worlds.

Just as northern Europe shared the originality and creativity too often carelessly assigned only to Italy, so also Italy shared in full measure the continuity and traditionalism too often carelessly attributed only to the north. This is clearly evident even in Italian thought and culture, fields in which the word Renaissance was first used and to which it is still applied with particular appropriateness.

Much importance, for example, has been attached to fourteenth- and fifteenth-century men's morbid preoccupation with death. It is well to remember that the first great representation of the dance of death—that in the Campo Santo in Pisa—comes from fourteenth-century Italy. We are accustomed to think of allegory as a medieval device, a peculiarly well-adapted response to the need of medieval Christians to understand works of classical literature in an acceptably Christian context. But the same use of allegory to Christianize pagan works, whose assumptions are often profoundly secular and hostile to Christian values, continued in the Renaissance, both in Italy and in northern Europe. Medieval scholars had allegorized Ovid; in the fifteenth century a professor of the humanities at the University of Florence still considered it useful to allegorize Vergil's *Aeneid:* Aeneas was the human soul, Dido represented the trammels of the flesh, Latium the promised land where at last the soul gratefully arrives. The survival and adaptation of the scholastic method is especially instructive. One of the great intellectual creations of the twelfth and thirteenth centuries, this method of analysis, organization, and debate remained a powerful and developing intellectual tool throughout the fifteenth and sixteenth centuries, and particularly in Italy. Indeed, the liveliest centers of scholastic philosophy in all Europe were the Universities of Padua and Bologna, and a line of brilliant commentators on Aristotle's *Physics* forms an unbroken bridge between the scientific and philosophical achievements of Oxford and Paris in the fourteenth century and the revolutionary discoveries of Galileo at the end of the sixteenth.

The implications of the word "Renaissance" or the complacent view Italian fifteenth-century intellectuals had of themselves are equally deceptive if they lead us to assume that the period was necessarily one of economic expansion. The conditions that nourish periods of cultural brilliance are various and complex. The experience of the Italian Renaissance suggests that a generalized prosperity is not always one of them.

The most striking evidence is demographic. In 1347 a merchant ship sailed from Tana in the Crimea to Messina in Sicily. On board were rats infected with the plague. Although the work of a single bacillus, the disease took several forms. Bubonic plague, so called from the buboes or swellings on the bodies of the victims and carried to humans by fleas from the sick rats, attacked the lymphatic gland system. Pneumonic plague, much more devastating, attacked the lungs. It was highly communicable and almost always fatal. From Sicily the Black Death swept the western Mediterranean littoral in 1347, raged in Italy, Spain, and France in 1348, reached Switzerland, Austria, Germany, the Low Countries, and England in 1349, and Scandinavia and Poland in 1350. Plague hammered Europeans again and again in the fourteenth and fifteenth centuries and continued its ravages, though with diminished intensity, in the sixteenth and seventeenth centuries. Reliable estimates of the loss of human life vary from 12 to 70 per cent, depending on the region, with a global loss for the years between 1348 and 1377 of no less than 40 per cent. For example, the population of the rural countryside around the Tuscan city of Pistoia had been about 31,000 in the mid-thirteenth century. In 1401 it was less than 9,000. The number of inhabitants of the city itself fell from 11,000 in 1244 to 6,000 in 1351 and to 3,900 in 1415. "No one wept for the dead," wrote a Sienese chronicler, "because everyone expected death himself."

The shock halted more than two centuries of European demographic and economic growth. Until far into the fifteenth century population variously declined, partially recovered, then fell again, or stagnated at a level well below that of 1347. Long-term economic development followed a similar pattern, a decline of industrial and agricultural production and volume of trade reflecting the shrinking markets and smaller labor force of the later fourteenth and fifteenth centuries. Italy was not exempt from the European-wide contraction. Indeed, it has become fashionable to speak of the "depression of the Italian Renaissance." The customs records of Genoa and Venice chart a decline in the volume of goods exchanged. The output of woolen cloth, Italy's most important manufacture, was smaller in the fifteenth century than at the end of the thirteenth. Florence, which had once produced as many as 100,000 bolts of cloth a year, was manufacturing only 30,000 in 1500. The cultural renaissance was not, as historians have long assumed, grounded on an expanding commercial and industrial activity, rising prosperity, and increasing wealth.

The material condition of Renaissance Italy, however, was less grim and much more complex than words like "depression" might suggest. Even in the later fourteenth and fifteenth centuries the consequences of demographic contraction were not entirely negative. Fewer workers meant higher wages; fewer mouths to feed meant lower prices for grain and a larger share of what the land produced for the survivors. There is evidence too that lower grain prices encouraged landowners and peasants to diversify their crops and give part of their time and labor to more expensive and profitable foods like wine, oil, cheese, butter, and vegetables. Abandoning marginal land, they devoted greater effort to improving the more fertile soils. South of Milan more than 90 kilometers of navigable canals and a host of smaller irrigation works were constructed between 1439 and 1476. Important drainage operations were undertaken in southern Tuscany and the Roman Campagna. Ordinary Italians in the fifteenth century probably ate more and had a more balanced diet than their more numerous thirteenth-century ancestors.

Italians faced more serious challenges than declining numbers: fiercer competition from foreign merchants and manufacturers and the loss of the monopolistic position on which their economic supremacy had for so long been based. They responded to these challenges too with skill and energy. To compensate for the decline in the export woolen industry, they concentrated on manufacturing silk, one symptom of a larger adaptation of the Italian economy to foreign competition: the concentration by Italian craftsmen on quality rather than quantity, on beauty rather than utility. In the fifteenth and sixteenth centuries Italy came increasingly to specialize in the manufacture and export of luxuries for the rich: artistic metalwork, decorative armor, elaborate furniture, bronzes, glass, ceramics, embroidery, fine leather goods, cloth of silver and gold. England clothed German burghers with serviceable woolens; Italy dressed German princes in silk brocades.

Ottoman expansion in the eastern Mediterranean, the competition of foreign merchants at Alexandria and Beirut, in the Bosphorus and Black Sea, and the establishment of a direct sea link with India by Vasco da Gama shattered Italy's monopoly of the spice trade. The foundation of successful banking houses in Castile, France, Germany, and the Netherlands in the fifteenth century broke its monopoly of international banking. Italian merchant-bankers adapted resiliently to changing economic circumstances. Not only did Italy continue to trade profitably in the eastern Mediterranean; in the later sixteenth century more pepper reached Venice via the Levant than 100 years earlier. Bankers rationalized the organization of their firms, generalized novel accounting techniques like double-entry bookkeeping, and developed more sophisticated instruments of credit and exchange. The Medici Bank was smaller than the great Florentine banks of the early fourteenth century; but in the days of its greatness it was better managed and more efficient.

The long downward trend given such impetus by the Black Death was reversed in the last decade of the fifteenth century. Demographic recovery, plainly discernible by the 1470's and 1480's, reached boom proportions in the sixteenth century, when many Italian cities doubled in size. Indeed, the sixteenth century was an age of economic expansion all over Europe. Every index, whether of industrial and agricultural production or volume of commercial and financial exchange, swung sharply upward. Italy shared in this expansive prosperity—as it shared in the earlier contraction. The Renaissance was an age both of catastrophe and of promise.

The word "Renaissance" has for many years suggested modernity as well as innovation and prosperity. In this perspective the Renaissance appears less as the rebirth or revival of a distant and glorious antiquity than as the origin and beginning of the modern world, the prototype of modern European civilization.

If we search fifteenth- and sixteenth-century Italy for the seeds of modernity, we will find them in abundance. Italians were the first to regularize and formalize diplomatic relations between states. They invented the resident ambassador, the permanent representative of one sovereign formally accredited to another, looking out for the interests of his home government and sending regular reports back to it on the situation and capabilities of the foreign state. The idea and practice of balance of power, the conscious manipulation and balancing of one power against another, of one coalition against another, so characteristic of the relations among European powers in the modern world, emerged for the first time in Italy toward the end of the fifteenth century. Realpolitik, political behavior divorced from religious and ethical norms, is universally practiced in the modern world. The most celebrated manual of realpolitik was written by an Italian in 1513: *The Prince* of Niccolò Machiavelli.

Ideas and institutions of an apparently prophetic modernism were common in other areas of life. The Medici Bank anticipated the modern holding company. A German sociologist has found the earliest clear expressions of bourgeois values in fifteenth-century Florence: the maxim that time is money; and the notion, so difficult for the aristocrat to grasp, that expenditures should not exceed one's income. Art historians point out that sixteenth-century Italian artists invented modern landscape painting and the still life and that the public buildings of Washington go back directly to architectural practices first made fashionable by Filippo Brunelleschi. Italian humanists founded modern historical scholarship, created the idea and practice of liberal education, established new scholarly disciplines like numismatics and epigraphy. An earlier generation used to call Petrarch the first modern man.

None of these statements is untrue. But their cumulative effect should make us uneasy—for two reasons. First, because it is also easy to cite personalities, ideas, or institutions that make the fifteenth century look like the end of an era rather than the beginning of a new one: the ascetic and visionary piety of the Dominican monk Savonarola, for example; or the taste of cultivated Italian aristocrats for medieval romances of chivalry; or the dependence of men of every condition on astrology and magic. Second, because the idea of the modern is itself problematical and ambiguous. We will reach a juster view of the Renaissance—and of our period too—by abandoning undue emphasis on modernity and by trying to understand it instead as a period of rapid and fundamental change, of transition from one firmly contoured civilization to another. Periods of transition—our own, the Renaissance, the two and a half centuries between Diocletian and Clovis, between antiquity and the Middle Ages—can be interpreted with equal plausibility as ages of new beginnings or of crises in traditional values and patterns of life. To the Roman historian the proliferation of the villa, for example, the great landed estates of the late empire, is evidence of fragmentation and decline, of the disintegration of the essentially urban city-state civilization of the ancient world. But to the medievalist a history of the villa is the prehistory of the manor and of manorialism, and it speaks to him of vigor and a creative adaptation to changing circumstance. Or take the spread of Christianity: a death blow to the secular assumptions of classical thought, but also the foundation of the new Christian civilization of the future. The identical situation exists in the Renaissance: on the one hand, a crisis of medieval institutions and values, strikingly apparent in the great ecumenical institutions of papacy and empire, in feudal government, in the very foundations of thought and feeling; but in a reversed optic an age of germination and novelty. It is therefore not surprising to learn that books with the apparently contradictory titles of *The Autumn of the Middle Ages* and *The Dawn of a New Era* are about the same period.

The new era, however, was not the modern one, if we use the word modern with the meaning it has, for example, in the phrase "modern art." For the assumptions of modern art—the revolutionary movement that began when Picasso painted his *Demoiselles d'Avignon* in 1907—are most hostile to those of Renaissance art, while modern taste and sensibility have been formed and satisfied not by Praxiteles and Raphael but by Greek archaic and Romanesque sculpture, the art of the steppes, Japanese prints, and African masks. Nor can we argue, to take one more example, that modern science began in the Renaissance. The Renaissance did indeed lay the foundations of Newtonian science; but in science as in art the period begun by the Renaissance ended in the late nineteenth and early twentieth centuries, notably with the physics of Planck and Einstein.

The present position of Western Europe in the world suggests a similar periodization. Until the fifteenth century Europe had been the docile pupil of Greco-Roman antiquity and of the more sophisticated cultures of the Far and Near East. After 1500 not only was Europe a cultural and techno-logical creditor; by the last decades of the nineteenth century the whole globe was the political and economic hinterland of the tiny western peninsula of the Eurasian land mass. In our own century this European domination of the world has disintegrated with incredible swiftness. Be-cause our own period too is one of rapid transition, its characteristically "modern" features point forward to an unknown future, not back to the Renaissance; whereas the seeds of modernity we discover in the Renais-sance are today the withered blossoms of a vanishing traditional past.

It is important to keep another fact in mind when we discuss the problem of the modern. Between us and the Renaissance lie the industrial-ization of the West and the French and Russian revolutions. The gulf is enormous, and it requires a very considerable imaginative leap to cross it. The jump will be easier if we remember that in the fifteenth and sixteenth centuries men still gave their political loyalty to persons rather than states. "Fatherland," "patrie," and "patria" normally meant the region or town where they were born, not the whole territory ruled by their prince. Wars were dynastic and personal and rarely involved national, to say nothing of economic, interests. When men revolted, their hope was to return to the "good old days" and the "good old law," not to create a new society. The economy was overwhelmingly agrarian, even in the most urbanized areas of the continent like north and central Italy. Society was landed and aristocratic. The political, economic, and social structure of Renaissance Europe was closer to that of the Roman Empire, Ming China, and feudal Japan than to contemporary Europe or America.

Let us therefore use the word Renaissance in a perfectly neutral sense to denote a particular period of time, roughly the years from the Black Death in the middle of the fourteenth century to the early seventeenth century, and not only in Italy but in all of Europe. We can (depending on the kind of material we are studying and our perspective on it) understand much of this period as the crisis time of medieval civilization; we can also see it as a period of creativity and new beginnings. Better still we should understand it as both: as a period of transition between one distinctive civilization and another. Looked at in this last perspective, the Renaissance was the beginning of early modern Europe, that is, of preindustrial modern Europe. And provided we keep firmly in mind that during the Renaissance Europe was an "underdeveloped" society, we can go further and say that Renaissance men built the foundations for the Europe which endured until the second half of the nineteenth century. (Since the two world wars it has been building a new sort of civilization whose contours are still only dimly discernible.)

In the transition from medieval to early modern Europe two developments are of particular interest and importance: the emergence of a vigorous lay culture in fifteenth-century Italy and the Lutheran revolution in Germany.

During most of the fifteen centuries between the fall of the Roman Empire in the fifth century and the Risorgimento, the national movement of the nineteenth century, foreigners ruled a disunited Italy. In the Middle Ages Italy was divided into three spheres of power: northern Italy and part of central Italy (notably Tuscany) belonged to the Holy Roman Empire of the German kings and was known as the *Regnum Italicum;* Rome and the rest of central Italy were under the sovereignty of the popes; southern Italy and Sicily formed a separate kingdom.

With the virtual withdrawal from Italy between 1250 and the early years of the fourteenth century of the ecumenical powers of empire and papacy, this division of power and the political order based on it collapsed. Effective imperial power in Italy broke down during the imperial interregnum of 1250–1275 and was never again restored. By 1300 the city states of Lombardy and Tuscany were in practice free and independent of their nominal feudal overlord. The removal of the papacy from Rome to Avignon in the early fourteenth century bestowed a similar de facto independence on the rest of central Italy; and when the popes sought to make effective their sovereign rights within the papal states after the return of the curia to Rome at the end of the century, they did so less as universal spiritual monarchs than as rulers of a particular Italian state. This relative freedom of action lasted for 200 years, until the French invasion of 1494 and the struggle of France and Spain during the first half of the sixteenth century to dominate the peninsula. Spain was the victor, and from about 1530 to the establishment of the national Italian kingdom in the nineteenth century, the house of Hapsburg, first the Spanish branch, then the Austrian branch, ruled in Italy. A notable characteristic then of the period we call the Renaissance is that it was the only period in the history of Italy between antiquity and the nineteenth century when Italians controlled their own political destiny.

Since antiquity northern and central Italy had been exceptionally dense with towns. Nowhere else in Europe was urban life more dynamic and sophisticated; nowhere was resistance to the claims of presumptuous overlords more tenacious. Wherever medieval cities flourished—in south Germany, the Netherlands, Catalonia, and Provence, as well as in Italy—resistance to political unification in the larger framework of a territorial state was particularly marked. In Italy civic particularism grew with the cities' ability to defend it. By the end of the thirteenth century their wealth and power had made them virtually immune to the interference of pope or emperor. The collapse of imperial authority and the withdrawal of the papacy to Avignon made permanent the de facto independence won in earlier struggles. The result was the atomization of the peninsula. Renaissance Italy, in its liveliest areas, was, like classical Greece, a congeries of fiercely independent, competing, warring city-states.

A sense of national identity was not entirely absent, for geography made it easy to visualize Italy as an intelligible unit, its frontiers drawn by Nature herself: on three sides the sea, to the north the barrier of the Alps. Dante had expressed the linguistic kinship of all Italians, and his *Divine Comedy* worked to make that kinship an effective linguistic unity. The recognized intellectual and artistic primacy of Italy in the Renaissance aroused pride in all Italians. That non-Italians were barbarians was as self-evident to them as the parallel conviction had been to the Greeks. In a famous canzone entitled *Italia mia* (1341–1342) Petrarch described Italy as "the loveliest country of the earth" and called on Italians to revive the ancient Roman virtues. By the fifteenth century it was a commonplace of humanist rhetoric that Italy was sacred soil where no barbarian had any right to be. The poignancy of the famous last chapter of Machiavelli's *Prince* flows from this conviction. Writing after Italy had become the battle ground of foreigner invaders, he quoted *Italia mia* and called for a virtuous ruler to arise and liberate Italy from the "barbarous domination that stinks in the nostrils of everyone."

Machiavelli believed passionately in liberty, but in a liberty that made unity impossible. To lament the failure of the independent city-states of Italy to unite is to read back the aspirations of the nineteenth century into an earlier and very different age. For the Renaissance idea of liberty no more implied unity than it implied democracy. In internal politics it meant freedom from the rule of one man or of one family; in international affairs it meant independence from foreign domination (and to the Florentine every non-Florentine was a foreigner). Statesmen often distinguished the interests of particular states from the interest of Italy as a whole, but they never doubted for a moment that there was a necessary connection between the independence of the individual state and that of Italy as a whole. The idea of unity would have destroyed the very bases of their rule; the practice of unity would have destroyed liberty itself, as they understood it. An Italian state did not exist. No one seriously imagined that it would be desirable to have one.

Yet though Italians did not achieve unity, a structure of order gradually emerged from the apparent chaos of the early fourteenth century. The process was bloody, for its mainspring was the desire of every statesman to aggrandize his territory, of every city to colonize as large a hinterland as possible. In 1395 the emperor Wenceslas raised the Milanese territories of the Visconti to the dignity of a duchy, giving its ruler, Gian Galeazzo (1385–1402), a factitious legitimacy. From the fastness of a fortress from which he rarely emerged, he directed his captains east against Verona, Padua, and Mantua; then south against Pisa, Florence, and Perugia. Although his successors rapidly lost his more distant conquests, he laid the permanent territorial foundations of a Milanese state in the Lombard plain. A decade later Ladislas of Durazzo, king of Naples, launched a campaign of aggressive expansion from the south. Marching north from Naples, he annexed part of the Papal States. In March, 1414, he took Rome, sacked the city, then entered the basilica of St. John Lateran on horseback to venerate the relics of the apostles. He moved on toward Florence; but he too died before he could reach the city, contemporaries said of poison administered by a Perugian courtesan in the pay of the Florentines. Although for centuries Venice had been an exclusively maritime power, she too expanded rapidly on the Italian mainland in the fifteenth century. A desire to secure the vital trade route from Venice to the Brenner Pass and the need to protect her food supply in the lower Po Valley and to buffer herself from the predatory attacks of the Milanese sharpened her aggressiveness. By the middle of the century she had built a compact territorial state which included Padua, Vicenza, and Verona, extended to the Brenner in the north and to the Lake of Como and the river Adda, her frontier with the duchy of Milan, in the west.

The gradual expansion of the strong and the loss of independence by the weak rationalized the political map of Italy. Five principal states emerged: the pontifical State, the Kingdom of Naples, the Duchy of Milan, the Republic of Venice, and the Republic of Florence. In the interstices were the military principalities. The lords of cities like Mantua and Ferrara, Rimini and Urbino, were professional warlords. Their territories were generally poor and mountainous. They recruited from the petty nobility and impoverished peasantry and maintained their independence and solvency by hiring themselves and their soldier subjects out to the five major powers as mercenaries. The tone of their courts was seigneurial and military; feudal and chivalric ideals lingered longer here than anywhere else in Italy. It is not surprising that the loveliest courtly romance of the sixteenth century, Lodovico Ariosto's *Orlando Furioso,* and the most elegant expression of the Renaissance idea of the gentleman, Baldassare Castiglione's *Courtier,* come from the aristocratic ambiance of these military courts.

The governments of the five large states combined the principles of aristocracy and monarchy in a rich variety of constitutional structures. The Papal States were an ecclesiastical principality composed of many small seigneuries and cities very imperfectly obedient to their elected sovereign; Naples was a feudal monarchy whose king shared political power with a factious and tumultuous baronage; Milan was a ducal despotism; Venice a republic ruled by a closed hereditary aristocracy; Florence a republic in flux. Everywhere but in Venice the pattern of change was from the rule of a few to the rule of one man or one family. Florence is typical. In the middle of the fourteenth century the city was a republic; 200 years later she was a grand duchy, ruled in hereditary succession by the Medici, who, having begun as merchant-bankers no cleverer or richer than a hundred others, rose in the fifteenth century by skillfully manipulating the levers of patronage and intimidation to become the respected political bosses of the city. By the sixteenth century they were princes and popes, allied by marriage to the greatest kings in Europe.

The social structure of the Italian states was rigidly inegalitarian. The Republic of Florence is again representative. In 1500 its population was approximately 70,000. Contemporaries distinguished three principal social groups. They called the members of the highest group *ricchi,* because they were the richest men in the city; *principali, grandi,* the "first citizens," because they monopolized political power and rotated the principal offices in the state among themselves; wise men, *uomini savi,* because they were men accustomed to the exercise of power, of wide experience of the world, traveled, and well educated; "members of the great houses" or, collectively, *le case,* because the visible signs of their wealth, power, wisdom, and magnificence were their houses, those enormous piles which dwarfed, then as now, all the other houses and shops around them: the Palazzo Pazzi built by Brunelleschi; Alberti's Palazzo Rucellai; Michelozzi's Palazzo Medici; and most impressive of all, the great Strozzi Palace of Cronaca. These men were not only rich and politically influential, they also enjoyed the highest social position in the city. Their families were old and famous in the history of the republic. They were *nobili* and exhibited noble virtues. Above all they were men, as the great historian Francesco Guicciardini memorably put it, with an appetite for fame and greatness, *uno appetito di grandezza.*

Below the patricians were the *mezzani* or *populari,* the commoners, the men of moderate means. To distinguish them sharply from the *grandi* some contemporaries called them the *populo minuto* (a confusing term because by the end of the eighteenth century the phrase had shifted its meaning and come to denote a proletariat rather than a middle class). They were shop-keepers, bakers, butchers, winesellers, druggists; painters and sculptors; carpenters and stonemasons, lawyers, notaries, permanent civil servants, and schoolmasters: men like Lucca Landucci, who owned a pharmacy opposite the Palazzo Strozzi and passed his life in the political, economic, and social shadow of that grim and serene façade; or like Niccolò Machiavelli, head of the second chancery, a salaried civil servant, dependent on the patronage of *grandi* like the Soderini, Ruccelai, or Medici, a man, as he described himself in the preface to *The Prince,* "of humble and obscure condition."

In terms of the guild structure of the city, the *grandi* matriculated almost exclusively in one or more of the seven major guilds—the *arti maggiori;* the *mezzani* comprised the fourteen lower guilds, the *arti minori.* In fact the guild affiliations of the two groups were even narrower than this suggests. Many members of the *arti maggiori* were "men of moderate means." This was especially the case in the guilds of druggists, notaries, and retail merchants. The *grandi,* on the other hand, monopolized the four great guilds of crucial importance and power: those of the cloth merchants (the *Calimala*), the wool manufacturers (*Arte della Lana*), silk manufacturers (*Arte della Seta*), and the bankers (the *Cambio*). The mentality and cultural horizon of the *mezzani* were therefore typically those of the shopkeeper and the craft guild which controlled their economic activities and gave them a limited participation in the city's government. They were men of property, but of property on a small scale. Their world was bounded by the shop over which they lived, the guild hall, and the parish church. They could read and write the vernacular; they had enough arithmetic to do their accounts. But their intellectual interests were narrow, traditional, and conformist.

Economic cleavage fed social discrimination and resentment. The patriciate looked down on the *popolo minuto*. They were, said Guicciardini, "poor and ignorant and men of little capacity." The *mezzani* feared, envied, emulated, and angrily resisted the domination of the patricians. What they wanted is made vivid for us by Machiavelli, for the most articulate spokesman of the Florentine *mezzani* was also the greatest political theorist of the age. His bias was antiaristocratic, and he thought that the best government for Florence would be a *governo populare,* a regime in which the people, that is, the *popolo minuto,* would participate fully in political life: for, as he wrote in the *Discourses on Livy:*

> One should always confide any deposit to those who have least desire of violating it; and doubtless, if we consider the objects of the nobles and of the people, we must see that the first have a great desire to dominate, while the latter have only the wish not to be dominated, and consequently a greater desire to live in the enjoyment of liberty; so that when the people are entrusted with the care of any privilege or liberty, being less disposed to encroach upon it, they will of necessity take better care of it; and being unable to take it away themselves, will prevent others from doing so.

This divergence of interest colored every aspect of life, not only in Florence but in every Italian city.

Below the *grandi* and *mezzani* were the masses, by far the largest social group in every Renaissance city. Contemporaries called them the poor (*poveri*), the pleb, the dregs (*infima plebe*); or the mob, the crowd, the vulgar, the multitude. About one-third of this group (or one-quarter of the city's people) was made up of the *sottoposti* of the guild of cloth manufacturers: that is, the wool carders, spinners, weavers, cutters, fullers, and so on who supplied the labor force of the wool industry, the backbone of Florentine economic life. The remainder was the varied mass of domestic servants (a very large group which included a substantial number of slaves—Tatars, Russians, Alans, Rumanians, even Greek Christians—imported from the East by the Venetians and Genoese); the apprentices and journeymen of the multitude of trades whose masters comprised the lesser guilds; the workers in the building trades. Men of this class were socially invisible and excluded totally from participation in the political life of the city. Guild regulation and municipal ordinance wove a tight network of oppression. Their lot was misery and want. Strictly controlled, totally dependent on their employers, they concentrated in the slums of S. Spirito and S. Croce. Our main evidence about them comes from court records: a stream of tales of violence and degradation, illiteracy, open and universally condoned exploitation, and a latent hatred which on rare occasions burst out in open revolt. A contemporary wrote about them: "If the lowest orders of society earn enough food to keep them going from day to day, then they have enough." The vast majority of Florentine political writers hardly mention them: Machiavelli's sympathy for the *popolo minuto* did not include the pleb. He wrote always—this indeed was his unquestioned assumption—as though the *grandi* and *mezzani* made up the totality of the population of the city.

Not only the pleb were excluded from political life; so also were the populations of the towns and countryside which the larger city-states subjected as they expanded. Venice ruled terra firma—as did Florence the steadily growing part of the old county of Tuscany she was coming to dominate—like a miniature colonial empire, with aristocratic governors appointed by the Senate or elected by the Grand Council. Venice was not a territorial state in the strict sense; it was a city-state linked to its dependent possessions on the mainland only as ruler and ruled. Her mainland subjects were not Venetian citizens. No representative institutions developed through which their desires and legitimate interests might influence Venetian policy. They felt no sense of community with Venetian ambitions, no sense of belonging to a larger unit that could command their loyalty and devotion. On the contrary, Venice treated them as colonials economically as well, by trying to make herself the entrepôt of every commercial transaction, forcing mainland merchants to buy and sell from and to Venetian citizens only, forcing Ravenna, for example, to give up importing goods directly from overseas and even from other parts of northern Italy. This is one reason city-states hired condottieri. The ruling class could not trust the loyalty of their own subjects.

For Further Reading

Brucker, Gene A., *Renaissance Florence.*
Burckhardt, Jacob, *The Civilization of the Renaissance in Italy.*
de Roover, Raymond, *The Rise and Decline of the Medici Bank, 1397–1494.*
Gilbert, Felix, *Machiavelli and Guicciardini: Politics and History in Sixteenth-Century Florence.*
Hay, Denys, *The Italian Renaissance.*

2   Humanism and Society

The *grandi* of the Italian cities are no longer important to us because they
were an exclusive and effective ruling class. They interest us because it was
their needs, their interests, their tastes and manners which, overwhelmingly, shaped Renaissance art and culture. In order to understand Renaissance civilization we must probe again the nerve of wealth and power. Let
us begin by looking at two concrete examples of the Renaissance elite, one
a Venetian aristocrat, the other a Florentine patrician family.

Andrea Barbarigo (1400–1450) was a typical Venetian aristocrat of
the fifteenth century. Since the main economic activity of Venetian nobles
was maritime commerce, he spent his youth learning this trade under the
quasi-official patronage of the Venetian state. As part of the pattern of
perpetuating a ruling class, Venice maintained several services for educating and launching young members of the aristocracy. They received a legal
apprenticeship in one of the city's busy commercial courts. Here they
learned the rudiments of commercial law and studied arithmetic and accounting. They were allowed to sail on the state's armed galleys (which
made yearly or twice-yearly voyages to England and Flanders, Constantinople and the Black Sea, or to Beirut and Alexandria) as "bowman of the
quarter-deck." As a bowman Barbarigo ate in the captain's mess with the
officers and established merchants, learning from their experience the
fundamentals of his trade; and most important of all he was allowed to
load a small cargo of his own without paying freight. These voyages were
his apprenticeship to the sea. They gave him experience at first hand of
trade and of commercial conditions abroad and, because he was able and
lucky, allowed him to increase the small capital sum of 200 ducats that was
all his widowed mother could give him to begin on.

Barbarigo prospered. By the time he was thirty he was active in the
main areas and departments of foreign trade, importing cloth from England, cotton from Syria, wool from Spain. In 1430, for example, the Senate
sent five galleys to Flanders. On one of these Barbarigo loaded six bales of
pepper. The galley on which he had rented space went directly to Bruges.
Here an agent sold the pepper and with the money bought English goods:
23 barrels of tinware and pewter and 23 bolts of woolen cloth. The money
involved had been transferred from Venice to Bruges to London by bills of
exchange. In the winter of 1430 Barbarigo disposed of his English imports
in Venice itself. He sold most of the cloth through his godfather's shop on

A.D.   1341   Petrarch crowned poet laureate on the Capitoline in Rome
        1353   Boccaccio's *Decameron*
        1375   Coluccio Salutati appointed chancellor of the Florentine Republic
        1404   Pier Paolo Vergerio's *Concerning Liberal Studies,* the first humanist treatise on education
        1414   Poggio Bracciolini discovers Quintilian's *De institutione oratoria* in the library of the monastery of St. Gallen in Switzerland
        1429   Leonardo Bruni finishes his *History of Florence*
        1440   Lorenzo Valla's *On the True Good* (or *On Pleasure*)
        1450   Pope Nicholas V founds the Vatican Library
        1456   Giannozzo Manetti enters the service of King Alfonso of Naples
        1462   Establishment of the Platonic Academy in Florence
    c. 1469   Marsilio Ficino finishes translating into Latin the dialogues of Plato, the first complete translation into any Western language
        1469   Birth of Erasmus
        1486   Pico della Mirandola, *Oration on the Dignity of Man*
        1505   Erasmus publishes Valla's *Annotations on the New Testament*
        1516   Pietro Pomponazzi's *On the Immortality of the Soul*

the Rialto, to which customers came from all over northern Italy; he sold the pewter in Apulia, Ferrara, and Verona. With the proceeds he prepared shipments to send in the spring of 1431 with the Venetian fleets going to the Levant. Again his plans were conditioned by the transportation facilities arranged by the Venetian Senate, which that year had decided to send one fleet of unarmed cogs to Syria and the usual three fleets of armed merchant galleys: one to Alexandria, one to Beirut, and one to Constantinople and the Black Sea ports. Barbarigo shipped to Beirut a varied consignment: Florentine cloth he had bought from the Venetian branch of the Medici; the remainder of his English cloth; sheepskins bought in Apulia after he had sold part of his English pewter there; canvas, used in the East to pack raw cotton in; and two bags of *grossi* (silver coins minted in Venice for export to the East). For the return trip to Venice his agent in Beirut bought spices and raw cotton at Acre in Palestine and 250 ducats' worth of gold thread from Constantinople which Barbarigo later shipped overland to London.

This is an abbreviated picture of Barbarigo's business activities in 1430 and 1431, but typical of his activity throughout his life, although in his later years (especially after his marriage in 1439 to a girl who brought him a dowry of 4,000 ducats, a substantial increase in his capital) his scope widened. He invested everything in trade, so much so indeed that once in 1442, at a time when he had about 10,000 ducats' worth of goods going and coming between England and Egypt, he had to pawn a ring to borrow 10 ducats. He was a true merchant of Venice.

The Strozzi family of Florence, after the Medici the greatest Florentine family of the Renaissance, were the same manner of men as Andrea Barbarigo. One branch of that extraordinary family is of particular interest, the one whose greatest member was Filippo di Mateo di Simone degli Strozzi, that is, Filippo, son of Mateo, son of Simone of the clan of Strozzi.

Simone, founder of the line, matriculated in the wool guild in 1397. With his father and a brother he was a partner in a wool manufactory. The firm's total capital was between 4,000 and 5,000 florins and the average return was 14 per cent, about 200 florins a year and the major part of his income. Simone also sold insurance on commercial shipments from western Mediterranean ports to Italy. The fee was between 2 and 5 per cent. Such private insurance transactions were a handsome supplementary income for men who had the financial security to make good the occasional losses. He also had money invested in land and urban real estate: a town house, a tavern, and four small farms. At the end of his life these properties and his household goods were valued at 4,500 florins. Finally, he invested in government bonds. In 1345 the commune had consolidated its obligations into a funded debt, paying 5 per cent annually. This communal debt was called the *monte*. Simone had 1,400 florins invested in *monte* bonds.

When Simone died in 1424, his sole heir was his son Matteo. Matteo's business activities and investments were much the same as his father's. In a census made in 1427 for purposes of taxation his name appears among those of 247 heads of family with more than 4,000 florins of taxable property, placing him in the upper 2½ per cent of the population, though well below the eighty-six patricians with fortunes of over 10,000 florins. Politics was his undoing. In the ruthless factional fighting of the ruling class, predatory taxation, confiscation, and banishment were favorite weapons. When Palla Strozzi, a distant cousin and Cosimo de' Medici's arch-enemy, fell in 1434, Matteo was involved in his ruin. Cosimo exiled him and forbade him to liquidate his real estate in Florence. A year later he was dead, leaving a wife and small children. By 1459 Alessandra, his widow, had sold most of the family property except for the ten-room house in town and one very small farm in the country; and as her three sons grew to manhood they took the path of exile in their turn, virtually penniless, their sole resource their more affluent relatives.

Filippo di Matteo degli Strozzi (1428–1491) left Florence in 1441. He went to work for some Strozzi cousins who had built up a commercial and banking firm in Naples. He worked his way up in the firm and ultimately took it over. So sensitive was his handling of risky ventures of international scope that he built up one of the greatest fortunes of his day and restored the splendor and reputation of his family. When the ban against him was lifted in 1466 he returned to Florence. In 1471 his fortune, almost entirely invested at that time in the firm (known in Florence, like the Medici bank, as a *bancho grosso*), amounted to 31,649 florins; by 1483 it had risen to 112,281; and in 1491–1492 it stood at the colossal sum of 116,000 distributed as follows: real estate, 17,000; personal and household possessions, including jewels, 12,000; cash 52,000; and business investments 35,000. His children married into the core of the Medicean oligarchy. In 1489 he began the Palazzo Strozzi. He was as splendidly housed in death as in life. His three sons buried him in Santa Maria Novella, in a family chapel decorated by Filippo Lippi and in a tomb by Benedetto da Maiano.

The Barbarigo and Strozzi were members of a tiny elite. The Venetian nobles numbered some 1,500 in a population of about 100,000. In Florence the 600 names on the tax lists of 1403 and 1427 included every man in Florence who could effectively manipulate the levers of political and entrepreneurial command. We shall not be far wrong if we imagine a ruling group in every Italian city of about 2½ per cent of the population. To the poor everyone in this group seemed rich; but of course some were much richer than others, and solvency varied from immense wealth at one extreme to near ruin at the other. When they lost their money, or if prince or despot confiscated their property, if their rivals banished them, if their line died out, families dropped out of the patriciate. At the same time there was a steady influx of new men into the top rank of the business and political community. An able ambitious man moved into the city from the countryside; he made money by trade and moneylending; he founded a merchant-banking company of international reach and made a great deal more money; he matriculated in a major guild, acquired citizenship, and bolstered a shaky social position by advantageous marriages; by spinning the necessary web of influential friendships and dependent clients he got himself elected or appointed to public office; if he remained fertile and lucky, he founded a dynasty. Older families might call him a parvenu; by the third generation, though, the family was unquestionably patrician.

The organization of economic life gave patricians an ample leisure. Their firms required careful and alert supervision; but slowness of communication allowed them to space out the crucial decisions of buying cheap and selling dear. Their wool or silk manufactory was run by a manager who shared the profits; the senior partner had only to see that it was run well. They normally leased their farms to tenants on a profit-sharing basis, called in Tuscany *mezzadria*. The farm rarely brought in more than 5 per cent; but the arrangement left the landlord free. Most patricians devoted their leisure to politics: to seeing that the rich also ruled. Simone degli Strozzi was prior in 1421 and for some months treasurer of Arezzo. His son Matteo went on diplomatic missions and held a variety of magistracies. The Venetian aristocracy sitting in the Grand Council elected all officers of state, served on commissions and as ambassadors, took their turn as military commanders and provincial governors. A typical Venetian noble interrupted his commerce in pepper, sugar, nuts, tin, copper, skins, wax, and pearls to govern Treviso on the mainland or to command the Venetian galleys at the defense of Candia against the Turks.

Men of this sort had the self-confidence of the rich, powerful, and successful. They were proud of their capacity to get to the top of the social heap and stay there, to staff the offices of state and church; to advise the prince on the government of the commonwealth. Shaped by their business and political activities, they were competitive and self-reliant, individualistic, calculating and daring. They were men of wide experience and international perspective, and at the same time passionately devoted to their city and to the grandeur of their families. They were in short a new kind of lay aristocracy, different in its needs and interests from the feudal nobility of earlier centuries. The chivalric code of that old nobility and the scholastic learning of the clerical university answered their needs very imperfectly. The ideal men of the past, the monk and the knight, were no longer useful models. It is therefore not surprising that they became the enthusiastic patrons of a "new learning," of humanism, an educational and cultural program that offered them an ideal of man more in harmony with what they were and what they aspired to become.

Humanitas, from which both "humanist" and "humanism" derive, is a classical word and a classical idea. Cicero used it to translate the Greek paedeia, education or culture. The second-century grammarian Aulus Gellius defined it as "knowledge and instruction in the good arts." Fourteenth- and fifteenth-century humanists revived the word. "To each species of creature," wrote one, "has been allotted a peculiar and instructive gift. Galloping comes naturally to horses, flying to birds. To man only is given the desire to learn. Hence what the Greeks called paedeia we call studia humanitatis. For learning and training in virtue are peculiar to man; therefore our forefathers called them humanitas, the pursuit of activities proper to mankind." Humanists were men who taught and studied the studia humanitatis, the humanities, the good, humane, or liberal arts (bonae artes, humanae artes, artes liberales). Their intellectual interests were primarily literary, rhetorical, historical, and ethical; they typically wrote poems, orations, letters, plays, histories, works of scholarship, and a very wide range of moral treatises. Their literary language was normally Latin, and their admired models were classical. Some of them, indeed, were almost literally persuaded that everything it was really important for mankind to know was contained in the literatures of classical Greece and Rome, that is, in the works of ancient pagans like Plato, Cicero, and Livy and of ancient Christians like St. Augustine and St. Jerome. We mean by humanism, then, an educational and cultural program based on the study of the classics and colored by the notion of human dignity implicit in the word humanitas.

Humanist intellectuals occupied an honored place in society and exercised educational, professional, and cultural functions rather different from medieval intellectuals. Medieval intellectuals were almost always clerics; the cultural institutions in which they worked were the monastery and the university; it was their function to train priests and to study, organize, explain, and pass on to their successors the traditional substance of the Christian faith. Italian humanists were more frequently laymen; they worked in secondary schools, printing offices, and informal academies; they were teachers, civil servants, and independent men of letters, very closely tied to the rich and powerful. The sons of grandi were their pupils; indeed, many princes, merchants, bankers, lawyers, and rentiers patronized humanistic studies and were themselves enlightened amateurs, while humanists were often men of remarkable political and social importance, moving as equals among the great. Petrarch was the friend of princes and nobles. A line of distinguished humanists—Coluccio Salutati, Leonardo Bruni, Poggio Bracciolini—were chancellors of Florence. They drafted the official correspondence of the republic; wrote, registered, collected, and published the acts of the citizens directly invested with power, and generally supervised the lower echelons of the civil service. By the criteria of education, office, property, and income, the social rank of their friends, and the respectability of their children's marriages they were virtually indistinguishable from patricians. Whereas medieval intellectuals had educated priests, therefore, it became the function of humanists to educate the ruling class of the Italian city-states and principalities and to provide them with a philosophy of man in harmony with their needs and aspirations.

At the heart of the Renaissance philosophy of man is an assertion of human dignity. "What a piece of work is a man! how noble in reason! how infinite in faculty! in form and moving how express and admirable! in action how like an angel! in apprehension how like a god! the beauty of the world! the paragon of animals!" Hamlet's words combine pagan and Christian themes of great antiquity, some from classical philosophy and literature like the celebrated chorus in praise of man in Sophocles' *Antigone,* others from the Bible, the Greek church fathers and the medieval mystics: God created man in his own image; he is God's special care; for his sake God made all things and himself became man; he rules the world, and all other created things in it are subservient to him; he joins in himself the mortal and immortal and bears in his own nature the image of the whole creation (for this reason man is called a microcosm or little world); no science, art, or doctrine escapes the penetration of his mind. Italian humanists and philosophers of the Renaissance attached great importance to these themes and discussed them in a series of treatises entitled *De hominis dignitate,* on the dignity of man. The most moving of them is Giovanni Pico della Mirandola's *Oration on the Dignity of Man.*

In Pico's view man's greatest claim to nobility is that he has no fixed position in the hierarchical chain of being which philosophers considered the fundamental principle of order in the universe. The traditional structure was a simple one: inanimate matter, plants, animals, men, angels, and God. Rocks exist, plants live. Animals, men, angels, and God not only exist and live, they also know, each in a manner appropriate to him. Sensible knowledge is proper to animals; rational knowledge is proper to men; intellectual or intuitive knowledge is proper to angels. God's mode of knowing is far above even intellectual knowledge and almost inconceivable to the limited capacities of human beings. Man's median position between animals and angels is reflected in the diversity of his cognitive faculties and the complexity of his mental operations. For though his appropriate faculty is reason, he shares sense and imagination with brutes and intellect with angels. He can therefore know in three different ways: through his senses, by reason, and by intuition (helped in this very often by God's grace). Pico took one important and novel step beyond this scheme. Emphasizing both man's capacity to know in different ways and his moral freedom and responsibility, he argued eloquently that man contains in his own nature the possibility of the most varied development, that he can freely choose to become akin to any being, become like a rock or plant or beast if he turns toward evil, like the angels if he turns toward good. Man, that is, defines his own place in the hierarchy of being, rising or falling in it according to the nobility or baseness of what he chooses to know and love. Man is potentially capable of becoming all things—he can be a human bear or lion, dominated by cruelty, lust, and greed; or he can keep his head among the stars, his eyes fixed on heavenly things, and become a human angel or even, in certain ecstatic states, his mind rapt in contemplation and separated from the body, a kind of mortal god.

The notion that each man should freely and harmoniously develop all sides of his nature is the root of Renaissance individualism and of some of the most characteristic emphases of Renaissance thought: the greater stress laid on moral philosophy than on logic and metaphysics; the importance attached by many thinkers to the freedom of the will; the rehabilitation of the active life and the conviction that human personality develops most fully in the context of family and civic responsibility; a more generously secular conception of happiness which broadens its conditions to include wealth, pleasure, health, and beauty as well as piety and virtue. Such shifts of emphasis and value implied no direct repudiation of traditional ideals. They were rather an effort to resolve some of the antitheses of the immediate medieval past by understanding them not as alternatives but as necessarily complementary. The ideal man, it was suggested, should be both rich and virtuous, excel in both arms and letters, not only contemplate divine things but also act prudently in the world to benefit his family, friends, and city. He will then be a true individual, not only because the soul of every human being is immortal and unique, individually created by God and equally precious to him, but also because he has activated all of his own unique potentialities. The type of the *uomo universale* expressed this ideal individualism in practice. The great humanist architect Leon Battista Alberti (1404–1472) was a Florentine patrician, playwright, poet, moralist, man of letters; mathematician, architect, archaeologist, and art critic; an accomplished singer and organist; in his youth a skillful runner, wrestler, and mountain climber; handsome and affable, admired by his contemporaries as the phoenix of the age, a new Socrates.

The positive value assigned to wealth by many Italian intellectuals of the Renaissance is a good example of this more inclusive view of human nature and the world. Medieval men, at least in theory, had admired poverty more than wealth and considered riches a hindrance to salvation, attitudes shaped by the ideals of a monastic culture and derived from the Biblical bias against wealth and from the teaching of ancient Stoic philosophers that happiness comes from virtue only and that neither misfortune nor lack of temporal goods can trouble the tranquillity of the true sage. Petrarch modified the ascetic ideal of poverty by suggesting the virtue of the golden mean, Horace's *aurea mediocritas,* and by pointing out that Cicero had not protested against wealth as such but only against the abuse of wealth. After 1400 what Petrarch had advanced reluctantly, Florentine and Venetian humanists systematically defended. Seeing the problems of getting and spending with the eyes of citizens who claimed proudly that their self-acquired wealth was the foundation of their city's greatness, they praised international commerce and banking and encouraged the rational quest for property and profit. They maintained that wealth is a necessary condition of happiness and helps to develop the moral life. Thus Alberti, in a fascinating book on the family, argued that whatever increases a man's power to benefit his family and city is a good. Riches certainly do this. They foster a dignified, honorable family life; they are indispensable if the city is to be adequately defended and appropriately embellished with statues, fountains, and public buildings. They free men to exercise virtues like benevolence and charity more effectively. They promote happiness. For it is just as absurd to imagine that we can be satisfactorily happy if we are ill or ugly or lonely as it is to think we can be happy if we are poor. Riches bring a noble spirit inner freedom and cheer. Therefore the wish to be rich and to be good are not incompatible. True happiness consists in the possession of both capital and virtue.

A parallel shift of emphasis gave positive value to the body. The nude, much neglected by painters and sculptors since the fall of Rome, regained much of the importance it had enjoyed in antiquity. During the High Renaissance the idealized human form was the central subject of art. In humanist educational theory and practice physical training began to receive a novel attention as an integral part of a liberal education. In 1440 the humanist Lorenzo Valla published one of the most famous books of the Renaissance, his *De voluptate* (On the True Good). The Epicurean interlocutor in the dialogue defends nature, pleasure, and the human body. Nature is good; following natural impulses is pleasurable. To follow nature is the path to virtue. Therefore, those who condemn pleasure condemn nature herself. All pleasure is good, *omnis voluptas bona est;* so we should not suffocate the spontaneous inclinations which bring us joy. Valla himself did not share these opinions. The Christian interlocutor criticizes the Epicurean for speaking of "nature" rather than God and opposes a Christian pleasure of the soul, foretaste on earth of the beatific vision yet to come, to physical *voluptas.* But other thinkers soon combined the arguments of

Valla's two interlocutors to form an influential and attractive Christian Epicureanism, best flavored perhaps in Sir Thomas More's praise of pleasure in the *Utopia*. The result was a gradual rehabilitation of the natural, an emphasis on the dignity of the whole man, body and soul, and a healthy respect for pleasure, defined by Valla as a "joyful movement of the soul" combined with "a suave well-being of the body."

For many centuries thinkers had distinguished the active from the contemplative life, preferred contemplation to action, and found the model of the contemplative life in the monastery. Renaissance intellectuals redefined contemplation, passionately defended action, and asserted that the best lives combine the two, just as they combine wealth and virtue, physical and intellectual pleasure. Petrarch began the change. He wrote a book in praise of contemplation called *On the Solitary Life*. The contemplative withdrawal he praised, though, was not monkish but scholarly, a retired and studious leisure devoted to literature and philosophy. Other scholars developed his argument. Truth, they said, is more important than action. Cicero's political activity benefited one city for a limited time, but his writings on how to live well and virtuously have benefited all ages. For actions die with the men who made them, but thought, triumphing over the centuries, endures forever. The man who acts judiciously is admirable; but the man who has been able, as Vergil says, to know the causes of things is a god among men. Let men give themselves to the active life insofar as their human nature, family affection, and love of homeland demand. But let them remember that they were born to contemplate celestial things and seek the highest good—knowledge of the truth.

The argument assumes already that the active life has legitimate claims. These claims were put with increasing vigor by men committed to civic life. Their major premise was an assumption about the relative powers of the two principal faculties of the soul, reason and will. The will is free and in our power, whereas our knowledge, as one humanist put it, is no more than rational doubt. The object of the will is to be good; that of the intellect is truth. It is therefore safer and better to will the good than to strain reason in abstract speculation. The first is never without merit; the latter can often be polluted with crime and then admits no excuse. From the superiority of will to intellect they deduced the superiority of the active life to speculation and a program of civic humanism which condemned intellectual pursuits divorced from political and social commitment. Wise men should actively occupy themselves with the affairs of their commonwealth. Man is a political animal whose overriding duty is to his family, friends, and country. Civic duties do not distract men from higher things; they perfect men. So the active life, which prudently manipulates human beings, is to be preferred to the speculative life which contemplates the divine. "To tell the truth," says Salutati in a striking passage, "I will boldly affirm and openly confess that I will happily give up to you and to those who lift their speculation to the sky, all other truths, if only the truth and reason of things human are left to me." Solitary speculation, the lonely search for truth and the unshared joy of its discovery, these are lesser goods. It is nobler to be always active in the service of one's country by increasing its wealth and occupying its offices. Man, said Alberti, is born to be useful to man; and every citizen is obligated, after God, to his country. Noblest of all, however, is the man who combines speculation and action, who joins wisdom and learning in fulfilling family obligation, military service, and civic responsibility. When Alfonso, king of Naples, asked the humanist Giannozzo Manetti, then in his service, what was the proper duty of man, Manetti answered: *agere et intelligere,* to act and to know; and Alberti defined man as a mortal but happy god because he combined capacity for virtuous action with rational understanding. Both men were echoing wonderful lines from Cicero's *De finibus:* "Just as the horse is born to run, the ox to plow, the dog to scent a trail, so man, as Aristotle says, is born to two things, to know and to act, and in this he is almost a mortal god."

Complementing the Renaissance philosophy of man was a profound and distinctive piety. The point is worth emphasizing, for the myth of the wicked Renaissance, that beguiling mixture of artistic splendor with poison, perversion, and paganism, is still with us. Murder was indeed too often the instrument of policy. Evidence of unusual sexual practice is readily available—the more so because Renaissance Italy ranks with eighteenth-century France and several periods in the art and literature of India and Japan as one of the major sources of erotica of classic merit. On the other hand there is no evidence that anyone was an atheist or passed from an admiration of classical literature to a worship of the pagan gods. Renaissance Italy was a Christian society where the temperature of piety was high. This does not mean that styles of piety remained the same. On the contrary, important changes were under way.

One such change was a growing hostility to scholastic theology. Fifteenth-century men attacked the great summas of the thirteenth and fourteenth centuries on several grounds. Their style was barbarous and therefore incapable of persuading men to love God and their neighbors. They were too complicated, hiding simple religious truths under a mass of riddles, enigmas, and syllogisms. Theological reformers regularly compared themselves to Hercules fighting the hydra (the entangling syllogisms. of scholastic theology) or to Alexander cutting the Gordian knot. Scholastic theology was disputatious and promoted contention rather than peace and concord. When the theologians raised knotty difficulties, opposed authorities *sic et non,* probed *quaestiones* in disputations and reconciled them by a subtle logic, they were rather pandering to their own dialectical pride than serving the faith. Finally, their effort to make theology a science, that is, to establish a systematically ordered body of true and certain knowledge derived from the certain but undemonstrable principles of revelation, was misguided, arrogant, and dangerous, for it produced only sophistry, arid intellectualism, emotional poverty, and lack of charity.

To this discredited theology Renaissance intellectuals opposed a piety which they claimed to be simpler, more pure, more personal and emotional, more eloquent, more humbly and accurately dependent on the divine text, directed less toward the presumptuous and inevitably disputatious goal of trying to *know* God in his fullness than toward the more human and possible aim of ardently loving him, more scholarly, more intimately and persuasively concerned with moral teaching. It was a learned piety; it was Biblical and patristic in inspiration; its orientation was ethical.

It was Petrarch who gave the phrase *docta pietas,* learned piety, its currency. Piety is knowledge, love and worship of God. Since piety is true wisdom also and since the philosopher is a lover of wisdom, the true philosopher is a man who loves God and true philosophy is necessarily a Christian philosophy, a *philosophia Christiana.* Petrarch knew, of course, that many ignorant, uncultivated men had achieved a noble sanctity. But a learned piety is nobler still. By learning he meant knowledge of classical literature. For piety and wisdom come from two sources—from the Christian God and from the ideas and examples of the greatest pagan ancients. Did not Cicero describe "one single god as the governor and maker of all things, not in a merely philosophical but in an almost Catholic manner of phrasing it, so that sometimes you would think you were hearing not a pagan philosopher but an apostle"? The idea of *docta pietas,* by assuming the harmony of Christianity and classical culture, defined for Renaissance men the proper relation between their enthusiasm for the antique and their firm commitment to Christian values.

The idea had other implications. True theology should be eloquent, a "union of piety and wisdom with eloquence." Its study should require historical sense, critical method, and knowledge of languages, notably Greek and Hebrew. True theology, in sum, should be Biblical; not a science but a positive wisdom, a holy learning derived from the holy page of Scripture. Examples of such a theology were conveniently at hand—the works of the Greek and Latin fathers. The simple Biblical piety Renaissance thinkers attributed to them justified their own aversion to scholastic method, their insistence on a return to the sources in their original languages, the normally exegetical form of their own theological work and the end they sought—an eloquent and vibrant personal piety joined to moral probity. Above all, the Biblical work of the fathers became a model for their critical study and correction of the Biblical text itself. Valla applied his passion for linguistic precision, his scrupulous flair for the way words gradually change their meanings, the philological techniques acquired in studying classical texts, to a critical probing of the text of the New Testament. Erasmus published Valla's *Annotations on the New Testament* in 1505, and the book influenced his own vastly more important Biblical and patristic studies.

Yet for Renaissance Christians learning and scholarship were always at the service of an ethical impulse. The end of humanist education was to teach men to live well and happily. From the many possible options offered by traditional Christian theology, Renaissance thinkers chose for special emphasis the freedom of the will and Christ's ethical teaching. From reading philosophy, they thought, man will learn to know himself, to recognize his own human dignity. This will encourage him to learn to live well and to flee all vices like the worst pest. The Bible, church fathers, and mystics teach the same lesson. From them the wise man will learn to hate vice and love the good, gradually learn, with God now helping his cooperative will, to live well and happily, and to die well, in the tranquil assurance of salvation.

For Further Reading

Garin, Eugenio, *Italian Humanism: Philosophy and Civic Life in the Renaissance.*
Goldthwaite, Richard, *Private Wealth in Renaissance Florence: A Study of Four Families.*
Holmes, George, *The Florentine Enlightenment 1400–1450.*
Kristeller, Paul Oskar, *Renaissance Thought: The Classic, Scholastic, and Humanist Strains.*
Martines, Lauro, *The Social World of the Florentine Humanists.*

3   Renaissance Art

The works of Renaissance artists, beautiful and civilizing in themselves, luminously supplement the evidence of texts and documents. "The good painter," wrote Leonardo da Vinci, "must paint principally two things: man and the ideas in man's mind." Because Leonardo and his contemporaries did indeed choose these as their subject, few sources make so attrac-

A.D.   c. 1255–1319   Duccio di Buoninsegna
     c. 1276–1337   Giotto
        1377–1446   Filippo Brunelleschi
     c. 1386–1466   Donatello
        1387–1455   Fra Angelico
        1401–1428   Masaccio
        1404–1472   Leon Battista Alberti
     c. 1426–1492   Piero della Francesca
     c. 1430–1516   Giovanni Bellini
        1431–1506   Andrea Mantegna
        1444–1510   Botticelli
        1444–1514   Bramante
        1452–1519   Leonardo da Vinci
        1471–1528   Albrecht Dürer
        1475–1564   Michelangelo
        1477–1576   Titian
     c. 1478–1510   Giorgione
        1483–1520   Raphael
        1494–1534   Correggio
        1511–1574   Giorgio Vasari
        1518–1590   Andrea Palladio
        1518–1594   Tintoretto
        1528–1588   Paolo Veronese

tively explicit the humanist philosophy of man as do Renaissance paintings, sculptures, and buildings.

The most distinctive artistic invention of the Renaissance was perspective. It distinguishes Renaissance painting from medieval painting. But not only that. Exact geometrical perspective is uniquely found in Western art between the early fifteenth and the early twentieth centuries. Wall paintings and mosaics from Pompeii suggest that an approximation of it was known to Hellenistic and Roman artists. Many Chinese and Japanese landscape painters were able, by empirical means, to achieve breathtaking illusions of distance. However, exact perspective construction—and more important the wish itself to depict objects in a unified space—was invented in Florence about 1420, remained perhaps the most important single characteristic of Western art until the Post-Impressionists, was unknown to any previous culture, and is absent from the art of all non-Western civilizations.

The invention of perspective threw open a window on the world. "I describe a rectangle of whatever size I please," wrote Alberti, "and I imagine it to be an open window through which I view whatever is to be depicted there." In the Renaissance the painting surface lost its opacity and became a clear pane through which we look into a world of rationally related solids, where the objects represented seem to have the same sizes, shapes, and positions relative to each other that the actual objects located in actual space would have if seen from a single viewpoint. Using a geometry of converging visual rays, perspective projects the illusion of a unified, continuous, and infinite three-dimensional space upon a two-dimensional plane. Probably invented by the architect Brunelleschi, with the sculptor Donatello and the painter Masaccio one of the seminal trio who founded the Renaissance style in Florence, and in Italy, and first described by Alberti, its principles and methods were fully worked out during the fifteenth and early sixteenth centuries by painter-theorists like Piero della Francesca, Leonardo, and Albrecht Dürer. The earliest surviving work of art that uses the new technique is Masaccio's fresco of the Trinity in the church of Santa Maria Novella in Florence, painted about 1427.

There is a suggestive parallel between the discovery of perspective in art and the renewed sense of historical distance which enabled Renaissance scholars and artists to understand antiquity more exactly and objectively. Medieval men had very little perspective on antiquity because no chronological line divided it from their own age. They knew only two great periods, one of light and one of darkness, before Christ and after Christ. They believed that the second great period of world history had begun with the simultaneous founding of the Roman Empire and the birth of Christ and that they themselves were living near the end of that same period.

Renaissance historians drew two sharp chronological lines instead of one. They invented the tripartite division of European history into ancient, medieval, and modern which even today remains the basis of our chronology. This new periodization of history modified profoundly men's sense of the past. Because the medieval historian believed that his own historical epoch had begun with the reign of Augustus, he was unconscious of the intellectual and imaginative gulf that had to be crossed in order to understand the ancient world. Apart from the inescapable fact that it was pagan, it could have for him no special character or style. The Romans were his contemporaries. The familiarity imposed on him by a theological periodization weakened his ability to see Rome as a culture complete in itself, quite different and separate from his contemporary world. By sharply dividing medieval from ancient history and their own age from the recent past, Renaissance historians ended this deforming familiarity. Their new periodization created the historical perspective on which the modern sense of history depends. They came to realize that a thousand years separated them from classical Rome. They realized too that this past was dead, that it formed a distinct historical period, remote, complete in itself, over. Disciplined by the insight that the arts and literature of antiquity were the historical expressions of a particular period and a unique society detached from their own, they gradually built up through the critical and historical study of ancient texts an image of ancient thought and institutions more nearly approximating ancient reality than any achieved before.

Nowhere is this imaginative reappropriation of the antique more striking than in the visual arts. A whole vocabulary of classical forms reentered Western art. Brunelleschi not only invented perspective. He went to Rome, studied the ancient ruins, and then subtly joined together columns and pilasters, arches and pediments in original buildings of incomparable harmony and grace. Painters and sculptors copied antique sarcophagi and collected coins and inscriptions. Inspired by the "excellent works of the Greeks and Romans," they covered the walls and ceilings of the peninsula with classical quotations: swags and garlands, Nereids and Tritons, fauns and nymphs; Roman armor, standards and trophies; the gods and goddesses of Olympus.

At the same time Renaissance representations of classical antiquity show a grasp and understanding of the ancient past qualitatively different from the medieval. Medieval artists had illustrated classical themes like the story of Dido and Aeneas. They had also reproduced classical motifs and forms, imitating from a coin the profile of a Roman emperor, or from a bas-relief the gracefully draped figure of a Roman matron. What is curious, though, in medieval art is the invariable disjunction of classical theme and classical motif. The Dido and Aeneas illustrating a manuscript of Vergil appear anachronistically as a medieval noble and his lady playing chess. Conversely, the Roman matrons who greet each other at Reims cathedral are the Virgin Mary and St. Elizabeth, for the scene is a Visitation. In the Renaissance, on the other hand, for the first time in more than 700 years, artists found for the substance of ancient literary texts historically and artistically appropriate forms. They reintegrated classical theme and classical motif. The classical deities shed their clothes and regained their ancient grace and attributes. A renewed consciousness of anachronism put Dido and Aeneas in classical dress. Ancient representations of Hercules were no longer used to represent David. A sharpening archaeological expertise re-created scenes from ancient history of enormous splendor and plausibility. This plausible rendering of classical themes is a fundamental criterion for defining the Renaissance in art. It is also tangible, and beautiful, evidence that new windows had been opened on the classical past.

The generalization of perspective and artists' enthusiastic admiration of the "excellent work of the Greeks and Romans" posed the central problems of Renaissance aesthetics, those of realism, harmony, and imitation. Perspective made it possible to represent the external world more realistically. It was, in a sense, a return to nature; and it gave new weight to the notion that the best painting is that which imitates nature successfully, a conviction the more solidly held because the injunction "follow nature" had been bandied about by moral philosophers for centuries. It is the function of the painter, wrote Alberti, "to render with lines and colors, on a given panel or wall, the visible surface of any body, so that at a certain distance and from a certain position it appears in relief and just like the body itself." Does this mean that it is the function of the painter to start us salivating before a bowl of fuzzed and bursting peaches? Certainly Renaissance artists and their audiences enormously enjoyed and valued representational virtuosity, the convincing rendering of transparent draperies, the sheen of pearls, subtle effects of cloud, storm, and light, the minute imitation of plants, animals, and fruits. Leonardo went so far as to call Narcissus the first painter because he saw his likeness reflected in a pool and to say that the "true painting" is a reflection in a mirror.

But the realistic imitation of nature was not the only function Renaissance painters thought their art should have. Representations of nature should be beautiful as well as accurate; and by beauty they typically meant the harmonious ordering of ideal forms, forms at once recognizably natural, but more beautiful than any actually observable in nature. A ravishing example is Raphael's *Galatea,* commissioned about 1510 by Agostino Chigi, a Sienese who made his fortune as a papal banker. The central figure of Raphael's fresco is the milk-white sea nymph Galatea, the beloved of Acis. Raphael learned her history and attributes from verses by

Theocritus and Ovid and from the contemporary Italian poets Angelo Poliziano and Pietro Bembo. Against a background of sky and sea veined like an antique marble, Nereids and Tritons, hippocamps and cupids, celebrate her triumph. The scene is a vision of antiquity consciously disciplined by archaeological expertise: the figures come directly from a Nereid sarcophagus. Raphael's successful effort to make the figure of Galatea an image of ideal beauty represents a conscious revival of the similar effort of ancient art. "To paint a beautiful woman," he wrote about the *Galatea* to his friend and patron Baldassare Castiglione, "I need to see many beautiful women. . . . But since there is a dearth both of good judges of what is beautiful and of beautiful women, I use as my guide a certain idea of the beautiful that I carry in my mind." This idea of the beautiful he derived in practice from the canons of classical art and from the example of ancient sculpture. The same idealizing impulse controls the tight geometry of the composition. Like every Renaissance artist, Raphael intended to imitate nature; but he regarded nature as ordered, harmonized by geometry, just as Copernicus and Kepler were certain they would find ideal geometrical patterns behind the confusing particularity of observed experience. Thus Galatea's head is at the apex of a triangle. The horizon divides the picture space into two equal parts, locked together in a musical harmony by intersecting circles: the three flying *amors* outline the circumference of the upper circle; the figures around Galatea mark the lower circumference of the other. In the center of rational nature is a beautiful human being.

Clearly, Renaissance art was a humanistic art, and not only because, like literary humanists, Renaissance artists admired and imitated antique models. Artistic activity in the high Middle Ages had normally been an anonymous communal enterprise controlled by the clergy and directed by ecclesiastical authority to orthodox religious ends. By the sixteenth century, humanists had replaced clerics as the typical "inventors" of the subject matter of works of art. It is not surprising, therefore, that Renaissance art is a learned art. Renaissance paintings must be read, for they were consciously designed to tell stories, teach lessons, and inculcate humanist ideals of knowledge, conduct, and piety. They are humanist also in style; for the harmonies of their composition derived from the harmony of the human body, "because from the human body," in the words of an Italian mathematician who also wrote an early treatise on double-entry bookkeeping, "derive all measures and their denominations and in it is to be found all and every ratio and proportion by which God reveals the innermost secrets of nature." Admiration of the harmony of his body and of the world arouses man's admiration and love of God; by imitating nature in his art man imitates the creativity of God and becomes himself a creator in the realm of art. Ideas such as these are one source of the romantic idea of artistic genius. When the great romantic historian Jules Michelet took one short step more and defined the Renaissance as the discovery of the world and of man, he peopled the whole peninsula with geniuses and created the image of the age which has ever since provoked admiration and contention.

For Further Reading

Benesch, Otto, *The Art of the Renaissance in Northern Europe.*
Berenson, Bernard, *The Italian Painters of the Renaissance.*
Panofsky, Erwin, *Renaissance and Renascences in Western Art.*
Shearman, John, *Mannerism.*
Wittkower, Rudolf, *Architectural Principles in the Age of Humanism.*

4   The Reformation: Doctrine

When in October, 1517, an almost unknown Augustinian friar named Martin Luther posted ninety-five theses against indulgences on the door of the castle church of Wittenberg, a small university town in the territories of Frederick the Wise, elector of Saxony, the Roman church had been for many centuries the most powerful ecumenical institution in Europe. From Cracow to Lisbon, from Edinburgh to Palermo, its teachings defined every man's faith. The spirituality of its saints shaped his devotions. Its priests baptized him when he entered the world and buried him when he died. Its authority and blessing touched rich and poor, priest and layman, noble and commoner, king and subject. The church united Western European society in one common corps of Christendom, made it one body whose head was Christ.

The organization of this universal church was monarchical, sacerdotal, and sacramental. Punishing blows had weakened its worldly power: the humiliation of Pope Boniface VIII by the king of France and the exile early in the fourteenth century of the papacy from Rome to Avignon; the Great Schism later in the same century, when the shocking spectacle of two and even three rival popes excommunicating each other provoked the calling of a series of councils to reform the church in head and members; the increasingly successful efforts of kings and princes to subject the personnel and property of the church in their dominions to their control. As

A.D. 1505 Martin Luther joins the Augustinian Order
       1512 Luther appointed professor of Holy Sciptures at the University of Wittenberg
       1516 First edition of the New Testament in Greek
       1517 Luther's theses against indulgences
       1518 Zwingli called to be minister at Zurich
       1520 Luther's *Open Letter to the Christian Nobility of the German Nation, The Babylonian Captivity of the Church,* and *On Christian Liberty;* Luther's excommunication
       1521 Diet of Worms
       1524 Erasmus defends the freedom of the will against Luther
       1525 Conrad Grebel baptizes Georg Blaurock: the beginning of Anabaptism; the Reformation established in Zurich
       1527 The Schleitheim Confession, first Anabaptist doctrinal statement
       1529 Colloquy of Marburg
       1531 Death of Zwingli at the Battle of Kappel
       1534 First complete edition of Luther's translation of the Bible
       1546 Death of Martin Luther
       1564 Death of John Calvin

---

early as 1420 a pope wryly observed: "Not the pope but the king of England governs the church in his dominions." On the other hand, in the area of faith and morals Roman claims had become more comprehensive, in the area of church government more sharply monarchical. Curial lawyers identified the universal church with the Roman church and the Roman church with its supreme head, the pope. Just as the universal church cannot err in matters of faith and morals, so the pope cannot err—one assumption behind the doctrine of papal infallibility. Lawyers also identified the church with the ecclesiastical hierarchy. In this perspective the church was an "empire" ruled by the laws, ordinances, and will of its sovereign, who inherited the powers and prerogatives attributed to the sovereign prince in Roman law: *Quicquid principi placuit legis habet vigorem* (The will of the prince has the force of law).

The ecclesiastical hierarchy monopolized the right to interpret Scripture and administer the sacraments, the objective exclusive channels of

God's saving grace: baptism, confirmation, penance, the Eucharist, marriage, ordination, and extreme unction. The clergy was the first order in society and a class apart, separated from the laity by the indelible mark of ordination. The basis of the priest's authority was his miraculous and unique power to change the Eucharistic elements into the very body and blood of Christ. The doctrine of transubstantiation was the only medieval contribution to dogma in the strict sense, as the Mass was the heart of medieval sacerdotalism. When the priest said, "This is my body," he transformed the sacramental bread and wine into the body and blood of Christ, while their accidents, everything about the elements perceivable to the senses, remained those of bread and wine. He reenacted on the altar the incarnation and crucifixion. God again became flesh, Christ again died sacrificially for man's salvation. By eating the body of Christ the communicant shared his death and resurrection; for, as St. Ignatius had written in the apostolic age, the sacramental meal is "the medicine of immortality." Only through the priest as mediator could this grace reach the laity. Clerical power and the preeminent position of the church in society rested on this monopoly.

Between 1517 and the death of John Calvin in Geneva in 1564 revolutionary changes shook this hierarchical, sacerdotal, sacramental church to its foundations. A handful of religious geniuses denied the authority of Rome, abolished the Mass, broke the priesthood's control of access to salvation, created original systems of Christian doctrine, and founded new churches and sects. In less than forty years they shattered the millennial unity of Western Christendom.

The first half of the sixteenth century was a tragic and heroic age, humanized for us by paradox and irony. Not the least of its ironies is that this revolution in the church has come to be called a "reformation."

Reformers believe that the institution they want to improve is fundamentally healthy and good. Martin Luther was not a reformer. He did not want to purify monasteries by enforcing their rules more strictly or by raising the spiritual and intellectual level of monks and friars; he wished to get rid of monasteries entirely. Like many of his contemporaries, he deplored abuses in the papacy; but he was as radically hostile to worthy popes as he was to unworthy ones, for he believed that the pope was Antichrist. His mature purpose was not to correct abuses in, for example, the sacrament of penance; he wanted to abolish the sacrament because it had no scriptural foundation. In spite of its name, the Protestant Reformation was not in any fundamental way an effort to reform the church in head and members; it was a passionate debate on the proper conditions of salvation. Its serious concern was not with abuses but with the very foundations of faith and doctrine. Protestants reproached the clergy not for ignorance or for keeping concubines but for teaching false and dangerous things. They did not attack the corruption of institutions; they attacked what they considered to be the corruption of faith itself. Luther intended to restore Biblical Christianity, but he made a revolution. Like Jesus, he brought not peace but a sword. He came not to reform but to destroy—and then restore.

Luther's beginnings were conventional enough. The son of a prosperous miner of peasant stock, he received a sound elementary and secondary school education, and at eighteen matriculated in the University of Erfurt. There he followed the usual course of study in the faculty of arts: logic, some literature and mathematics, ethics, physics, and metaphysics, taught, wherever possible, from Aristotelian texts interpreted by members of the Nominalist school descended from the great fourteenth-century philosopher William of Ockham. He received the B.A. in 1502 and the M.A. in 1505. Obeying his father's wishes, he next enrolled in the faculty of law, the normal road to high office in church or state. He had just become a law student when, returning to Erfurt after a visit to his parents, he was caught in a thunderstorm and thrown to the ground by a bolt of lightning. In a moment of terror, fearful of death and possible damnation, he cried out: "St. Anne, help me, I will become a monk." Within a month, over the angry protests of his father, he joined the mendicant order of St. Augustine.

The next years were for Luther a period of the most intense torment, anguish, and doubt. He was, apparently, in every way a model monk: he was obedient, chaste, and studious; he obeyed the rule of his house and order; he ignored no discipline, penance, or religious exercise. But no peace came. His monkish good works brought no inner security. The more humbly he meditated on the majesty and justice of God, the more intense became his own feeling of sinful unworthiness. In the last year of his life, in the preface to a collected edition of his works he described the root of his despair: "Though I lived as a monk without reproach, I felt that I was a sinner before God with an extremely disturbed conscience. I could not believe that He was placated by my satisfaction. I did not love, yes, I hated the righteous God who punishes sinners, and secretely, if not blasphemously, . . . I was angry with God." God is just, a righteous God. Luther suffocated with the overwhelming sense that he was weak and impure, and that every effort he made to satisfy God's justice and righteousness, to merit salvation, was a failure. While he was saying his first Mass in 1507, he was so terrified by the disparity between his own sinfulness and God's justice, so appalled that a man as base as he should presume to transform the wafer and wine into the body and blood of Christ, that he almost collapsed.

In 1511 Luther's superiors transferred him from Erfurt to Wittenberg, and in 1512 he became professor of Holy Scriptures at the town's new university. He read voraciously: St. Augustine, the mystics, scholastic theology, humanist commentaries and editions of the Bible. He lectured on Genesis, the Psalms, and finally Paul's Epistle to the Romans. He found his solace and solution in St. Paul:

> At last, by the mercy of God, meditating day and night, I gave heed to the context of the words, namely, "In it the righteousness of God is revealed, as it is written, 'He who through faith is righteous shall live.'" (Romans 1:17) There I began to understand that the righteousness of God is that by which the righteous lives by a gift of God, namely faith. And this is the meaning: the righteousness of God is revealed by the Gospel, namely, the passive righteousness with which merciful God justifies us by faith, as it is written, "He who through faith is righteous shall live." Here I felt that I was altogether born again and had entered paradise itself through open gates.

By the end of 1516 Luther had won his private battle. His terror before an angry God subsided and a tranquil assurance of God's mercy calmed and fortified him. His struggle to *earn* salvation gave way to a total passivity and trust and faith in Christ. Holding firm to Paul's belief that man is justified by faith alone without the works of the law, he came to believe that God's justice is a free acquittal of the guilty. He knew he was no less sinful now than he had been before, but he was totally convinced that God, in his purely gratuitous and mysterious mercy, had chosen him for salvation.

Between 1517 and 1520—haphazardly, without premeditation, under the pressure of events—Luther drew the consequences of his hard-won understanding that man is justified by faith alone. In the spring of 1517 a Dominican friar arrived near Wittenberg to sell indulgences, part of a campaign arranged by Pope Leo X, the archbishop of Mainz, and the Augsburg banking house of Fugger to raise money for rebuilding St. Peter's in Rome. In the early sixteenth century an indulgence was the transfer by the pope of superfluous merit accumulated by Christ, the Virgin Mary, and the saints to an individual sinner in order to remit all or some of the temporal penalties for sin later to be suffered in purgatory. Papal doctrine held that such transfers of divine credit could benefit not only the living but the dead as well. The Dominican salesmen even promised that as soon as a coin dropped into the collector's box a soul would fly up out of purgatory to heaven. Luther was horrified at this caricature of what he conceived to be the true economy of salvation. Because he believed that man was justified by faith alone, he argued that the pope could remit only those penalties he had imposed himself. He denied that saints had superfluous credits or that merit could be stored up for subsequent use by others. He branded indulgences as positively harmful, for actually imperiling salvation by giving simple people the dangerous impression that they could buy their way into heaven.

Luther's theses were the work of a reformer. He was attacking abuses and superstitions that had grown up around the sacrament of penance. But during the controversy aroused by his attack—which Pope Leo X momentarily brushed aside as a "monk's quarrel"—Luther drew more radical consequences from his unshakable conviction that salvation comes not from ourselves but through faith in Christ the Redeemer. Faith in Christ implies, he felt, the unique authority of the word of God revealed in Scripture; the Bible is the *only* source of religious truth because it is the concrete locus of the Word of God, the written record of the revelation of God in Christ, the channel through which God reaches those to whom he has granted the grace of faith. Looking one day for new Biblical arguments with which to buttress his criticisms of indulgences, he compared the Latin and the Greek texts of the verse traditionally cited as the scriptural authority for the sacrament of penance. The Vulgate, the Latin translation of St. Jerome, reads, "Do penance"; he found in the Greek, conveniently available to him in the recently published edition of the Greek New Testament by the great humanist Erasmus of Rotterdam, the rather different injunction, "Be patient." With a logic devastating for traditional belief and practice, he decided that the sacrament had no scriptural foundation and must consequently be abolished. Astonished, but undismayed, Luther found himself the leader of a revolutionary attack on the Roman Church.

Three celebrated tracts of 1520—*An Open Letter to the Christian Nobility of the German Nation, The Babylonian Captivity of the Church,* and *On Christian Liberty*—sum up the work of demolition. In them Luther attacked every fundamental assumption on which the medieval church had rested. Since only Scripture is infallible, popes and councils can, and have, erred. Not only was the pope's claim to preeminence in Christendom a usurpation; the pope was Antichrist: "O pope, not most holy, but most sinful. O that God from heaven would soon destroy thy throne and sink it in the abyss of hell." He called most Christian the opinions of Hus and Wycliffe, long branded by the church as notoriously heretical. To the rejected sacrament of penance he added the sacraments of confirmation, marriage, holy orders, and extreme unction. By rejecting holy orders he erased the distinction between a spiritual estate (pope, bishops, the secular and monastic clergy) and a temporal estate (kings, princes, nobles, merchants, craftsmen, and peasants), the distinction between priest and laymen, thus ending, as he put it, "the detestable tyranny of the clergy over the laity." In its place Luther put his conception of a priesthood of all believers. Because all Christians share one baptism, one gospel, one faith, and one church, he argued, they are equal in the realm of the spirit, all

alike members of a single spiritual estate, all priests. He struck at the heart
of sacerdotalism by redefining the sacrament of the Eucharist. He denied
that the Mass was a repetition of Christ's sacrifice on the cross. He denied
the doctrine of transubstantiation. He denied that the sacrament worked, as
medieval theologians had taught, by its own innate virtue and power. On
the contrary, since men are justified only by faith, the sacrament must be a
function of the faith of the recipient. Here is the root of Lutheran individualism. The faith which makes the sacrament effective is one's own,
given by God freely and gratuitously to each individual to whom he
chooses to be merciful. The individual soul stands alone before its savior
and creator.

Arguments like these were not the commonplaces of a "monk's quarrel." In October, 1520, a papal bull of excommunication reached Wittenberg. Luther burned it publicly. The next year the emperor summoned him
to appear before the Diet, meeting at Worms. On the evening of April 18,
1521, Luther stood before his king and the representatives of the German
nation. He was asked to recant his books. He replied in German:

> Unless I am convinced by the testimony of the Scriptures or by clear reason
> (for I do not trust either in the pope or in councils, since it is well known that
> they have often erred and contradicted themselves), I am bound by the Scrip-
> tures I have quoted and my conscience is captive to the Word of God. I cannot
> and I will not retract anything, since it is neither safe nor right to go against
> conscience. May God help me! Amen.

The next day, April 19, Charles V answered in French, a reminder that
the German king was a foreigner in Germany. His statement is as moving,
as true to the characters and vision of the man who spoke it, as was
Luther's:

> It is certain that a single friar errs in his opinion which is against all of
> Christendom and according to which all of Christianity will be and will always
> have been in error both in the past thousand years and even more in the
> present. For that reason I am absolutely determined to stake on this cause my
> kingdoms and seigniories, my friends, my body and blood, my life and soul.
> For it would be a great shame to me and to you, who are by privilege and
> preeminent standing singularly called to be defenders and protectors of the
> Catholic faith, if in our time not only heresy but even suspicion of heresy or
> decrease of the Christian religion should through our negligence dwell after us
> in the hearts of men and our successors to our perpetual dishonor.

The emperor condemned Luther as an obstinate heretic and put him under
the ban of the empire.

Luther summed up his teaching in two lapidary formulas: *sola fide*
("by faith alone") and *sola scriptura* ("by Scripture alone"). They answer

the fundamental religious question, "What is the proper relation between man and God?" by attributing as much as possible to God and as little as possible to man. Man's principal faculties are his intellect, by which he distinguishes truth from falsehood, and his will, by which he distinguishes good and evil and orders his moral life. Luther's estimate of human nature was uncompromisingly pessimistic. Human reason is deformed and blind, incapable of saving truth. The human will is in bondage, free only to choose among different degrees of sin. All goodness, truth, and virtue come from God: all weakness, falsehood, and sin come from nature, especially human nature. Apart from God's grace, the human condition is hopeless. "It is not only the privation of a property of the will," wrote Luther in his commentary on the Epistle of St. Paul to the Romans, "nor only the privation of light in the intellect, of virtue in the memory; but the absolute privation of all righteousness and of the power of all strengths, of body and soul, of the whole man interior and exterior. Further, there is in man a positive inclination to evil, a disgust for the good, a hatred of light and wisdom, a delight in error and darkness, a flight from and abomination of good works, a race toward evil."

This assessment of man, so different from that of the Italian humanists, may seem hard and cruel; but for Luther and for thousands of his contemporaries it was demonstrably full of peace and sweetness, because, as Luther put it in this same commentary on Romans, "it teaches us to seek all assistance and all salvation, not from ourselves, but from without, through faith in Christ." For the doctrine of *sola fide* emphasizes both man's nullity and God's merciful concern for his salvation. Man is saved by faith without the works of the law. His own deeds, his own merit, count for nothing. He has no merit. Man cannot cooperate in his own salvation. Nothing he can do by his own effort brings him closer to God. If God were merely just, he would surely damn him. But God is also merciful; and so, mysteriously, gratuitously, he chooses to save some men, freely acquitting them of their guilt. Although they have been, are still, and will remain sinful, he gives them faith and considers them just. They, in turn, though fully conscious of their unworthiness, become joyfully confident, exactly as Luther had himself, of God's mercy and believe firmly that Christ has shed his blood for their salvation. Justification by faith alone, delicately balancing pessimism about man against optimism about God, is the cornerstone of classical Protestant theology.

Sola scriptura is a special case of *sola fide*. Because fallen man is morally and spiritually helpless, he cannot reestablish contact with God. God must reestablish contact with man. He does so through the incarnation of his Son. He justifies man by mercifully granting him faith in his son, who is also his Word, as in the memorable opening of the Gospel of John, that Word who is also named Wisdom, Christ, Redeemer, Second Person of the

Trinity, and the canonical Scriptures. For man receives the gift of faith by hearing and reading the Bible. Since Christ is the author of the written Word, the Eternal Word can be known from the written Word. This is why the sermon, that is, the explication of a portion of God's Word, dominates the Protestant church service and why Luther saw the Bible as the only infallible source of religious truth.

Locating the sole source of religious truth in Scripture was not an ideal way of ensuring Christian unity, for Biblical texts can be and have been interpreted in a bewildering number of different ways. Catholic and Protestant alike believed that true understanding of Scripture was a gift of the Holy Spirit. They agreed too that individuals should not interpret Scripture as they pleased; that could only mean that everyone was free to go to hell in his own way. But while Catholics institutionalized the Spirit's guidance in tradition, in the pope, and in the church, Protestants either claimed that the Spirit gave them individual guidance, or argued, in the face of all evidence to the contrary, that the Bible is simple, clear, and easy to understand. The difficulties inherent in such claims became obvious as soon as other reformers, guided, as they firmly believed, by the Holy Spirit, began to interpret Scripture as personally as Luther had done. Each considered his own interpretation normative; each attributed other interpretations to the inspiration of the devil. From these divergent readings of Scripture sprang new varieties of Protestantism. In the sixteenth century the most important were Zwinglianism, Calvinism, and Anabaptism.

Huldreich Zwingli (1484–1531), the reformer of German Switzerland, was, after Luther, the most creative theologian of the century. In 1519 he began to preach the gospel in the Grossmünster in Zurich. Luther influenced him profoundly. By the end of 1520 he had made the two fundamental Lutheran principles the heart of his theology: justification by faith alone and the sole authority of Scripture. He drew many of the same consequences from these principles that Luther did; he attacked monasticism, relics and the veneration of saints, and purgatory. He preached predestination and the bondage of the will and the reduction of the sacraments from seven to two.

Zwingli's originality was to spell out the consequences of *sola fide* for liturgical and sacramental simplification more consistently and radically. In liturgy and decor Zwingli was the first Puritan. Offended by corporeal representations of divine things and by the sensuousness of the traditional service, he banished from his church the "trills" of music and the "luxuriously and sleekly" painted images of saints. He broke up the organ in the Grossmünster and knocked out its stained glass windows, for he wished his congregation to have ears only for the Word of God and eyes only for

Scripture. The Gesù in Rome has become the symbol of a Catholic interior: blazing with gilt, stucco, and marble, smoky with incense, its theatrical perspectives reverberating with the serpentine polyphony of Palestrina and the massed bronzes of Gabrieli. Zwingli created in Zurich the representative Protestant interior: whitewashed walls, plain benches for the congregation, a wooden table and a simple wooden cup for the celebration of the Supper.

Zwingli's "sacramentarianism," the denial of the Real Presence of Christ in the sacramental elements of the Eucharist, came from his passionate concern to reduce religion to its essentials. Like Luther, Zwingli rejected the Catholic Mass; in 1525 he persuaded the town council to abolish it in Zurich. Both Luther and Zwingli rejected the doctrine of transubstantiation as unscriptural, implausible, and a scholastic sophistry. But Luther remained convinced that Christ was present in the sacrament, arguing both that his real body and blood coexisted in and with the substances of bread and wine and that the efficacy of the sacrament depended on the faith of the believer. Zwingli went further. If man is justified by faith alone, if God grants us this faith through hearing his Word, if the virtue of the sacrament depends on the believer's faith, then it must follow that the sacrament of the altar is not a channel of grace and that the Eucharistic Christ is not objectively present in it. The Lord's Supper or communion service is therefore not a physical partaking of the body and blood of Christ, but a spiritual eating, a commemorative service celebrated in memory of the redemptive death of Christ.

The differences between Lutheran and Zwinglian teachings about the sacrament of the altar reflect different interpretations of Biblical texts. In October, 1529, Luther and Zwingli met at Marburg in Hesse, hoping to heal the breach between them and present a united front to the Catholics. Their dialogue posed vividly the problem of authority lurking in the idea of *sola scriptura*. Luther began the debate by chalking on the tabletop Christ's words of institution: *Hoc est corpus meum* ("This is my body"—Matt. 26:26). Johannes Oecolampadius, the reformer of Basel, replied for the Zwinglians, saying that in this sentence the word *est* or "is" meant *significat*, "represents" or "stands for." And to prove that the word ought to be understood symbolically, he cited the sixth chapter of John, where Jesus promises eternal life to whoever eats his flesh and drinks his blood, but lest his disciples take him literally, explains: "It is the spirit that quickeneth; the flesh profiteth nothing" (John 6:63). Oecolampadius concluded that Jesus meant us to eat his body symbolically and spiritually, not literally and physically. But Luther with his customary massive certainty stood by his own reading of the text: "I won't argue about whether *est* means *significat*. I rest content with what Christ says, and He says: *This is my body.* Not even the devil can change that. Therefore believe in the pure word of God and glorify Him." A rapid exchange between Luther and Zwingli ended the debate:

Zwingli: We urge you too to give up your preconceived opinion and glorify God. I do not give up my text either, and you will have to sing another song.
Luther: You are speaking in hatred.
Zwingli: Then let John 6 cure your ignorance.
Luther: You are trying to overwork it.
Zwingli: No! No! This text will break your neck.
Luther: Don't brag. Our necks don't break so fast. You are in Hesse now, not in Switzerland.

Clearly Luther and Zwingli had different spirits. Each thought his spirit holy; each accused the other of spiritual witchcraft and insinuated that he was inspired by the devil.

Although *sola scriptura* means that scripture is normative both in faith and in morals, Luther and Zwingli relied on the Bible primarily to guide them in matters of faith and doctrine. The interest and importance of the Anabaptists is that they understood *sola scriptura* to mean a minute and literal ordering of human life according to the commandments of the Sermon on the Mount, and used the Bible primarily as a model of behavior.

Anabaptism arose during the early stages of the Reformation in Zurich among members of Zwingli's circle who protested his gradualism and demanded an immediate break with all antiscriptural ceremonies and doctrines. It crystallized as a distinct variety of Protestantism on January 21, 1525, when Conrad Grebel, a layman and the son of a wealthy Zurich merchant, rebaptized a former priest named Georg Blaurock, who in turn rebaptized the other men and women present in his house. They called themselves Brethren. (Their enemies named them Anabaptists, or "re-baptists," in order to bring them within the jurisdiction of an ancient law of the Justinian code carrying the death penalty for rebaptism.) The Swiss Brethren produced their first important doctrinal statement, the Schleitheim Confession, at a synod which met in February, 1527. After twenty years of persecution, sporadic excess, and near extinction, the sect received its permanent doctrine, organization, and name from Menno Simons (1496–1561). The Brethren were first called Mennonites in the 1540's.

Anabaptists ordered their lives according to three fundamental principles: adult baptism, separation from the world, and the literal observance of Christ's commandments.

Biblical literalism is picturesque, touching, and morally formidable. A few Anabaptists babbled like infants because Jesus commanded them to become like little children; or persuaded credulous virgins that it was impossible for them to be saved without sacrificing their virtue, for, they argued, the Lord said that only he who is willing to part with what he holds most dear to him can enter the Kingdom of Heaven. All Anabaptists refused to swear oaths because Jesus said, "Swear not at all"; and because Paul advised the Corinthians not to go to law, they spurned lawyers and never went to court. Reading that the earliest Christians held their property in common, they broke the locks on their cellar doors, shared their goods with one another, and lovingly practiced evangelical communism. Christ said, "Resist not evil" and ordered Peter to sheath his sword. Anabaptists were normally pacifists and nonresistant in the face of persecution.

They rightly believed that a life so different from the lives of ordinary men could be led only apart from the world. Anabaptists were separatists who preferred to live in segregated communities as far removed from "civilization" as possible. They were, in a sense, Protestant monks, though their ascetic withdrawal embraced men, women, and children. As citizens only of heaven, they rejected the state, civil government, civil coercion, and even the idea of a Christian magistracy. They refused to bear arms, to hold civil office, or to serve the state in any capacity. All creatures, they believed, were either good or bad, believers or unbelievers, in the world or out of the world, Belial or Christ. The good must have no truck with the wicked.

The sign of their separation, of their repentance and rebirth in Christ, of their membership in a society of believers who had consciously chosen Christ, was adult or believers' baptism. Baptism is the sociological sacrament; it links the individual to society. Infant baptism presupposes a church; adult baptism creates a sect. Luther, Zwingli, and later John Calvin retained and defended the ecumenical conception of the church inherited from the Middle Ages. To Anabaptists who argued that membership must be restricted to true believers, to those with faith, they answered that since no reliable criteria existed to distinguish the elect from the hypocritical majority, the Word of God, purely preached, must be available to everyone. Since the ecclesiastical community must therefore include everyone, every child must be initiated into it by infant baptism, just as circumcision initiated male infants into the holy community of Israel. Anabaptists, on the other hand, consciously chose Christ as adults. They formed a voluntary association of true believers, a gathered society of the regenerate; thus they considered infant baptism meaningless. Their ecclesiastical organization was the voluntary congregation, the conventicle, and they founded the first sixteenth-century sect, a type of religious association that was to flourish in the modern West, especially in Britain and the United States.

By 1530 Western Europe was seething with theological debate and controversy. The most creative phase of the religious revolution was over. Every conceivable doctrinal and ecclesiological position had apparently been formulated, adopted, and defended. It remained to organize and order, to make the classical statement of what Protestantism had become. This was the achievement of John Calvin (1509–1564).

Calvin was born in Noyon, a small town in northern France, a quarter of a century after Luther and Zwingli. His father was a prosperous notary, his background solidly middle class. He received an admirable education. He studied scholastic philosophy and theology at the University of Paris and law at the Universities of Orléans and Bourges. He mastered patristic and contemporary theology, and practiced the humanist's historical and philological techniques of textual criticism. His first book was a humanistic commentary on the *De clementia,* an ethical treatise by Seneca. Between the publication of this commentary in 1532 and the end of 1533, he had what he later laconically described as a "sudden conversion." He fled from France and settled in Basel, where, in 1536, he published the first edition of the *Institutes of the Christian Religion.* He was barely twenty-six.

Calvin's *Institutes* is the summa of classical Protestantism. Reworked and expanded constantly over the next twenty years, beautifully written, keenly and subtly argued, it organized the theological insights of the first generation of reformers into a clear, comprehensive, and effective statement. Calvin restated the fundamental Lutheran and Protestant doctrines: the unique authority of the evangelical standard and justification by faith alone. Zwingli and the Strasbourg reformer Martin Bucer shaped his view of the sacraments and bequeathed to him their puritanical passion for whitewashed simplicity and decorum. And although Calvin, like Lutherans, Zwinglians, Anglicans, and Catholics, feared, hated and persecuted the Anabaptists, one important tendency of Anabaptism penetrated his Protestantism: its concentrated drive to maintain the moral purity of the community of the faithful by an elaborate discipline. The idea of an ecclesiastical discipline enforced by the ban (and the character and emphasis Calvin gave to the idea of predestination) are the two most characteristic details of this majestic book.

The purpose of Calvinist discipline was to keep the Lord's Supper from profanation by making sure that everyone's life and manners were exemplary and that the beliefs of every member of the community conformed to the teaching of the *Institutes,* which the city council of Geneva declared in 1552 to be "well and saintly made, and its teaching the holy doctrine of

God." To ensure that all adult members of the church attend the Lord's Supper unspotted by heresy, blasphemy, or wickedness, a Consistory of elders sought minutely to regulate their thought and action. During the long period of Calvin's ascendancy in Geneva (1541–1564) they prosecuted fornication, fighting, and swearing, laughing or sleeping in church, promiscuous bathing, card playing, and dancing. They forbade theatrical performances and tried to close the taverns and replace them with community eating houses furnished with Bibles. If wrongdoers refused to mend their ways, they were excommunicated, banned from the society of their fellows and from the Supper. If they laughed at excommunication, they were handed over to the secular authorities for punishment. The "fraternal correction" of the Consistory touched high and low, and disciplined a commonwealth whose holiness astonished Europe. Geneva, wrote the Scottish reformer John Knox in 1556, "is the maist perfyt schoole of Chryst that ever was in the erth since the dayis of the Apostillis. In other places, I confess Chryst to be trewlie preachit; but maneris and religioun so sinceirlie reformat, I have not yit sene in any uther place."

Calvin emphasized predestination in order to reinforce the central truth of justification by faith alone, in order to make forever clear the greatness of God and the nullity of that "teeming horde of infamies," man. He wished to make inescapably plain that the Holy Spirit and God's grace were sovereignly independent of man's will and works. By his eternal and immutable counsel God ordains some to salvation and eternal life, others to eternal damnation. The salvation of the elect is an act of God's free mercy, taken with no regard whatever for human merit. The condemnation of the reprobate is an act of God's justice. Why, we painfully ask, does God take pity on some but not on others? There is, says Calvin, no other answer but that it pleased him to do so. God chooses some few and rejects the rest "for no other reason than that he wills to exclude them." His judgment is just and irreprehensible, although man's puny reason cannot grasp it. The reprobate, then, are incomprehensibly but rightly condemned. But this is not all. Because the reprobate are justly condemned, they are condemned by their own fault. "Accordingly, man falls as God's providence ordains, but he falls by his own fault." Calvin himself confessed the doctrine a horrible one: *Decretum quidem horribile fateor.*

For Further Reading

Bainton, Roland, *The Reformation of the Sixteenth Century.*
Erikson, Erik H., *Young Man Luther: A Study in Psychoanalysis and History.*
Monter, William, *Calvin's Geneva.*
Wendel, François, *Calvin: The Origins and Development of His Religious Thought.*

5   The Reformation: Society

From Wittenberg and Zurich, Strasbourg and Geneva, in printed books, popular pamphlets, and broadsides, by preaching, through personal contacts between monks and priests, commercial travelers and students, the sweetly cruel good news of revolutionary Protestantism penetrated to peasant and aristocrat, to craftsmen and merchants, in virtually every territorial and city-state of Europe. For the first time in centuries, religious doctrines were in open competition, and for a few years individuals had the freedom to choose among them. Why did some men remain Catholics? Why did others become Lutherans or Zwinglians or Calvinists? Why did still others become Anabaptists?

Protestant penetration of the peasantry offers an initial perspective on the dialogue of ideas and interests in the Reformation era, the more interesting because the first phase of the Lutheran religious revolution coincided with a violent peasant revolt (1524–1525), the last and most desperate of a series of uprisings that had begun in the fourteenth century. The clearest statement of peasant grievances, the so-called Twelve Articles of the Peasants in Swabia (January–February, 1525), began by demanding for every congregation the right to choose its own pastor to "preach to us the Holy Gospel purely and clearly, without any human addition, doctrine or commandment." The most important article was against serfdom: "It is the custom hitherto for men to hold us as their own property; and this is pitiable, seeing that Christ has redeemed and bought us all with the precious shedding of His blood, the lowly as well as the great, excepting no one. Therefore, it agrees with Scripture that we be free, and we will to be so."

The relation between peasant grievances and evangelical Lutheranism in these demands is not a simple one. The grievances themselves were not new: for at least two centuries peasants had protested against serfdom, tithes, restrictions on their right to use the common fields, woods, streams, and meadows, and against their landlords' efforts to raise rents and increase labor services. Very frequently too in the past peasants had drawn on the spiritual egalitarianism of the New Testament to buttress radical claims for social and economic reform. Even the election of priests by the congregation was common in medieval Germany. On the other hand, the Lutheran bias of the articles is plain enough. While Luther no more caused the Peasant Revolt than Voltaire caused the French Revolution,

A.D.　1509–1547　Reign of Henry VIII of England
　　　1515–1547　Reign of Francis I of France
　　　　　1516　Concordat of Bologna
　　　　　1519　Election of Charles V as emperor
　　　　　1521　Diet of Worms; beginning of Hapsburg-Valois wars
　　　1524–1525　Peasant Revolt in Germany
　　　　　1525　Battle of Pavia; Francis I taken prisoner
　　　　　1526　Defeat of Hungarians by the Turks at the Battle of Mohács
　　　　　1527　Sack of Rome by an imperial army
　　　　　1528　Basel and Berne accept Reformation
　　　　　1530　Diet of Augsburg; German Protestant princes declare faith in the Augsburg Confession
　　　　　1534　Day of Placards; Act of Supremacy
　　　　　1538　Geneva accepts the Reformation
　　　　　1540　Society of Jesus approved by the pope
　　　　　1542　Roman Inquisition established
　　　　　1545　Opening of the Council of Trent
　　　　　1546　Death of Martin Luther
　　　　　1547　Battle of Mühlberg: Charles V defeats the Protestant Schmalkaldic League
　　　1547–1553　Reign of Edward VI of England
　　　1547–1559　Reign of Henry II of France
　　　1553–1558　Reign of Mary of England
　　　　　1555　Religious Peace of Augsburg on the principle of *cuius regio, eius religio*
　　　　　1556　Abdication of Charles V in Spain and Empire; accession of Philip II of Spain
　　　　　1559　Peace of Cateau-Cambrésis: end of Hapsburg-Valois wars

some of his doctrines were used to sanction it. (To pillage a monastic landlord was easier when it could be believed that monasticism was a perversion.) One of Luther's most famous books was named *On Christian Liberty*. An idea like the priesthood of all believers suggested more secular equalities. Above all, Luther embodied for the peasants the promise of the gospel itself and the hope that on new foundations of Biblical Christianity would soon arise a new and more just society.

Luther himself answered the peasants in his *Admonition to Peace: A Reply to the Twelve Articles of the Peasants in Swabia* (April, 1525). About the article condemning serfdom he said:

> This is making Christian liberty an utterly carnal thing. Did not Abraham and other patriarchs and prophets have slaves? . . . Therefore this article is dead against the Gospel. It is a piece of robbery by which every man takes from his lord the body, which has become his lord's property. For a slave can be a Christian, and have Christian liberty, in the same way that a prisoner or a sick man is a Christian, and yet not free. This article would make all men equal, and turn the spiritual kingdom of Christ into a worldly external kingdom.

Luther wrote another tract about the peasants a month later, *Against the Robbing and Murdering Hordes of Peasants,* in which he urged princes and nobles to unite, smite, slay, and stab, "remembering that nothing can be more poisonous, hurtful, or devilish than a rebel." Luther only encouraged landlords to do what they were doing already; and he had no illusions about the German nobles; he called *them* "furious, raving, senseless tyrants." But it was the peasants who died. "Should someone wish to erect a victory monument because he has defeated the rebellious peasants," wrote the greatest German artist of the period, Albrecht Dürer, "let him use this design." The projected monument is a column. Around the base are cattle, sheep, and pigs; farther up are baskets of bread, cheese, eggs, and fruit; from the shaft hang a milk churn, agricultural implements, a cage of chickens; on the top sits a peasant with a sword plunged between his shoulder blades.

Until the end of his life peasants formed the majority of the large audiences that gathered to hear Luther preach in Wittenberg. Clearly Luther could and did find converts among the peasantry. Yet the alliance of Lutheran church and secular prince, forged in the crisis of 1525, and the ecumenical repression of the revolt by lords secular and ecclesiastical, Catholic and Protestant, made most peasants apathetic conformists. When they had freedom of choice they preferred to join a sect, apart from the state church; otherwise, they adopted docilely the religion of their prince.

The response of the urban population offers a different perspective on the spread of Protestantism. The free imperial city of Augsburg is a representative example. During Luther's and Zwingli's lifetimes the city, which almost a century before had provoked an admiring Italian to remark that the burghers of Augsburg were better housed than the kings of Scotland, was at the zenith of its prosperity, famous for the manufacture of textiles, clothes, shoes, and books and home of some of the largest and richest trading and banking firms in Europe. The profits of the house of Fugger from trade, royal moneylending (the Fuggers were the principal bankers of the Hapsburgs), and mining concessions in the Tyrol (silver), Hungary (copper), and Spain (mercury) averaged more than 50 per cent each year between 1511 and 1527. Anton Welser-Conrad Vöhlin and Company traded with Venice and Antwerp and helped finance the first Portuguese voyages to India. The Hochstetters manipulated the market with unprecedented bravura and became the most hated monopolists of their day. Herwarts and Grossembrots, Paumgartners and Rems, were other merchant bankers of the same stamp. Below these international tycoons was a middle class of guild masters, shopkeepers, local merchants and manufacturers, the master printers and the owners of small manufactories producing fustian and linen. At the bottom were the journeymen, the *armen Weber* (poor weavers), the workers in the building trades, and domestic servants.

The religious choices of the inhabitants of Augsburg corresponded to their positions in the social hierarchy. The merchant-bankers remained Catholic, while in the early 1520's Lutheranism attracted a majority of the independent masters and many workers. During the peasant war, Anabaptist missionaries held secret meetings in cellars and gardens and, according to local chroniclers, converted some 800 people, mostly poor weavers. The arrival of Zwinglian preachers in 1526 complicated the religious life of the city even more. By 1530 Catholicism was in full retreat except among the very rich; the Council had broken the Anabaptist hold on the workers by executions and expulsions; Luther retained many adherents among the middle class of citizens; and the sympathies of the government were Zwinglian. In one German city, then, during one decade, 1520–1530, when its inhabitants had relative freedom of religious choice, financial capitalists remained loyal to the traditional faith, petty manufacturers and shopkeepers became Lutherans, and workers turned to Anabaptism.

It is a hopeless enterprise to try to explain a pattern of religious choice of this sort by supposed affinities between particular systems of theological doctrine and the interests and aspirations of particular social classes. There is no innate harmony between Lutheranism and the psychological and ethical needs of petty manufacturers. Luther's social and economic teachings were exceptionally primitive, rooted in the traditional world of the peasant rather than in that of the nascent capitalist. At other times and places his doctrines captured kings, princes, knights, urban patricians, and peasants. Anabaptism, to be sure, found its converts principally among the disinherited—a doctrine so uncompromisingly hostile to established society it could hardly do otherwise—but Conrad Grebel was a Zurich patrician and several leaders of the sect were aristocrats. And it would be absurd to argue that Fuggers, Welsers, and Hochstetters remained Catholics because sixteenth-century Catholicism justified the acquisitiveness of monopolists and moneylenders. They remained faithful to Rome because they had loaned vast sums to their Catholic emperor, Charles V; they were fettered to him with hoops of gold. Every interest which held them to the Hapsburgs held them to the traditional faith as well.

It is not surprising then that Augsburg's pattern of religious choice was not the only one. Paris offers instructive variations. Between 1520 and 1530 the relatively small numbers of Protestant converts came from two main groups: intellectuals, mostly clerics connected with the university, and the urban working class. By the 1530's the social composition of Parisian Protestantism was more varied. During the night of October 17–18, 1534, Protestants papered the walls of the city with scurrilous placards attacking the Mass. Even the king found one on the door of his bedroom at the château of Amboise. The government reacted by burning as many of the culprits as it could catch. The surviving lists of men and women caught or condemned in absentia record their ranks and occupatiohs. Most of the individuals listed were members of the working, lower-middle, and middle classes. One group consisted of journeymen dyers, weavers, masons, cooks, and carpenters; another of substantial entrepreneurs, goldsmiths, printers, and minor civil servants. A larger group was made up of modest artisans and retail traders: bookbinders, engravers, hatters, cobblers, illuminators, cabinetmakers, bakers, grocers, and four singers from the royal chapel choir. The lists also record a scattering of quite different types: a theologian and four Augustinian monks, the poet Clément Marot, several aristocrats and their wives, and a handful of rich merchants. In later decades Calvinism made enormous progress among the aristocracy and gained many adherents among the more substantial burghers. Conversely, petty artisans, shopkeepers, and workers, the masses of the capital, turned into some of the most fanatical Catholics in Europe.

Sixteenth-century European towns had roughly similar social structures, and similar tensions and bitterness everywhere separated class from class. The financial power of the merchant-bankers threatened the independence of guild masters, who, in turn, were transforming their journeymen into workers and themselves into small capitalist entrepreneurs. Each cordially hated the other. Sixteenth-century religions were to a large extent socially and economically neutral. They could and did appeal to any urban social group, just as they found adherents also among peasants and nobles. Local conditions determined the pattern of choice. What makes local diversity intelligible during the years when townsmen had reasonable freedom of choice among competing churches and sects is the tendency of members of different social groups to choose different religious affiliations. One result was almost invariably the same: the religion of the poor was different from the religion of the rich. By 1540 the wealthier citizens were Catholic in some towns, Lutheran in others, Zwinglian or Calvinist in still others. And in each town a religion different from that of the wealthy polarized the sentiment and piety of petty artisans, journeymen, and workers. Religions were becoming ideologies.

Only among princes have we enough evidence to examine the sociology of conversion at the level of the individual.

The economic and political advantages of a Lutheran conversion seem so obvious that the difficulty is rather to account for the fact that throughout Luther's lifetime the princely majority in the German Diet was Catholic. The aim of the German princes was the same as that of the more powerful and successful monarchs of Western Europe: to make themselves the untrammeled masters of a sovereign state. Becoming a Protestant gave a prince a new and widely admired reason for resisting his nominal overlord, the Catholic emperor. It fulfilled that very old ambition of secular rulers to be "pope, archbishop, bishop, archdeacon, and deacon" in their own territories. For the Protestant ruler automatically became *summus episcopus* ("head bishop," though some preferred the more classical Pontifex Maximus) of an autonomous territorial church: he controlled ecclesiastical patronage and appointments; he reformed abuses and supervised morals; he enforced uniformity of faith and liturgy on his subjects; in practice he even defined doctrine. Breaking with Rome also made him richer; he could dissolve monasteries and confiscate their land. He could not keep everything for himself. Too many vested interests were involved. But Margrave Philip of Hesse, one of the most important Protestant princes, managed to keep a typical 40 per cent.

Yes not even these advantages could tempt a majority of the princes into the Protestant camp. In the first place, conversion was a revolutionary act, risky and dangerous. From 1520 until his death in 1546 Luther was an excommunicated heretic under the ban of the empire. Charles V was determined to repress heresy. In 1547 he invaded the electorate of Saxony with Spanish troops and defeated the Protestant Saxons at Mühlberg. The elector was captured and imprisoned. Refusing to abjure his faith, he lost his electoral title and much of his territory. In the second place, a Catholic prince could win by persuasion and blackmail almost as much added power and wealth as the Protestant gained from a dangerous conversion. His tactic was to extract concessions from Rome in exchange for each move he made to suppress heresy: an expansion of the jurisdiction of his courts over the clergy; permission to tax the clergy regularly; a bull empowering him to visit monasteries and reform abuses; complete control of ecclesiastical appointments. The result for Catholic as for Protestant was a territorial church under princely control.

Clearly no simple formula will explain the religious choices of the German princes. One elector of Brandenburg was a zealous Catholic; his son, whose political and economic interests were no different from his father's, became a Lutheran. For Albert of Hohenzollern, cynical grand master of the Order of Teutonic Knights, reform appears to have been indistinguishable from secularization. In 1525, on Luther's advice, he renounced his clerical calling, secularized the order's lands, and made himself the first duke of Prussia. Others embraced the new faith because they believed that what Luther said was true. Princes remained Catholics for reasons equally varied. Some, like the prince-bishops, felt their own power and legitimacy to be inextricably intertwined with that of Rome. Some feared that religious revolution would turn into social revolution. "Do not fail to realize," wrote Duke William of Bavaria to his brother in 1527, "that a creed which allows each man to interpret his faith according to his taste and will must breed civil disobedience and ultimately rebellion and bloodshed." Others were as certain as Charles V that "a single friar errs in his opinion which is against all of Christendom," and would have as willingly renounced their states as their religion.

Princely conversion is important because the choices of princes determined the religious geography of Germany. Freedom of religious choice for most burghers, peasants, and knights—for everyone except princes and the ruling oligarchies of independent city-states—a freedom always relative at best, lasted barely twenty years. By the 1540's repression and persecution had radically curtailed it. As the coercive governments of city-states and principalities enforced religious uniformity within their territories, the religious preferences of magistrates and princes overwhelmed those of citizens and subjects. By mid-century the *ius reformandi,* the right to order the religious affairs of a territory, had become an attribute of princely sovereignty. The subject enjoyed only the *ius emigrandi,* the right of emigrating to a state whose prince's religion was the same as his. Just as the personal decisions of sovereigns determined war and peace in this dynastic age, so their personal theological convictions determined the fate of the Reformation in their states. The religious Peace of Augsburg (1555) made this novel sovereignty of the prince's conscience part of the public law of the empire. It allowed electors, princes, and imperial cities to choose between Catholicism and Lutheranism, and it made the religious choices of rulers binding on their subjects.

"He who rules a territory determines its religion." This is the phrase in which lawyers of a later generation defined the German religious settlement in 1555. The same principle increasingly shaped the religious choice of individuals everywhere in Europe. In 1542 an invigorated and militant papacy established a Roman Inquisition to discover, try, and judge heretics. It successfully rooted out almost every trace of Protestantism in Italy. The personal devotion of Charles V, the crusading tradition of the Spanish monarchy, and a popular piety kept hot and sharp by attacks on the large Jewish and Muslim minorities assured the Catholicity of the Spanish kings. Systematic persecution effectively suppressed dissent among their subjects. The government expelled Jews and Muslims. Inquisitors suspicious enough to jail the founder of the Jesuit order and the archbishop of Toledo, primate of all Spain, made the country equally uncongenial to Protestants. Powerful inducements also bound the Valois kings of France, Francis I (reigned 1515–1547) and Henry II (1547–1559), to the Catholic church. They needed papal support both in their struggle against the Hapsburgs and to accomplish their dynastic ambitions in Italy; while even before Luther's attack on indulgences an agreement with the papacy—the Concordat of Bologna (1516)—had consolidated their hold on the French church. They too, after a few years of comparative laxity, moved vigorously against heresy. At the death of Henry II in 1559 the vast majority of Frenchmen were Catholics.

The case of England is especially instructive, the more so because the English Reformation began as a constitutional rather than a religious crisis. No properly religious motive complicated Henry VIII's ecclesiastical policy. In theology Henry was a good Catholic all of his life. He had even attacked Luther in print, and a grateful pope had conferred on him the title *Defensor fidei* (defender of the faith). Nor did he break with Rome in order to strengthen his control of the English church and clergy. His powers were already as great as those the king of France acquired under the Concordat. He disposed freely of all important ecclesiastical benefices. He taxed the clergy. The laws known as praemunire restricted appeals to the papal court and protected royal courts from clerical interference.

Henry's motives were personal and dynastic: he wanted a male heir and his wife, Catherine of Aragon, had given him only daughters. Besides, he was in love with the charming Anne Boleyn. Since scripture forbids a man to marry his brother's wife, and Catherine was the widow of Henry's older brother, Arthur, only a papal dispensation had made it possible for Henry to marry her. Now he wished the pope to annul the marriage his predecessor had sanctioned. In ordinary circumstances he would have had no difficulty. Reconciling canon law and the exigencies of royal coupling had for centuries been a major subject of negotiation between popes and princes. But the circumstances were not ordinary, and the pope refused.

Henry's wife was Charles V's aunt; and Charles, whose army had sacked Rome in 1527, had too much power to be resisted.

Henry therefore took by force what he could not get by negotiation. To create a legitimate authority in England to annul his marriage, he forced the clergy to recognize him as head of the church in England "as far as the law of Christ allows" (1531). As the Archbishop of Canterbury put it: *Ira principis mors est* (The anger of the prince is death). Then, pushed by the king and his great minister, Thomas Cromwell, Parliament, kept in session from November, 1529, to April, 1531, legislated the independence of the English church. The Act of Appeals (February, 1533) cut every judicial link with Rome and made the Archbishop of Canterbury's court the highest and only legitimate ecclesiastical tribunal for English cases. The archiepiscopal court promptly annulled Henry's marriage to Catherine, and in the autumn Anne Boleyn gave birth to the future Queen Elizabeth. (An Act of Succession confirmed the child's legitimacy.) Finally, the Act of Supremacy (November, 1534) made Henry without qualification the "only supreme head in earth of the church of England called *Anglicana Ecclesia.*"

Like the German princes, Henry was now *summus episcopus,* lay bishop of his church and kingdom. It followed that the religion of his people must be the religion of the church's head. Doctrinal deviation was at once heretical and treasonable: Henry established the Anglican *via media* (middle way) by burning heretics in pairs, papists on one side and Anabaptists or "Lutherans" on the other. During the last years of his reign, and again in the reign of his Catholic daughter Mary, some Protestants expediently exercised the *ius emigrandi,* going into exile in Switzerland and Germany. The more elastic consciences of the majority created the sixteenth-century paradigm of *cuius regio, eius religio.* Nimbly following the doctrinal preferences of their sovereigns, Englishmen were Roman Catholics in 1529, Henrican Catholics from 1534 to 1547, moderate, then extreme Protestants under Edward VI (1547–1553), Roman Catholics once more under Mary (1553–1558), and again moderate Protestants under Elizabeth I.

In the Middle Ages the Western church had been a European corporation. During the first half of the sixteenth century it broke apart into a large number of local territorial churches—national churches, princely churches, provincial churches, even churches confined to the populations of a single city or, as in Poland, of a single aristocratic estate. Secular rulers exercised a predominant control over these churches: whether a church was Protestant or Catholic in doctrine, appointments to its offices, taxation of its members, jurisdiction, administration, and discipline were in their hands. In this perspective the Reformation appears as an aspect of the emergence of the sovereign state and the culmination of the long medieval struggle between secular and clerical authority. In the sixteenth century the balance of power swung decisively and finally from church to state and from priest to layman.

These results were unintended, for it had been the dream of the great reformers to give all glory to Christ and to restore the one, true universal church to its pristine splendor. Nor were the results achieved without resistance. The triumph of the territorial church and the coercive claims of Europe's secular rulers to be the religious arbiters of their dominions sucked religion into the fundamental political struggle of the age: that between royal and princely efforts to unify the state and centralize its administration and the defense of local and corporate privilege, the "liberties" of nobles and clergy, monasteries and universities, provinces and cities. For some Protestants and Catholics refused to emigrate because their religion differed from their king's; these resisted bitterly when he tried to convert them. If their king was Protestant, as in England, aristocratic reaction fought him under the banner of Catholicism. Where he was a Catholic—and most European monarchs ultimately became the allies of a reformed and reinvigorated Catholicism—Protestantism secured its political base at the level of the principality, province, or city, and the slogans of groups resisting the encroachments of centralizing monarchs were evangelical. The competing religions were as neutral politically as they were economically and socially. But just as religious choice reflected social cleavages, so too did political divisions take on a religious coloration. Once the struggle between centralizing "absolutism" and the defense of local "liberties" fused with the struggle between Catholicism and Protestantism, Europe stood on the threshold of a century of civil and religious war.

From this fortuitous sixteenth-century alliance of Protestantism with the defense of traditional "liberties" has sprung an irony as odd as the Reformation's name: the popular association of Protestantism with liberalism and democracy. Sixteenth-century Protestants were neither liberal nor democratic. On the contrary, most of them were elitist persecutors, like almost everybody else. Apart from their theology, their most valuable legacy to the future was precisely their failure to reunite Europe in a Protestant faith. The continent was to remain religiously fragmented. The broken shell of uniformity encouraged intellectual and religious diversity. It made possible, in time, a tolerance and liberal temper inconceivable in the age of the Reformation.

For Further Reading

Cohn, Norman, *The Pursuit of the Millennium.*
Dickens, A. G., *Reformation and Society in Sixteenth-Century Europe.*

Hillerbrand, Hans J., *The Reformation: A Narrative History Related by Contemporary Observers and Participants.*
Olin, John C., *The Catholic Reformation: Savonarola to Ignatius Loyola: Reform in the Church 1495–1540.*

6   The Counter Reformation

Not all the religious reformers of the sixteenth century were Protestants. Even before Luther's time there had been some monastic reform in Italy, and humanists in the papal services had reproached the Church's leaders in Rome for their lack of spirituality and their vices. Quite independently of Rome's influence, reform of the Church had also begun in Spain under Ferdinand and Isabella. But these beginnings of change, important as they were, scarcely deserve to be called a Catholic Reformation; they were inspired either by persistent medieval spiritualism or by new humanistic theories of the contemplative life. They differed greatly from those which would be carried out after 1536 partly as a response to Protestantism. Reformers like Gasparo Contarini, Reginald Pole of England, and Francisco Jiménez of Spain held similar, quite aristocratic conceptions of the devout life; thus their programs, both monastic and educational, lacked the repressive, regimental character of later reforms inspired by the ominous Cardinal Caraffa and St. Ignatius of Loyola. Indeed, the early generation found their influence insignificant in Rome, and were swept aside by Caraffa, who as Pope Paul IV instituted harsh changes reinforced by an Inquisition.

In any discussion of Catholic reform, therefore, the principal focus must be on Rome and the papacy, not on monastic or regional changes. In Rome complacency about spiritual matters, combined with a myopic concern for Italian affairs, made the popes of the sixteenth century overconfident. The Church had never been without critics of Luther's sort; thus Pope Leo X and his cardinals saw no cause for alarm when the monk posted his ninety-five theses on the door of the castle church of Wittenberg.

This complacency explains the papacy's failure to respond to Luther's charges of corruption. Time after time Rome had triumphed over reform movements, and Leo X saw no reason for abandoning time-tested weapons for controlling men of Luther's stamp. The last great reform movement, Conciliarism, had strongly threatened papal sovereignty but at the Council of Constance (1414–1417) the papacy had emerged victorious. The principal north European reformer, John Hus, had been burned at the stake as

A.D.

1528	Founding of the Capuchin order
1536	Commission of Cardinals established by Pope Paul III to reform the papal court
1540	Founding of the Society of Jesus
1542	Roman Inquisition established by the papal bull *Licot ab initio*
1545–1547	First session of the Council of Trent
1548	Publication of the *Spiritual Exercises* by St. Ignatius of Loyola
1549	Death of Pope Paul III
1551–1552	Second session of the Council of Trent
1555	The Peace of Augsburg, religious-political settlement of Germany; Gian Caraffa elected as Pope Paul IV
1558	Diego Laynez elected general of the Society of Jesus
1559	Death of Pope Paul IV
1560	Carlo Borromeo launches Catholic "model" reform as archbishop of Milan
1562	Neo-Scholasticism stimulated by publication of the *Loci Theologici* of Melchor Cano
1562–1563	Third and final session of the Council of Trent
1564	Revised *Index of Prohibited Books* promulgated by Pope Pius IV
1568	St. John of the Cross founds the discalced Carmelites
1572	St. Bartholomew's Day Massacre in France
1573	Veronese called before the Inquisition to defend the orthodoxy of his painting
1575	St. Philip Neri reforms and extends the Oratory
1582	Death of St. Theresa of Avila
1584	Publication of the Jesuit educational program, the *Ratio Studiorum*
1586	Robert Bellarmine publishes Volume I of *Disputation Against the Heretics of Our Times*
1609	St. Francis of Sales publishes the *Introduction to the Devout Life*
1629	Edict of Restitution restores much land to the Roman Church in Germany
1648	Peace of Westphalia

a heretic immediately after the council, thus demonstrating that papal control over church doctrine could be transformed into brutal political action. This example overawed later centuries. Several times Luther and his supporters feared that like Hus his life might end at the stake.

So long as papal control over doctrine remained secure—and this control was strengthened in the period between Constance and Luther—Rome did not fear reformers. Moreover, the Conciliarist challenge taught the popes that reformers could threaten their authority only if some king or prince supported their cause. The French monarchy had used the Conciliarists to gain concessions on church taxes and offices. Conflicts over money and church offices had to be kept separate from theology; thus the papacy strove to make its peace with secular rulers. Both kings and popes actually wanted to keep the Church as it was, a source of revenue for nephews and favorites, and the bargains they struck led to a decline of papal influence in northern Europe, and to a progressive nationalization of the French, English, and Spanish churches. But in Germany, a patchwork of territories where bishops often exercised great secular power, no settlement had been reached with the princes. Papal influence, and therefore papal revenues, remained high, which encouraged the princes to support "reform." Therefore, while Leo X considered the possibility of another alliance between secular princes and otherworldly reformers remote, that is just what developed under Luther.

By late 1520 Rome had lost control of the Church in Germany. Its initial responses had been based on the pope's power to define church doctrine. In the fifteenth century Pope Pius II had decreed that an attack on his power or even an appeal to a church council was heretical. But few German princes took these decrees seriously. If Luther was to be burned, it must first be proved that not merely his conduct but also his preaching and theology were heretical. Recognizing this necessity, Leo X sent his best theologians to debate Luther, but he underestimated how much his spiritual authority had been undermined. Indeed, the worldliness of Rome had its counterpart among several German princes.

In several places in Europe the popes could cancel the right of priests to preach or administer the sacraments, order their books burned, and possibly have them imprisoned, tried, and burned as heretics. But in Germany this was not so. Papal power to enforce edicts and excommunications depended on local Church officials; if they joined the rebel princes supporting Luther, Rome's control was lost. Careful diplomacy with the princes and victory in the theological war with Luther were, between 1520 and 1536, the papacy's only recourse. These weapons proved ineffectual because the papal diplomats could not gain the cooperation of the secular rulers. Lutheranism spread across northern Germany, and other reformers rebelled in Switzerland, France, England, and even in Italy itself.

Appeals for a church council had been made in Germany almost from the start, to the papacy's horror. But only the pope could call such a council, and no pope would do so unless he was sure that he could control its proceedings. Charles V, Holy Roman Emperor, who had his own grievances against the papacy as well as against the Lutherans, wanted a council, but his principal enemy, Francis I, king of France, opposed him because the Lutherans curtailed Charles's military power. Indeed, the Catholic Francis even allied himself with the heretic Germans in the long Hapsburg-Valois wars of the sixteenth century.

As questions of church reform and doctrine sank into the abyss of court politics and war after 1520, Europe's rulers failed to grasp what effect Luther's call to action would have on their subjects. Princes and popes accustomed to ignoring public opinion scarcely noticed the hot anger against corrupt and lazy clergymen which began to sweep across northern Europe. Since the opinions of the bourgeois, peasants, and minor nobles were of little consequence to the court politician, the Reformation became a social revolution without the rulers of Europe recognizing it.

Negotiations, theological debates, and war continued, with the Protestants holding the initiative until 1536. In that year Pope Paul III, whose motives for reform were of the most pragmatic sort, acted to curtail financial abuses and sexual license in Rome. At first improvements were sporadic, since the self-perpetuating clique of Italian families controlling the papacy was slow to awake to the Protestant threat in Italy and to the need for reform. Paul III even came to believe a church council necessary, though he dreaded the prospect and delayed calling it until he believed that the papal nuncios could control its proceedings. Finally, after a tricky agreement with Charles V, and after numerous delays, the Council of Trent began work in 1546. Papal power had become stronger by then, especially under Cardinal Caraffa's influence; the Vatican once again took an interest in the Church beyond the Italian frontiers. As cardinal and as Pope Paul IV after 1555, Caraffa combated abuses and immorality, while remaining rigidly conservative on matters of doctrine. Caraffa's program became the Counter Reformation.

Before 1542 investigations of heresy had been a local affair; Caraffa's "Holy Office" made them a papal matter. Soon no one was above suspicion. Even some cardinals were questioned as the atmosphere in Rome became tense. The extremely devout Bernardino Ochino, head of the newly founded Capuchin order and a prominent reformer who had chosen to remain loyal to Rome, fled to Protestant Geneva when "invited to Rome," afraid that the Holy Office intended to charge him with heresy.

Ochino was not the only reformer confronted with the terrible choice between flight and conforming to Caraffa's orthodoxy. The "Erasmians" and those who placed moral and Biblical teachings above existing practice were silenced, as courts which could imprison or burn persons for heresy imposed a generally Thomistic, thirteenth-century conception of the faith and the Church.

Thus, by 1546, papal power over the Church had been restored. Charges of immorality lost significance as a result of Caraffa's proceedings in Rome. Consequently, when papal officials at the Council of Trent proposed that doctrine be the first subject on the agenda, the majority of prelates agreed. Considering the size of the Church and the thousands who had the right to attend, the number present—only about fifty voting members—was small. After the council's initial decision, neither Charles V, the Protestants, nor "Erasmian" reformers could have much influence. Papal nuncios, Dominican theologians, and the Italian clergy joined to prevent any diminution of papal power or compromise with the Protestants. Having at last perceived the dangers of Protestantism, the papacy was now ready to maneuver and, if need be, to send armies to destroy its enemies. Papal diplomats controlled the council in almost every proceeding. Hopes for church unity were doomed from the beginning, for in the first, year-long session, Luther's teachings on justification, grace, free will, and the Mass were pronounced anathema.

In rejecting Lutheranism, the council extended the papal foundations of the Counter Reformation to the Church as a whole. It acted very cautiously on doctrinal questions, for there was considerable danger that in rejecting one heresy it might create others. Trent's formulation of church doctrine, although grounded on an old-fashioned Thomistic world view and refined by two hundred years of scholasticism, would stand firm for centuries.

Within the Church itself, on the other hand, the revitalization of thirteenth-century conceptions of knowledge, nature, and the universe would lead to the harassment of some of the boldest speculators and greatest scientists of the era, like Leonardo Bruni and Galileo. Moreover, Trent's declaration that the Latin Vulgate of St. Jerome was the sole canonical text of the Bible blighted historical scholarship on the early Church and the life of Jesus. The work of preparing critical editions of church fathers continued among Catholic scholars, especially since the Council of Trent had upheld church tradition as a source of faith and doctrine, but historical investigation as such declined after 1560, and subsequent heavy censorship by the Church made the scholar's life precariously dependent on the Inquisition in many parts of Europe.

At later sessions the council decreed the suppression of the office of "indulgence seller" and the strengthening of the powers of the bishops. The latter proposal would have reduced royal power in most dioceses far more than papal power, and for this reason the decrees were not accepted in strong states like France. In recognition of the need for better education of priests, new or revived religious orders, like the Oratory, were designed to complement the decisions at Trent. The council lasted, with three long intermissions, until 1563; then Pope Pius IV's bull *Benedictus Deus* confirmed its decrees, reasserted papal authority, and made it clear that further discussion was unnecessary. In the same year Pius issued strict rules for religious art and a revised *Index of Prohibited Books*. An ascetic quality unknown for centuries settled over Roman life.

Departing from its policy of ignoring spiritual concerns in favor of Italian politics, the papacy again adopted a global view of the Church as a God-sanctioned spiritual authority. Kings and princes would, of course, count for more in the opinions of papal diplomats than ordinary souls, but the need to minister to the millions of faithful had once again been recognized. Much remained to be done to regain control of the spiritual forces in Europe, even in states which had remained Catholic. But the bold statements about stamping out heresy once again took on meaning under Paul IV and his successors. The papacy inspired many devout young persons to follow its commands. Ignatius Loyola, founder of the Society of Jesus, made obedience to the "Hierarchical Church" the first rule in his *Spiritual Exercises,* the most influential devotional tract of the era. Loyola and the Jesuits followed Caraffa's lead, blindly accepted papal dogma, and then grew spiritually militant through traditional devotions. Between 1540 and 1555 the Society of Jesus grew rapidly, becoming a dominant force in the Counter Reformation. Through the Jesuits, who took on the task of educating princes and aristocrats, the Church prepared a new Catholic elite.

Free now of charges of license and corruption, the papacy once again assumed diplomatic leadership in Europe, claiming to be a force for peace, but, at the same time, a force for the suppression of Protestant nations. It assumed the burden of winning back heretics throughout Europe. Germany, then France and England, and finally the Netherlands became battle grounds where Jesuits, priests, and papal-supported troops converted and combated heretics. The papacy's overambitious ally in Spain, Philip II, made the Counter Reformation more political than ever as he sought to extend Catholic-Spanish power. By 1572 the Counter Reformation had developed into its final militant stage, subordinating its peacemaking role and helping to provoke war and violence until 1648.

For Further Reading

Chadwick, O., *The Reformation.*
Evenett, H. O., *The Spirit of the Counter-Reformation.*
Jedin, H., *History of the Council of Trent.*

Building the Early Modern State

7   The Golden Age of Spain

The history of sixteenth- and seventeenth-century Spain is full of extraordinary contrast, of victories and failures, of wealth and poverty, of supreme cultural achievements and also of degradation, drudgery, and despair. For most of this period Spain expended its resources and manpower on war in northern Europe. For decade after decade, Spanish troops, and mercenaries paid with Spanish money, marched and countermarched across the Alps, the Netherlands, and Germany, fighting people who seemed as alien to them as the Indians of America.

This preoccupation with northern Europe was new to Spanish history and is all the more striking when set against Spanish disunity and poverty at home. The culture of Spain was Mediterranean, and throughout the Middle Ages contacts with the north of Europe had been insignificant. But all this changed as a result of the dynastic accidents of the Hapsburg family, marriages, births, and deaths which ultimately united the Spanish crown with the great possessions of that family in Germany and the Netherlands. This Hapsburg unity, if anything, remained the long-term cause for Spanish involvement in northern Europe. Charles V, who ruled Spain from 1516 to 1556, was also the Holy Roman Emperor, sovereign duke over the provinces in the Low Countries, Burgundy, Austria, Styria, and almost innumerable other, lesser territories in addition to being king of Bohemia and Hungary, and Duke of Milan, Naples, and Sicily. As part of this great Hapsburg Empire, Spain was called upon to play a very special role in European affairs. The course of Spanish history was determined by this Hapsburg link in one of the most politically and socially disruptive periods of modern times, beginning with the Reformation and ending with the Peace of Westphalia in 1648.

Charles V, and then his son Philip II (1556–1598), also made northern Europe the center of Spanish interest because of mercantilist

A.D. 1545 Opening of Potosi mines, Bolivia

      1556 Abdication of Charles V; his son, Philip II, becomes king of Spain

      1557 Bankruptcy of Spanish Crown

      1568 Outbreak of revolt in Netherlands

      1571 Victory of Lepanto, against Turks; repression of revolt of the Moriscos

      1575 El Greco arrives in Spain

      1579 Disgrace and arrest of principal minister, Antonio Pérez

      1584 Direct Spanish intevention into French civil wars

      1587 Sir Francis Drake destroys Spanish fleet at Cádiz

      1588 Defeat of the Spanish Armada

      1591 Revolt of Aragon

      1597 Bankruptcy of Spanish Crown

      1598 Death of Philip II: Philip III, his son, becomes king; Lope de Vega presents *Arcadia*

      1605 Cervantes publishes Part I of *Don Quixote*

      1609 Expulsion of the Meriscos

      1612 Suárez publishes *De Legibus ac Deo Legislatore*

      1616 Spanish forced to leave Japan

      1621 Rise to power of Count Duke Olivares

      1628 Zurbarán, the painting *St. Serapion*

      1630 Velázquez completes painting *Vulcan's Forge*

      1640 Revolt of Catalans and Portuguese

      1643 Defeat of Spanish army by French at Rocroi

notions. With New World treasure and Netherlands trade the Hapsburg Empire seemed to form the basis for a very powerful state. To keep these lands and interests together in a period of revolt, Charles V and Philip II raised taxes until they provoked rebellion in Spain itself, and permanently dislocated and damaged the Spanish economy.

For Spain, Hapsburg rule meant subordination of national interests to those of the whole empire. Charles V believed that God had given him power to keep peace among all his diverse subjects, and to protect them from all enemies, be they Turks or French. To accomplish this purpose, Charles claimed, he had the right to call for military and financial aid in any part of his vast domain. Charles's Spanish subjects accepted this traditional, feudal principle of kingship, despite the alien origins of their ruler and his interests. Their submission brought them decades of fighting against France, against Lutheran rebels, against Turks, and, finally, against Calvinists.

But for these wars, Hapsburg rule would have had little impact on Spain. Charles V did not wish to impose common laws or a centralized government on all his possessions. He exploited Spain's resources but otherwise was prepared to leave the country to its own devices. For the Spanish people, Hapsburg rule was all giving and no receiving.

Spain's traditional enemies threatened her trade and security. The Spanish conquest of Granada in 1492 had cleared the peninsula of Muslim rule but had not eliminated Muslim-Turkish power in the western Mediterranean, or freed the Spanish mind of centuries-old fears and suspicions of foreigners. Turkish fleets harried the seas between Spain's east coast and her possessions in southern Italy. Would this Turkish presence cause Spanish Muslims to rise against the Christians? North African pirates, though not a serious military threat like the Turks, persistently raided and pillaged merchant vessels and coastal towns, forcing Spain to maintain a large fleet of galleys. How long would this expensive nuisance endure? The Spanish had hoped that the potent Hapsburgs would bring help from the north against these traditional enemies, but aside from a minor campaign in North Africa, Charles did nothing for them.

Under Philip II, Hapsburg imperial concerns continued to determine Spanish policy. Since Philip himself was not Holy Roman Emperor, keeping the peace in Germany was left to Philip's uncle and later to his cousins. But for all that, Spanish involvement in northern Europe did not decrease: Philip himself, after all, ruled the Netherlands. Though the Spaniards could hope for little territorial gain, Philip's involvement there, and in Burgundy, made France and Spain mortal enemies throughout the sixteenth and seventeenth centuries. Furthermore, dynastic ambition had led Philip to marry Henry VIII's daughter, Mary Tudor, heir to the English throne. This

EUROPE 1559-1600

Spanish Hapsburgs
Austrian Hapsburgs
Venetian possessions
Holy Roman Empire boundary
× Battle

again embroiled Spain in dangers from which little gain could be expected. Would the Spanish also have to pay for armies to suppress rebellions in England? Only the defeat of the Armada in 1588 by the English navy prevented this from happening.

To encourage the Spanish people to fight and to make economic sacrifices, Charles and his descendants exhorted the Spanish aristocracy and clergy to accept as a divine mission the task of preserving political order and religious orthodoxy in Europe. Had they not defeated the Muslims with God's help? This refrain pervaded Spanish politics and culture throughout her "golden age." Now the Hapsburgs wanted the Spanish, as the strongest, most orthodox, and "purest" people in Europe, to police Germany and the Netherlands, control France, and invade England, this last after that kingdom had fallen to a heretic queen, Elizabeth. This incredible program actually appealed to Spanish noblemen; not all the responsibility for Spain's later decline lies on Hapsburg shoulders. The Spanish nobility, overstocked with younger sons and short on money, was attracted by military commands, booty, and land in northern Europe. Since both Charles V and Philip II were very devout themselves, and since the Spanish nobles made at least a semblance of being so too, belief in Spain's divine mission was not difficult either to rouse or to sustain.

The "holy wars," as they were described to the taxpayers, began under Charles V in the 1520's, against Turks, Lutherans, and their allies, the French. Then in 1568, a rebellion broke out in the Netherlands which required large armies, notably those commanded by the great Duke of Alba, to repress Calvinists and rebels in provinces which had already become economically crucial to the survival of the Spanish empire in Latin America, and to Spain herself. Later, in 1618 during the reign of Philip III (1598–1621), after a twelve-year truce, Spain attempted to reconquer the Netherlands, and in doing so became involved in the general European war. Decline seemed inevitable after the failure of the Armada, but the Spanish struggled on. Neither of Philip II's successors, Philip III and Philip IV, nor able minister-favorites like Olivares, were able to break the mold which had shaped Spanish policy since the 1520's. Thus a crusading spirit, sustained by a tarnished chivalric code and by fanatical preaching against foreigners and heretics, gave coherence to what were in actuality mere dynastic claims. Various wily ambassadors who understood *raison d'état* attempted to base policy on real Spanish interests, but they failed.

Spain's huge American profits, especially the gold and silver from Mexico and Peru, were thus squandered. Many royal ministers were painfully aware of this waste and of the disastrous economic and commercial effects of borrowing and inflation. But policies did not change; reason was never allowed to penetrate the shield of prayers and hopes which held Spain together—even after the destruction of the great Armada. Spanish agriculture was also sacrificed to these wars; the *mesta* (large-scale sheep raising) meant higher revenues for the state than grain or cattle. Consequently crop failures brought starvation for Spaniards already living on a subsistence level. Taxes on commercial transactions, and policies favoring merchants dealing in war materials and colonial products, led to the decline of traditional Spanish industries. After decades of docility and support for their kings, peasant and aristocratic rebellions became more frequent as conditions worsened. Since strong regional identities persisted, entire provinces, not merely aggrieved classes, rose against the Hapsburgs.

The unity of Aragon, Catalonia, Castile, and other Spanish provinces (and Portugal for a time) was never very solid. The ties had originally been little more than dynastic, and the Hapsburgs failed to make them more substantial. Neither centuries of crusading, nor the Muslim enemy, nor even common economic interests had brought unity to the Spaniards. They had no common political institutions, for even ∴e Church was controlled by nobles with regional interests. Spain never got what it most needed in the sixteenth century: quiet and isolation from Europe's turmoil. The colonization of the New World was essentially a Castilian effort, not a Spanish one, and so were the wars in northern Europe. Since Charles and Philip gave offices to those who served Hapsburg interests most zealously, the Castilians came to dominate not only foreign affairs but also internal administration. The Hapsburgs seem to have sincerely intended to uphold provincial laws, but their Castilian officials became increasingly hostile to regional political interests.

Despite his close attention to the endless reports and letters which he received when he was abroad, Charles was an absentee ruler for twenty-three of his nearly forty years on the Spanish throne. And though Philip II and his successors rarely left Spain, their government became increasingly remote from the country. Philip II picked Madrid as his capital and stayed there because it was the geographic center of the peninsula. He and his descendants virtually ceased to travel outside Madrid; the royal presence nearly always meant the king's Castilian officials. Fewer and fewer Cortes (consultative assemblies) were held, and Castilian practice became the model for the entire peninsula.

The extension of Castilian influence, no matter how offensive in other provinces, was inevitable, for Castilians paid proportionately more taxes and served the royal administration more faithfully and longer than the others. The consequences of this subtle Castilianization of the monarchy in the long run were to be disastrous. Provincial Spaniards began to look upon the monarchy itself as foreign; gradually Hapsburg officials, and finally Hapsburg policies, came under attack. The Revolt of Aragon in 1591 should have been a warning to Philip II, but he was too obsessed with the Dutch rebels to look into its causes. Instead he merely crushed the uprising.

But if Spain underwent enormous difficulties, these in no way impeded an extraordinary spiritual and cultural flowering. Along with the hardships came the exhilaration of conquering an empire of gold in America, and of playing the leading role in the salvation of all peoples from heresy. To many Spaniards it seemed that God had chosen them once again to play a special role in the world, and had given them the gold and armies to do it. This attitude helps explain the enormous spiritual vitality of the art and literature of Spain during the Golden Age.

Spiritual fervor, rigid orthodoxy, and firm convictions about man's place in the universe, and the social hierarchy graded from popes, kings, dukes, merchants, on down to peasants, pervaded the Spanish cultural and political achievement under the Hapsburgs. The *Spiritual Exercises* of St. Ignatius of Loyola (1491–1556) quickly became an extremely influential devotional work. It had enormous political and literary consequences as well, accompanied as it was by a monastic way of life to which its readers might adhere, and strict obedience to the pope. St. Theresa of Avila's (1515–1582) *Way of Perfection* contributed to the general Spanish religious and political dominance of Europe by appealing to women to reform the Carmelite order, and to found new monastic houses.

Spanish sculpture and architecture during the Golden Age had less impact on the rest of Europe, chiefly because the great Italians, notably Michelangelo and Bernini, continued to make Rome the capital of Europe in those arts. In painting, however, the unique spiritual intensity found in Loyola's thought manifested itself in a long and impressive list of primarily religious painters. Though Greek by birth and trained in Italy, El Greco (1547–1614) captured Spain's spiritual mood during his productive years in that country. The ascetic quality of El Greco's Spanish style jars with its modernity; only the asceticism survived in the works of Zurbarán (1598–1664) and Murillo (1617–1682). Sure in their faith, almost deintellectualized, the Spanish religious painters reflected the mood of a people with a divine mission in the world, and also, as in Murillo's paintings of commoners, the popular, more humane aspect of religion. Unafraid as they were of either sentimentality or harshness, Spanish religious artists stressed the themes of love in the Holy Family, the sufferings and miracles of the saints, and the miracles of the sacraments.

Secular painting reached its apogee in the court portraits of Velázquez (1599–1660). Whether in the face, dress, or hair of a little princess, or the massive body of Philip IV, Velázquez created a glow in his portraits which suggest that those he painted, be they kings or dwarfs, were set apart from the world.

By contrast, the political and religious idealism of Spain also inspired pathos and satire. The revived courtly poetry and manners of the sixteenth century could be ridiculed in plays and novels. Cervantes (1547–1616) accomplished the almost impossible task of satirizing chivalry without making *Don Quixote* unbelievable in the eyes of his contemporaries. His great novel, an incomparable picture of all aspects of Spanish society in his day, portrays sympathetically the contrasts between Spanish idealism and the harsh social and economic realities of Spanish life.

The last years of the sixteenth century proved crucial for Spain's future. Forced by exhaustion and defeat to curtail his imperial ambitions, Philip II had a splendid opportunity to examine critically the aims of the Spanish crown in Europe. But he was surrounded by partisans of the old northern-oriented policy whose only "solutions" to local dissent were military repression and the Inquisition. These same men continued to govern under Philip III and, in spirit, even under Philip IV. The government of Spain had become monolithic, racist, rigidly Catholic, and unable to conceive of any way of obtaining its ends except by force.

Sacrifices and hardships still seemed worthwhile to Hapsburg ministers, clergymen, and the Castilian nobility, but by 1600 the rest of Spain had come to resent paying taxes and furnishing troops without obtaining anything in exchange. Yet dissidents scarcely dared attack imperial policy, not only because they feared reprisals against their persons but because they still believed that kings had the right to manage foreign affairs any way they pleased. Defense of provincial liberties, therefore, became the rallying cry of non-Castilians. Despite further signs of breakdown and violence in the 1630's and 1640's, the monarchy refused to change its policy or to remove objectionable officials. The provincials protested, refused to cooperate with hated officials, and then took up arms. Too late, Olivares, Philip IV's great minister, attempted halfway reforms but without curtailing the northern war against the Dutch rebels and France. He failed to placate the provinces. Rebellions broke out in Catalonia and Portugal in the 1640's, the rebels joining with the French against their own government.

Spanish dominance in Europe had been based on unity and orthodoxy at home as much as on American silver and on military might. The Catalan revolt undermined unity, and Spanish power slowly declined. The war ended in 1659, but for the rest of the seventeenth century and into the eighteenth the Hapsburg legacy stifled the intellectual and economic life of the country. Wars and the crusading ideology had welded together an orthodox and snobbish aristocracy and clergy which held all the reins of power in the state. Intellectual life had been crippled by censorship and the Inquisition, which had been used against anyone protesting against either official theology or state policy. At last, even the combination of despair and hope that had sustained the last generation of great poets and artists— Lope de Vega, Murillo, and Velázquez—gave out. What remained was only fear: of foreigners and of the unknown. Spain's greatness was no more. The culture of the *Sieclo d'Oro* remained, but politically much had been lost, most obviously (and most disastrously) the northern lands that were to become the Dutch Republic.

For Further Reading

Elliott, J. H., *Imperial Spain 1469–1716.*
Lynch, J., *Spain under the Hapsburgs,* Vol. I.
Mattingly, G., *The Defeat of the Spanish Armada.*

8   The Rise of the Dutch Republic

Although the dramatic rise of the Dutch Republic to the status of a major power in the seventeenth century could not have occurred if it had not had a healthy and efficient political organization, the republic had few of the characteristics of a modern state. It was a loose confederation of provincial estates, themselves nothing more than confederations of towns and privileged groups, and continually in conflict over hopelessly complicated problems of sovereignty. In addition, each province had a stadtholder, usually a prince from the House of Orange, who sometimes acted as an executive but remained constitutionally an officer of the sovereign provincial estates. In a way the republic was a curious medieval relic, an improbable institutional platypus, rather than a prototype of a national political organization of modern times.

Since it was undeniably a success, the Dutch Republic raises some interesting questions: Was monarchy, absolute or constitutional, the only viable answer to the organizational problems posed by the sixteenth- and seventeenth-century transformations in Europe? That question aside, what special circumstances made the Dutch success possible?

On the eve of the revolt against the Hapsburgs, the Netherlands constituted even less of a national unity than the other countries of western Europe. As late as the fifteenth century the Dukes of Burgundy had acquired a number of independent territories in the Low Countries, and during the first half of the sixteenth century their Hapsburg successors had added still others. The result was essentially a personal union. Culturally Flanders and Brabant were united with the north by the common Dutch language. But the court, as well as the southern Walloon provinces, spoke French. Economically, the Netherlanders were a heterogeneous lot. Rural, sometimes backward provinces were thrown together with the most advanced and most urbanized regions in Europe: Flanders, Brabant, and Holland. Politically, in spite of princely efforts, the provinces guarded their independence, cooperating, as it were, only in order to thwart efforts to make them cooperate. The Estates General did not represent the nation; it was a mere congress of provincial embassies. Centralist ideas existed only among the professional jurists of the prince's councils. The high nobility, although participating in these councils, were too self-centered to be concerned with centralizing reforms.

However, after Emperor Charles V had abdicated (1556) and Philip

A.D. 1556 Abdication of Charles V of Hapsburg as Lord of the Netherlands; succession of Philip II of Spain

1559 Philip II leaves Netherlands and returns to Spain, which becomes center of his government; beginning of opposition of higher nobility against government of king's confidants in the Netherlands

1566–1567 First outbreaks of large-scale revolts as well as iconoclastic movements against the Church; Philip II sends the Duke of Alva to suppress the uprising; William of Orange flees the country

1572 Successful attack of William of Orange, who occupies provinces of Holland and Zeeland

1576 Other provinces join the rebellion (Pacification of Ghent

1579 Walloon nobility defects from the rebellion (Treaty of Arras); Alexander of Parma commander of the Spanish troops

1581 Revolutionary Estates General depose Philip II as Lord of the Netherlands

1584 Assassination of William of Orange

1585 Parma takes Antwerp; rebels withdraw behind the great rivers

1588–1609 Dutch drive the Spanish out of the northern Netherlands: attempts at liberation of the south fail

1609–1621 Truce between Republic of the United Netherlands and Spain

1625–1648 The Republic joins the anti-Spanish coalition

1648 Peace of Westphalia: de jure recognition of independence of the Republic

II had transferred the center of government to Spain (1559), this high nobility, having lost the prominent position it had held under Charles V, became the first rallying force in the revolt against Spanish rule. The nobles formed a league under William, Prince of Orange, to protect their interests, but their actions provided a catalyst for widespread popular discontent. Population pressure, inflation, and lagging wages had a particular impact on the Netherlands with its highly advanced and vulnerable economy. Earlier, the discontented groups had not been very homogeneous, a fact which helps to explain why Charles V had succeeded in maintaining an uneasy political balance. Now they came together, helped by the widespread demand for religious toleration, the ideological bond between the otherwise dissident groups.

Since the late 1550's the Calvinists had been strengthening their organization, and by the early sixties they were alarming the authorities by forcibly freeing jailed preachers and smashing religious images. Such outbreaks occurred mainly in the socially disturbed southern industrial regions, where a temporary economic crisis attracted discontented burghers as well as workers to the Calvinists. Their organization, like that of the Huguenots in France, had a military as well as a religious function. After the collapse of a movement among the higher nobility, the lower nobility took recourse in 1566 to what was supposed to be a nonviolent action. This triggered a revolt in the cities, marked by wild, iconoclastic acts against the Church, symbol of law, order, and the establishment. Against such an improbable coalition of nobility, bourgeoisie, and industrial workers, the government of Philip II was isolated and powerless.

The same disharmony which had caused the revolt, however, was also responsible for its failure. The violent behavior of the lower classes reminded many members of the nobility and higher bourgeoisie of the interests they shared with the government, and in the spring of 1567 the movement collapsed.

At this point peace might have been restored had Philip II not instituted a reign of terror and revenge. Too many people, compromised in the early rebellion, had fled the country; their only hope of return lay in a revolution under William of Orange. Orange himself went through a remarkable change in exile; he realized that narrow class interests had ruined the revolt and that his only hope was to unite nobility and bourgeoisie. A political genius of the first order (crafty as the serpent and innocent as the dove of Scripture), William of Orange prepared the ground patiently, stressing in his propaganda a program of constitutionalism and toleration.

In 1572 William invaded the Netherlands from the east and the south. His attack failed, but a separate invasion by the so-called Seabeggars, pirates supported by a leavening of freedom fighters, provided him with a foothold in the coastal provinces of Holland and Zeeland. In spite of furious Spanish assaults he managed to consolidate his position. It was of incalculable importance that William's first government was organized in the province of Holland, where the nobility was far less important than in the southern provinces, and where the guilds lacked the strong influence on town government of their counterparts in Flanders and Brabant. Power lay in the hands of a merchant clique that was willing to support William, provided the ultimate authority resided in their provincial estates. Although not much inclined to Calvinism, most of the merchants were not very enthusiastic Catholics either, and they were willing to adopt the faith of William's comrades for political reasons. Moreover, Catholic Church properties were a convenient source of revenue essential to finance the war.

The situation became more complicated in 1576 when the other provinces rejoined the revolt against Spain. The Flemish and Brabant towns had a long history of class war, with the guilds, now the driving revolutionary force, opposing the patriciate and the nobility. The Walloon provinces were the strongholds of the nobility, who joined the revolt out of disappointment with Philip II's policy, but who still cherished the idea of an aristocratic government under the king. The southern grandees did not want to accept William of Orange, an equal, as their leader, but William cleverly staged a number of democratic coups in Brussels, Ghent, and other southern cities. Thus the savior of oligarchy in Holland had become the hero of guild democracy in the south.

William tried desperately to reconcile the clashing social groups behind a national program to be carried out by the Estates General, which now assumed legislative power. However, the southern nobility now found good reason to seek reconciliation with the Spanish king. Their battle cry was defense of Catholicism against Calvinist extremism. Wherever they came to power the Calvinists unleashed a reign of terror. William tried hard to make them accept a Peace of Religion, a real charter of toleration. The extremists were not interested in peace, however, and often only super-ficially in religion. The Flemish cities and the nobility were old enemies, and this was a life-or-death struggle. The Walloon provinces, strongholds of the nobility and Catholicism, finally signed a treaty with the king (1579) and ended their rebellion; the revolutionary hardliners in the Estates General pushed through the deposition of Philip (1581), declaring solemnly that a tyrant who broke his contract with his people could law-fully be removed from power. The process of polarization was completed. Military power was going to decide the outcome of the conflict. Philip II's new governor general, Parma, skillfully blending mercy, moderation, and military force, had conquered the whole of the south and northeast, including Antwerp, by 1588, at which time he was preparing for the final invasion of Holland and Zeeland. The rebels were weakened by the assassination of William of Orange (1584) and by the nearly lethal assistance of unreliable or inept governors like Anjou, the youngest of Catherine de Médicis' dismal brood, and by Leicester, Queen Elizabeth's "sweet robin." They managed to hold out, however, and then the defeat of the Spanish Armada and the Spanish involvement in the French civil war enabled them to drive the Spanish from the north and to negotiate the Twelve Years' Truce (1609). In spite of some weak Dutch attempts after 1621 to reconquer Flanders and Brabant, the boundaries of the military stalemate of 1609 persisted, and were formalized in the final peace treaty of 1648.

Dutch historians have oft deplored the separation of the Low Countries, which they interpret as a defeat for the Netherlands' national community. However that may be, this rupture was a decisive factor in the success of the Dutch Republic. The struggle between nobility and guild-democracy in the south, resulting in the failure of William of Orange's attempts at a Greater Netherlands Confederation, suggests that social and political conflicts would have ripped this construction apart if all the provinces would have been liberated. Moreover, in such a larger political construction, encompassing the present-day Low Countries, the presence of three equally strong provinces in the Estates General, Flanders, Brabant, and Holland, would have precluded any harmonious development of central government; but the province of Holland could easily dominate the northern rump state. The rapid economic expansion of the Dutch in the seventeenth century could not have occurred without their merciless blockade of Antwerp: southern capital, skills, and manpower flowed to the north, so that instead of competing with the north, the south contributed to its blooming.

Strong leadership was also an ingredient in Holland's expansion; the merchant patriciate knew how to tend its interests better than monarchs generally did. And above all, the enigma of the rise of the Dutch Republic can be explained by the fact that it was small enough to be run as a mercantile city-state, but large enough to defend itself against princely conquerors. When England and France overcame their lack of social cohesion and other weaknesses, the republic would be in danger. But that did not happen until late in the seventeenth century.

Nevertheless, the first half of the century was a period of continuous political and religious crisis and threatening social revolt. The troubles began immediately after the conclusion of the Twelve Years' Truce with Spain. The oligarchy had forced the truce upon an unwilling war party because its regular European trade was suffering severely from the war and the financial situation was appalling. The war party was led by Prince

Maurice of Orange, commander of the army, and by orthodox Calvinists, who considered any agreement with the "Spanish Papist-beast" an offense against God. The colonial lobby also joined the war party to protect their interests in the Spanish and Portuguese overseas possessions which brought the powerful city of Amsterdam to the side of Prince Maurice. This war party would not have succeeded had not the lower classes and lesser provinces, jealous of Holland's leadership, endorsed its coup d'état in 1618. The prestige of die-hard Calvinism among the lower classes gave this alliance much of its dynamism.

It was characteristic of the times that the whole conflict had been built around the purely theological clash between liberal Arminians and orthodox Predestinarians. The Holland politicians supported the Arminians, partly out of conviction, partly because the Arminians accepted the power of the state over the church. Prince Maurice chose the orthodox party without understanding much about the theological subtleties. He won, but it was again characteristic for the purely political significance of this theological conflict that after the coup d'état the prince did not give his orthodox allies the power and influence they had demanded. On the other hand, most members of the Holland patriciate conformed nominally to the Calvinist rigorists and remained in or soon returned to power. After 1625 Frederick Henry of Orange, Maurice's successor, made use of the same coalition to impose his war policy and his alliance with the France of Richelieu (1635), but he could not prevent the Holland oligarchy, reinforced since the late 1620's by the return of Amsterdam to its side, from regaining power and imposing the Peace of Westphalia (1648) upon an unwilling war party.

This pattern of power alternating between the Orangists and the mercantile patrician factions has remained a distinctive feature of the Dutch Republic. Each shift involved a coup d'état, but these were dull, bloodless affairs compared to the political upheavals in England and France. The Orangist coup d'état of 1618 cost only one life, that of the Grand Pensionary of Holland, Oldenbarneveldt. Other Orangist coups occurred in 1650 and 1672, the former totally without violence and the latter proving fatal only for the leaders of the republican faction, the brothers De Witt.

The return to power of the republican faction in 1650 and again in 1702 indicates that the oligarchic government and the hegemony of the province of Holland were deeply rooted in the social and political structure. Popular commotions were never strong enough to bring about a successful revolt. At the same time the influence of the Orangist war faction throws light on the ambiguous position of the republic: the economic nature of the state seemed to justify the peaceful city-state mentality of the patrician faction; on the other hand it became increasingly clear that the republic was not a city-state but rather a small and vulnerable nation with the wealth and duties of a great power. The alternation between mercantile and expansionist regimes offered a pragmatic solution to the problems posed by an impossible situation. It was precisely the illogical and anti-quated character of the Dutch constitution that maintained an efficient bourgeois economic policy and provided military protection in time of danger.

For Further Reading

Geyl, P., *The Netherlands in the Seventeenth Century.*
————, *The Revolt of the Netherlands.*
Wilson, C., *The Dutch Republic.*

9   The Collapse of France

In the sixteenth century the only state that seemed capable of curbing Hapsburg power, notably the might of the Spanish armies, was France. Under Francis I (1515–1547) the French monarchy seemed to shrewd observers, including no less an authority than Niccolò Machiavelli, the very model of a large kingdom—politically stable, efficiently centralized and administered, and possessed of a magnificent court and a powerful army. Francis was admired and envied by kings and ministers all over Europe, chiefly because he seemed to wield enormous powers over his subjects, in assessing taxes. The claims to absolute power and the magnifi-cence of the châteaus on the Loire River were indeed impressive.

A closer look, however, reveals weaknesses. French kings did not have to convoke the Estates General to levy taxes, to be sure, but large numbers of powerful, wealthy, and privileged subjects could not be taxed at all. To raise money from the church and from members of the third estate, they had to negotiate with bishops, town councils, and other assemblies. The French government resembled those of other European states more than some foreign observers realized.

On the other hand, Francis and his descendants held almost absolute control over the church, especially after the Concordat of Bologna (1516), which assured the king the right to select the abbots and bishops of the realm, who controlled enormous wealth. This patronage gave Francis great

A.D. 1559 Peace of Cateau-Cambrésis; death of Henry II
      1561 Colloquium of Poissy
      1562 Outbreak of civil war between Protestants and royal troops
      1572 St. Bartholomew's Day Massacre
      1574 Death of Charles IX; assembly of Millau, establishes firmer government for French Protestants
      1576 Jean Bodin publishes *Six Books of the Republic;* Estates General of Blois, seeks religious compromise and fails
      1578 Duke of Anjou invades Low Countries; founding of the Order of the Holy Spirit
      1579 Publication of the *Vindiciae contre Tyrannes*
      1580 Publication of the first edition of the *Essays* of Montaigne
      1587 Battle of Coutras, first pitched battle won by the Protestants
      1588 Revolt of Paris against Henry III
      1589 Assassination of the Guises, on Henry III's orders; assassination of Henry III
      1590 Battle of Ivry, victory of Henry IV against the Catholic League
      1593 Henry IV abjures Protestantism
      1595 Henry IV absolved of his heresy by Pope Clement VIII
      1597 Siege of Amiens
      1598 Treaty of Vervins, ends war between France and Spain; Edict of Nantes

power and large revenues. Moreover, royal control of the intellectual and cultural life of the kingdom was nearly complete. Francis I had the reputation of being one of the leading patrons of the arts and learning, his greatest coup being the attraction of Leonardo da Vinci to France.

When Lutheran teachings began to spread in France they therefore caused little stir. A few humanists, to say nothing of Francis' own sister, found the new religion attractive, but once its heretical character was recognized powerful institutions of suppression swung into action. The Sorbonne, the high court of the Parliament of Paris, and the Assembly of Bishops all condemned Luther's position, and France remained overwhelmingly Catholic throughout the first storm of religious reform.

Not for long; the ideas of John Calvin were not so easy to suppress as those of Luther. Perhaps because he had been born and educated in France, Calvin's doctrines proved congenial to many Frenchmen. And his conception of church government admirably suited tastes of French dissident social groups. Francis I had established his absolutist regime over the opposition of many provincial nobles and town oligarchs. Both groups resented his centralized government bitterly. Thus after about 1555 Calvin's ideas caught on in many sections. Under Francis' successor, Henry II, it seemed that tiny sects were springing up everywhere, holding Bible-reading sessions and prayer meetings at homes and gathering clandestinely to hear newly arrived preachers from Calvin's headquarters in Geneva. First artisans and merchants, then important local leaders, then royal officials and even noblemen began to be found in these secret meetings. From town to town the proselytizers moved, organizing gatherings and making converts.

Calvinism hit France at a particularly unpropitious moment for the Crown. The eroding Hapsburg-Valois wars had exhausted and bankrupted the country. Popular rebellions similar to the peasants' wars in Germany flared in rural districts, while in towns unemployment and general misery left artisans and the *menu peuple* ripe for riots and civil war. Population increases combined with currency devaluation continued to send prices soaring. However, these problems alone do not explain the popularity of Calvinism in France; the strongest support of the "new religion" came from groups who opposed royal absolutism without regard for the economic troubles of the times. Francis I and Henry II had allowed two families, the Guises and the Montmorencys, to accumulate an inordinate amount of power, rousing many jealousies. By 1555 they controlled most important government posts along with many rich places in the religious hierarchy; in some provinces they ruled almost like kings with their own armies. Francis had the strength and wit to hold the Guises and Montmorencys in check, but Henry could not control them. They soon clashed

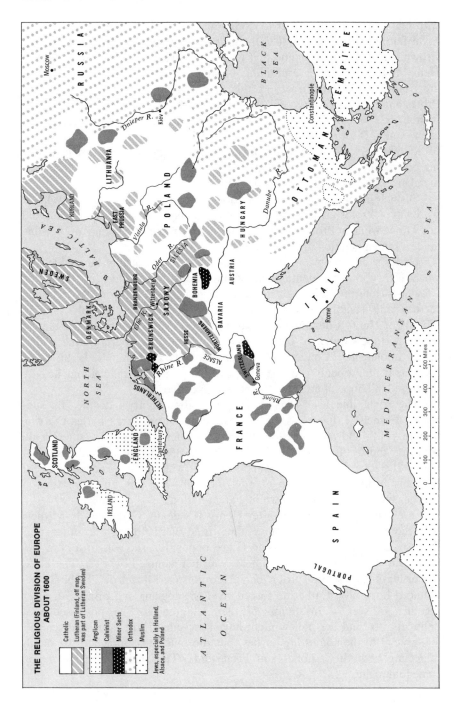

THE RELIGIOUS DIVISION OF EUROPE ABOUT 1600

Catholic

Lutheran (Finland, off map, was part of Lutheran Sweden)

Anglican

Calvinist

Minor Sects

Orthodox

Muslim

Jews, especially in Holland, Alsace, and Poland

with one another in an effort to dominate him. Both had married into the royal family, which meant that their rivalries posed a grave threat to the Crown. Thus at the very time that Calvinism was spreading across France, Henry found his power crumbling because of the rivalries of these two great families. Perhaps because of his very weakness, Henry persecuted the Protestants far more severely than Francis had. They were condemned without trial or inquisition; mere hearsay was sufficient for burning a man at the stake. Both royal and petty local officials were pressed to prove their orthodoxy by zealously rooting out heretics in a desperate effort to terrify his people into submission. Henry even had Ann du Bourg, a prominent member of Parliament, immolated for heresy.

Suspicion, fear, and false accusations spread across France. Few knew who was a Protestant and who was not—indeed, many royal officials did not know what a Protestant was. For some, mere ownership of a Bible made a man a heretic.

Under such circumstances social upheaval was probably inevitable, but when Henry was accidentally killed in a jousting accident in 1559, the Calvinists interpreted his death as a sign of God's favor. Abandoning secrecy and stealth, they began to hold their services openly. Within months of Henry's demise they held a general synod in Paris itself almost within a stone's throw of the chief civil and religious courts of the realm. Great nobles like Condé and Coligny followed by hundreds of other prominent men openly espoused the cause. With royal officialdom heavily infiltrated, all hope of crushing the new faith collapsed.

The royal line itself was in jeopardy after Henry's death. His successor, Francis II, lived less than a year. Francis' brother, Charles IX, was a mere youth and dominated by his mother, Henry's widow, Catherine de Médicis, and by the Guise faction. When Charles died in 1574 the third of Henry II's sons, Henry III, became king, but while he was more intelligent than his brothers he lacked energy and will—he was no more than a courtier trying to wear the crown of a great nation.

In effect, for two decades after Henry II's death, Catherine de Médicis was the virtual ruler of France. She tried hard to restore order and domestic serenity and over strong Guise opposition she sought a compromise with the Calvinists. "Le couteau vaut peu contre l'Esprit" (The knife is worthless against the spirit), her able minister, Michel de l'Hôpital, announced hopefully. Catherine forced rival theologians and princes to meet together to seek a resolution of their differences. She possessed real political gifts, and her policy might have succeeded if the issue had seemed less crucial to the contesting parties, but she failed to appreciate the depth of feeling of both Catholics and Protestants. Thus her reasonable policy came to naught.

Guises and Montmorencys, Protestants and Catholics, subverted her efforts at every turn. Amid confusion and unrest the Protestants swiftly increased their strength. By 1562 there were more than 2,000 congregations in France, really different sects which quarreled among themselves almost as bitterly as they resisted the Catholics. In that year war broke out between the Guises and Montmorencys. Catherine became a virtual prisoner of the Guises, who unleashed a religious terror, burning and jailing Protestants wherever they could apprehend them. Rival armies clashed in Paris and other cities, then scourged the countryside killing and looting. For thirty years this war raged sporadically, interspersed with occasional truces but never producing a clear-cut victory for either side.

Then on August 24, 1572, came the St. Bartholomew's Day Massacre. With Catherine's knowledge, the Guises prepared to assassinate all the Protestants in France. In the capital fanatics smashed down doors, stabbed the heretics in their beds. In a matter of days as many as 30,000 Calvinists including Coligny, admiral of France, were brutally murdered. Even this dreadful slaughter did not destroy the new faith, however. The conflict went on, each side gradually improving its organization. On the Catholic side, an unofficial holy league sprang into existence to help the Guises crush out the heretics wherever they could be found. Help came to the Calvinists from Protestant groups in Holland, England, and Germany, while the fanatically religious Philip II of Spain dispatched men and money to the Catholic cause.

The long conflict finally came to a head in 1588. Acting in conjunction with Philip II, who launched his great armada against Protestant England at this time, the Guises seized power in Paris. In this crisis Henry III decided that the political threat of the Guises was greater than the religious threat of the Protestants. He arranged to have the Duke of Guise murdered in his very presence during a royal council. Still the chaotic struggle went on, and a few months later Henry III was himself assassinated. Before his death he had named the Protestant leader, Henry of Navarre, as his heir, but French Catholics would not accept a Protestant king. For ten years more the fighting raged on. Finally Navarre, abjuring Protestantism, came to terms with Rome. In 1598 peace was finally restored to France.

To make sure that it would endure, Henry IV declared a general amnesty and issued the Edict of Nantes, granting religious and political freedom to all his subjects. The Protestants, called Huguenots, formed a kind of state within a state. Henry did not find this congenial, but he realized that he had no choice. Accepting this limitation on his authority, he worked feverishly to expand the commerce of France, and he rebuilt her devastated cities. But in 1610, despite all his efforts to persuade his countrymen to forget the past, he was himself assassinated. Civil and religious war again erupted, not to end until 1624 when Cardinal Richelieu took over the reins of government.

For Further Reading

Elliott, J. H., *Europe Divided, 1559–1598.*
Kingden, R. M., *Geneva and the French Protestant Movement 1564–1572.*
Neale, J. E., *The Age of Catherine de Medici.*
Roelker, N., *Queen of Navarre, Jeanne d'Albret, 1528–1572.*

10   Elizabethans and Puritans

Among the great powers to arise on the Atlantic, England came last, shortly after Spain and France. In the hundred years between the mid-fourteenth and mid-fifteenth centuries, Englishmen had to cope with a drastic reduction of population by the Black Death, a prolonged economic stagnation, and the sporadic outbursts of the Hundred Years' War against France. They suffered too the consequences of feudalism in dissolution—a disputed crown, the collapse of effective national and local administration, the corruption of justice, and private wars among noble chieftains at the head of bands of mercenaries. The picture was not entirely black, for these same years saw the virtually complete disappearance of servile status, some prosperity among those of the lower orders lucky enough to survive, and a flourishing university life; nor was there any diminution of the nation's artistic impulse, whose greatest legacy in this century was the perpendicular style, the last and perhaps loveliest expression of Gothic architecture. But the gradual working out of a new stability after the middle of the fifteenth century was welcome, great malefactors aside, to the whole country.

The Tudors, ultimately victorious in the dynastic struggle, were heirs to this gratitude. They carried further the stabilization begun under the last Yorkist kings and brought the country safely through Reformation, Counter Reformation, and the threat of a Spanish invasion. Though it was absolutist in principle and often harsh and corrupt in execution, Tudor policy in its main intentions coincided with the deepest aspirations of Englishmen until nearly the end of the sixteenth century.

The brilliantly engineered despotism of Henry VII (1485–1509)—a wily, grasping, pacific, and extremely able monarch—was based on refurbished machinery of the royal household. He left the monarchy firmly

A.D. 1485   Battle of Bosworth; accession of Henry VII

1509   Death of Henry VII; accession of Henry VIII

1529   Fall of Cardinal Wolsey

1529–1536   Reformation Parliament

1536–1540   Dissolution of the monasteries

1540   Execution of Thomas Cromwell

1547   Death of Henry VIII; accession of Edward VI

1553   Death of Edward VI; accession of Mary I

1558   Death of Mary I; accession of Elizabeth I

1563   Thirty-Nine Articles; Statute of Apprentices

1570   Elizabeth I excommunicated by Pope Pius V

1587   Execution of Mary, Queen of Scots

1588   Defeat of the Spanish Armada

1600   East India Company chartered

1603   Death of Elizabeth I; accession of James I

1611   Authorized Version (King James Version) of the Bible

1618   Beginning of the Thirty Years' War

1625   Death of James I; accession of Charles I

1628   Petition of Right adopted; assassination of the Duke of Buckingham

1629–1640   Period of personal rule: the "Eleven Years' Tyranny"

1640   Short Parliament (April–May); Long Parliament convenes in November

1641   Execution of the Earl of Strafford; Irish Rebellion begins

1643   Death of John Pym

1642–1646   First Civil War

1645   Execution of William Laud, Archbishop of Canterbury

1648   Second Civil War; Pride's Purge

1649   Execution of Charles I

1653–1658   Protectorate under Oliver Cromwell

1658   Death of Oliver Cromwell, succeeded as Lord Protector by his son Richard

1660   Restoration of Charles II

1662   Beginning of the "Bartholomew Ejections" following Act of Uniformity; expulsion of ministers creates English Nonconformity

1670	Secret Treaty of Dover between Charles II and Louis XIV
1678	Popish Plot
1679	Habeas Corpus Act
1679–1681	Exclusion crisis
1681–1685	Charles II rules without Parliament
1685	Death of Charles II; accession of James II
1688–1689	Glorious Revolution replaces James II with William of Orange and Mary; Bill of Rights; Mutiny Act; Toleration Act
1689–1697	War of the League of Augsburg (King William's War)
1694	Bank of England chartered; Triennial Act; Death of Queen Mary
1697	Treaty of Ryswick
1701	Act of Settlement
1702	Death of William III; accession of Queen Anne
1702–1713	War of the Spanish Succession (Queen Anne's War)
1707	Act of Union with Scotland
1713	Treaty of Utrecht
1714	Death of Queen Anne; accession of King George I
1721	Sir Robert Walpole becomes Prime Minister

---

established, financially solvent, and of no mean account in European affairs. Much of this legacy was wasted by his son, Henry VIII (1509–1547), an intelligent, cruel, self-indulgent Renaissance prince. Henry fancied himself a warrior and could seldom be bothered with the hard business of day-to-day governing; the inherited machinery was worked, therefore, by his chancellor Cardinal Wolsey, who gathered power and wealth into his own hands with a magnificence of style that far outdistanced his efficiency. The forms did not long survive Wolsey's fall in 1529. To deal with the administrative problems posed by the Reformation, new ad hoc institutions were created, still cast, however, in the medieval mold of government by essentially judicial bodies. Some, like the Court of Augmentations and the Court of First Fruits and Tenths, which dealt with the main financial consequences of the Reformation, had only a brief existence. Others were permanent, or were intended to be so. The main precedent was the Court of Star Chamber, which had evolved in the fifteenth century to deal with public order, a field in which the common law was notoriously defective. In the sixteenth century were added the Court of Requests, to deal with poor men's causes; the Councils of the West and the North, to govern those remote and rebellious regions; and, in Elizabeth's reign, the Court of High Commission, with a broad mandate over ecclesiastical affairs. Providing swift, cheap justice in contrast to the convoluted, hardened, and costly procedures of the regular common law courts, these Tudor creations formed a parallel and at least potentially competitive system of justice. But the rivalry remained latent, and the courts were, on the whole, popular.

A more fundamental change in the Tudor constitution grew from two further instances of the medieval process known as "going out of court," whereby one after another institution of the royal household (the origin of all medieval government) had separated itself from the household to become an established, bureaucratic department of state, still subject to the ultimate power of the king but free from his day-to-day interference. Under Thomas Cromwell, Henry VIII's chief minister in the 1530's, the key office of secretary of state—the king's closest confidential servant who had acquired a special importance in foreign affairs—made this transition and began its evolution, by division, into the principal ministries of modern central government. So too the king's council, hitherto an informal body of royal advisers, emerged as the Privy Council, a more regularized committee of ministers who decided and implemented policy. Not many aspects of English life escaped the scrutiny of "conciliar government" in the century between the Reformation and the Civil War. To finance, defense, diplomacy, and religion were added the supervision of foreign trade and the new efforts at colonization, the regulation of the quality and consumption of goods, the organization of apprenticeship, and efforts to solve the chronic problem of poverty, culminating in the Poor Law of 1601, which guaranteed state aid to the destitute, probably the most important piece of social legislation before the nineteenth century. But such measures were a far cry from modern welfare legislation. The intention behind them was profoundly conservative—to keep the country quiet and men in their places; the machinery was not that of enlightened humanitarianism but of social police.

The reach of Tudor policy far exceeded its grasp. Unlike modern governments, Tudor ministers had neither an army, nor police, nor corps of salaried, responsible civil servants to implement their policies. In the localities they had to depend on the justices of the peace, unpaid officials drawn from the ranks of nobility and gentry. Created in the fourteenth century to help keep the peace, the J.P.'s had by the sixteenth century become administrative officers as well as judges. Locally, their often selfish and tyrannical rule worked because English society was hierarchical and deferential. In the sixteenth century they were more or less effective instruments of national policy as well: a degree of cooperation was assured because they held their posts at the pleasure of the Crown and because in general they supported the dynasty and its intentions. But individuals among them could ignore legislation they did not like—against enclosures, for example, or against Catholics or Puritans. Tudor government depended on mutual accommodation between the Crown and the landed classes, a system that could not survive an estrangement.

In the Middle Ages, it has been said, Parliament was an occasion rather than an institution—a periodic meeting of the king's council reinforced by the summoning of feudal magnates and, at times, representatives of the freemen of the counties and towns. As it grew into an institution, Parliament divided into two parts. The representatives of the lesser nobility (the knights) came together with representatives of the towns to form the House of Commons, merging two potentially powerful segments of society that in other countries were likely to remain separate. The greater nobles and the bishops were thus left to evolve formally by the early sixteenth century into a House of Lords.

At the opening of that century, the future of Parliament was not bright. It was cumbersome and inconvenient, and kings would gladly have dispensed with it, had it not been necessary to them for two reasons. The highest form of declared law, the statute, required parliamentary assent. This power never degenerated into a formal and occasional exercise in registration, nor was it supplanted (though it was supplemented) by the royal prerogative of legislating by proclamation. When Henry VIII said that he at no time stood so high in his estate royal as when he was in his parliament, he was speaking more than flattery: ultimate sovereignty rested in the king in parliament. The use of statutes to accomplish the Reformation confirmed this function of Parliament, feeding a tradition of necessary association that could not easily be undone. Still more important was the requirement that Parliament consent to taxation. Had Henry VII succeeded in his intention of endowing the Crown through careful financial management, this power might have lost much of its significance. But the extravagance of Henry VIII, the inefficiency of the tax system, and above all, the drastic rise in prices wrecked such hopes. Still, Tudor monarchs summoned parliaments as seldom as possible, and when one was summoned, they and their ministers made certain that it was carefully managed.

After the reign of Queen Mary and her marriage to Philip II of Spain, anti-Catholicism became a major factor in English life, in the ensuing century inextricably linked to hatred of Spain, the foremost Catholic power as well as a colonial giant to be felled. Queen Elizabeth I (1558–1603) rode the crest of this wave of religious and secular patriotism. The queen could be perverse, mean, and petulant; she could procrastinate almost endlessly; her appetite for flattery was unceasing; and her involvements with favorites like the Earls of Leicester and Essex were embarrassing or even dangerous. She was at times the despair of her ministers. Yet she was intelligent and tough-minded, courageous, and (perhaps even in her apparent follies) capable of playing a role brilliantly. She was a consummate politician, able to manage her ministers and to dominate an increasingly rebellious Parliament, now by scolding them like an outraged governess in a nursery, now by giving in graciously to their complaints. In her hands the Tudor constitution reached the pinnacle of its success, though by the end of her reign more and more signs of trouble were appearing.

The defeat of the Spanish Armada in 1588 and the country's growing awareness of its good fortune fed a swell of creative energy bursting out in all directions—in exploration, in economic life, in intellect—that is almost without historical parallel. Broad-windowed country houses proclaimed the end of strife that had subjected architecture to the needs of defense; their style, adapting medieval forms, owed little to the classicism so rapidly advancing on the Continent. This independence of Continental models was paralleled in other fields. In music, the English reached a level of accomplishment they were never to attain again. A school of English historians and antiquaries laid the intellectual foundations for the struggles of the next century. The new learning, imported early in the century and of such importance in the reworking of English government and religion, had been assimilated; so had the Calvinist infusion of mid-century. Now theologians built a distinctive Anglican theology, led in Elizabeth's reign by the great transmitter of medieval tradition, Richard Hooker. In literature the age was preeminent, adding to a cluster of poets and dramatists of whom any nation might be proud three transcendent geniuses in Edmund Spenser, Ben Jonson, and William Shakespeare.

The finest works of the Elizabethan renaissance actually appeared in the reign of James I (1603–1625). But the Elizabethan constitution did not survive the change in dynasty so well as did Elizabethan culture. For all his abilities, James I did not have the art of the Tudors. But even had he had it, his lot would have been little easier: he was heir to Elizabeth's troubles too.

James I of England was also James VI of Scotland. He had come to the Scottish throne as an infant, following the forced abdication of his mother, Mary, Queen of Scots, who after twenty years as a prisoner and center of innumerable Catholic plots was executed by her cousin Elizabeth. His claim to the English throne lay through his great-grandmother, whose father, Henry VII, had married her to the then king of Scotland. The prospect of England promised James liberation in three directions—from the tutelage of the Scottish nobles who had made a mockery of his philosophical commitment to royal absolutism and the divine right of kings; from the leaders of the Scottish Church, the most radical of Calvinist establishments outside Geneva; and from the chronic poverty of his native country. On all three counts he was destined to disappointment.

From the 1570's opposition had been growing in the House of Commons. By clever management and by occasionally yielding, Elizabeth and her ministers had managed to keep it within bounds, but in James's reign it reappeared with new virulence, a vocal minority able from time to time to draw active or tacit support from less committed but increasingly discontented members. In 1604, some of the Commons presumed to lecture the king, in an *Apology,* about their interpretation of the constitution and their privileges; James, no mean scholar and fond of pontificating, lectured back. The issue was thus joined in a way that helped to defeat every effort of the king's essentially conciliatory policy.

James faced similar opposition in religion. The Elizabethan church had aimed at comprehension—absorbing into the national church the widest possible range of religious views, omitting only those Catholics who threatened the security of the country. But agreeing to differ on points of theology was far from satisfying to the more ardent spirits inspired by a Calvinism much more corrosive than the mild Calvinist infusion that had gone into the Thirty-Nine Articles. "Puritans" were dedicated to purifying the church of all remnants of popish superstition. Some of them wanted, moreover, to replace the bishops by a presbyterian form of church government, like that in Scotland; others, more radical, wanted to dispense with all centralized ecclesiastical rule in favor of congregational autonomy, or Independency. To a king whose convictions were put succinctly in his famous aphorism "No bishop, no king," the Puritan program was anathema. Again James was willing to compromise or at least to hear the objectors out, but the Puritans came to the Hampton Court Conference in 1604 determined not to yield an inch and drove the king to uphold a similarly rigid position. The one positive result was a decision to retranslate the Bible: the "King James" or Authorized Version appeared in 1611.

Opposition in church and state was sporadic; financial difficulties pressed continually. James had expensive tastes, a family, and an unfortunate weakness for favorites. But as his costs rose, his income did not. Much of the capital of the Crown—the royal lands—had been sold to help pay for the war against Spain. The rigid tax system produced nothing like a fair return on values, and the general rise in prices caught not only the

Crown in an inflationary squeeze but landowners and businessmen as well, making them the more reluctant to consent to new taxes.

The leaders of the opposition and much of its residual strength were to be found among the gentry, that range of middling landowners who had been the major beneficiaries of the sale of monastic lands by a needy Crown. The depression of the 1590's and the steady rise in prices severely hurt men whose standard of living had been rising. Not all of them were willing to keep down expenditure or to run their estates (or to have them run) in a business-like fashion, the more necessary as capitalistic methods spread in agriculture. The luckiest were those whose estates held timber or mineral resources, or on whose lands a growing town encroached. Some were able to enlarge their fortunes by the profits of office. But wealth, whether rising or declining, is an insufficient explanation of growing hostility among the gentry to interference by the central government. They were accustomed to rule in their localities; the state's very reliance on them increased their natural pride and their pretensions. More and more of them were educated in the "public schools" like Eton and Winchester, originally founded to train boys for the priesthood, in Oxford and Cambridge, or in the Inns of Court, England's "university" of the common law. Not that these young gentlemen were well educated or that they turned scholars or professional men; but they got a certain finish that increased their sense of superiority as a privileged order to be defended against encroachments. Whatever the precise balance of economic and social factors, there is no doubt that the gentry were outgrowing the Tudors' leading strings.

To a remarkable degree the ambitions of the gentry had come to center on Parliament: as natural leaders of their communities, they felt they belonged there; it sat at Westminster, where the fashionable world also assembled, and good behavior there might earn favorable notice and open possibilities of office. Peers, the titled aristocrats, sat in the House of Lords as a matter of right. But their sons, who were commoners at law (unlike Continental aristocracies), and the heads of prominent gentry families sought election to the Commons. They gradually took over the representation of England's towns, which counted far more seats than the counties for which sons of peers or leading gentry might naturally stand. The townsmen, with their limited vision, were happy enough to get out from under the burden of parliamentary attendance, to avoid paying wages to their representatives when gentlemen were willing to serve for nothing, and perhaps to bargain for favors in return for choosing one eager gentleman rather than another. The Crown was under constant pressure to increase the number of seats, and from 298 members in the first Parliament of Henry VIII the membership rose to 467 in the first Parliament of James I.

Neither king nor parliamentary opposition wanted to abolish the other or to bring about a revolution, let alone modern limited monarchy. Both Parliament and the king looked backward, James and his advisers to royal powers under the Tudor constitution, the members of Parliament to their own interpretation of that constitution and their place in it, and further to the idea of an unbreakable "fundamental law." Although this law invariably covered the privileges of each of its interpreters, it was no mere selfish rationalization: the notion itself has a certain moral impressiveness, and to the more articulate of its believers, it represented actual historical truth as a creative if mistaken generation of scholars had disinterred it. Both sides set to searching out precedents and, of course, found them. Historians today agree that the best precedents were nearly all on the king's side: the royal prerogative had been an inexhaustible storehouse of power to deal with new situations as they arose, and privileges, historically, flowed from royal grace. But the prerogative had never been defined; the early seventeenth-century conflict lay between increasingly discordant efforts to define the extent of royal powers. As their claims grew more irreconcilable, both sides were forced into extreme actions that no one would have predicted or wanted.

In James's reign, the principal disputes concerned money and foreign affairs. The king and his ministers tried to escape from the pinch of inflation on one side and grudging and inflexible parliamentary supply on the other by a series of expedients—a prerogative upward revision of customs, a statesman-like proposal to commute feudal dues in exchange for a regular parliamentary grant, devising ingenious monopolies to increase particular trades, placate the powerful, and fill the royal coffers. All the expedients failed. In foreign policy, James's intentions were admirable. A peaceable man, he started his reign by ending the war with Spain, but to those who remembered the Armada and feared the pope, this was compromising with the devil. The situation worsened when the Thirty Years' War broke out in 1618. The Protestant champion in the first stage of the war, the Elector Palatine of the Rhine, was the husband of James's daughter. But while public and parliamentary opinion was strong for intervention, it was equally unwilling to pay for a land war. James's opponents were, however, free with advice, whereas the king held that foreign policy was for his determination and that Parliament had no right to meddle.

The opposition in the Commons had created a number of procedures—the committee of the whole house, not subject to the usual rules, was one—to increase its chance to discuss or obstruct royal policy, and certainly James and his ministers managed Parliament less well than their predecessors: the House of Commons, in the famous phrase of one historian, had won the initiative. James added to his difficulties in 1616 by dismissing the chief justice of the Court of King's Bench, Sir Edward Coke, so providing the parliamentary opposition with its first leader of genius. As a minister under Elizabeth, Coke had yielded to no one in violent pursuit of suspected traitors, but in the courts he emerged as an equally fanatical defender of the common law. The king contended, quite correctly, that the judges, holding office at his pleasure, were his servants, "lions under the throne," as Sir Francis Bacon called them. But Coke, holding to his passionate belief in the supremacy of the law, precipitated his dismissal by refusing to consult in advance about decisions. When he entered the Commons in 1621, he brought his formidable learning to bear against the king. Under his guidance, the old medieval process of impeachment was revived —a procedure in which the Commons prosecute and the Lords try—and turned against corrupt ministers and monopolists, against Coke's archrival, the Lord Chancellor Sir Francis Bacon, and Lionel Cranfield, Earl of Middlesex, the London merchant who had become James's principal minister in the twenties. Impeachment remained a formidable if cumbersome weapon for dealing with dangerous or beaten opponents into the next century.

When James's reign ended in 1625, no final conflict was in prospect; within five years his son Charles I (1625–1649) had made it inevitable. As Prince of Wales, Charles and the Duke of Buckingham, his favorite as he had been his father's, had gone off to Madrid to arrange a Spanish marriage, much valued by James, highly unpopular among his subjects. The suit was rebuffed, the rejection rankled, and after his accession Charles and Buckingham decided on war against Spain, a brief, inglorious episode that, like an equally disastrous quarrel with France in 1626–1627, brought no advantages and considerably worsened the financial situation. The House of Commons had refused the king the customary life grant of customs revenues known as tunnage and poundage; Charles proceeded to collect them without authorization and resorted to forced loans as well, victimizing those who refused on principle to pay. Coke's reply to the king's desperate and unwise moves was the resounding if ineffectual Petition of Right in 1628, declaring it illegal to collect money without parliamentary consent, to quarter troops in private households, to imprison without showing cause, or to apply martial law to civilians—to all of which Charles had resorted to get his way. Meanwhile the ascendancy of the foolish and irresponsible Buckingham had alienated both Lords and Commons; foiled in an attempt at impeachment in 1626 by the king's dissolving Parliament, and again in 1628 by a prorogation, they were at last cheated of their victim by an assassin in 1628. By that time, many of the moderate opposition leaders had withdrawn, either to support the king or to the sidelines, leaving the zealots in control, above all the noisy demagogue Sir John Eliot. When the stormy parliamentary session of 1629 was ended by a dissolution, the Commons ordered the Speaker held in his chair while they passed three hysterical resolutions condemning as enemies of England anyone who paid the unauthorized tunnage and poundage, advised its collection, or introduced innovation in religion. Charles determined to rule without calling another parliament.

As an exercise in government, the "Eleven Years' Tyranny" was not unimpressive. The financial problem was dealt with by a careful husbanding of resources, a ruthless and unpopular enforcement of often forgotten feudal rights, and many other expedients, the most famous of which was a decision to extend the collection of ship money—for the outfitting of warships—from the port towns, which had traditionally paid, to inland towns. When an opposition leader, Sir John Hampden, refused to pay, the judges upheld the king's right, with only one dissent, a decision no doubt correct in law, but one that brought the judiciary into still further contempt, as other arbitrary acts of government were helping to discredit the once popular conciliar courts like Star Chamber. The government also made a last attempt at effective enforcement of old social legislation—commercial regulations, for example, and limitation of enclosures—and at firm central administration of the poor law. These actions further alienated many among the gentry and the merchants who disliked central interference with what they deemed their own proper concerns. Such opponents were primarily motivated, no doubt, by selfish and narrowly defensive considerations, but dubious motives merged with or were transmuted into a principled protest against the uncertainties and unfairness of arbitrary government and in the end were not untinged with nobility.

Two men came increasingly to determine government policy in the 1630's and to dominate the dark imaginings of the opposition. One was Thomas Wentworth (later Earl of Strafford), who had stood out against Buckingham in 1627 and had been imprisoned for refusing the forced loan. The next year, however, appalled by the excesses of some of his colleagues, he emerged as a king's man, a step true to his anti-Puritanism and his essentially loyal, authoritarian nature, but one that labeled him a turncoat in the eyes of a resurgent opposition. Wentworth was first put in charge in the north of England and then, after 1633, in Ireland, where he ruled effectively and despotically, careless of the dangerous resentments he was creating; in 1639, he was called back from Ireland to deal with the mounting crisis. The other man was William Laud, Archbishop of Canterbury after 1633, narrow, dedicated, and determined to put the internal government of the church in order. His emphasis on ritual and discipline offended the lively anti-Catholicism of the country, already alarmed by the intense and open Catholicism of Charles's queen, Henrietta Maria of France, and by the teachings (perhaps unnecessarily provocative) of a new school of theologians who, turning against the Calvinist heritage in Anglicanism, inaugurated what has come to be known as the "high church" tradition. Wentworth and Laud spoke of their policy of "Thorough," a resolute determination to rule justly and efficiently, as they saw it, against all obstacles, an impolitic course that ultimately brought both of them and their king to the scaffold.

The precipitating blunder was a decision to impose the Anglican prayer book on Presbyterian Scotland. The resulting Scottish rebellion had to be suppressed, and the shortage of funds made resort to Parliament a necessity. The Short Parliament in 1640 ended in deadlock, but the new parliament, reluctantly summoned at the end of that year and famous as the Long Parliament, met determined first on a reckoning with Strafford, who was believed ready to turn his Irish army against England. When it became clear that the attempt at impeachment would fail in the Lords, the Commons substituted a bill of attainder, declaring Strafford guilty of treason, and forced it on the unwilling Lords and the grief-stricken king by mob action and the threat of worse to come. He was beheaded in 1641. Laud too was imprisoned, but not put to death until 1645. Once Strafford's execution had removed the prime villain, Parliament turned to pass a series of reforming statutes. It provided that it could not be dissolved without its own consent, required that a parliament be called every three years, declared ship money illegal, and demolished much of the machinery that had been brought into disrepute, including the conciliar courts. Charles had little choice but to consent.

In January, 1642, having already turned London against himself, Charles made the fatal blunder of invading the House of Commons to arrest five leaders who, forewarned, had fled; the king then left his capital. He was still willing to make some concessions, even to the extent of agreeing to the exclusion of bishops from the House of Lords. But he found the sticking point in a demand that Parliament be given control of the armed forces, now vital to the suppression of a rebellion that had broken out in Ireland. In June, in the Nineteen Propositions, Parliament demanded control of the executive power as well. Charles raised his standard at Nottingham in August, and the Civil War began.

In November, 1641, in a vote on a manifesto called the Grand Remonstrance, nearly half of the Commons had swung to support the king. On this, and on the sympathy of most of the nobility and of much of the country, the king was able to rely. Still, the pattern of loyalties in the Civil War was extremely complex, reflecting personal and regional rivalries, ambitions and resentments, mixtures of interests and beliefs that varied from individual to individual, perhaps a clash of generations as well—at any rate the royalist members of the Long Parliament were younger, on an average, than the supporters of the parliamentary cause. The usual geographical generalization is that north and west were more likely to be royalist, the wealthier south and east parliamentary, but exceptions abound.

Without a king and without many of its members, Parliament ruled by ordinance, negotiating an alliance with the Scots, reconstructing the army, and launching England on the road to presbyterian church government. The most remarkable innovation was in the field of finance, where the invention of the excise and a prototype of the later land tax for the first time broke through the inflexibility of medieval taxation. The genius behind this parliamentary program was John Pym, a brilliant manipulator who had served in the parliaments of the twenties, established his ascendancy in the Short Parliament, and managed Strafford's trial and attainder; Pym was able to get his way by a consummate playing off of conservatives and extremists in the House. But after his death in 1643, Parliament did not recover its effectiveness, and the initiative passed to the army. While the bulk of the officers had gone over to the king, the "New Model" Army created for Parliament threw up its own leaders under the command and inspiration of an obscure country gentleman named Oliver Cromwell. Victories began to fall to him in 1644, and in 1646 the king fled to the Scots and surrendered.

Parliament and army fell out. Immediate issues like disbanding and arrears in pay were superficial reflections of deeper divisions. A victorious army, thirsting for further reform, resented its technical subordination to a self-satisfied and ineffective assembly. Parliament feared the growing radicalism of the army. This clash had its religious dimension in that Parliament was committed to a curious blend of presbyterian organization and civil supremacy, abhorrent both to true theocratic Presbyterians like the Scots and to the religious enthusiasts in the army who have been lumped together under the catch-all term "Independents." In normal times such profound questioning of the organization and purpose of civil society would have been kept in obscurity by the restraints of the traditional forms of social hierarchy. But those restraints had disappeared in the Civil War, and the army became a seedbed of radicalisms, the most famous of them the doctrines preached by the Levellers, who have been claimed, with some if not entire justice, as ancestors of modern democratic thought. Cromwell's enormous authority helped him to control his enthusiastic subordinates, but he found the necessary political ballast in his son-in-law, Lieutenant General Henry Ireton, a profound, conservative political thinker who was the author of the succession of draft constitutions that punctuate the negotiations of the late 1640's; Ireton's death in 1651 was a perhaps fatal blow to the prospects of stability of a Cromwellian regime.

Cromwell and his associates negotiated seriously with the king to preserve the monarchy and the changes that had been accomplished. Charles invariably eluded them, reaching a peak of deviousness when he agreed to accept a presbyterian church and so launched the Scots against the English in the second Civil War in 1648. Cromwell, a profoundly religious man, was likely to conclude, once he had been convinced of a course of action, that God had spoken to him; he finally came to believe that it was necessary to get rid of Charles Stuart, "that man of blood." Parliament was purged of its reluctant members, and Charles was seized and brought to trial before a specially created tribunal whose lawfulness he refused to recognize. He was convicted on the charge of high treason against the state and executed on January 30, 1649.

By 1651 Cromwell had suppressed the bitter resistance in Ireland and Scotland. Meanwhile England had been ruled as a republic by the remnant left after Colonel Pride's purge, the Rump, a rule increasingly inept and corrupt. In 1653 Cromwell went down to the House with troops and drove the members out. He then tried the experiment of a parliament elected by Independent congregations, an assembly of considerable respectability and much radicalism that was so occupied with talk and projects that it in turn was dissolved. Finally, under the first written constitution, the Instrument of Government, Cromwell undertook to rule as Lord Protector, a monarch in all but name, with a powerful Council of State, a submissive single-chamber legislature, and indispensable support from the army. The nature of Cromwell's military rule was emphasized in 1655 when the country was divided into districts, each in charge of a major general, its monarchical nature reinforced in 1656 when a second chamber was added to Parliament.

Although much was done, most of the wide-ranging reforms canvassed in the 1640's and in the short-lived "Barebones Parliament" of 1653 remained unenacted. Cromwell found himself, moreover, forced by the realities of power into policies and attitudes that would have shocked him when he had sat as a back-bench member of Parliament. Despite his genuine commitment to religious toleration, he had to deal harshly with troublemakers among the fanatics, including the Levellers and the Fifth Monarchy Men under whose influence he had passed at certain stages in his career. Even his neutered parliament caused him trouble, forcing him to dissolve it as soon as possible. His war with Spain (which won England Jamaica) was a policy Elizabethan enough for any Puritan taste, but Puritan England also fought the Dutch, who were Protestants, in the interests of trade. What Cromwell and his major generals set out to do, above all, was to make England into a godly commonwealth, by reforming the church and universities and by enforcing a moral revolution. These policies were not calculated to endear him to ordinary men; still, for those whose Puritan motivation was deep, these were magnificent years. The memory of this attempt at a new society survived among men of a Puritan persuasion for a century and a half and made its contribution to a new reforming impulse in the nineteenth century. The intensity of the Puritan vision survives in its two greatest literary monuments: John Bunyan's *Pilgrim's Progress,* and *Paradise Lost,* the greatest English epic poem, the last superb embodiment of a prescientific religious universe, by Cromwell's Latin secretary, John Milton.

Cromwell had steadily resisted advice to make himself king, though his institutions and his style edged more and more toward monarchy. After he died in 1658, he was succeeded by his ineffectual son Richard. But it was only a matter of time before the Stuarts were restored. In 1660 General George Monk, the commanding general in Scotland, came down to England with Presbyterian support, and recalled the remaining members of England's last legitimate Parliament—the Long Parliament—which dissolved itself. The new Parliament, encouraged by the conciliatory Declaration of Breda issued by Charles II from his Continental exile, recalled him as king in May, 1660.

In law, the whole period since 1642 was a blank, yet much was changed in the restored state and church. The statutes of 1641 still stood, and the machinery of conciliar government was not reerected; Charles's principal minister in the first years of Restoration was the Earl of Clarendon, one of the reformers of 1641 who had gone over to the royal cause. The financial inventions of the 1640's were carried over, and feudal dues were finally abandoned in exchange for a parliamentary grant. The Navigation Act that had been passed in 1651 was reenacted and expanded into a code of regulations that governed England's trade with her colonies and foreign countries for more than a century and a half. The church came more fully under royal (or ministerial) control after 1664, when an agreement that the clergy would no longer tax themselves removed the major reason for maintaining a more than nominal existence for Convocation, the Church's legislative body. The greatest change in the church, however, grew from the fierce loyalty to Anglicanism evident in the Parliament elected in 1660. Accommodation with the Puritans was rejected, even with the Presbyterians who had done so much to bring about the Restoration; a series of statutes—the so-called (and probably miscalled) Clarendon Code—deprived a fifth of the parish clergy who refused to subscribe to the Thirty-Nine Articles and to use the Book of Common Prayer and visited a number of civil disabilities on laymen who refused to conform to the Anglican Church. Thus the early 1660's saw the creation of a body of Dissenters or Nonconformists; the old Anglican ideal of comprehension had been abandoned, with far-reaching consequences in the religious, social, and political life of England.

Charles II could rely on the loyalty to both church and king of a Parliament and most of a country determined that the experiments of the 1640's and 1650's would not be repeated. He was himself extremely skillful; he had a standing army, as his father had not; as his reign advanced, more and more effective use was made of "the influence of the Crown"—the distribution of pensions, offices, and honors to gain political ends. With all these advantages he was able to dispense with Parliament for the last four years of his reign. But the finances continued in a bad way, despite the improvements made, and the notorious subsidies he got from Louis XIV of France were smaller in fact than in fame. What he won was won by politic yielding and clever management. Even so, opposition developed, based on the "country" as opposed to the court, and able to play on a residual Puritanism among the proscribed and sometimes persecuted Dissenters. At the end of the 1670's, in the midst of anti-Catholic hysteria provoked by baseless rumors of a "popish plot," the proposal was made to exclude Charles's brother, James, from the succession to the throne because of his open Catholicism. On this issue, men of country and court persuasions condensed into parties, nicknamed Whigs and Tories. In their pursuit of James, the Whigs overreached themselves in 1680–1681. Parliament was not called again in the reign, the town corporations were systematically remodeled to secure their loyalty, and the Whig leader Shaftesbury fled the country in 1682. With these developments to reinforce the monarchical loyalties of most of the country, James II succeeded to the throne in 1685 with broad support and even some enthusiasm.

Stupid and bigoted, James threw away all his advantages by a resolute attempt to restore Catholicism—not only by suspending laws against Catholics (and incidentally Dissenters) but, in the end, by trying to insinuate Catholics into positions of authority in the church, the universities, and the army. Any hope that this policy might disappear with James's death collapsed when his long-barren second wife, Mary of Modena, bore him a son in 1688. The threat to the church cracked the loyalty that had been expressed in doctrines of divine right and passive obedience. Although there was no national uprising, a coalition of Whig and Tory leaders issued an invitation to William of Orange, stadtholder of the Netherlands, to come to England, an invitation fully welcome to him, since gaining the English throne would mean bringing England firmly into the coalition against Louis XIV, of which William was the leader. His claim to England was more, however, than his being the Protestant champion of Europe: his mother was a daughter of Charles I, and his wife was Mary, the elder daughter of James II by his first, Protestant wife, Clarendon's daughter. When William landed in England and started his long march toward London, James's support gradually evaporated, and he fled to France. In violation of all constitutional logic, a Convention Parliament declared the throne vacant and offered it jointly to William and Mary.

Known since as the Glorious Revolution, this change of rulers was celebrated in the eighteenth century as yet another deliverance—by a curious coincidence it came exactly a century after the defeat of the Armada—and consecrated by the superb rationale of John Locke's second treatise on government, it became the basic political legend of a hundred and fifty years. The reality, as always, was more complex. The apparent harmony of the Revolution no more than interrupted fifty years of political violence, to which indeed the change of rulers added a new dimension. At no time in English history was party feeling so strong as under William and Mary or under Mary's sister Anne (1702–1714); it was grounded in differences about the exclusive claims of the church against the Dissenters, about the role of the king (the return of the Stuart pretenders from France remained a possibility down to 1715), and above all about who was to be in office. In an interesting transition, it was the post-Revolution Tories who took over the political footing and the ideology of the country orientation that had underlain pre-Revolution Whiggism; and, appropriately, some leaders of this new Toryism overreached themselves in 1714, as the Whigs had done thirty years before, by intriguing for a restoration of the Jacobite pretender. This and the unpopularity of the Peace of Utrecht, which Anne's Tory ministers had negotiated to end the War of the Spanish Succession in 1713 destroyed Toryism as a political force, however loyal obscure country gentlemen remained to Tory principles. When Queen Anne died childless in 1714, the crown passed uncontested, under terms of the Act of Settlement of 1701, to the elector of Hanover, who became King George I; he was descended from the marriage of the daughter of James I to the Elector Palatine of the Rhine.

The "Revolution Settlement" is the name given to a series of statutes passed in a dozen years or so after 1689, guaranteeing that parliament would meet annually and that the life of a parliament would be limited to three years; that the king would be Protestant; that judges would hold office during good behavior instead of at the king's pleasure, so ensuring their independence; that Dissenters could practice their religion openly, though they were not relieved of the civil disabilities visited on them by the Clarendon Code. The Bill of Rights of 1689, with the Habeas Corpus Act of 1679, provided a set of broad guarantees of the liberty of the subject. To these statutory provisions must be added as further insurance of the permanence of the settlement the act of union in 1707 that merged England and Scotland into the United Kingdom of Great Britain, and the new, firm basis given to government finance by the founding of the Bank of England in 1694 and the regular organization of the national debt in the following year.

In the Revolution, Parliament had secured its existence and its rights as an indispensable partner in the governing process. But it was by no means the dominant, and was far from an equal, partner. Although the king was limited in some ways that he was not before 1688, he was still the active head of government: ministers were responsible to him, not Parliament; he was in, not above, politics. But the party disputes, like the religious disputes that had so fully engaged men's attention in the seventeenth century, wore themselves out in sterility. Thanks to the astute political management of Sir Robert Walpole, the leading minister (he rejected the then pejorative term "prime minister") from 1721 to 1742, and to his perfection of the use of royal "influence," thanks too to the desire of Englishmen to be left alone to get on, to make money, and to live quietly, England had by the 1720's entered a period of political stability. She was no longer an example of violence to be abhorred, but an example of liberty—real, if partial—to be admired and imitated by eighteenth-century reformers elsewhere.

For Further Reading

Ashley, Maurice, *England in the Seventeenth Century.*
———, *The Greatness of Oliver Cromwell.*
Bindoff, S. T., *Tudor England.*
Elton, G. R., *England under the Tudors.*
Kenyon, J. P. (ed.), *The Stuart Constitution.*
Neale, Sir John, *Elizabeth I and Her Parliaments.*
———, *The Elizabethan House of Commons.*
———, *Queen Elizabeth.*
Ogg, David, *England in the Reign of Charles II.*
Plumb, J. H., *The Origins of Political Stability in England, 1675–1725.*
Stone, Lawrence, *The Crisis of the Aristocracy, 1558–1641.*
Trevelyan, G. M., *The English Revolution, 1688–1689.*

11   The Thirty Years' War

Historians are fond of stressing the importance of the Scientific Revolution of the seventeenth century, and of the opening up of vast economic opportunities in Asia, the Americas, and Africa for Europeans. But they often fail to mention how insignificant or even irrelevant these developments appeared to the overwhelming majority of Europeans who lived and fought in that age. The discoveries of Brahe, Galileo, and Harvey in physics and physiology went unnoticed by Europe's ruling elites. The founding of trading companies in America by Sir Walter Raleigh, for example, did not much influence the prevailing modes of social and political life for decades. Turning their backs on these pioneering efforts and enormous opportunities, Europeans squandered most of their energies in a massive war.

The violence broke out first in 1618 and soon extended all across the continent. It was much more brutal and destructive than either the earlier feudal conflicts or the more modern wars which began during the reign of Louis XIV in the late seventeenth century. Not until the twentieth century would the Western world again know the wanton pillaging, raping, and killing of a semiguerrilla force which no government could command. As the last great war of the condottiere generals, those men who hired themselves out to governments, then raised armies which preyed on the peasants and townsmen, the Thirty Years' War stands unique—a series of bloody campaigns in which civilians often suffered more grievously than soldiers.

Actually war had geen raging sporadically in Europe since the 1520's. In Germany the assassination of Henry IV in 1610 only delayed a resumption of the struggles between France and the Hapsburgs, a struggle reminiscent of the wars of Charles V and Francis I a century earlier. In the Netherlands the Dutch readied themselves for another clash with the Catholic power of Spain. In Italy the French and Spanish prepared to resume their contest for control of the passes across the Alps.

It would have been understandable, if not necessarily sensible, had the powers clashed over control of foreign empires, of trade routes and rich farmlands, or if social conflicts had triggered the fighting. Instead, they spilled their blood and treasure over relatively minor religious differences and spilled more for pure dynastic aggrandizement. Europe's elite—the kings, diplomats, scholars, and churchmen—took little interest in science or far-off lands.

Why they indulged in such madness so soon after such disasters as the

A.D.   1612   Ferdinand II becomes king of Hungary and Bohemia
       1618   Defenestration of Prague
       1620   Battle of White Mountain
       1621   End of the Spanish-Dutch truce
       1623   Maximilian of Bavaria receives electoral vote held pre-
              viously by Palatinate
       1624   Richelieu enters and soon dominates royal council;
              French-Dutch treaty
       1626   Defeat of Danish troops in Brunswick by Count Tilly
       1629   Edict of Restitution
       1630   Electoral Assembly of Regensburg insists on Wallen-
              stein's resignation; Gustavus Adolphus lands in north-
              ern Germany, is subsidized by France
       1631   Capture and massacre of Magdeburg
       1632   Battle of Lützen, Hapsburg defeat; death of Gustavus
              Adolphus
       1634   Assassination of Wallenstein
       1635   Treaty of Prague; French declaration of war against Spain
       1636   Capture of Corbie by the Spanish
       1639   Revolt of the Nu-Pieds in France
       1640   Revolts of the Catalans and the Portuguese
       1643   Defeat of the Spanish by the French at the Battle of
              Rocroi; war between Denmark and Sweden
       1646   Invasion of Bavaria by Swedish and French troops
       1648   Peace of Westphalia

Armada and the bloody religious wars in France attracted the attention of some of the best minds of Europe during this thirty years of war: men like the statesman Sully, the philosopher Thomas Hobbes, and the lawyer Hugo Grotius. Such men agreed that no single ruler, but rather the awful reality of European power politics, explained the wasteful conflict. Hobbes put it clearly when he said that violence was the natural result when nations either sought to conquer other nations or feared being themselves overrun. In the early seventeenth century every country of Europe fell into one or another of these categories, if not into both.

The exhausted and bankrupt powers of the Holy Roman Empire had seen the Treaty of Augsburg (1555) as no more than a truce, not as a permanent solution of the religious question. Gradually treasuries were replenished and the new generation of nobles grew to fighting age. The German Jesuits injected a revived religious zeal among Catholics, and Calvinist preachers preyed with equal force on their followers in Augsburg and the Palatinate. (No account of the Calvinists had been taken at Augsburg except perhaps a tacit agreement to burn them as heretics, but by 1600 this faith had made important inroads among the nobility and bourgeoisie of the Netherlands, France, Scotland, and England.)

In 1585 the city of Cologne, which had been under Lutheran control, reverted to Rome. This heralded a Catholic revival in northern Germany, a Lutheran stronghold. Jacques Callot's great engravings vividly depict the inquisitions, hangings, burnings, and general misery that plagued the region in the following years. The balance of power swung back and forth erratically until in 1618 a rebellion in Bohemia triggered a general war which, shifting from district to district, endured for thirty years.

Once the balance of forces had been destroyed, state after state struggled brutally for dominance in the Holy Roman Empire. (The playwright Bertolt Brecht, writing with the equal carnage of World War I in mind, recapitulated the horror of the era graphically in *Mother Courage.*) The many tiny principalities of the empire formed Protestant and Catholic leagues. Religious differences were magnets attracting the ambitions of the great Catholic families, the Hapsburgs and the Wittelsbachs, who formed foreign alliances with the pope and with Spain, thus enmeshing Germany in the larger struggles of the Counter Reformation. Similarly, German Protestants allied themselves with French Huguenots and with the English and the Dutch.

With the continent thus divided, the youthful Hapsburg king of Bohemia, Ferdinand, sought to restore the imperial policies of Charles V. In alliance with his Spanish cousins he launched a reckless campaign to exterminate Protestantism from the empire. In his own Bohemia he levied heavy taxes on Protestants and closed their churches. Powerful Protestant

THE THIRTY YEARS' WAR 1619-1648

nobles would not tolerate such treatment. Bohemia being an elective monarchy, they deposed Ferdinand, choosing the Protestant prince Frederick of the Palatinate as king. Frederick knew, of course, that this meant war, but he counted on aid, especially from James I of England, his father-in-law. James, however, unlike most kings of the epoch, disliked fighting. Besides, he had no money for foreign campaigns. He did nothing. Since Frederick could offer them little to fight war but a good cause, the Lutheran princes of Germany also refused to help. Ferdinand, on the other hand, swiftly obtained a powerful army led by an excellent general, Count Tilly, appointed by Maximilian of Bavaria, whose Catholic zeal was reinforced by the desire to snatch the electoral hat from his relative Frederick's head along with the Bohemian land. Spain also provided Ferdinand with money and troops. Thus between Spanish forces striking from the Rhine and Bavarians from Bohemia, Frederick's army was smashed at the Battle of White Mountain outside Prague in 1620.

At this point the Bohemian conflict seemed a mere incident. Actually it was the prelude to a continent-wide disaster, for which Ferdinand was chiefly responsible. Interpreting the reasonable refusal of the Protestant states to support Frederick's hopeless cause as a sign of weakness, he unleashed the terrible Counter Reformation throughout his domains. Hapsburg officials invaded every principality, imposing harsh taxes and wiping out the cherished rights of nobles and businessmen. All the German princes found the freedom they had won from Charles V in the sixteenth century now in grave danger. The fate of Frederick of Bohemia heightened their alarm; Ferdinand treated him as a renegade, deposed him, and gave his land and his electoral authority to Maximilian.

Although no united resistance emerged, warfare now became general. The king of Denmark, unwilling to stand by idly while Ferdinand's Spanish allies controlled the Palatinate, attacked the Rhineland with an allied force only to be defeated badly. Ferdinand's brilliant General Wallenstein then wrecked havoc on the Lutherans of northern Germany. Now the war took on a life of its own. Most of the fighting had been done, according to the custom of the time, by mercenaries. When after years of costly campaigning the rulers ran out of money, the mercenaries extracted their wages in the form of plunder, rape, and senseless destruction. Troops of armed men roamed the countryside in search of peaceful towns to loot. They blackmailed entire communities, pillaged churches and monasteries. No nationality or religious faith was safe from attack; no noble too prestigious, no peasant too poor, to escape their hunger for booty. Ragged hordes of camp followers followed each armed band, scavengers feeding on the wreckage. For months and for years armies of from 10,000 to 40,000 men subjected Germany to senseless slaughter and pillage, all in the name of religion. Only the generals profited, attacking whom they pleased without consulting the princes whose standards they carried, setting themselves up practically as sovereigns in captured territory. Wallenstein even became the acknowledged ruler of the Protestant duchy of Mecklenburg.

Military success led Ferdinand in 1629 to issue the Edict of Restitution ordering the return to Rome of all church lands seized in the Protestant principalities since 1552. This was a direct blow at the north German Lutheran and Calvinist princes and also, of course, a revocation, at least of the spirit, of the Peace of Augsburg. At the apogee of his power, Ferdinand summoned the German princes to meet with him at Regensburg and called upon them to join him in a war against the Dutch. He considered this as a fair exchange with his Spanish cousins for the help they had given him in Bohemia, but the German princes saw the situation differently—they refused; what is more, they forced Ferdinand to discharge the unpopular General Wallenstein.

Ferdinand was still the strong man of central Europe, but foreign powers alarmed by the imbalance of forces he had created were beginning to intervene. French envoys moved unobtrusively among the princes at Regensburg. The French, guided since 1624 by the astute Cardinal Richelieu, allied themselves with the Dutch and began to challenge the Hapsburgs in Mantua and other parts of Italy. More significant, a new force, King Gustavus Adolphus of Sweden, now threw his weight into the conflict. Seeking to restore his Mecklenburg relatives to their lands, he marched a well-organized army, sustained by Protestant zeal and French money, into Germany. Combining political and military skills astutely, he formed an alliance with Protestant Brandenberg and Saxony, and in 1631, at the Battle of Breitenfeld, defeated an imperial army. Thereafter he swept over the Rhine and in a series of successful battles advanced clear to Munich. While his troops pillaged Bavaria, his Saxon allies captured Prague.

In desperation Ferdinand restored Wallenstein to command of his army. Wallenstein then marched into Saxony, leaving a trail of wreckage in his wake. But after months of maneuvering and destruction he was finally defeated by Gustavus on the field of Lützen, although Gustavus was killed in the battle. For a time Wallenstein seemed more of a threat to Ferdinand than to his enemies. Ferdinand, however, undermined the general among his own junior officers and then discharged him; soon thereafter he was murdered. Ferdinand then pressed the war against the Swedes, gaining slowly. Sweden's Brandenburg and Saxon allies, tired of the war and fearful of Swedish designs on Pomerania, were soon ready to abandon the contest. After winning an important victory at Nördlingen in 1634, Ferdinand was able to negotiate a peace under his own harsh terms at Prague in 1635. He was now free to help the Spanish in the Netherlands.

That war had gone badly for Spain, but Ferdinand might well turn the tide. To prevent this, France declared war on Spain and increased its subsidies to the Swedes and to another of Ferdinand's foes, Bernard of Weimar. This was a desperate gamble for Richelieu, for Spain was the greatest power in Europe and his own resources were limited. The French army was small and ineptly led and the royal treasury was almost empty. But the cardinal was convinced that the Hapsburgs posed a threat to all

Europe; the risk had to be taken. With Spain also almost exhausted by the long and costly struggle, the outcome seemed to depend upon which side first collapsed rather than which could win a military victory.

The tide went first one way, then the other. French prospects looked bleak in 1639 when a popular uprising occurred in Normandy, but Richelieu successfully suppressed these rebels. Then in the early 1640's French troops took both Alsace and the vital Alpine passes. Rebellions in Spanish Catalonia and in Portugal forced the chief Spanish minister Olivares to pull troops back from the Netherlands to restore order. Finally, in 1643, French forces won a decisive victory over the finest units of the Spanish army in the Battle of Rocroi.

Such was the chaos of the times, however, that each victory caused counterbalancing shifts among the contesting forces. After Rocroi the Dutch began to fear the French more than the Spanish. Similar realignments occurred in northern Europe. The Hapsburgs gave up their dream of reclaiming Protestant church lands, and after four years of negotiations, constantly complicated by the shifting fortunes of war and the outbreak of civil disturbances in various districts, the exhausted rivals signed the Peace of Westphalia in 1648. A bewildering exchange of territory and money took place among the German states. Sweden was given a place in the German diet. France got control of Metz, Verdun, and Toul, along with part of Alsace. The Dutch and Swiss achieved their independence. And as for the original cause of the war, religion, the delegates agreed merely to reestablish the principle laid down at the Peace of Augsburg in the previous century: each prince would determine the religion of his people now, even if he was a Calvinist. As a result the Hapsburgs drove all Protestants from their land, and many of the Lutherans and Calvinist princes compelled their Catholic subjects to choose between conversion and emigration.

After thirty years of war much of Germany lay in ruins, the fields untilled, the forests untended, the towns devastated, their crafts and industries destroyed. One-third of the population had died either in battle or from plague, malnutrition, or similar war-related catastrophes. Recovery would take decades if not whole centuries. Such were the terrible consequences of this enormous and bloody conflict for Germany and most of the rest of Europe.

But at Westphalia no one really expected, despite these terrible losses, that a long or a just peace had been achieved. The war between France and Spain continued unabated until 1659. Elsewhere the settlement had been made by exhausted powers but powers perfectly willing to consider resuming the struggle once their strength had been recovered. Indeed, one of the reasons why Sweden had conceded peace at last had been her growing concern over the other Baltic powers. At best a precarious balance had been reached. The nations returned to more regional interests. But at least for the moment peace had returned to Germany.

For Further Reading

Clark, G. N., *The Seventeenth Century.*
Holborn, H., *A History of Modern Germany.*
Wedgwood, C. V., *The Thirty Years' War.*

12   The Rise of Modern Political Thought

The fundamental changes that transformed Europe in the sixteenth and seventeenth centuries produced corresponding changes in the ways men thought about politics. Within roughly 200 years, beginning with Niccolò Machiavelli and ending with John Locke, political philosophers recognized and responded to these changes—the slow emergence of secular politics and the irremediable splintering of religious unity—by devising a theory for the modern state.

The essential ideas underlying political thinking in the Christian Middle Ages had been fairly simple: fallen man required controls; repressive political institutions are the kind of check that sinful humanity had invited after Adam. On the positive side, kings and judges also had the task of aiding men to lead a Christian life in this world by giving them their rightful place in the hierarchy of society and enabling them to respect the men and institutions that existed for the protection and propagation of the True Faith. Of course, while it was easy to agree on these propositions, priests and statesmen, theologians and philosophers, interminably, often bitterly, debated over what they meant in practice: How was authority to be divided between pope and emperor? Who was to appoint the higher functionaries of the Roman Catholic Church—the secular or the religious arm? Over these intensely practical issues, supporters of one side or the other had wrangled for centuries, and which side prevailed depended more on the fortunes of diplomacy and arms than on the logical merits of the case. When Machiavelli, early in the sixteenth century, founded modern political thinking, he did nothing to settle these disputes, but much to suggest that they were becoming irrelevant.

It is significant that Machiavelli was a product of Renaissance Florence —a diverse, sophisticated urban culture and small though potent city-state

A.D.   1494   Invasion of Italy by French troops

1513–1521   Niccolò Machiavelli writes *The Prince* and *The Discourses on the First Ten Books of Livy*

     1517   Martin Luther posts 95 theses on church door at Wittenberg; Reformation usually dated from this moment

     1525   Sack of Rome

1562–1594   Series of religious wars in France

     1572   St. Bartholomew's Day Massacre in Paris, slaughter of the Huguenots

     1576   Jean Bodin publishes *Six Books of the Republic*

     1594   Henry IV takes Paris

     1610   Henry IV is assassinated

1618–1648   Thirty Years' War

     1642   Civil war begins in England

     1649   Charles I of England beheaded

     1651   Thomas Hobbes publishes *Leviathan*

     1656   James Harrington publishes *The Commonwealth of Oceana*

     1658   Oliver Cromwell dies

     1660   Restoration of the monarchy in England; Charles II (1660–1685)

     1661   Louis XIV of France assumes sole rule after death of Mazarin

     1670   Baruch (Benedict de) Spinoza publishes, anonymously, *Tractatus Theologico-Politicus*

1685–1688   Reign of James II in England

1688–1689   Glorious Revolution; James II dethroned; William and Mary

     1690   John Locke publishes *Two Treatises of Civil Government,* written ten years before

struggling for expansion and survival amid a ruthlessly competing group of similar states fighting for similar stakes. An experienced public servant and a keen observer, Machiavelli witnessed this spectacle without any illusions; a classicist and a pagan, he was not surprised to find that the princes of the Church behaved quite as viciously as their secular enemies. In 1512, when the shifts of political fortunes compelled Machiavelli to retire, he used his involuntary leisure to put down his reflections on politics in orderly form, and wrote two books that were to become classics in political theory: the *Discourses on the First Ten Books of Livy,* a set of aphorisms and short essays on ancient and modern politics, and *The Prince,* a disenchanted little book that would shock readers for centuries.

Freed as he was from religious convictions or superstitions, Machiavelli saw politics as a purely secular affair. It was, quite simply, the combat of men in search of power. Since men are all alike—all brutal, all selfish, all cowardly more or less—politics must follow universal rules, rules as applicable to Machiavelli's day as they had been to ancient Rome. The successful ruler therefore is the man who has studied his fellow man, both by reading history and by observing his contemporaries, and is willing to exploit their weaknesses. This cool prescription arose not from some supposed lack of moral sense, which many of his readers professed to detect in Machiavelli, but from his deeply pessimistic appraisal of human nature. The prince (so runs his most notorious maxim) must be both lion and fox: he must both terrorize and deceive his subjects. While Machiavelli did not have a taste for despotisms—in fact he greatly preferred sturdy, self-reliant republics—his own time, he thought, was too corrupt to permit any alternative to the kind of ruthless Renaissance despot that he saw all around him.

Machiavelli was a master stylist, pungent and vigorous, and from his own day on he found apologists eager to clear him from the widespread charge that he gloried in evil; he was, his supporters insisted, a scientist of politics who saw the world more clearly than others and reported what he saw with his own peculiar lucidity. This is an inadequate, or at least incomplete, view of the man: he was, first of all, a product of his time, in which the techniques he appraised so clinically were widely practiced; what was to shock other countries and later ages did not shock his compatriots and contemporaries. In addition, he was a man of passion: he was passionately committed to the active life; he was passionately hostile to the papacy for inviting foreign invaders to Italian soil for its own political profit. But while his supposed "scientific attitude" was not all he represented, it was his particular contribution to political theorizing: Machiavelli successfully detached politics from ethics and from theology, and presented it as a secular activity to be practiced and studied for its own sake. It was a fateful legacy.

Machiavelli was so intent upon establishing the autonomy of politics that he had little to say about religion apart from his comments on papal diplomacy. Yet, in the very decade in which he wrote his masterpieces, Martin Luther was to place religious questions squarely into the center of political speculation. For the Protestant reformers—for John Calvin and the others quite as much as for Luther—politics was something of an embarrassment. As good and in many respects perfectly traditional Christians, they were provoking and leading a great rebellion while, at the same time, they preached submission. They agreed with Catholic theologians at least in this: one of the primary duties of a Christian man was to obey constituted authority, no matter how wicked it might be. The evil king was a scourge sent by God, to be endured rather than resisted. As we have seen, Luther denounced the German peasantry in the most brutal terms for rising up against its princes; while he found many of their demands reasonable, he could not accept their defiance of those whom the Lord had set above them. Again, in 1559 Calvin counseled the French Huguenots to remain peaceful subjects of their Catholic rulers; while he could not help sympathizing with the sufferings of his coreligionists, the sin of rebellion seemed to him inexcusable. But in a Europe irrevocably split apart, with Catholics and Protestants equally unwilling to surrender to the other and equally insistent that their own faith was the only true one, and with regions, cities, even families divided in their religious allegiances, such inculcation of passivity could not remain a tenable policy for long. By the 1570's, therefore, two distinct theories had emerged to deal with the new situation: one, most exhaustively stated in Jean Bodin's *Six Books of the Republic,* devalued religion in behalf of a revived antique idea—sovereignty; the other, best represented by the anonymous pamphlet *Vindiciae contra tyrannos,* developed into a full-fledged system the rudimentary medieval notion that it might be lawful to resist the tyrant. These theories pointed in opposite directions while they tried to deal with the same issue: the first, stressing the right of the ruler over all subjects within his jurisdiction, moved toward the idea of modern absolutism; the second, by concentrating on the right of the subject against the impious tyrant, moved toward the idea of modern constitutionalism. Hobbes and Locke, the two greatest political theorists of the seventeenth century, while they agreed on much, became the supreme representatives of these two strands.

Thomas Hobbes was born in 1588, the year, as he himself liked to point out, of the Spanish Armada. And all his long life was spent in a time of turmoil, a virulent combination of religious, political, economic upheaval that England had not seen for more than a century and a half, a civil conflict culminating with the killing of Charles I and the establishment of a commonwealth under Cromwell. These events, combined with

Hobbes's philosophical materialism, shaped his political thinking: the *Leviathan,* one of the great books in the literature of political theory, appeared in 1651, two years after the execution of the king. The greatest evil in the world, Hobbes insists, is civil war; the central task of the political thinker, therefore, is to find the way to civil peace. In pursuit of this task, Hobbes developed a rigorously consistent system of rule and obedience, securely founded on his view of human nature. Man's most distinctive quality, Hobbes argued, is egotism—the pursuit of pleasure and the avoidance of pain at the expense of others. It is no peaceful pursuit; goods are scarce, and men always want more than they have: "I put for a general inclination of all mankind, a perpetual and restless desire for power after power, that ceaseth only in death." Employing that favorite metaphor of seventeenth-century political theorists, the state of nature in which men exist without the dubious benefit of political institutions, Hobbes argued that given human nature, such a state must be a "war of every man against every man," an orgy of mutual suspicion inevitably issuing in mutual murder, a life without morality or comfort or civility—"solitary, poor, nasty, brutish, and short."

But Hobbes saw man as equipped with reason as well as with the desire for pleasure and power, and man's enlightened search for self-preservation would therefore lead him to abandon the disastrous state of nature for a system of political order secure enough to forestall civil war and strong enough at the same time to protect all subjects. It is precisely because men are so egotistical that the state must engross all possible power. "Covenants, without the sword, are but words, and of no strength to secure a man at all." It follows that men must, figuratively and literally, give up their swords to the sovereign—"that great Leviathan . . . that mortal God"—whose control is absolute.

The theory sounds terrifying, but its logic is impeccable, and its bearing, be it noted, is wholly secular and wholly utilitarian. There is only one justification for the state: its capacity to keep order. The old sources of authority—legitimacy, tradition, religious foundations—were of no interest to Hobbes at all. While Hobbes refuses to allow the subject any right to resist the sovereign, the task of the sovereign is to protect the subject, and rebellion against him only proves the sovereign unfit to rule. Hobbes's utilitarian theory thus poses an interesting paradox: revolutions are illegal, but successful revolutions make the new regime legitimate, through their very success; Hobbes was interested not in tyranny—he was an individualist, and his theory was, after all, not hostile to any form of government, even republics—but in the logic of politics.

Great works of the mind rise above, and last beyond, the occasion that brought them forth, but they will always bear the marks of their origins.

Hobbes wrote during and against civil strife; thirty years after him, when the republican interlude was over and the Stuart monarchy had been restored, Locke would write during and against a different menace: the possibility of a Catholic succession in a Protestant, or at least Anglican, country. The brother and heir to Charles II was a declared and determined Roman Catholic, and even before his accession in 1685 as James II it was clear that his reign would mortally offend the vast majority of Englishmen. Locke's political writings came out of this atmosphere; they are a notable attempt to formulate the right to resistance while, at the same time, guaranteeing the state enough power to rule effectively. Locke wrote his *Two Treatises of Government* before the Glorious Revolution of 1688 which expelled James II and brought in the Protestants William and Mary, but he published them after that revolution, in 1690. Intended as the justification for future action, they came to be read as the justification of a triumphant revolution.

Like Hobbes, Locke used the device of a prepolitical state of nature, but to different effect. In their original condition, Locke argued, men enjoyed the right to "life, liberty, and estate," and it was obvious that they would contract to found a political society only because in such a society these rights would be better protected than they would be without a state. The civil power thus established had the right to make laws, and reserved enough authority to make them stick, but it existed quite clearly only for the sake of the public good. A government was thus distinct from, and the servant of, society. It followed, as Locke did not fail to point out, that there were certain conditions when societies might legitimately refuse their obedience to their government, especially when the government had betrayed its trust, when it invaded the inviolable rights of all men, when, in a word, it degenerated from a government of laws into a despotism.

Locke took good care to define the reasonable powers of the state widely enough to make legitimate rebellion a rarity. Still, he enunciated a significant set of principles which would acquire a certain explosive verve in the eighteenth century, in France and in Britain's American colonies: government is a sacred trust; men have imprescriptible rights; revolution is a last but always a possible resort. Much like Hobbes in this as well, Locke founded this trust and these rights not on theological or historical arguments, but on the philosophical theory of human nature. Thus, while Locke was scarcely a secularist himself, and while his theory was hedged around with conservative caution, he pushed political thinking into modernity.

For Further Reading

Aaron, R. I., *John Locke.*
Allen, J. W., *Political Thought in the Sixteenth Century.*

Chabod, Federico, *Machiavelli and the Renaissance.*
Dickens, A. G., *Martin Luther and the Reformation.*
Dunn, John, *The Political Thought of John Locke.*
Franklin, Julian H., *Jean Bodin and the Sixteenth-Century Revolution in the Methodology of Law and History.*
Gerbrandy, Pieter S., *National and International Stability: Althusius, Grotius, van Vollenhoven.*
Gilbert, Felix, *Machiavelli and Guicciardini.*
Goldsmith, Maurice M., *Hobbes's Science of Politics.*
Gough, J. W., *John Locke's Political Philosophy.*
Krieger, Leonard, *The Politics of Discretion: Pufendorf and the Acceptance of Natural Law.*
McShea, Robert J., *The Political Philosophy of Spinoza.*
Monter, Edward W., *Calvin's Geneva.*
Pelikan, Jaroslav, *Spirit vs. Structure: Luther and the Institutions of the Church.*
Plamenatz, John, *Man and Society, Vol. I.*
Raab, Felix, *The English Face of Machiavelli.*
Reynolds, Beatrice, *Proponents of Limited Monarchy in Sixteenth-Century France: Francis Hotman and Jean Bodin.*
Ridolfi, Roberto, *The Life of Niccolò Machiavelli.*
Sabine, George H., *A History of Political Theory.*
Smith, Russell, *Harrington and His "Oceana."*
Strauss, Leo, *The Political Theory of Hobbes.*
Vreeland, Hamilton, *Hugo Grotius, the Father of the Modern Science of International Law.*
Wendel, François, *Calvin.*

Toward One World

13 The Commercial Powers

The spectacular discoveries of the fifteenth-century European navigators opened a new chapter in the history of mankind. Portuguese exploration of the African coasts and islands and Columbus' discovery of a totally new world began a quest which brought most of the earth into the scope of European man. All over the world Europeans forced themselves into the ken of people who had been living in relative isolation and self-sufficiency. This dramatic and painful process, which lasted until the end of the eighteenth century, began a gradual movement toward one world and a system of international relations affecting the daily lives of people in every corner of the earth. After a brief halt in the nineteenth century, a new wave of exploration and colonization created the reality of today, with all its problems and tensions: this is the heritage of European expansion.

The age of discovery was filled with tumultuous events as small bands of adventurers penetrated into strange new worlds in pursuit of profit and dreams, and as their discoveries were consolidated into vast empires by following generations, the excitement and drama continued. It is paradoxical that the sixteenth-century colonial conquests were made by Spain and Portugal, two countries that did not play very large roles in the European commercial life of the time. The chief commercial powers were not especially interested in colonial expansion, nor were they worried by the Treaty of Tordesillas (1494) by which Spain and Portugal had confidently divided up the overseas world between themselves.

From the strictly commercial point of view the discoveries had come too early, before the European economy had been integrated into a single market, an integration that was necessary before the intensive colonial exploitation of the seventeenth and eighteenth centuries could take place. At the beginning of the sixteenth century Europe still consisted of a number of small regional economic systems. Although interregional trade was profitable and important, the economy was still predominantly agrarian.

A.D.   1494   Treaty of Tordesillas divides overseas world between Spain and Portugal

1570's   First raids by English and Dutch on Spanish empire in South America; breakdown of Portuguese monopoly in the Indian Ocean

1600   Foundation of English East India Company

1602   Foundation of Dutch East India Company

1609   Foundation of Bank of Amsterdam

1619   Foundation of Bank of Hamburg

1621   Foundation of Dutch West India Company

1624   Dutch drive English out of spice trade of the East Indies

1629   Dutch obtain rights to trade at Arkhangelsk

1635   Foundation of Compagnie française des îles d'Amerique

1639   English establish themselves in Madras

1651   Navigation Acts in England, directed against Dutch trade

1652–1674   Period of Anglo-Dutch wars; peace of 1674 results in division of colonial spheres of influence between England and Holland, in which East Indies go to the latter and America to England

1689–1713   Period of Anglo-Dutch coalition wars against France of Louis XIV

1713   Peace of Utrecht gives England trading rights in Spanish American empire; decline of the Dutch

The Mediterranean was the most important of these regional econo-mies. It was centered in Venice, which, besides dominating the Mediter-ranean trade, was the almost exclusive channel through which luxury goods from Asia reached the rest of Europe. The northern European economy was dominated by the Hanseatic League, while the Netherlands and Eng-land dominated that of western Europe.

These commercial powers profited far more from colonial exploitation than did Spain and Portugal, which could not absorb all the exports of their colonies or market them effectively elsewhere on the continent. Spain was drained of her American silver by foreign merchants, and in spite of direct access to Asian producers, the Portuguese could not force Venice out of the spice market. When more diversified colonial products, such as sugar, tobacco, coffee, tea, Brazilian wood, and textiles were produced in the seventeenth century, the Iberian nations proved even less capable of con-trolling their distribution.

However, in the sixteenth century it was not easy to predict which of the commercial powers would dominate the growing European market. Regional trade was expanding, creating markets to absorb the products of colonial exploitation. The emphasis was, however, shifting from luxury goods to grains and manufactured products like cheap textiles. In the first half of the sixteenth century Antwerp seemed to get the lead, profiting from its crucial location, as well as its thriving local industry and strong home market. Annual imports into the Netherlands amounted to seven guilders per capita around the middle of the century; comparable figures were one and a half guilders for both England and France. Nevertheless, Antwerp's trade was still too exclusively dependent upon luxury goods and its money market. The final shift of the European staple market toward the Nether-lands came with the rapid increase of bulky seaborne trade, and for various reasons, among which the course of the Netherlands' revolt looms very large, Amsterdam, not Antwerp, became the center of this commerce.

One more step in the integration of the European economy was neces-sary to bring this about. The relative autarky of the regional economic systems was based upon their agricultural self-sufficiency. The Netherlands were the one exception: a highly urbanized area which imported a part of its food supply, mainly grains, from the Baltic. Amsterdam specialized in this trade. By around 1500 the Dutch Baltic fleet already equaled that of the Hanseatic League, and Dutch ships dominated traffic through the Danish Sound. In the second half of the sixteenth century population pres-sure began to cause grain shortages in the Mediterranean area, some of catastrophic magnitude. Although the Hanseatic League tried to exploit this situation, the Dutch, already specializing in the grain and other bulk trades, easily won this valuable market. They had developed a new type of cheap, efficient freighter, the "flute" or "flyboat," which was too much competition for the old-fashioned Hanseatic carriers. Philip II of Spain confiscated whole Dutch fleets in his harbors during their rebellion against his authority, but it became clear even to his slow-working mind that Spain needed the services of the Dutch. Economic considerations prevailed over political and religious ones. After his troops had occupied Antwerp (1585), the trade and financial activity of that city shifted to Amsterdam, and this business, grafted upon the existing northern shipping and trade, produced Amsterdam's remarkable rise. In the seventeenth century, it was the financial and trade center of the Western world.

Thus, by the beginning of the seventeenth century, the struggle to control the European market had been decided. Venice declined to the status of a secondary regional market and soon could not even defend its monopoly of the Levant trade in the Mediterranean financial market against Genoese, English, and Dutch rivals. The Hanseatic League's cumbersome political structure made it impossible to carry out an efficacious economic policy. Its strength was increasingly undermined by the rivalries of its members; Hamburg, for example, prospered at the expense of the other towns. Late in the sixteenth century the League lost the last remnants of the English cloth trade with Germany. South German cities like Augsburg and Nürnberg suffered from the decline of their overland trade with Venice, which the Dutch absorbed.

The powerful kingdoms of France and England failed to profit from the shifts in European trade patterns. France was too much weakened by civil war to play an active role, while England's trade was too little diversified to challenge the Dutch. Moreover, in the expansion of strictly commercial capitalism, mercantile expertise and the availability of credit were crucial, and governments could do little to create such facilities. Even under Colbert, when France had an infinitely more powerful government than at the beginning of the seventeenth century, French expansionist commercial policy was largely a failure: a convincing illustration of the prevalence of efficiency and competitiveness over government protectionism. In the Netherlands both expertise and credit were abundantly available. The Dutch also profited from inertia. In a time of slow communications, once-established trade patterns were not easily changed, which helps to explain why the English failed to market their own cloth or find outlets other than the Dutch ones.

Still another element entered into the Dutch success. Successful commercial operations were best carried out by small, specialized, mercantile communities. All the great commercial centers began as independent city-states, or urban leagues like the Hansa, in which government policy was geared to commercial needs. At the end of the sixteenth century it had become increasingly clear, however, that commerce had to be supported by some state power to prosper. Such power did not have the overwhelming impact upon trade movements that the more efficiently organized nation-states of the eighteenth and nineteenth centuries had, but it was substantial. The smaller, defenseless commercial centers succumbed. The Netherlands Republic was large enough for the time being to defend its trade against the larger but poorly organized monarchies.

Yet the intricate trade system upon which the Dutch prosperity rested was precariously balanced. Of the various branches which came together in Amsterdam, Dutch observers considered Baltic grain the "mother trade." Baltic products had to be exchanged for other goods, and herring figured large in these transactions. But herring were caught along the coasts of England and Scotland. The fishing industry also needed salt, which was imported from Spain, France, and (later) the West Indies. Trade with Spain and France brought in wine and silver. Silver helped pay for Baltic commodities and for imports from the East Indies. Further revenue came from shipping and from financial operations. Essentially, the Dutch had only services to offer; they could survive only as long as their seaborne trade went on uninterruptedly in all of its interdependent branches. As an envious English observer puts it, the Dutch were like "a fair bird suited with good borrowed plumes; but if every Fowl should take his feather, this bird would rest near naked." To defend their host of unarmed freighters, a large naval force was vital, but the Dutch also relied upon that typical, and usually fragile, device of the weak: the appeal to international law, in which they became experts, from the time of Hugo Grotius (1583–1645) onward.

During the course of the seventeenth century it became clear that England was the only power that could challenge the Dutch. In colonial enterprises it had preceded the Dutch by many decades; as early as the 1570's the English had made effective inroads into the Spanish-American empire. The Dutch had a strictly commercial conception of colonization, and lacked the surplus population to provide their American enterprises with sufficient settlers. Consequently they contented themselves with the control of the trading ports in the Antilles, vital for their smuggling trade with Spanish America and the slave trade. They accepted the loss of New Amsterdam to England in the 1660's without much regret, and in much the same spirit they abandoned their holdings in Brazil to Portugal (1630–1657).

Economic competition between England and the Netherlands became much more bitter after 1650. English commercial interests pushed a hesitant Cromwell to pass the Navigation Acts and launch the first of a series of Anglo-Dutch wars (1652–1654), an example followed less hesitantly by Charles II in 1665. The situation became even more perilous for the Dutch when the French defender of mercantilism, Colbert, brought France into the economic war against Holland. This Anglo-French coalition almost finished off the Dutch in 1672. Dutch trade, however, showed a remarkable resilience. To a great extent the maxims of the late sixteenth century still held true. Navigation acts were hard to enforce against cheap Dutch shipping. Colbert's prohibitive tariffs hurt France as much as the Netherlands. His trading companies lost money. Yet, despite the fact that as late as the 1690's the Dutch merchant fleet, totaling 568,000 tons, was still more than three times as large as that of the English, England's was increasing.

The Dutch Republic finally succumbed under the financial burden of protecting itself during the coalition wars against Louis XIV. Bearing the lion's share of the cost of the Anglo-Dutch army (1689–1713) it had to abandon naval superiority to the English. After the Peace of Utrecht (1713), the English reaped the profits of the opening up of Spanish America and the Dutch sank to the level of a second-rate power.

Other than purely military and financial causes account for the Dutch decline. American products, in which the Dutch never had shown much interest, became much more important for the European market. A different type of colonial exploitation came to the fore, as the powers sought to market industrial products in their growing overseas settlements. With the increasing importance of industry, an exclusively mercantile economy was bound to decline. An even heavier blow was the gradual disappearance of the staple-market type of European trade, made obsolete by improved communications in the eighteenth century. The Netherlands remained an extraordinarily strong financial center, but its commodity market and its political power declined.

The eighteenth-century emergence of France and England as commercial, colonial, and increasingly industrial powers, based upon large populations and great natural resources, produced a different, world-wide economic contest, demanding a much more intensive mobilization of national resources, and a different conception of imperialist economic policy. In this new configuration, small, strictly commercial powers could play only a minor role.

For Further Reading

Barbour, V., *Capitalism in Amsterdam in the Seventeenth Century.*
Penrose, B., *Travel and Discovery in the Renaissance, 1420–1620.*
Rich, E. E., and Wilson, C. H. (eds.), *The Economy of Expanding Europe in the Sixteenth and Seventeenth Centuries* (Vol. IV of *The Cambridge Economic History of Europe*).
Wilson, C., *Profit and Power.*

14 The Ottoman Empire

In the second half of the thirteenth century the shattered lands of Anatolia seemed a singularly unsuitable locale for the rise of a new world empire. Devastated for some two centuries by the conflicts of local dynasts whom the Seljuks were increasingly incapable of controlling, Asia Minor sank into chaos after the crushing victory of the Mongols at Köse-dagh in 1243 swept from it the last vestiges of centralized authority. The history of the origin of the new Turkish principality which arose in the extreme northwest of the peninsula under the leadership of Osman I (1290?–1326) is obscured by legends created at a later date, but the new state emerging clearly into history with Orkhan I (1326–1359), the second sultan of Ottoman tradition, was based on a combination of military and religious forces which gave it both its initial impetus and its remarkable staying powers.

The conquest of Anatolia in the eleventh century had been largely the work of warrior groups known as *gazis* whose common tie was their devotion to the jihad, the holy war spreading the faith of Islam by force of arms. At first of mixed origin, then increasingly Turkicized in the twelfth and thirteenth centuries through new migrations, the *gazis* formed a separate frontier society which spearheaded the Muslim advance toward the West, and it is among them that we should seek the roots of the Ottoman state with its fundamental marcher characteristics. Far removed from the centers of Seljuk power, in an exposed position bearing the brunt of Byzantine counterattacks, the Ottomans depended only on their stubborn dedication to the Muslim cause and on their military prowess for their survival. The traditional suspicion of frontiersmen for effete sedentary cultures increasingly opposed the *gazis* to the weakening Seljuk rule and freed them from the onus of its collapse. Even their militant Islamic faith differed from the learned and strictly orthodox beliefs of the Seljuk court. Undisturbed by theological speculations, devoted to popular practices and mystical beliefs of dubious orthodoxy brought to them by wandering dervishes, the Ottoman *gazis,* to their great advantage, could paradoxically both share the superstitions of the local non-Muslim population and rally the allegiance of other Muslim groups as the true sword-bearers of Islam against the Infidel.

Leaving behind them the East, where Muslim chieftains opposed them as unorthodox upstarts and barbarians, the Ottomans turned first to the West, where they could exploit the enthusiasm they aroused for the holy

A.D.	1326–1359	Reign of Orkhan I
	1359–1389	Reign of Murad I
	1365	Ottoman capital shifted to Andrinople in Thrace
	1371	Ottoman defeat of the Serbs on the Marica
	1389	First Battle of Kossovo
	1402	Defeat of Bajazet I Yilderim by Tamerlane
	1444	Ottoman defeat of the Christian "Crusade" at Varna
	1448	Second Battle of Kossovo
	1451–1481	Reign of Muhammad II the Conqueror
	1453	Ottoman capture of Constantinople by Muhammad II the Conqueror
	1514	Ottoman defeat of the Safavids at Caldiran
	1517	Ottoman capture of Cairo; surrender of Mecca
	1520–1566	Reign of Suleiman I the Magnificent (Kanuni)
	1521	Ottoman capture of Belgrade
	1522	Ottoman capture of Rhodes
	1526	Ottoman defeat of the Hungarians at Mohács
	1529	First Ottoman siege of Vienna; Ottomans acquire Algerian bases
	1534	Ottoman capture of Tabriz and Iraq
	1536	Ottoman alliance with Francis I of France
	1547	Larger part of Hungary ceded to the Ottomans
	1555	Ottoman-Safavid peace
	1571	Battle of Lepanto
	1606	Peace of Sitvatorok
	1630	*Memorandum* of Koça Bey
	1641–1687	Reign of Muhammad IV; abolition of the *devşirme*
	1656–1676	Ottoman revival under Köprülü viziers
	1683	Second Ottoman siege of Vienna
	1696	Capture of Azov by Peter the Great
	1697	Eugene of Savoy's defeat of the Ottomans at Zenta
	1699	Peace of Karlowitz
	1703–1730	Cultural revival under Ahmed III
	1718	Peace of Passarowitz
	1724–1730	Victories of Nadir Shah in Transcaucasia
	1726–1742	Opening and closing of the first Turkish press
	1757–1774	Reign of Mustafa III; Ayans granted official status
	1774	Treaty of Kuçuk Kaynarca
	1783	Russian annexation of the Crimea

1792	Treaty of Jassy
1793	Selim III proclaims the "New Order"
1798–1799	Napoleon's campaign in Egypt
1801	Russian annexation of Georgia
1804	Serbian revolt
1822–1830	Greek war of independence
1826	Massacre of the Janissaries; Ottoman fleet sunk at Navarino
1829	Treaty of Andrinople
1833	Treaty of Unkiar-skelessi
1839	Hatt-i Serif of Gulhane; beginning of the Tanzimat period
1840	Treaty of London concedes Egypt to Muhammad Ali
1841	Straits Convention
1853–1856	Crimean War
1856	Hatt-i Humayun
1876	Mihrdat Pasa proclaims the Ottoman Constitution
1877	Ottoman Constitution allowed to lapse
1878	Congress of Berlin
1883	Creation of Public Debt Control
1908	Formation of the Committee of Union and Progress (Young Turks); Constitution restored
1909	Deposition of Abdul-Hamid II

war and the quarrels of Byzantine and Balkan rulers. Little more than a quarter-century after Orkhan had made Brusa (Bursa) his capital, his son Murad I (1359–1389) moved to Andrinople (Edirne) in Thrace. Thereafter, the Ottomans always considered "Rumeli" (the land of the Romans) as against "Anadolu" the core of their empire.

Until they crossed into Europe, the Ottomans were hardly distinguishable from a number of other Anatolian successor states, but the great victories of Murad at the Marica (1371) and in the first Battle of Kossovo (1389) gave him mastery of the Balkans at the same time as he asserted his domination over the Anatolian princes. At his death on the battlefield of Kossovo, the Muslim dynasts of the East, the Christian princes of Serbia and Bulgaria, and the Byzantine emperor himself were tributary to the Ottoman sultan. The Christian failure to take advantage of Tamerlane's rout of Murad's successor, Bajazet I Yilderim, at Ankara in 1402, and of the subsequent decade of wars between Bajazet's sons sealed the fate of Constantinople. Muhammad I (1413–1421) pursued a cautious policy of consolidation, but his son Murad II (1421–1451) and his more famous grandson Muhammad II the Conqueror (1451–1481) turned back to an all-out military policy of conquest and annexation. The Anatolian beys were again reduced to obedience, the Hungarians and Balkan princes defeated at Varna (1444) and the second Battle of Kossovo (1448). Finally, in 1453, Constantinople fell after a four months' siege. The city's position necessarily made of it the capital of the new empire, which was as much European as Anatolian.

This triumph of Muhammad II after eight centuries of Muslim assaults ensured his fame, but Turkish expansion had not yet reached its high-water mark. Christian bridgeheads were swept from the Balkans, Rhodes was captured, Italy seriously threatened, while at the other end of his empire Muhammad II defeated the new Turkoman state of the Akkoyunlu (White Sheep) created in northeastern Asia Minor and Iran by Uzun Hasan. The Conqueror's son Bajazet II adopted a more cautious policy, but the crowning conquests were added by his son and grandson, Selim I the Grim (1512–1520), and Suleiman I the Magnificent (1520–1566). The establishment of Ottoman sovereignty in the Crimea and south Russia in the days of the Conqueror had given the Turks control of the Black Sea. (In 1569 plans were even made for a Volga-Don canal which would give them access to the Caspian and Central Asia.) At Caldiran in 1514 Selim routed the new Persian dynasty of the Safavids, who had succeeded Uzun Hasan, and whose militant Shi'ite creed had rallied many of the heterodox elements among the Turkoman tribes; Suleiman went on to take Tabriz, their capital, and to conquer Iraq. In the south, Selim's armies swept across Syria into Egypt, and forced the Muslim Holy Cities of Mecca and Medina to acknowledge his suzerainty. In the West, making the most of the Emperor Charles V's difficulties with Francis I of France and the Protestant princess of the Schmalkaldic League, Suleiman extended his control over the Mediterranean. Aided by Algerian corsairs who accepted his overlordship and provided him with a fleet, he defeated Venice and her allies of the Holy League at Prevsna in 1548. On land, the sultan crushed the Hungarians at Mohács in 1526; by 1547 he had forced the Hapsburg empire to recognize his control of much of Hungary and to pay a yearly tribute. Hampered by overextended lines of communications, the Ottomans failed to capture the imperial city of Vienna which they attacked in 1529, but by the middle of the sixteenth century most of Eastern Europe, Western Asia, and North Africa, together with the Mediterranean and Black seas, were in their hands.

The spectacular victories of the Turks owed much to the remarkable leadership of the first ten sultans and to the support they commanded as the champions of Islam. But the crucial element seems to have been their absolute yet flexible military ideology—the raison d'être of the *gazi* state. Unencumbered by the elaborate traditions of earlier Islamic civilizations in Arabia and Iran, the Ottomans bent all circumstances to their advantage with the shrewd adaptability of frontiersmen. Both fanaticism and tolerance they profitably exploited, and they learned many useful techniques from their enemies. The Ottoman fleet that came into being in the sixteenth century copied Venetian models; European renegades contributed knowledge of firearms and helped to make Ottoman siege and field artillery invincible. Long before the creation of the world empire, the system of recruitment known as the *devşirme* (child tribute) replenished the ranks of the Turkish army by conscripting able-bodied Orthodox Christian boys and forcibly converting them to Islam. Yet until the sixteenth century Christian contingents continued to serve among the Ottoman forces and were even rewarded with fiefs. All means were acceptable if they served the ends of the holy war.

As late as the victory of Muhammad II over Byzantium, the Ottoman realm was still largely in an embryonic state, retaining many features of the original marcher principality, but in the century which culminated in the reign of Suleiman I, to whom Ottoman tradition gives the significant title of *Kanuni* (the Lawgiver), it was transformed into a full-fledged Muslim world empire, albeit one exhibiting a number of idiosyncratic features.

The basic form and institutions of the Ottoman state followed the classic Muslim pattern, since the sultan was the eternal defender of the faith. By the sixteenth century, faced with the growing threat of the Shi'ite Safavid empire in Iran, Turkish Sunnite orthodoxy increased in rigidity. The unalterable law of Islam, the *Shariat,* embracing both religious and

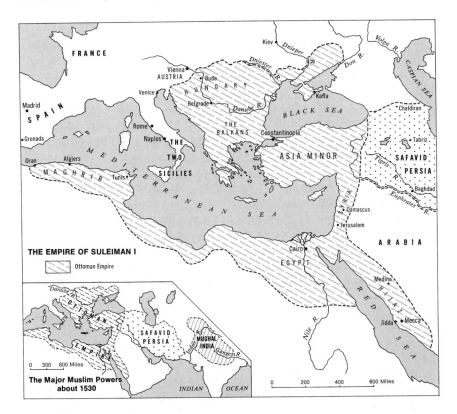

THE EMPIRE OF SULEIMAN I

Ottoman Empire

The Major Muslim Powers about 1530

secular spheres, was the law of the empire, and in fact received more direct application and support from the Ottomans than from any other Muslim ruler.

In spite of its orthodoxy, however, Ottoman society was rigidly compartmentalized in a thoroughly atypical pattern. The Muslim subjects of the sultan were barred from a significant role in the government. The imposition of second-class status on non-Muslim *zimmîs,* who paid the poll tax and were excluded from office, was not surprising, nor was the tolerance which permitted and (up to a point) protected their existence. Earlier caliphs had acted in the same manner. The division along religious rather than ethnic or even cultural lines of the non-Muslim communities or *millets* created by Muhammad II for the Orthodox, Armenians, and Jews was not unusual, since this too fitted the theocratic Muslim tradition. The remarkable feature of the *millets* was their exclusive and hermetic nature. Their members could not move from their community except through conversion to Islam; they were segregated from the rest of society as they had not been in the earlier caliphates, and their religious leaders, Patriarchs or Grand Rabbis, were held responsible for all the activities of their coreligionists, secular as well as religious. The *millets* were politically and culturally self-contained, contact between Muslims and non- Muslims reduced to a minimum.

Similarly, and still more amazingly, Muslims were also segregated in a special class isolated from the administration of the state. The majority of the population belonged in this class, and all the religious leaders had perforce to be drawn from it, but its contribution to the government outside of the "Religious Institution" took only one official form: service in the feudal cavalry known as *sipâhîs,* to which those eligible brought their own equipment and retainers, and for which they were rewarded with hereditary fiefs called *timars* or *zi'āmets,* depending on their size, from which they collected the taxes which provided their revenue. All other offices were closed to them and their children.

The strength of the empire rested neither on the Muslim majority nor obviously on the *millets,* but on the hierarchy of the *Kapi Kullari,* commonly known as the "Slave" or "Ruling Institution." All members of this group were legally slaves of the sultan; all were born Christians and converted to Islam primarily, though not exclusively, through the *devşirme;* and all were trained by the state for their official functions. The slave status carried no social stigma, but divested the *kullars* of any personality outside the service of their master. Forbidden to contract legal marriages, to have acknowledged children, or to own private property, paid, advanced, demoted, or even executed at the sultan's will, they were totally dependent on him, and their honors and possessions reverted to him at their death. The most famous component of the *Kapi Kullars* was the crack regiments of the Janissaries, who formed the backbone of the Ottoman army, but all officials, from the palace cooks and gardeners to provincial governors and the Grand Vizier himself, were drawn from the Slave Institution. By this remarkable, if precariously balanced, tour de force, the Ottoman empire obtained a superlative group of administrators, entirely devoted to their duties (since they were isolated from the interests of the rest of the population), undistracted by personal allegiances and preoccupations, and dependent for their careers and their very lives on the demonstration of their efficiency and loyalty. Simultaneously, their nonhereditary status precluded the formation of a powerful ruling elite which might threaten the authority of the sultan.

The hierarchy of the Ruling Institution provided a formidable instrument for the centralized absolutism which characterized the Ottoman state. A number of similar structures focused on the capital likewise promoted the cohesion of the empire and the all-inclusive might of its ruler. Islamic theology still admitted of no clerical body in a spiritual or sacramental sense, but in practice the learned *Ulemas* represented the Religious Institution. Now for the first time they were grouped under a hitherto nonexistent religious head of the state, the *Sheyh-ül-Islam*. In the same way, the local interpreters of the *Shariat,* the *kadis* or judges, were answerable not to the provincial governors, but to the two *Kadiaskers* residing in the capital. Finally, after 1530, the granting of feudal *timars,* once the prerogative of local dignitaries, was removed to the jurisdiction of the sultan. Hence, no external or internal element was in a position to interfere with the absolutism of the central government controlling the separate compartments of state which were too isolated from one another to present any serious threat. Even the danger of family rivalries, perpetually present in a polygamous society without a clear law of succession and consequently vulnerable to harem intrigues, was allayed by the decree of the Conqueror that all male relatives of the reigning sultan were to be executed at his accession: ". . . to whomsoever of my sons the Sultanate shall pass, it is fitting that for the order of the world he shall kill his brothers. Most of the *Ulema* allow it. So let them act on this."

Under the reign of Suleiman the Magnificent, the cresting wave of *gazi* enthusiasm, the elaborate if rather inhuman *kullar* system; the technological superiority in war; the supervision of the state in all matters; the continuing tolerance which gave asylum to the Jews fleeing from Spanish persecution and benefited from their skills; the wealth derived from the east-west trade which made of Brusa a major Mediterranean mart where the spices and cottons of India were exchanged for the woolens of Florence, the silks of Gilan, or local brocades—all these things made possible for a time a continuation in the pattern of conquests, a superlative bureaucracy, and a government far superior to that of most of its contemporaries. The Ottoman Empire dominated not only the Muslim world but much of the Mediterranean as well.

In 1571, five years after Suleiman's death, the Christian world rejoiced immoderately at the victory of Lepanto, where at long last an Ottoman fleet had been defeated by the ships of a new Holy League. Lepanto, however, was a minor triumph, another century at least would have to pass before any serious alteration in the political balance took place. But Ottoman strength slowly began to weaken in the seventeenth century. The most immediate manifestation of change was an ending of further Muslim conquests. Occasional fragments of territory were still added, but after more than two centuries of almost unbroken victories, the Ottoman armies now began to falter. They could not break through the opposition of the Hapsburgs in Europe, of Russia in the Ukraine, or of the Safavids in Iran. The walls of Vienna from which Suleiman had retreated in 1529 remained unbreached. Control of the Mediterranean passed out of Ottoman hands, while far to the east, Muslim fleets failed to sweep the Portuguese new-comers from the Indian Ocean. Russian expansion gradually blocked the alternate overland routes to Central Asia and its wealth. At Sitvatorok in 1606, the sultan Ahmed I agreed for the first time to a negotiated peace with the Infidel. Within twenty years the great Safavid ruler Shah Abbas I (1587–1629) wrested away Baghdad and the Armenian border provinces from the Turks. By 1699, after the failure of the second siege of Vienna (1683), the victories of Peter the Great at Azov (1696), and of Prince Eugene of Savoy at Zenta (1697), the Ottomans, as the defeated party, surrendered Hungary (except for the Banat of Temesvár), Transylvania, Croatia, the Morea, and most of Dalmatia to the westerners at the Peace of Karlowitz (1699). Three years later, Russia's presence on the Black Sea was conceded by the temporary abandonment of Azov. The high-water mark of Ottoman might was a thing of the past.

Western travelers noted the parlous state of the Turkish empire torn by violent rebellions and economic crises. Ottoman intellectuals such as Koça Bey, in his famous *Memorandum* presented to the sultan Murad IV in 1630, and Haci Halife in 1653 tried to suggest remedies for the military and economic disasters. But a combination of internal failures and external circumstances seemingly beyond control were turning the tide against the Ottoman Empire in which the vital *gazi* tradition had finally died, leaving only a monumental but cumbersomely expensive and increasingly hide-bound structure.

Internally, the state could not maintain the precarious balance of its superhuman machinery. The absolute centralization and efficiency of the administrative structure, which had been the source of its strength, de-pended ultimately on the perfection of the rulers at its apex. The early sultans had fulfilled the onerous demands of their office with remarkable dedication, but the system of selecting the ruler militated against the con-tinuation of this pattern. The merciless decree of the Conqueror was abandoned by the end of the sixteenth century, but its substitute was if anything more disastrous. All princes, except the sons of the sultan, were herded from childhood into separate palace apartments where they were confined for life in total isolation from the world, deprived of normal human experiences, and all but uneducated. A decree of 1617 granting the succession to the oldest member of the ruling house rather than to the sultan's sons ensured the accession of one of these "Caged Princes," neces-sarily unprepared for his duties, if not altogether unfit, and as such the puppet of one of the rival factions.

The growing strain of wars requiring larger and better armies gradually made obsolete the feudal *sipâhî* cavalry, which was no match for the technological advances of seventeenth-century warfare. More and more reliance was placed on the paid Janissary contingents. Not only did the expense of their upkeep strain the finances of the state, but their indispensability predisposed them more and more to violence and blackmail. Demanding higher pay and greater benefits, among these the right to pass their status on to their sons, thereby destroying the fundamental character of the Slave Institution, they became a hereditary Muslim privileged class, especially after the abolition of the *devşirme* by Muhammad IV (1641–1687). The Janissaries exploited the growing weakness of the sultans in order to crush any opposition to themselves, push their commanders into the Grand Vizierate, and play kingmakers. Between 1590 and 1634 they were to all purposes masters of the capital, while dissident *Celâlî* bands roved the countryside, terrorizing the villagers. The Ruling Institution was beginning to crumble.

External circumstances aggravated the crisis. By the seventeenth century, the discovery of new sea routes to the East left the great Ottoman markets, which had depended on overland trade, stranded in a backwater. The mass of cheap silver imported from the New World swamped the Turkish economy, cutting the value of the standard Ottoman coin, the silver *akçe,* almost in half as early as 1584 and precipitating an uncontrollable inflation. Ottoman currency was driven from international markets as the balance of trade turned against the empire and brought widespread poverty and discontent in its wake. Western technology surpassed Turkish traditional methods, frozen by the Muslim guild system.

Caught in an inescapable spiral of difficulties, forced to support an enormous bureaucracy on a still primitive economy increasingly inadequate to the task, the Ottoman Empire began to give way in all sectors. The frontiers cracked, the *sipâhîs* became obsolete at the very moment when the state could no longer afford a paid army. The system of land tenure and taxation tied to the military conquests, which provided new lands for fiefs granted to the *timariots* who in turn served as tax collectors, broke down, and in the absence of adequate fiscal machinery or revenue, the state was forced to farm out and increase the taxes, intensifying both the poverty and the anger of the population. Ruined by inflation, the *timariots* and peasants swelled the ranks of the malcontents, while the underpaid bureaucracy grew incompetent, venal, and restive.

Perhaps the crucial element blocking any alleviation of the difficulties was the arrogant assumption of Muslim superiority which the Ottomans had inherited from their predecessors and which had been reinforced by their own sweeping victories. The first sultans had been willing to acquire valuable techniques from their foes, and their tolerance had won the loyalty of the majority of their subjects. Muhammad the Conqueror still read

Greek books, encouraged humanists, and had his portrait painted by Gentile Bellini, but in the more rigid orthodox Muslim empire of Suleiman I, the Ottomans came to believe that nothing of conceivable worth could be learned from the barbarous infidels. Non-Muslim subjects, who controlled most of the empire's trade and finances, came under increasing oppression and were prevented from contributing their talents to the state. Religious opposition blocked the printing of works in Turkish until the eighteenth century, even though the Jewish, Armenian, and Greek communities had maintained presses for centuries. The enormous technological and intellectual advances which thrust Western Europe into the modern era were contemptuously ignored by the Ottomans.

Some officials were aware of the danger and sought to avert it. Between 1656 and 1676 the Köprülü Grand Viziers achieved a real revival. The Janissaries were temporarily crushed, finances were improved through confiscations and a tax reform, non-Muslims were shielded, and an artistic renaissance was encouraged. The capture of Crete from the Venetians increased the prestige of the empire. But the reformers provided no real solutions. The goal proposed for the state was merely a return to the institutions of Suleiman Kanuni and a reassertion of the fundamental Muslim tradition. By the end of the century the failure of the second siege of Vienna and the disastrous Peace of Karlowitz demonstrated the ineffectiveness of the reform.

With the loss of its power and prestige, extenal pressures on the Ottoman empire increased. As far back as the sixteenth century, Francis I of France had been granted a monopoly of trade with the Ottomans and the protectorate over the Christian shrines in Palestine. By the eighteenth century these concessions had turned into the famous "Capitulations" which gave Westerners quasi-control of Ottoman trade and all but extraterritorial status in the empire. Because of their contact with the Christian subjects of the sultan, who acted as middlemen, Westerners first extended to them some of their own privileges and immunities, then began to see themselves as the perpetual guardians of their interests. The French were acting as protector of Catholics from the eighteenth century, the Russians of the Orthodox a little more than a century later. Ultimately, Protestant missionaries from England and America played a similar role. Under these circumstances, the Christians came to look outside the empire for help in moments of difficulty and to render the state only a divided allegiance. This trend was intensified by the importation of nationalist ideas from the West in the course of the nineteenth century. The Ottomans on their part began to suspect indiscriminately the loyalty of all their non-Muslim subjects. The components of the empire increasingly pulled asunder.

Simultaneous with the alienation of minority groups, the vacuum left by the steady disappearance of the *timariots* was filled by the powerful tax farmers, who developed into a hereditary privileged class. These *ayans,* absentee landlords of great estates, exploited the declining economy and interposed themselves between the government and the peasantry to the detriment of both. Supported by armed bands of the dispossessed, usurping the power of the local governors, given official status by a decree of Sultan Mustafa III (1757–1774), some of the *ayans* succeeded in forming local dynasties in Rumelia and Anatolia which successfully defied the central authorities. Signs of separatism began to show in distant border areas.

By the beginning of the eighteenth century, the recognition of Western military superiority and the example of Russia's transformation under Peter the Great were leading some Ottomans to consider Westernization. But progress was slow. The first reaction to the crisis under Sultan Ahmed III (1703–1730) was to retreat into epicureanism, mysticism, and prodigality, which enhanced Ottoman culture but only deepened the gulf between the wealthy ruling class and the mass of the people. Humiliating defeats continued to accumulate: all Hungary, north Serbia, and part of Wallachia were lost at the Peace of Passarowitz (1718). Nadir Shah of Iran harassed the eastern front. Finally Ahmed III was toppled from the throne and some reforms were introduced with Western help into the obsolete Ottoman army. Through most of the century, however, these attempts produced few significant reforms. The main alterations were still purely technological in nature. The Turkish printing press finally authorized in 1726 was shut down in 1742 after producing fewer then twenty books.

The factor most operative in pushing the Ottomans onto a resolute path of Westernization was probably the constant increase of Russian power. The shock of the Treaty of Kuçuk Kaynarca (1774), which recognized Russia's control of the entire northern coast of the Black Sea, extended to her the system of Capitulations, and acknowledged the czar's protectorate over subjects of the sultan, was deepened in 1783 by Catherine the Great's annexation of the Khanate of Crimea, the first major loss of a primarily Muslim territory. Almost simultaneously, Napoleon's expedition threatened the safety of Egypt, and Russia annexed the semi-independent Christian kingdom of Georgia in 1801, thus threatening Transcaucasia and the eastern provinces of Turkey. The problem now facing the empire was clearly one of life and death.

Formidable obstacles still confronted the reformers. The *ulemas,* fearing for the purity of the faith, the Janissaries, worrying about losing privileges, and the *ayan* beys bent on thwarting any move toward centralization, joined together to oppose change. The government, furthermore, no longer controlled its finances. The proclamation by Selim III (1789–1807) of a "New Order" reorganizing the army, ending many abuses, reforming tax-

THE OTTOMAN EMPIRE, 1792 AND 1878

Ottoman Empire (1792—main map;   1878—inset map)

---------- Ottoman boundary, 1792   (— - — - approximate limits)

North African states under Ottoman suzerainty, 1792

Areas under autonomous and tribal rulers

Vassal states, 1878

(YEAR)   Areas lost (1774-1792, main map;   1792-1878, inset map)

TRIB. = Tributary   IND. = Independence won   BR. PROT. = British Protectorate

The Balkan Peninsula, 1878

ation, and establishing permanent Turkish embassies in European capitals provoked a coalition of the *ayans* of Rumelia and the Janissaries which ended in the deposition and murder of Selim and the massacre of most of the leaders of the reform party. Nearly twenty years were needed by Selim's successor, Mahmud II (1808–1839), to undercut the power of the *ayans* of Anatolia, the so-called *Derebeys* or "Valley Lords," and to win over the religious authorities. Then he challenged the Janissaries, who were finally slaughtered in 1826.

The annihilation of the Janissaries opened the way for the period of reforms known as the Tanzimat. The first major decree, the Hatt-i Sherif of Gulhane, proclaimed in 1839 in the presence of representatives of foreign powers, guaranteed the basic rights of life, liberty, and property, and promised military and fiscal reforms. This statement of principles was implemented by a series of centralizing measures: the final revocation of all *timars;* the control of religious foundations or *vakfs* and the diversion of their revenues to the state; the creation of ministries, administrative committees, and provincial assemblies of notables; the promulgation of a new penal code; the opening of technical schools. Since Christians had not been given sufficient reassurances or representation in the provincial councils, and to justify in Western eyes the Ottoman's claim to be a European power, the Hatt-i Humayun of 1856 complemented the earlier decree by abolishing the system of *millets* which had segregated non-Muslims, and ending the secular powers of their various religious heads. Liberty of conscience was guaranteed to all, as were security and property; Christians became eligible for civilian offices. Finally, in 1876, under the leadership of Mihrdat Pasha, a constitution was announced and a constitutional assembly elected.

Yet these extensive reforms failed to achieve their objectives in the face of lukewarm support and heavy traditionalist opposition. A radical transformation of the government was theoretically possible through the assimilation of the new regulations to governmental *kanuns* or decrees authorized by Muslim tradition, but as long as the sacred *Shariat* remained the law of the land, two mutually hostile systems were forced into uneasy coexistence. Western institutions were at best skin deep, and no machinery existed for their implementation. The spread of nationalist ideas, first among the minorities but eventually in the Turkish ruling class, was incompatible with the concept of a Muslim empire based on a community of faith and not on national or cultural origins. Moreover, the new ideas exacerbated the antagonism between the state and the minorities, which exploded into violence. Separatist tendencies first manifested themselves in the Serbian risings of 1804 and 1815 and the Greek war of independence of 1822–1830. But the insurrections were not restricted to Christian areas: rebellions in Bosnia and Albania, the establishment of a quasi-independent Egypt under Muhammad Ali by 1840, and the rise of Arab nationalism were all indices of the general disintegration of the empire. The economic situation continued to deteriorate. Large-scale high-interest loans from the West only made matters worse, and in 1875 the Turkish government was forced to repudiate its obligations. In 1883 a Public Debt Control created to protect the debtors' interests infringed on Ottoman sovereignty by giving foreign powers some supervision of the revenues and financial administration of the state.

The main underlying purpose of the reforms—the safeguard of the imperial territory and the solace of national pride—was also lost in the

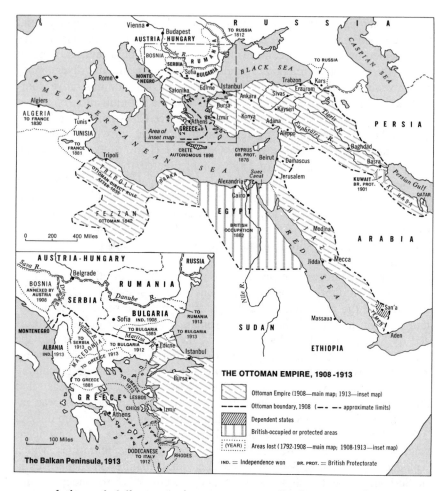

THE OTTOMAN EMPIRE, 1908-1913

- Ottoman Empire (1908—main map; 1913—inset map)
- --- Ottoman boundary, 1908 (— · — · — approximate limits)
- Dependent states
- British-occupied or protected areas
- (YEAR) Areas lost (1792-1908—main map; 1908-1913—inset map)

IND. = Independence won   BR. PROT. = British Protectorate

The Balkan Peninsula, 1913

accumulation of failures during a century of almost continuous war. Serbian autonomy was won at the Treaty of Andrinople in 1829, Greece became independent the following year, Egypt was autonomous by 1840. Support for the rebels came from England, France, and Russia, who had jointly destroyed the Ottoman fleet at Navarino in 1826. Russia advanced in both Thrace and Transcaucasia. Fear of Russia's expansion in Central Asia, which threatened British interests in Iran and India, and of her control of the Dardanelles, briefly extorted in 1833 through the secret clauses of the Treaty of Unkiar-Skelessi, alarmed the Western powers and led to the Crimean War of 1853–1856, which gave a breathing spell, but no more, to the Ottoman government. In the famous phrase of Czar Nicholas I, "the Sick Man of Europe," unable to function under his own power, lived only at the mercy of outside forces and to serve their interests. In 1878 the Congress of Berlin, under the "honest brokerage" of Bismarck, partitioned Bulgaria, gave Bosnia-Herzegovina to Austria, proclaimed the independence of Serbia, Rumania, and Montenegro, granted Russia the city of Batum with part of Transcaucasia, and established the French in Tunis and the British on Cyprus, while demanding still further reforms.

Westernization like all other methods seems to have failed. A violent traditionalist reaction under the new sultan Abdul-Hamid II turned once more to political and religious fanaticism. The promised constitution died stillborn in 1877; a policy of repression and terror was launched against the minorities. As new pieces of territory were wrenched from the empire and the violence of nationalism grew apace, as plan after plan, frustrated by the dead hand of traditionalism failed to function, the thoughts of intellectuals veered from reform to revolution.

For Further Reading

Coles, P., *The Ottoman Impact on Europe.*
Davison, R., *Turkey.*
Lewis, B., *The Emergence of Modern Turkey.*
Lybyer, A. H., *The Government of the Ottoman Empire in the Time of Suleiman the Magnificent.*
Saunders, J. J., *The Muslim World on the Eve of Europe's Expansion.*
Vaughan, D., *Europe and the Turk: A Pattern of Alliances 1350–1700.*
Wittek, P., *The Rise of the Ottoman Empire.*

15   European Voyages of Exploration

In the early fifteenth century Christian Europeans knew less of the world beyond their borders than had the ancient Greeks or Romans. To the south and east of Europe lay a crescent of Islamic states, whose rulers willingly allowed trade with infidels but opposed penetration by Europeans into their territories. Journeys to China, like those of the Polos a hundred and more years before, were impracticable, since Muslims barred the path. West of Europe lay the Atlantic Ocean, the "Green Sea of Darkness," considered impassable by Christian and Muslim alike. Indeed, in 1400 Europeans lagged far behind Asians, particularly the Arabs and the Chinese, in the ability to sail for long distances over open water.

A.D. 1415 Portuguese capture of Ceuta
      1433 Cape Bojador rounded by Gil Eannes
      1482 Building of Elmina Castle (São Jorge da Mina)
      1484 Discovery of Congo estuary by Diogo Cão
      1488 Doubling of Cape of Good Hope by Bartolomeu Dias
      1492 Discovery of America (Bahama Islands) by Christopher Columbus
      1494 Treaty of Tordesillas
      1497 Voyage to North America by John Cabot
 1497–1498 Voyage to Calicut (India) by Vasco da Gama
      1500 Discovery of Brazil by Pedro Cabral
      1510 Portuguese capture of Goa
      1513 First sighting of the Pacific by Núñez de Balboa
 1519–1521 Conquest of Mexico by Hernán Cortés
 1519–1522 Circumnavigation of the world (begun by Ferdinand Magellan, completed by Sebastián del Cano)
      1529 Treaty of Zaragoza
 1531–1538 Conquest of Peru by Francisco Pizarro
 1534–1535 Exploration of Gulf of St. Lawrence by Jacques Cartier
      1553 Voyage to Archangel by Richard Chancellor
 1576–1578 Search for the Northwest Passage by Martin Frobisher
      1585 Planting of first English colony in North America (Roanoke Island, North Carolina)
      1596 Voyage of Willem Barents to Novaya Zemlya
      1600 Founding of the English East India Company
      1602 Founding of the Netherlands East India Company
      1606 Discovery of Australia by Willem Janszoon
      1642 Discovery of Tasmania and New Zealand by Abel Tasman

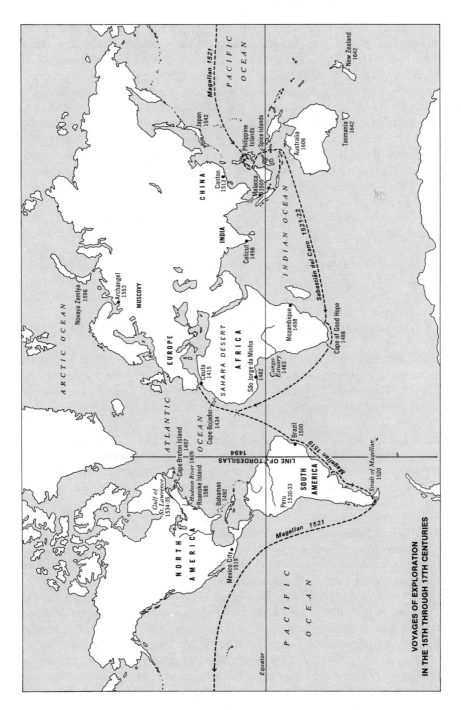

VOYAGES OF EXPLORATION
IN THE 15TH THROUGH 17TH CENTURIES

Yet by 1700 European navigators had found their way into every ocean, had plotted the outlines of all continents but Australia, and knew what the Greeks and Romans never guessed, that all the salt seas of the world are one. A combination of audacity, religious zeal, commercial enterprise, and technological advance made this achievement possible. Cut off from direct access by land to the precious metals, silks, and spices of the East, western Europeans of the late Middle Ages decided to seek the Asian trade by sea. If this necessitated fighting, so much the better. Not only was there a long tradition of crusading, especially in the Iberian peninsula, but a military career, with glory and loot as its rewards, was a desirable—for many young men of the day, the only desirable—occupation. European ships, too, were being rapidly improved, and by the end of the fifteenth century were larger, more seaworthy, and better armed than Asian vessels. The art of navigation was advancing, with the development of nautical tables, more accurate measuring devices like the astrolabe, backstaff, and ship's log, and refinements in the construction and use of the compass and mariner's chart. The essential prerequisite of successful maritime exploration, the ability to sail into the open sea and return safely and accurately to a point of departure, had been mastered.

The beginning of the European Age of Discovery is usually dated from the capture by the Portuguese of Ceuta, on the North African coast opposite Gibraltar, in 1415. During the remainder of the fifteenth century Portuguese explorers, inspired initially by Prince Henry the Navigator and later by King John II, slowly made their way down the western African coast as they searched for a path to the Indies. In 1488 Bartolomeu Dias doubled the Cape of Good Hope. A decade later Vasco da Gama pioneered the route to Calicut in India, and by 1513 the first Portuguese ship had reached Canton. In the meantime, under the leadership of Alfonso d'Albuquerque, the Portuguese had established bases at Goa in India (1510), Malacca on the west coast of the Malay Peninsula (1511), and Ormuz in the Persian Gulf (1515). For the better part of the following century they were able to dominate the sea routes in the South China Sea and Indian Ocean and between Asia and Europe.

Meanwhile, a navigator in the service of Spain had begun carving out a different kind of empire. In 1492 Christopher Columbus (Cristoforo Colombo) sailed across the Atlantic to the Caribbean, and in three subsequent voyages (1493–1504) discovered most of the major islands in that area and part of the eastern coast of Central America. Columbus believed that he was pioneering a route to the Far East, and it was only gradually that his masters realized that a "New World" stood in the path of an explorer seeking Asia by sailing west. The Portuguese were disconcerted by Spain's entry into a field they regarded as their own, but a compromise was engineered. By the Treaty of Tordesillas (1494), the two powers "divided" the world by running an imaginary line north and south 370 leagues west of the Cape Verde Islands on the west coast of Africa. All new lands to the west of this meridian were to belong to Spain; everything to the east of it was to be Portuguese.

The empire the Portuguese created was mercantile, and consisted of a chain of bases on the African and Asian coasts linked and protected by sea power. The Portuguese were never strong on land in Africa or Asia, and never tried to be; to have created a territorial empire against the wishes of the local rulers would have been beyond their strength. In the New World, on the other hand, there were no states capable of withstanding the Spaniards. In about 1520, by which time most of the Atlantic coasts of Central and South America had been plotted and it had become clear that there was no way through the Americas into the Pacific (first sighted by Núñez de Balboa in 1513), the age of the conquistadors began. Possessing horses and firearms, neither of which had been seen before in the New World, the Spaniards were able to conquer huge stretches of territory with very small numbers of men. Mexico fell to Hernán Cortés in 1519–1521 and Peru to Francisco Pizarro in 1531–1538. Other conquistadors established Spanish rule in the intervening areas. Thus the whole of Central and South America (with the exception of Brazil, which became Portuguese because it lay east of the demarcation line of 1494 and because it had been discovered by a Portuguese, Pedro Cabral, in 1500) was gradually turned into a Spanish colonial empire.

The Americas soon began to yield gold and silver in abundance and provided land suitable for European colonization, but the Spaniards still hoped to find their own trade route to the East. In 1520 Ferdinand Magellan (Fernão de Magalhães), a Portuguese in Spanish employ, discovered the straits that bear his name, passed through them, and crossed the Pacific Ocean to the Philippines. There he was killed, but his lieutenant, Sebastián del Cano, brought one of Magellan's ships home to Spain around the Cape of Good Hope, thus completing the first circumnavigation of the world.

The wealth obtained by the Portuguese and Spaniards from their overseas possessions encouraged other Europeans to imitate them. During the reign of Henry VIII of England a ship from Bristol, commanded by a Venetian, John Cabot (Giovanni Caboto), made the first trans-Atlantic journey—the first at any rate since the voyages of the Vikings in the eleventh century—to North America, touching at Cape Breton Island and Newfoundland in 1497. Jacques Cartier, in the service of Francis I of France, explored the St. Lawrence River and estuary in a series of voyages between 1534 and 1541. These discoveries, however, did not lead to colonization, or even to occupation. The English and French and, later, the Dutch had the same aim as the Portuguese and Spaniards; they wanted their own sea route to Asia. Since the Iberian powers discouraged competitors in the South Atlantic, other Europeans were obliged to seek their fortunes to the north. In the end neither the Northwest Passage (to the north of Canada) nor the Northeast Passage (north of Norway and Russia) proved practicable, but in the process of searching for them men like the Englishmen Hugh Willoughby and Richard Chancellor (1553), Martin Frobisher (1576–1578), Davis (1585–1586), and Henry Hudson (1609–1610), and the Dutchman Willem Barents (1594–1596) greatly increased Europe's geographical knowledge.

In the seventeenth century the pattern of European discovery and expansion changed. The revolt of the Dutch against Spain roughly coincided with the period (1580–1640) during which the Spanish and Portuguese crowns were united. As a result, the Dutch were able to harm Spain effectively by attacking Portugal overseas. They soon drove the Portuguese from the west coast of Africa (though only temporarily from Angola), and from Ceylon, the Spice Islands, and Malacca. The English, too, after the founding of the East India Company in 1600, appeared in Asian waters in ever increasing strength, and took commercial supremacy away from the Portuguese in India, and later in China. Whereas the Spanish and Portuguese navigators and explorers had been in the service of their sovereigns, the Dutch and English sailed the oceans of the world as agents for commercial concerns, the great East India Companies. For these companies the profit motive was preeminent; they did not encourage exploration for its own sake or for reasons of glory or religion. The discovery of the northeastern coast of Australia by Willem Janszoon in 1606 was not the result of a planned reconnaissance but of an error in navigation. Abel Tasman sailed to Tasmania and New Zealand in 1642, but his employers, the Netherlands East India Company, made no attempt to profit from what he found. It was not until the late eighteenth century, with the coming of the age of scientific exploration, that the last remaining major geographical puzzle, the location and extent of Terra Australis, was solved, and not until the nineteenth that the penetration of the interior of the non-European continents as opposed to the charting of their coastlines was seriously undertaken.

A direct result of Europe's Age of Discovery was the Atlantic slave trade. A traffic in black Africans arose almost as soon as the Portuguese made their first probes down the West African coast in the fifteenth century. Not, however, until the development of the sugar, cotton, and tobacco plantations in the New World from the seventeenth century onward did the trade reach substantial proportions. Africans were transported across the

Atlantic to provide a labor force when it was found that neither the indigenous Amerindians nor imported white indentured servants were able or willing to work the plantations and mines. Initially handled by the Portuguese on their own account or as agents of the Spanish government, the trade was progressively taken over by the British, Dutch, and French. It lasted for approximately 450 years, only coming to a gradual end during the latter half of the nineteenth century. In all, somewhere in the region of 10 million slaves were carried to the New World. The total population loss to Africa, however, was much greater. To the number of slaves landed in the Americas must be added the men, women, and children who died during the infamous "Middle Passage" across the Atlantic, to say nothing of those who died on the African coast while awaiting transshipment, or while in transit from the interior to the coast, or in the wars between African states that were directly attributable to the slave trade.

The effects on tropical Africa of four and a half centuries of continuous and systematic plundering of its human resources were profound. The slave trade inhibited political, economic, and social development, culled out the young and healthy from a population already debilitated by endemic disease, and created or exacerbated intertribal and interstate hostilities. For hundreds of years Africans fought and enslaved one another to meet an insatiable overseas demand for black labor.

The Age of Discovery and the ensuing first phase of European expansion thus produced very different results in different parts of the world. In Asia, trade was the primary European object, and the great chartered companies vied with one another and with competing Asian traders for the profits of an increasingly valuable commerce. Before the end of the eighteenth century few thought in terms of permanent European territorial dominion or ownership. In the Americas, by contrast, land-grabbing and colonization were the accepted objectives from the beginning. The local inhabitants were everywhere conquered, and then destroyed, incorporated into European empires or colonies, or driven farther and farther into the interior, defeated by the white man's diseases as well as by his guns. In Africa, except in the far south, the only significant European interest was a traffic in human beings. No colonization took place, no agricultural crops were produced for export, and no industry developed.

For Further Reading

Albion, Robert G. (ed.), *Exploration and Discovery.*
Curtin, Philip D., *The Atlantic Slave Trade.*
Nowell, Charles E., *The Great Discoveries and the First Colonial Empires.*
Parry, J. H., *The Age of Reconnaissance.*

16   India: 1500–1750

The unification of the whole Indian subcontinent under a single political
authority had been the aim of many ambitious rulers, but only two dynasties, the Mauryas in the third century B.C. and the Tughluqs in the fourteenth century, had achieved this goal, and they only briefly. A new, and
quite self-conscious, movement toward political domination of the whole
region began in the sixteenth century under the Mughal dynasty and
reached fruition at the end of the seventeenth century. The Mughal empire
began to dissolve almost at the moment of its greatest territorial expansion,
thus seeming to repeat the history of its predecessors, but the transference
of many of its institutions, as well as the memory of imperial control, to the
new political hegemony established by the British at the end of the eighteenth century gives it a special dimension in the history of India.

    While contemporaries did not regard the arrival in 1526 of a new
group of Turks under Babur as particularly significant, the subsequent
history of his dynasty marks 1526 as the beginning of the modern era in
India. The search for methods of political integration that characterized the
reigns of Akbar (1556–1605) and Aurangzeb (1658–1707), the establishment of important commercial relationships with the European powers,
and the growth within the empire of new and dynamic regional forces
represented by the Marathas, all linked the empire of the Mughals with
modern India.

    Babur, the founder of the empire, was a Turkish chieftain who had
established a small kingdom at Kabul after having been driven out of his
principality in Central Asia by other Turkish tribes. This new Turkish
intrusion is one more reminder that India was never isolated, despite the
many unique features of its culture, but was continually being affected by
events on its borders from Central Asia and China to the Near East.
Babur's empire, stretching from Kabul through the Punjab and the Gangetic
plain to Bengal, was temporarily lost under his son Humayunto Sher
Shah, one of the Afghan chieftains who had gained power in the last years
of the Delhi Sultanate, but was regained by his grandson Akbar.

    Territorial expansion and political centralization were the dominant
themes of Akbar's long reign. Agra was the Mughal capital, and from this
strategic position control was maintained over the Punjab, the Gangetic
heartlands of the old sultanate, and, somewhat tenuously, Afghanistan.
Akbar began expanding toward the south and east, conquering the Mus-

A.D.   1510   Portuguese capture Goa
          1526   Defeat of the Lodi Sultan by Babur
     1526–1530   Reign of Babur
     1530–1538   Reign of Humayun
          1538   Death of Guru Nanak
     1538–1555   Interregnum under Sur dynasty
     1555–1556   Humayun restores Mughal authority
     1556–1605   Reign of Akbar
          1565   Fall of Vijayanagar
          1600   British East India Company receives charter
     1605–1627   Reign of Jahangir
     1628–1658   Reign of Shah Jahan
          1634   English begin trading in Bengal
          1639   Founding of Fort St. George, Madras
     1658–1707   Reign of Aurangzeb
          1674   Shivaji crowned king of Marathas; French found
                 Pondicherry
          1690   Founding of Calcutta
          1708   Death of Guru Govind Singh
          1739   Nadir Shah raids Delhi
          1742   Marathas raid Bengal
     1744–1748   War between French and British in India

lim kingdoms of Gujerat, Malwa, and Bengal, which had been independent
for more than a century. The ruthlessness of this expansion, especially in
areas where there was strong resistance, is typified in the account of
the conquest of Gujerat by one of Akbar's generals: "We burnt and
destroyed the towns of Kari and Kataria. . . . We realized an enormous
booty, and after plundering and destroying nearly three hundred villages
in the course of three days, we re-crossed the Rann. After crossing, we
destroyed the districts of Malia and Morbi."

Since to control an empire in India was always more difficult than to
acquire one, Akbar's administrative and political arrangements are of
particular interest. Previous Muslim rulers had drawn their main support
from their Turkish military commanders, but these officers were not inclined to strengthen the sultan's power at the expense of their own. Akbar,
however, forged an alliance with the Rajput chieftains, who were Hindus,
thus creating a counterweight to the powerful Turkish commanders. The
Rajput princes had become independent during the last century of the rule
of the Delhi sultans, and the conquest of their strongholds was necessary
before Akbar could expand southward. But in contrast to his treatment of
the independent Muslim rulers whom he deposed and whose territories he
incorporated into the empire, Akbar allowed the Rajput rulers who submitted to retain their lands. The allegiance of the Rajput chieftains to the
Mughal empire was cemented by marriage alliances between Akbar and
princesses of the leading Rajput families; thus for the next 150 years,
groups that had traditionally been most resistant to Muslim rule provided
security to the Mughal dynasty.

A concomitant of the Rajput compromise was Akbar's general policy
of religious accommodation. This was not analogous to the toleration of
the modern Western world but to the latitudinarianism of early Hanoverian
England. The fundamental religious dilemma posed for Muslim rulers in
India was the fact that the vast majority of Hindus could not be brought
into the Islamic fold. The problem had long been "solved" by a practical, if
uneasy, acceptance of the continuance of Hindu rights along with an
emphasis on the priority of Islamic practices. By giving virtual religious
equality to Hinduism, Akbar obtained a more positive basis of support for
his dynasty, and at the same time freed himself from deference to the
opinions of the *ulemas,* or Muslim theologians, who intransigently demanded that the rulers seek the spread of Islam and the destruction of
idolatry. Akbar's abolition of jizya, the special tax imposed on non-Muslims, and his granting the Hindus permission to build temples were regarded by orthodox Muslims as proof of his apostasy.

Akbar also strengthened royal power by rationalizing the procedures
for assessing and collecting land revenue. The central portions of the em-

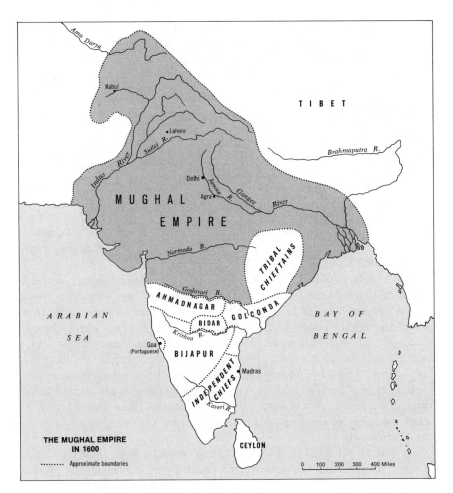

THE MUGHAL EMPIRE
IN 1600

········ Approximate boundaries

0   100   200   300   400 Miles

pire were surveyed, and fixed assessments replaced the arbitrary demands of the tax collectors. The empire was divided for administrative purposes into provinces, and these were then divided into districts and subdistricts. Officials were paid in cash rather than in land, an attempt to solve one of the most persistent problems of earlier Indian rulers. Granting of land, or *jagirs,* had been common among both Muslim and Hindu rulers, but this deprived the central treasury of income and provided officials with territorial bases for building up their own authority. Akbar did not succeed in regaining all the land that had been alienated in the past or in paying all salaries in cash, but he moved the empire in the direction of centralization and away from the old political pluralism.

Under Akbar's successors, Jahangir (1605–1627) and Shah Jahan (1628–1658), territorial expansion and centralization continued. By the middle of the century the Mughals had extended their power over the Muslim sultanates of the Deccan, although the two most powerful, Bijapur and Golkunda, acknowledged Mughal suzerainty without surrendering their territorial integrity.

The graceful elegance associated with the art and architecture of the Mughal dynasty reached a high point during the reign of Shah Jahan, when Indian and Persian artistic forms were combined in what was perhaps the only genuinely creative synthesis of elements from Islamic and Hindu culture. Miniature paintings reflecting both Persian and Indian sensibilities portray a style of courtly life that, while light and delicate, had also a kind of mannered formalism. The architectural forms favored in Shah Jahan's time survive in the great palace complex in the Red Fort at Delhi as well as in the famous Taj Mahal at Agra, the most splendid of the numerous tombs with which the Mughals memorialized their fame.

Aurangzeb (1658–1707) realized more completely than any other Indian ruler the ancient dream of the chakravartin, the king who would bring all of India under his sway. Fifty years of warfare pushed the frontiers of the empire almost to Cape Comorin in the extreme south, brought Assam for the first time under Muslim rule, and maintained control over the tribesmen on the northwest frontier. Yet this great empire disintegrated within thirty years of Aurangzeb's death, for the internal stresses were working against its preservation even at the beginning of his reign. He had come to the throne after a fierce struggle against his three brothers and his father, and the factionalism this had engendered expressed itself in widespread uprisings.

As with all Muslim rulers who sought to control a great empire in India, Aurangzeb's principal problem was to find support for his regime. Akbar had turned to the Rajputs, but the alliances he had formed, while still of importance, had been weakened during the wars of succession. Personal religious convictions and his understanding of the political situation led Aurangzeb to emphasize the Islamic nature of the empire. He gave prominence in the administration to Muslim commanders, tried to set standards of manners and morals that conformed to the Islamic ideal, and supported Islamic "truth" against Hindu "falsehood." He replaced Hindu officials with Muslims, discouraged Hindu religious practices offensive to Islam, and beat a general retreat from the easy pluralism of Akbar's regime. There was no widespread persecution, but Hindu temples, notably at such places of peculiar sanctity as Benares and Mathura, were destroyed. And while Muslims could not replace the numerous minor Hindu tax officials, fewer Rajputs received high appointments in the army.

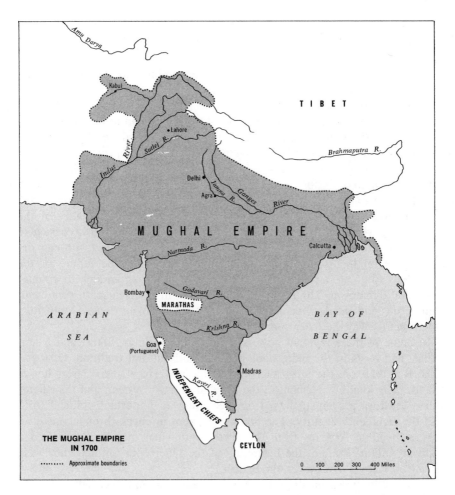

Aurangzeb's religious policies naturally roused resentment, but they were not an important factor in the weakening of the imperial structure. Public opinion, as representing the feelings of the Hindu masses, can scarcely have existed as a political force. The Rajputs of Marwar, one of the largest of the Rajput states, rebelled in the second half of the reign, but this resulted from Aurangzeb's attempt to annex their territories, not from religious zeal. The Rajput rebellions were contained with a fair measure of success, not only by Aurangzeb but also by his weak successors, and the Rajputs maintained their alliance with the Mughals well into the eighteenth century. In the Punjab, the Sikhs' militant desire for political independence, not their response to Aurangzeb's religious policy, led to a violent but unsuccessful uprising that ended with the execution of their leader. They remained hostile to the Mughals, but only late in the eighteenth century were they able to win independence.

The chief causes of the decline of the empire are almost certainly related to the social and economic costs of expansion. For twenty years war was carried on in the Deccan first against Bijapur and Golkunda, and then against the Marathas. The cost of this fighting had to be borne by the old imperial provinces. Taxes were apparently raised so high that the peasants in some areas rebelled against the tax collectors, while in others they fled from the land. Aurangzeb was continuously occupied with fighting in the south, and his absence from the center of political power in the north contributed to the breakdown of local authority. The economic crisis of the empire was thus part of the political crisis: the growing inability of the imperial government to control the regional forces that had always been so strong in India. Aurangzeb's attempt to shore up his empire through dependence on the Islamic community was defeated by the failure of the Mughals to create an administrative mechanism strong enough to counter regional dynamism. The result was the growth in the eighteenth century of numerous independent centers of power, which acknowledged only in a perfunctory way the suzerainty of the emperor.

Some of these regional powers, notably the Rajputs, Sikhs, and Marathas, had roots in the indigenous political and cultural tradition. Of these, the Rajputs were the most ancient, but the poverty of their desert homeland, their long involvement in the Mughal military system, and their fierce clan loyalties prevented them from becoming an important political force in the eighteenth century. The Sikhs were kept in check through pressures from invading Afghans from the north, and when they finally created a strong military state at the beginning of the nineteenth century, they were confronted by a new power, the British.

The Marathas, on the other hand, made their influence felt in almost every part of India, and in the middle of the eighteenth century seemed likely to become the successors to the Mughals. From fortresses in the hilly country south of Bombay, they had carried on guerrilla warfare against Aurangzeb for twenty years. Their leader, Shivaji (1627–1680), who was crowned king in 1674, claimed a special role for the Marathas as defenders of Hinduism and enemies of the Muslim invaders. Early in the eighteenth century his chief minister, the Peshwa, seized power and under his leadership the Marathas expanded rapidly, bringing most of central India and large areas of the Deccan under their control. At the same time the kingdom lost its unitary constitution and became a confederacy of military commanders who carved out territories for themselves. The Marathas captured Delhi and controlled the emperor at times, but they never substituted a Maratha for a Mughal as emperor. Like all the other Indian rulers of the time, whether Muslim or Hindu, they sought formal legitimization of their power through recognition as officials of the empire.

The Marathas reached the height of their power in 1761, but they were then defeated at Panipat, the historic battlefield north of Delhi, by a combination of Afghan and Mughal forces. The individual Maratha chieftains, however, particularly the rulers of Indore and Gwalior, remained formidable powers, and it was they, not the Mughals, who challenged the British in the late eighteenth and early nineteenth centuries.

Other centers of independent power were formed out of provinces of the empire by the Mughal governors, but not through rebellion or by explicitly defying imperial authority. Gradually the empire lost control over revenue and appointments, including that of successors to the governors. In the Deccan, the viceroy established his independence from Delhi in the 1720's, as the Nizam of Hyderabad. (This dynasty remained the most important Muslim ruling house in India up to 1948.) The governors of Oudh, the province in the fertile central plains north of the Ganges, became independent a little later, and vied with the rulers of Hyderabad for control of the imperial court.

Bengal, the third of the great provinces to become independent, had not been in the mainstream of the political and cultural life of India during the Mughal period, but assumed a new status in the eighteenth century. Trade, which had formerly moved inward toward the great imperial cities, now responded to the demands of European, Armenian, and Arab merchants for such products of Bengal as textiles, sugar, and indigo. This trade was never of great importance to the Indian economy as a whole, which remained overwhelmingly dependent upon local agricultural production, but high profits made it especially attractive to foreign merchants. By the middle of the eighteenth century the French and the English were engaged in a bitter struggle in India to dominate this commerce. The defeat of the French by the British was an aspect of the world-wide struggle of the two great powers, but it was hastened by the superior trading position of the East India Company in Bengal. The French in India were dependent upon the political and financial support of Paris, but the English used the profits of the Bengal trade to maintain a high degree of autonomy from home control.

Once the French were defeated, the East India Company's economic power brought it in conflict with the Nawab of Bengal, who by this time was aware of the threat that the foreign powers posed to the integrity of his government. In 1756 the new Nawab, Siraj-ud-daulah, sought to prevent any further encroachments on his sovereignty by driving the English out of their settlement at Calcutta. The English, along with a group of powerful

Hindu merchants, responded by supporting a rival claimant to the throne, and overthrew Siraj-ud-daulah in 1757 at the Battle of Plassey. The next eight years were marked by a series of quarrels between East India Company officials and the new Nawab, and in 1765 a decisive change in the political history of India took place. The Company forced the Mughal emperor to recognize its right to collect the revenue of Bengal. Within twenty years the East India Company was the actual ruler of Bengal.

The establishment of British power in India was thus not the result of military invasion but of participation, in a manner familiar to Indian political history, in a dynastic struggle. The expansion of British territorial control beyond Bengal in the next fifty years also conformed to a recognizable Indian pattern, the new power using the resources of the Gangetic heartland to conquer the rest of India. Mughal administrative institutions, although decayed and ramshackle, still existed in many areas, and everywhere local rulers acknowledged the suzerainty of the emperor, even though he had long since ceased to exercise authority beyond the walls of Delhi. The East India Company itself issued its coins in the emperor's name until 1835.

But emphasis on continuities in styles and patterns of political experience should not mask the changes resulting from the British conquest. The government established in Bengal at the end of the eighteenth century sought to maintain the old legal and judiciary system; that it was unable to do so was an indication that the new state carried with it values and presuppositions that made necessary different forms of administration. Technological advances in communications, particularly the telegraph and railway, combined with the nineteenth-century understanding of the role of the nation-state to permit a degree of political control and an integration of government and society unique in Indian history.

For Further Reading

Ahmad Aziz, *Islamic Culture in the Indian Environment.*
Habib, Irfan, *The Agrarian System of Mughal India.*
Ikram, S. M., *Muslim Civilization in India.*
Spear, Percival, *A History of India,* Vol. II.

17 Japan and China

Japanese historians refer to the late fifteenth and early sixteenth centuries as the "warring states period," the time when the country came closest in all of its history to complete disunity. Shoguns of the Ashikaga family continued to reign in Kyoto, but were powerless outside their own small domain. The imperial court, impotent as before, lacked the means even to keep up its ceremonial role in the style of previous times. The only true effective political units were the domains of virtually autonomous provincial daimyos. Though the total number of these at any one time might run into the hundreds, there were never more than twenty or thirty with large domains, and these ruled at most a few provinces. Warfare among them was so frequent that there was practically no time when the entire country was at peace.

Three military men accomplished reunification between 1568 and

A.D.   1542   Portuguese merchants first reach Japan
                  1568   Oda Nobunaga in control of Kyoto
                  1582   Nobunaga assassinated; rise of Hideyoshi
         1592, 1597   Abortive Japanese attempts to conquer Korea
                  1597   First persecution of Christians in Japan
                  1598   Death of Hideyoshi
                  1600   Tokugawa Ieyasu victor at Sekigahara
                  1603   Establishment of Tokugawa shogunate
                  1638   Suppression of Christian rebellion at Shima-
                         bara
                  1640   Seclusion and exclusion policies in effect
   Early 17th cent.   Unification of Manchu tribes of China by Nur-
                         hachi
                  1644   Peking captured by Manchus and made capital
                         of the Ch'ing Dynasty
         1661–1722   Reign of K'ang-hsi Emperor in China
         1675–1683   Ch'ing conquest of south China
         1688–1704   Cultural brilliance during Genroku calendrical
                         era in Japan
         1736–1796   Reign of Ch'ien-lung Emperor in China
                  1793   Mission of Lord Macartney to Peking
                  1853   Perry expedition forces end of Japanese ex-
                         clusion policy
                  1867   Abdication of last Tokugawa shogun

1615. The first of these, Oda Nobunaga, puppetized, then removed from office, the last Ashikaga shogun. By the time of his assassination in 1582 he had conquered a formidable block of territory in the central provinces. His lieutenant Toyotomi Hideyoshi, a man of peasant stock, completed the military victories over the central daimyos, and the pacifying alliances with the more distant of them, that restored an effective national government for the first time in nearly 200 years. Hideyoshi's palace at Momoyama gave its name to a brief period of brilliant, if gaudy, virtuosity in the visual arts. The age, in fact, was one of vigor and dash in all aspects of society. Overseas commerce flourished, and attempts to conquer Korea in 1592 and 1597, while abortive, seemed to forecast a national policy of overseas expansion.

The third reunifier was Tokugawa Ieyasu, a member of a minor daimyo family who had risen to national prominence as Nobunaga's vassal and later Hideyoshi's ally. In 1600, two years after Hideyoshi's death, he won the battle (at Sekigahara) that established him as the successor to Hideyoshi's power, though he did not finally destroy Hideyoshi's family until 1615, a year before his own death. Ieyasu's greatest achievement was to give legitimacy and continuity to the new national government, a feat he accomplished by having the emperor confer on him the hereditary title of shogun.

Japan's first contact with Europeans had occurred in 1542, when Portuguese merchants visited its shores. They were followed in the next few years by traders and missionaries from other Catholic countries. The Europeans in Japan had dealings with numerous local rulers, as well as with the principal figures in the central government. The Japanese learned from the West the use of firearms and certain other military techniques that aided reunification. Tobacco was another Western import. However, the most important aspect of Western culture introduced was surely the Christian religion. By late in the sixteenth century the number of Japanese Christians may have been as high as 150,000. Whole domains of western Japan were converted when their daimyos became Christians. Nobunaga was friendly to the Christians, in part because he saw the Buddhist church as an impediment to political unification. From the time of Hideyoshi, however, a reaction set in. Japanese rulers came to mistrust Christianity, then reject it. They began to suspect that European missionary activity might be a prelude to political conquest by the Spanish king (as they knew it had been in the Philippines). Furthermore, the zealous devotion of Japanese Christians convinced the authorities that fidelity to their religion took priority with them over the obligations of Japanese subjects.

The persecution of Christians began under Hideyoshi, in 1597. Ieyasu's attitude was intermittently intolerant (because he was a pious

Buddhist) and tolerant (because he wished to encourage foreign trade). The appearance in 1600 of Dutch and English merchants, the first northern Europeans in Japan, increased Japanese fear of Roman Catholicism by acquainting them with the religious warfare of post-Reformation Europe. Moreover, it gave them the idea that trade was possible without Christianity, for the Protestants in the Far East were not interested in proselytizing.

Rebellion by the Catholic community of Shimabara, in Kyushu, in 1638 spelled the doom of Christianity in Japan, and with it of unrestricted commerce with European countries. The government, which itself used Dutch technical advice and material to win its bloody victory over the rebels, feared the disruption that might result in the future if foreign Christians were to make league with Japanese dissidents. The result was a radical policy of seclusion (prohibiting Japanese from traveling abroad) and exclusion (prohibiting foreigners from visiting Japan) that lasted from 1640 to 1853. The only exception to the rule was to permit a handful of Chinese and Dutch merchants to trade under strict shogunal surveillance in the West Kyushu city of Nagasaki. In the meantime the practice of Christianity by the Japanese was stamped out with utter ruthlessness.

The Tokugawa political and social system lasted for more than two centuries. Its architects' aims had been to ensure peace and the perpetuation of Tokugawa family power, and in this they were remarkably successful. Politically, the keystone of the system was a balance between central and peripheral authorities, a characteristic historians call "centralized feudalism." Socially, it was the sharp differentiation of the military from the working classes, and the hereditary privileges of the former.

At the apex of the Tokugawa state was the shogun, a hereditary monarch whose title was military, but who came more and more to resemble a civilian-bureaucrat king. The shogun through his government (bakufu, or shogunate) performed two functions. He controlled directly his own extensive lands. These comprised about one-quarter of the agricultural land of the country situated mostly in the central provinces of Honshu from the Kanto Plain to the Kyoto-Osaka region, but also including outlying commercial, strategic, and mining centers. The remaining territory of the country was divided into approximately 260 han, or feudal domains. The shogun's jurisdiction over these lands and their rulers, the daimyos, did not extend to internal governance or taxation, but he strictly regulated their external relations by preventing alliances or warfare among them or with the outside world. He required certain dues from them, such as road building and aid in castle construction. Most important, from the middle years of the seventeenth century he required each daimyo to perform "alternate attendance" (sankin kōtai), that is to reside at his capital,

Edo (now Tokyo), on a regular basis one year out of every two. Thus he kept the daimyos under observation and forced them to divert to double residences of a suitable level of grandeur income that might otherwise have been spent on defense.

The daimyos were ranked by size of domain and further grouped into three classes according to the closeness of their feudal relationship to the shogun. The inmost group, the *shimpan* daimyos (cadet lords), were heads of side branches of the Tokugawa family. In addition to governing their domains, which tended to be large and strategically located, the cadet lords were regularly consulted about shogunal policy. However, they were rarely permitted to assume regular administrative offices in the shogunal bureaucracy. Shogunal heirs were chosen from this group when the direct line failed. The second group were the *fudai* daimyos, or hereditary vassals. The family founders had been vassals of the Tokugawa from the 1580's, the band of warriors from Ieyasu's native province of Mikawa with whose support he won the empire. Newly raised to the rank of daimyo after the Battle of Sekigahara, they governed the 140-some domains (typically small and centrally placed) that Ieyasu had carved out for them from the territory he had conquered. The *fudai* daimyos filled the chief administrative positions of the shogunal government.

The third group were the *tozama* daimyos, or "outside lords." Their ancestors had been domain lords coequal with the Tokugawa before 1600. Some had been allies of Ieyasu at Sekigahara, some neutrals in the fight. Only a few of the late-fifteenth-century daimyos who survived into the Tokugawa period had been enemies in 1600. Notably these were the lords of Satsuma (in southern Kyushu), Hizen (in northern Kyushu), and Chō-shū (in western Honshu), three territories too remote and powerful to be easily destroyed. The Tokugawa made peace with them, and they accorded the shogun grudging obeisance as a price for their survival. They, and the *tozama* group as a whole, were "outsiders" in several senses. Their domains tended to be in the remote peripheral provinces. They were on the average larger than other domains and had a larger measure of freedom in internal affairs. Throughout the period the shogunate continued to claim as a right of suzerainty the power to confiscate or relocate any *han*. With *shimpan* and *fudai* domains this was a real power, but after the first few years the shogunate lacked the will or the practical means to dispossess the larger *tozama han*. The penalty which the *tozama* lords paid for their relative autonomy and security was that they had virtually no voice in national affairs, which were under the jurisdiction of the shogunal government.

The shogun, daimyos, and samurai formed a governing class set off by strict marks of behavior and treatment from commoners. Samurai men wore swords as caste marks, but with the coming of peace the purely military character of the caste changed. They remained a pensioned and privileged aristocracy, and they continued to perform administrative and judicial functions. Since they were always the most highly educated group in society (along with the Buddhist clergy), they manned the learned professions—medicine, teaching, and scholarship.

The majority of the population were peasants, and the land tax which they paid to feudal rulers was the chief form of public revenue. Beyond collecting taxes and overseeing the administration of justice, the military classes left village government in the hands of a self-perpetuating local elite. Rural economy was always somewhat restricted by technical backwardness, and sometimes especially so because of plagues, floods, or other natural disasters. Yet, there was a gradual increase in the Tokugawa period both in the quantity of farm products and in the part retained by peasants for their own consumption.

A growing merchant class created numerous commercial centers throughout the country, in most of the "castle towns" as well as in the major cities of the shogunal domain: Edo, Osaka, Kyoto, and Nagasaki. The traditional Japanese attitude toward merchants was ambiguous. In accordance with a Confucian prejudice against commerce, their theoretical and legal status was near the bottom of society. Yet, samurai and daimyos needed the economic services of merchants and rewarded them with a considerable degree of favor. An important theme in the economic and social history of the period is the growing indebtedness of the government and the samurai to the merchant class.

To complete the picture of the political and social system in the Tokugawa period one must mention the emperor and his court in Kyoto, totally isolated from politics and from political affairs of every kind. Though the imperial institution reemerged into politics at the close of the period, its importance until then was wholly as a vestigial center of the indigenous national religion and as a symbol of the unity of the country and the legitimacy of the government.

Peace and prosperity produced a cultural renaissance that reached its greatest brilliance in the Genroku calendrical era (1688–1704). The haiku (17-syllable poems) of Basho, the puppet plays of Chikamatsu, the novels of Saikaku, and the woodblock prints of Moronobu bespeak an urban civilization of considerable refinement.

Education broadened under Tokugawa rule. In the seventeenth century the samurai class progressed from rough, spartan soldiery to a cultural elite, largely through domain-sponsored academies of the Neo-Confucian persuasion. Education then trickled down to the commoner classes, mostly to city-dwelling males, but increasingly by the nineteenth century even to peasants and to women. By the end of the period Japan may have ranked as high in point of literacy as the most advanced countries of western Europe.

Japanese history of the mid-seventeenth to mid-nineteenth centuries is devoid of dramatic institutional developments. Warfare was stilled; rulers of varying ability succeeded one another in orderly fashion; change was slow. Cities grew, but the population of the country remained remarkably stable (at about 30 million) from 1720 to 1850. The outside domains grew more independent, the central government more bureaucratic. There were evidences of sluggishness in the shogunate's rule and even of a relative enfeeblement in contrast with certain of its feudatories. Yet Tokugawa power was far from collapse when the West intruded. The collapse as it actually happened was the direct result of the shogunate's failure to solve with its traditional means an unprecedented problem—the threat to national security occasioned by the forced end of seclusion by the United States in 1853.

It was fortuitous that Americans should have been the people to open Japan. Before long others more powerful or with longer-established interests in the Far East would certainly have acted, and within months after the initial overtures Japan faced a concert of powers (including Great Britain, France, and Russia) demanding diplomatic and trade relations. The unequal treaties with all the powers granting extraterritoriality for their nationals in Japan were accepted at gunpoint between 1854 and 1867.

Acquiescence in this national humiliation stirred up fierce internal opposition. The leading protesters were outside domains traditionally aloof or hostile, such as Satsuma and Chōshū. Some critics could be found far closer, among the cadet lords and in cliques of shogunate officials out of power. Until 1860 the quarrel raged at the daimyo and upper samurai level, but then it spread to the lower samurai and the commoners. At first critics attacked specific shogunal policies, but increasingly in the 1860's their aim was more radical—to supplant the Tokugawa with a new and more effective ruling group.

From the beginning the antishogunal movement appealed to the name of the emperor, as the superior legal and moral authority from which the shogunate claimed its legitimacy. Some imperial courtiers joined the ranks of the dissidents, and the Kyoto court itself furnished a base from which they attacked the shogunate. The victory over the shogunate in armed confrontation from 1866 to 1868 was called an imperial victory, though the true heirs to the Tokugawa were a coalition of activists from samurai and courtier ranks who fought with the armed and fiscal backing of the great western *tozama* domains, Satsuma, Chōshū, Hizen, and Tosa.

China, too, in this era was dominated by a powerful regime; indeed, the rulers of the Ch'ing, or Manchu, dynasty were the most successful foreign conquerors in Chinese history. The story of how the Manchu* people succeeded in conquering and ruling China from 1644 to 1911 begins in the far northeast several decades before the end of the Ming. The Ming government maintained control over the regions north of the Great Wall by delegating authority to the chiefs of local tribes, which it attempted to keep divided and weak. However, in the first decades of the seventeenth century, while the Ming court was absorbed in enervating factional quarrels, the chieftain of one Jurchen tribe, Nurhachi, unified the area now known as Manchuria through a combination of military campaigns and marriage alliances. He organized the Jurchen warriors into companies of 300 men, grouped first under four, and later eight, divisions called Banners, each identified by its own flag. Tribal leadership had been hereditary, but the eight Banners were placed under the command of seven of his sons and one nephew, and Banner officers were appointed by Nurhachi. The companies and Banners were not autonomous combat units, but pools from which troops were mustered when needed. In time, Chinese and Mongol Banners were also organized.

It was this form of military organization that enabled Nurhachi's successors to conquer China. In 1616 Nurhachi proclaimed himself emperor of the Later Chin dynasty, and in 1625 established his capital in present-day Mukden. This was a momentous move, for Mukden was in an agricultural area, settled and cultivated by Chinese. To rule a sedentary population required methods and institutions far different from those suited for nomadic tribes, and Nurhachi met the challenge by choosing the only model available to him, the Chinese system of civil administration.

Nurhachi died in 1626, but the trend toward adoption of Chinese institutions continued under his successors. The Six Ministries and Censorate were established in Mukden in 1631. Chinese scholar-officials, some of whom had previously served the Ming, were appointed to the highest positions in the civil administration as well as in the armies. As bureaucracy supplanted the looser forms of tribal organization, the power of the ruling clan over the tribes and of Nurhachi's sons within the clan increased. Equally important, the Chinese system of government enabled the Manchus to win the allegiance of the Chinese gentry, and to administer territories conquered by Manchu armies.

The proclamation of the Ch'ing (Clear) dynasty at Mukden in 1636 set the stage for the conquest of China. Rebellions had broken out in north China in the 1630's, and in 1644 the rebel army of Li Tzu-ch'eng captured

---

* The name Manchu, the origin of which is obscure, was not adopted until 1635; it is used here for the sake of convenience.

Peking. When the Ming general Wu San-kuei called on the Manchus for aid, Banner troops streamed into north China and rapidly dispersed the rebels. The Manchus then occupied Peking themselves and proclaimed it the capital of the Ch'ing dynasty.

Remnants of the Ming armies withdrew to the south, where they set up satrapies, which were tolerated by the Manchus for several decades. But this anomalous situation could not be permitted to continue, and as soon as the Manchus felt secure in the north, south China and Taiwan were subjugated (1675–1683).

Military conquest was an impressive feat, but the major task facing the Manchus was ruling the vast and populous empire. The Manchu people comprised perhaps 2 per cent of the population of China. How were they to maintain internal cohesion and political supremacy?

In order to safeguard Manchu racial and cultural identity, the traditional clan system was preserved, marriage with Chinese was forbidden, and Manchuria was blocked off to Chinese emigration. Some of these barriers eventually broke down, and the Manchus came to adopt many Chinese customs, but until the twentieth century they did not become assimilated.

Superior military power had enabled the Manchus to conquer China, and steps were taken to ensure the preservation of military supremacy. Banner units were stationed at strategic locations throughout the empire. Small units, overlapping commands, the periodic transfers were among the measures designed to prevent any commander from becoming dangerously independent. Efforts were made to encourage the continuance of military prowess in the peacetime garrisons, and Manchus were forbidden to engage in manual labor or commerce. By the late eighteenth century inactivity and financial corruption led to the deterioration of the Banner forces, but by that time the Ch'ing had consolidated power through other means.

The Manchus realized that to govern China, the cooperation of the Chinese, above all, of the gentry class, was necessary. The house therefore ruled in much the same fashion as a native dynasty. This was the key to their success, and their greatest achievement. As a visible symbol of submission, Chinese were required to braid their hair in the Manchu queue, but in general, they were allowed to retain their own customs. Attempts to abolish Chinese women's practice of binding their feet and to encourage Chinese scholars to learn the Manchu language failed and were soon abandoned. Only minor alterations were made in the political organization inherited from the Ming. The civil service examination system continued to be the principal method of recruiting officials and of fostering ideological indoctrination and intellectual conformity. The hierarchy of examinations was complex, but basically unchanged from the three stages—district, provincial, and metropolitan—of Ming times. Examination requirements for Manchus were less rigorous, but of course the overwhelming majority of the more than a million degree holders at any given time were Chinese. Only a small percentage of the 40,000 or so officials were Manchu. Most of these held key posts in the central government or the military, while the day-to-day administration of the empire was conducted by Chinese.

China proper was divided into eighteen provinces, most of which were grouped into pairs to form larger units; as under the Ming, the governors of provinces and the viceroys of paired provinces were jointly responsible for the areas under their jurisdiction. Until the nineteenth century, the majority of viceroys were Manchus, while most governors were Chinese. The lowest level of direct administration was the district, of which there were some 1,400 to 1,500 with an average population of about 200,000, each under the supervision of a Chinese district magistrate. On the local level, the system of dividing the populace into units of 100 and 10 households was also retained.

In the capital, the Six Ministries and the Grand Secretariat headed the bureaucracy. Each ministry had two presidents, one Manchu and one Chinese, and four vice-presidents, two Manchu and two Chinese. There were equal numbers of Chinese and Manchus in the Grand Secretariat and in the Censorate as well. A new body, the Grand Council, created in 1729, eventually replaced the Grand Secretariat at the top of the government apparatus. It concentrated on urgent matters, while the Grand Secretariat handled more routine affairs. This innovation eased the task of the emperor, but ultimate authority and responsibility remained in his hands, and the system worked smoothly only when an emperor exercised this authority.

The ruling house was fortunate enough to produce two outstanding emperors during the first 150 years of the dynasty, whose combined reigns amount to almost one-half of the entire Ch'ing period. The K'ang-hsi Emperor (1661–1722) was an energetic and conscientious administrator and an able military leader. In addition to subjugating south China, he conquered Mongolia. Through holding special examinations and sponsoring important scholarly projects, such as the compilation of the *History of the Ming* and the *Complete Poems of the T'ang Dynasty,* he demonstrated his desire to rule as a Confucian monarch, and attracted a large number of the most eminent Chinese scholars to the service of the dynasty. Although at first many Chinese had naturally been hostile to the alien conquerors, by the end of the reign of the K'ang-hsi Emperor it is probable that the vast majority of the population, including the gentry guardians of the Chinese tradition, looked on the Manchu monarch as the legitimate possessor of the Mandate of Heaven.

Under the K'ang-hsi Emperor's grandson, the capable Ch'ien-lung Emperor (1736–1796), the Ch'ing reached its zenith. Tibet, after several revolts against Ch'ing influence, was made a protectorate. Ili and Turkestan were conquered, adding more than 6 million square miles of territory. By the late eighteenth century, the largest area in the history of China was under the administrative supervision of the imperial government. The record of the reign was marred by corruption during the last two decades, owing largely to eunuch influence. In 1796 the Ch'ien-lung Emperor retired, not desiring to appear unfilial by remaining on the throne longer than his illustrious grandfather. A son succeeded him, but the old emperor, still vigorous, retained real power until his death in 1799, making his rule the longest in Chinese history.

In retrospect we can see that the mid-Ch'ing was the twilight of traditional Chinese civilization. Within the eighteen provinces, peace reigned, commerce prospered, and the gentry devoted themselves to the finer things in life. Exquisite lacquer and porcelain wares were produced in unprecedented quantities, for export to appreciative connoisseurs in Europe as well as for domestic consumption. Scholars delved more deeply and more thoroughly into the classical past than ever before, even challenging the authenticity of parts of the accepted Confucian canon. Poets debated whether technique, moral content, feeling, or inspiration was the essence of great poetry. In *The Dream of the Red Chamber,* China's greatest novel, Ts'ao Hsueh-ch'in portrayed the decline of an aristocratic family and suggested that escape from this world was the only solution to the sorrow and futility of human love.

On the lower levels of society there were fewer pleasures and simpler worries. The long period of peace, combined with the widespread use of crops introduced from abroad which could be grown on previously uncultivated soil, such as the sweet potato, the peanut (used for cooking oil), and maize, caused a population explosion. By the end of the eighteenth century the population of China may well have reached the 300 million mark. Pressure on the land was intense, and when in 1796 a rebellion inspired by a combination of religious fervor of the Buddhistic White Lotus sect and animosity toward the Manchus broke out in north China, it spread rapidly among the discontented peasantry. The rebels were not well organized, but the Banner forces were ineffectual. The years spanning the turn of the century were spent in the slow and costly suppression of the rebellion.

The White Lotus Rebellion was quashed and the crisis seemed to have passed. No one could have foreseen that the barbarian emissary, the Englishman Lord Macartney, who had come in 1793 to petition for trade privileges and who had graciously been granted an audience in spite of his perverse refusal to kowtow before the Son of Heaven, was the herald of a new order, which within a few generations would humiliate and ravage the glorious empire of the Ch'ing.

For Further Reading

JAPAN

Ernst, Earle, *The Kabuki Theatre.*
Hibbett, Howard S., *The Floating World in Japanese Fiction.*
Keene, Donald (ed.), *Anthology of Japanese Literature from the Earliest Era to the Mid-Nineteenth Century.*
Reischauer, Edwin O., and Fairbank, John K., *East Asia: The Great Tradition.*
Tsunoda, Ryusaku, William Theodore de Bary, and Donald Keene, *Sources of Japanese Tradition.*

CHINA

Ch'ü, T'ung-tsu, *Local Government in China under the Ch'ing.*
Ho, Ping-ti, *The Ladder of Success in Imperial China.*
Ts'ao Hsueh-ch'in, *The Dream of the Red Chamber.*

18   Aztec and Inca Civilizations

Once the Spanish monarchs Ferdinand and Isabella had been convinced that Columbus had discovered an extensive archipelago of hitherto unknown islands, they began to build an empire in this New World with astonishing speed. Their conquistadors became leaders in that explosive geographical expansion whereby Europeans discovered more territory in seventy-five years than in the previous thousand. In this brief period, these remarkable men, variously impelled by curiosity, thirst for gold, and missionary zeal, found the Pacific Ocean and traversed its enormous expanse; explored great rivers (the Amazon, the Magdelena, the Mississippi, the Orinoco, the Plata); conquered a region larger than forty Spains; and sailed their tiny ships around the world. The men, hitherto unknown, who accomplished these extraordinary feats did so with little aid from the Crown, which shrewdly gave only formal authorization to act in the name of Spain. The bold conquistadors invested their own blood and fortunes, driven in the hope of winning honor and riches.

When the Spanish reached mainland America they encountered three different civilizations: those of the Aztecs, the Mayas, and the Incas. They

B.C.	5000	Beginnings of agriculture in Mexico
	2000	First Peruvian ceremonial centers
	900	Chavín unification of Peru
	800	Olmec unification of Mesoamerica
A.D.	300–600	Teotihuacan empire
	600–800	Huari and Tiahuanaco empires
	900	Fall of classic Maya civilization
	1400–1519	Aztec empire
	1438–1538	Inca empire

were greatly impressed not only by the gold to be looted, but also by the sophisticated, metropolitan character of these peoples of Mexico and Peru. In Mexico they found cities to rival and perhaps surpass those of Europe; in Peru, an empire of heroic magnitude. They marveled at these civilizations set in the midst of Indian country, and, happily for historians, they wrote about what impressed them: the ferocity of the Aztecs; the talented craftsmen of Cholula and Cuzco; the intellectual and scientific achievements of the Mayas; the efficiency of the Inca administration and its social security system; the immense pyramids and temples that studded the cities and towns of two continents.

The first step toward civilization, the cultivation of maize, beans, squash, and other plants, had been taken in the Mexican highlands about 5000 B.C. or perhaps still earlier. Knowledge of cultivation spread rapidly from this center, reaching as far south as Peru during the fourth millennium B.C. In area after area, farming stimulated experiments with local plants, and some of these (especially potatoes and manioc) became staples more important than those originally diffused from Mexico. The effects of cultivation on population and society differed, however, from area to area. In Mexico, Central America, and the northern and central Andes, where environmental and historical circumstances favored genuinely productive agriculture, and where reliable sources of protein (such as fish, wild game, or domestic meat animals) were abundant, cultivation led to a rapid expansion of population.

Within this broad territory, civilization developed only in Mesoamerica (Mexico and northern Central America) and the central Andes (Peru and Bolivia). These areas possessed two advantages which were largely responsible for the growth of their civilizations: a concentration of population in relatively restricted zones, and an integrated yet ecologically diversified environment with multiple centers of innovation and diffusion. Dense populations in restricted regions provided the background for urbanism and the personnel to fill the many roles required by a highly specialized society. The interchange between centers in different situations guaranteed the flow of stimuli across the whole area and gave rise to the expansive tendencies that led to the formation of states and empires.

These ancient American societies had in common features essential to all civilizations: intensive agricultural economies; large concentrated populations; intensive social stratification; a high degree of occupational specialization; governmental authority that cross-cut kinship and locality; statewide organization of food production; efficient distributive systems covering large areas; standing armies; diversified patterns of settlement; monumental architecture; and the concentration of major public functions in a limited number of centers (usually, but not always, cities). In addition they had features that some of their Old World counterparts of the sixteenth century lacked. Church and state were so closely linked as to be practically the same institution. Clans, lineages, and other kinship units were institutionalized within the political structure. Land was owned either by the kinship groups or by the state itself, not by individuals or families. On the other hand, none of the American civilizations had iron technology, draft or riding animals, the plow, wheeled vehicles, firearms, or true seagoing ships.

Since they had developed in different environments and under different historical conditions, these people evolved, in spite of their similarities, into different kinds of societies, with different goals and organized on different principles. Throughout most of their history the Mesoamericans and the inhabitants of the central Andes were isolated from each other. Certain basic innovations, such as the cultivation of maize, pottery making, and metallurgy, spread from one area to the other, or outward from the intervening territory. At no time, however, was there the sort of direct contact between Mesoamerica and Peru that was so common in the history of the nations of the Old World.

The earliest Mesoamerican civilization, that of the Olmecs, evolved along the Gulf of Mexico some time before 1000 B.C. After about 800 B.C., it exerted influence on the social and religious organization of an area extending from the Valley of Mexico to modern El Salvador. We do not know just how this expansion took place, but it seems to have spurred the development of civilization all over Mesoamerica.

To the north, especially in the Valley of Mexico, large cities soon grew up. During the Christian era the competing imperialistic designs of the major cities colored the whole history of the Mexican highlands. City after city—Teotihuacán, Tula, Azcapotzalco, and many others—rose to power and was then destroyed. Teotihuacán, founded about the time of Christ, became the largest city ever built in preconquest Mesoamerica. Its people established the largest of the ancient Mexican empires, extending from the Valley of Mexico to the highlands of Guatemala and lasting from about A.D. 300 to 600.

By the early sixteenth century the Aztecs of Tenochtitlán, along with their uneasy allies Texcoco and Tlacopán, dominated Mexico, holding sway over much of the southern part of the country. The Aztecs were an incredibly bloodthirsty people, and their empire was more a military machine than a political state. They left conquered governments intact, sending out armies on a regular schedule to collect tribute. They were more concerned with taking prisoners to be sacrificed by tens of thousands to Huitzilopochtli and other gods than with the peaceful administration of conquered territory. In a sense, the Aztec dominion was not an empire at all, but an immense battle ground on which their conquest was ever being refought. The only real integrating element was provided by the merchants, a special class of state-controlled capitalists who traded widely through Mexico while serving also as ambassadors, spies, and at times soldiers.

In the tropical country to the south, especially in the Petén area of Guatemala, the Maya civilization developed. This was a nonurban society; a dispersed and essentially rural population was organized around ceremonial centers which were the seats of government, commerce, and religion, but which largely lacked the residential districts that would have made them into cities. The Olmecs had discovered the rudiments of writing and the calendar, and the Mayas improved these—as well as the science of astronomy—into complex, sophisticated intellectual systems. The classic Maya civilization of the Petén was based on tropical slash-and-burn farming, rather than on intensive agriculture. Eventually (about A.D. 900) the ceremonial centers disintegrated when the constantly increasing population outstripped a diminishing food supply. Outlying Maya areas, especially in Yucatán, continued to flourish but were repeatedly conquered by the great cities of Mexico. What the Spaniards found in Maya country were the decimated, "Mexicanized" remnants of a once great civilization, its ceremonial centers abandoned and in ruins, the remaining noble families locked in a bitter civil war.

Peruvian civilization had its beginnings on the desert coast, where the first ceremonial centers were built about 2000 B.C. Small states, organized very much like those of the classic Mayas, extended over parts of the coast and highlands. About 900 B.C. one of these, the Chavín civilization, underwent an expansion very much like that of the Olmecs, spreading throughout the northern half of Peru. For a millennium and a half thereafter, the

PRE-COLUMBIAN EMPIRES

0   500   1,000 Miles

people of this area were organized around ceremonial centers similar to those in the land of the classic Maya.

Meanwhile cities were growing up in southern Peru, outside the area of Chavín influence. About A.D. 600 two of these, Huari and Tiahuanaco, carved out empires that, between them, included all of Peru and Bolivia and part of northern Chile. However, these empires, and the cities that founded them, survived only two or three centuries. Thereafter southern Peru and Bolivia reverted to a purely rural world of little tribal groups living in villages. These tribes engaged in incessant feuds. The Huari conquerors, however, had carried urban life and imperialism to northern Peru. Cities soon replaced the old ceremonial centers there, and one of them, Chan Chan, conquered much of the Peruvian coast.

Surprisingly, the final and greatest round of empire building originated in the rural south, not in the urban north. First the Incas, combining military ingenuity with diplomatic finesse, subjugated many of the little tribes of the southern Peruvian highlands. Then, their armies expanded by units from the new provinces, they conquered all of the Andean coast and highlands, from northern Ecuador to the Maule River in central Chile. They brought all of this territory under a single administrative system, establishing the rule of Cuzco in every province. This system was both complex and efficient. Inca governors subdivided the entire population of the empire into groups of ten persons, and were thus able to control the activities of every farmer and craftsman. Men paid taxes in the form of labor. An up-to-date census was kept in the capital and a thoroughgoing social security system neutralized the effects of localized droughts and other natural disasters. Almost all of the population of the Inca empire—including the people of Cuzco, the capital "city"—lived in little villages. The few real cities allowed to survive were those that posed no threat to the integrity of the empire.

The Spanish conquest of these large, far-flung, culturally advanced, and warlike civilizations was swift. Mexico was crushed in three years, Peru in six. How did a handful of European adventurers manage to overrun such vast stretches of territory with such seeming ease? The Spanish enjoyed the advantages of cannons, horses, superior personal armor, and fleets of almost impregnable sailing ships. They were also constantly reinforced by new arrivals from Spain. These advantages, however, cannot explain the victory of so few over so many, especially since the Indians were fighting on their own terrain; the answer lies in the weaknesses inherent in the Indian societies.

For one thing, the Indians were completely immobilized when deprived of their emperors. The Spaniards kidnapped both the Aztec and the Inca emperors; until each was killed his absence paralyzed resistance because the pyramidal political systems depended on decisions being made by the semidivine individual at the top. Still more important in the case of Mexico was the burning hatred of the provincial peoples toward their Aztec over-lords. The army that conquered Tenochtitlán was really an Indian army captained by a few Spaniards. Similarly, the permanent civil war in the Maya country played no small part in the fall of Yucatán. The Maya groups would not unite against the invaders and could therefore be crushed one by one. The same situation existed in Peru, where the Incas had the added disadvantage of being overextended. Their empire was so large, and communications so difficult across the mountains and desert, that a second capital had been established at Quito. The Spanish arrived in Peru near the end of a disastrous civil war between two royal brothers, one based in Cuzco and the other in Quito. By adroit diplomacy the Spanish succeeded in prolonging the civil war, sometimes intervening on one side and sometimes on the other. While the Inca armies destroyed each other, the Spanish gradually took over the territories that the Indians were too busy to administer, until, after six years, they owned the whole empire.

For Further Reading

Coe, Michael D., *The Maya*.
————, *Mexico*.
Lanning, Edward P., *Peru Before the Incas*.

19 Spain and Portugal in America

The Spaniards did much more than explore, intrigue, and pillage in the New World; they worked to implant a Christian, European civilization in a domain that eventually stretched from California to Patagonia. Their empire included the viceregal capitals at Mexico City and Lima; mining camps such as Guanajuato in Mexico and Potosí in upper Peru; Asunción in the middle of South America a thousand miles from Buenos Aires, Santiago de Chile, Quito, Bogotá, Caracas, Havana, Guatemala City, and, far across the Pacific, Manila in the Philippines. By the seventeenth century some of these towns competed in size and significance with European cities and easily outshone the largest English, French, and Portuguese settlements overseas.

Even before the heroic age ended, Spain began to devise an administrative system to control its empire. The first voyage of Columbus was a somewhat haphazard affair, but arrangements for the second were carefully supervised, and thereafter all colonial affairs were regulated, from the time a would-be emigrant applied for a permit to leave Spain through the disposal of his estate after his death in America. The House of Trade was established in 1503, the Laws of Burgos governing Spanish-Indian relations were drawn up in 1512, the Council of the Indies was organized in 1524. Indeed every action was so minutely prescribed by law that one needed a license to hunt for wild pigs on a Caribbean island. So many thousands of ordinances were passed that only with great difficulty were they codified and published as the massive, four-volume *Recopilación de Leyes de los Reynos de las Indias* (1680). The forest of laws continued to grow so rapidly that later attempts to issue an up-to-date compilation always failed. From the Supreme Council of the Indies in Spain, presided over by the king himself on important occasions, down through the viceroys and judges to lesser officials, a host of functionaries struggled to maintain the economic and political interests of the Crown. Regional

A.D. 1492 Columbus reaches the New World

1500 Cabral lays basis for Portugal's claim by landing in Brazil on his way to India

1519 Cortés begins the conquest of New Spain (Mexico)

1524 Council of the Indies established by Spain

1535 Antonio de Mendoza, first viceroy in Spanish America, begins rule in Mexico; Lima, Peru, is founded by Pizarro

1549 Permanent settlement of Brazil begun by Governor Thomé de Souza, and the Jesuits begin missionary labors

1550 Bartolomé de Las Casas and Juan Ginés de Sepúlveda debate at Valladolid whether the Indians are natural slaves according to Aristotle's doctrine

1551 University charters granted for universities in Mexico and Peru

1580 Philip II annexes Portugal and her empire, a "captivity" lasting until 1640

1624 Dutch begin their 30-year rule in Pernambuco, Brazil

1680 Publication of the Spanish colonial code: *Recopilación de Leyes de las Indias*

1759 Jesuits expelled from Brazil

1767 Jesuits expelled from Spanish America

1780 Unsuccessful rebellion by Tupac Amaru against Spanish rule in Peru

variations of laws and institutions developed, but this ponderous, complicated bureaucracy managed to hold the empire together for more than three centuries.

The Spanish sovereigns also had great authority and responsibility in ecclesiastical matters, owing to papal concessions in establishing the system of church-state relationship known as the Patronato Real. The Crown agreed to maintain the church in the Indies, but in return exercised pontifical powers except in purely spiritual matters. No church, monastery, or hospital could be built without the king's permission; no priest or friar might go to America without his express license. In the administrative, economic, and juridical affairs of the church in the New World he was dominant.

The Portuguese sovereigns obtained similar powers in Brazil, but in other respects Brazil differed significantly from Spanish America, for it was only one part—and for long not the most important part—of a sprawling aggregation of territories ruled from Lisbon. Portugal's colonial administration was loose and weak; she had so many other cares that she could not protect Brazil from foreign interlopers. Throughout a part of the sixteenth century, France powerfully rivaled Portugal in Brazil. Philip II of Spain annexed Portugal and all her overseas possessions in 1580, and until 1640 Brazil was an unwilling part of the Spanish empire. The Dutch established themselves in Pernambuco in 1624 and were expelled only thirty years later.

Brazil was poor, too, compared to Spanish America. The Indians that the Portuguese encountered were largely nomadic, and thus were no easily harnessed labor force to be exploited the way the sedentary and organized Aztecs, Incas, and Mayas were exploited by the Spaniards. Ecclesiastics sought to protect the Indians in the Spanish empire, but no widespread battle was fought to protect the Brazilian Indians, despite the notable labors of the Jesuit António de Vieira in the seventeenth century. Brazil had to import Negro slaves, an expensive operation, and though she became the world's leading exporter of sugar for a time, it was only late in the seventeenth century that gold was found in Minas Gerais. Brazil's combined agricultural and mineral production never sufficed to support a population as large as that of Spanish America: some 3 million people inhabited Brazil in 1800, mostly along the coast, while 18 million were found widely dispersed in the Spanish possessions.

The rhythm of history was different too. The sixteenth century was the exciting, dynamic period in Spanish America when Hernán Cortés, Francisco Pizarro, and other epic heroes made the great conquests and society was established: the "forgotten" seventeenth century was a quiet time with few significant events. In Brazil, on the other hand, only in the seventeenth century did the bandeirantes begin their dramatic explorations and slave raids which ultimately won tremendous areas for Portugal. Urban life was less important in Brazil; economic and political power was concentrated largely in the hands of the great plantation owners.

Everything in Brazil was on a simpler basis. The imperial organization that made Spanish America a paradise for bureaucrats did not exist in Brazil; the Church was poor and could not indulge in the ostentation practiced in Spanish America, where half of the land and other property was Church-held. The Holy Office of the Inquisition was not formally established in Brazil, and Jews played a significant role in commercial life. No printing press was set up, no university founded, and a quiet, almost vegetative provincial society grew up. At the end of the colonial period when Napoleon's invasion of Portugal sent the royal family scurrying across the Atlantic for safety, the women of Rio de Janeiro were so unacquainted with the ways of the world that when they saw the Portuguese court ladies debarking with shaved heads they hastened to cut off their own hair, not knowing that shipboard vermin, not Portuguese fashion, had decreed this drastic measure.

Another contrast between the Iberian empires in America lay in their relations with the native populations. In Brazil Indians played only a minor role, but in Spanish America the thorny question of their proper treatment was a dominant problem. In their effort to govern the natives, Spaniards adapted some institutions from their own medieval experience of fighting against the Muslims and created others to meet the needs of New World conditions. The determination of the Crown and the Church to Christianize the Indians, the need for labor to exploit the new lands, and the attempts of some Spaniards to protect the Indians resulted in a very remarkable complex of customs, laws, and institutions which even today leads historians to contradictory conclusions about Spanish rule in America. The encomienda system, by which groups of Indians were assigned to Spaniards, a device to provide labor and goods to the Spaniard and protection and religious instruction for the Indians, was both stoutly defended and bitterly attacked throughout the sixteenth century by Spaniards themselves. The imperial policy of attempting to "civilize" the Indians by urbanizing them produced many curious results, and in the end destroyed large numbers of natives. Academic disputes flourish on this debatable and in a sense insoluble question, but there is no doubt that cruelty, overwork, and disease resulted in an appalling depopulation. There were, according to recent estimates, about 25 million Indians in Mexico in 1519, slightly more than 1 million in 1605.

Spain made efforts to mitigate the travail of the Indians by appointing official "Protectors" and by setting up special courts to try cases involving

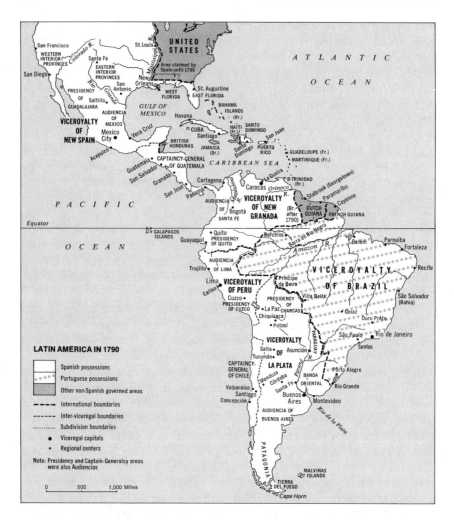

LATIN AMERICA IN 1790

Spanish possessions

Portuguese possessions

Other non-Spanish governed areas

— — — International boundaries

------ Inter-viceregal boundaries

.... Subdivision boundaries

● Viceregal capitals

• Regional centers

Note: Presidency and Captain-Generalcy areas
were also Audiencias

0   500   1,000 Miles

natives. The Crown dispatched numerous investigating groups and tried
many stratagems, in the sixteenth century particularly, to ensure that Indians would be brought under Spanish rule by peaceful means alone, and
be persuaded to accept Christianity by reason instead of by force. To
achieve this end Bartolomé de Las Casas and his brother Dominicans
preached the faith without the backing of the sword in Chiapas, and Vasco
de Quiroga established his utopian communities in Michoacán. In many
places a system of Indian segregation was worked out by friars and royal
officials to protect them from Spaniards bent on exploiting them. This

device, employed throughout the colonial period, culminated in the famous Jesuit missions of eighteenth-century Paraguay. Throughout the more than three centuries of Spanish rule in America, the difficult, indeed, impossible, double purpose of the Crown—to secure revenue and also to Christianize the Indians—inevitably led to angry disputes and evil compromises, along with some glorious episodes.

Looking back on the total encounter of Spaniards and Indians from the vantage point of the modern world with its multiplicity of cultures, two aspects of this confrontation hold special interest. For the first time in history one people—the Spaniards—paid serious attention to the culture of the peoples they met, because they felt a burning desire to establish a new Jerusalem in America. Protestantism had shattered the unity of Christendom in Europe, but many Spanish ecclesiastics saw in the New World a bright and shining opportunity for spiritual conquest. Many writers then and later pointed out that Luther and Cortés had been born about the same time: one to destroy Christian unity in Europe and the other to create a new community free from religious dissensions which were splitting the Old World asunder. To achieve this dream the souls of Indians must be won, and this could be done, the Spaniards believed, because the Indians were like soft wax, capable of being molded into true Christians. To accomplish this task the zealous friars learned the Indians' languages, familiarized themselves with their culture, and sought to make Christian doctrine intelligible to the Indian mentality.

The second, even more striking aspect of the Spanish-Indian relationship was the controversy which developed in the sixteenth century over the just method of treating the Indians. This issue led Spaniards to grapple with the ultimate problem—the nature of man himself. Of all the ideas churned up during the early years, none had more dramatic implications than the attempts some Spaniards made to apply to the natives the Aristotelian doctrine of natural slavery: the idea that one part of mankind is set aside by nature to be slaves in the service of masters born for a life of virtue. The scholar Juan Ginés de Sepúlveda sustained this view with great tenacity and erudition and concluded, without having visited America, that the Indians were in fact such rude and brutal beings that their forcible Christianization was both expedient and moral. But many ecclesiastics, most notably Bartolomé de Las Casas, opposed this idea scornfully, drawing upon divine and natural law as well as their own experiences in America. The controversy became so heated and the king's conscience so troubled over the question that in 1550 Charles V ordered the suspension of all expeditions to America while a junta of theologians, jurists, and officials, gathered at the royal capital of Valladolid, listened to the arguments of Las Casas and Sepúlveda. The Crown supported neither contestant fully, for Charles preferred to avoid clear-cut decisions whenever possible. But the basic law of 1573, designed to cover all future expeditions, required that future conversions be peaceful; "conquests" were henceforth to be called "pacifications."

In both Iberian empires, as in the colonial settlements of North America, there developed an "American" spirit which created a sense of alienation from the European powers and eventually led to a desire for independence. In both Brazil and Spanish America a mixed society grew up, unique in some respects because of the variety of the cultural and racial combinations that it produced. As the Liberator Simón Bolívar declared at the Congress of Angostura in 1819:

> It is impossible to say to which human family we belong. The larger part of the native population has disappeared. Europeans have mixed with the Indians and the Negroes, and Negroes have mixed with Indians. We were all born of one mother America, though our fathers had different origins, and we all have differently colored skins. This dissimilarity is of the greatest significance.

One final contrast between the two Iberian empires remains to be discussed. Fearing enemy attacks, Portugal discouraged writing about Brazil and suppressed publications concerning it, but in the Spanish empire an extraordinary wealth of documentation was produced. Columbus started the practice of writing about the New World, and many Spaniards followed his example. The conquest so excited the imagination of Spaniards that they came to look upon it as the greatest event since the coming of Christ. As the conquistadors roamed over vast areas and the missionaries attempted to Christianize millions of Indians, they collected historical materials and wrote histories on a monumental scale. This concern that the record of their deeds be known and the nature of the overseas lands be described led the Council of the Indies to establish the office of a Cosmographer and Cronista Mayor whose function was to write the history of the Indies on a continuous basis.

Both empires prospered more in the eighteenth century than ever before. Iberian paternalism and exclusivism continued in both economic and political affairs, but a certain Enlightenment influence mitigated its rigors. The monarchs improved the efficiency of their imperial machinery, and economically at least, as the century ended, their immense empires were enjoying a kind of Indian summer.

Particularly in Spanish America, the cities manifested all the outward signs of opulence. Imposing public buildings and churches had been built. The arts flourished. Centers of learning abounded on a scale unknown in the English, French, or Portuguese colonies. There was a school of mines, for example, in Mexico City, an astronomical observatory in Bogotá.

Colonial literary culture proliferated: men of letters, scientists, historians, and priests kept many a New World printer busy. Even viceroys "were often men of education and personal distinction, some of whom dabbled in arts and letters and held literary salons in the viceregal palace."

This luxury and refinement was something of a façade, for as that perspicacious traveler Alexander von Humboldt noted about 1800, a fearful gulf separated the elite from the masses: "The architecture of the public and private edifices, the finery of the ladies, the tone of society, all announce a refinement with which the nakedness, the ignorance, and vulgarity of the lower people form the most striking contrast."

Revolutions convulsed these colonial societies in the years following 1810, heralding a generation of turbulence and confusion. These years of liberation—following the events of 1776 in the United States and the French Revolution—led to the overthrow of the Iberian empires in America and the beginnings of a new kind of civilization.

For Further Reading

Boxer, Charles R., *The Golden Age of Brazil, 1695–1750.*
Freyre, Gilberto, *The Masters and the Slaves.*
Gibson, Charles, *Spain in America.*
Haring, Clarence H., *The Spanish Empire in America.*

20   The Settlement of North America

Almost a century elapsed between Columbus' discovery of the New World and the beginning of settlement in the temperate parts of North America. During that time Spain spread northward into Mexico and Florida from its Caribbean bases, but the lands farther north remained largely ignored. They appeared to house no gold, no fabulous cities, no advanced civilizations. Explorations along the eastern shore of the northern continent were often frustrating. Every river seemed to lead endlessly inland; the fabled Northwest Passage proved as elusive as the Seven Cities of Cíbola.

Instead of quick wealth and easy access to the Orient, those who probed North America encountered a vast expanse of dense forest, sparsely occupied by primitive natives. Unlike their ethnic relatives in the Mexican highlands, Central America, and the Andes, the peoples north of the Rio Grande were living in the Stone Age. Without metal tools (except for an

A.D.   1497   John Cabot reaches North America
           1513   Ponce de León establishes Spanish claim to Florida
           1524   Giovanni Verrazano explores coast of North America
           1534   Jacques Cartier explores St. Lawrence River
         1560's   French attempts to settle in Florida thwarted by
                    Spain
           1565   Spanish found first permanent settlement north of
                    Mexico at St. Augustine, Florida
           1607   First permanent English outpost established at
                    Jamestown, Virginia
           1608   First permanent French outpost established at
                    Quebec
           1609   Henry Hudson claims part of North America for the
                    United Provinces
           1619   First Negroes brought to British America as forced
                    labor; Virginia begins representative assembly
           1620   Separatists found Plymouth Colony
           1630   Great Migration to America begins; Massachusetts
                    founded
         1630's   Connecticut, Rhode Island, and New Haven colonies
                    founded
           1633   Colonization of Maryland begun
           1636   Harvard College opened
           1638   A Swedish settlement founded on the Delaware
                    River
         1640's   Civil wars in England cause shift in migration pat-
                    terns
           1655   Dutch from New Netherland conquer New Sweden
           1660   Stuart monarchy restored
         1660's   Legal definition of Negro slavery begun in Virginia
                    and Maryland

1663 Charles II grants Carolinas to eight proprietors

1664 British seize New Netherland

1675–1676 Bacon's Rebellion in Virginia; King Philip's War in New England

1682 William Penn founds Pennsylvania

1684–1689 Dominion of New England places several colonies under royal authority

1685 Revocation of the Edict of Nantes in France spurs Protestant migration to America

1689–1713 King William's War

1691 New Massachusetts charter puts colony under royal authority; Plymouth Colony and Maine included in new Massachusetts boundaries

1693 College of William and Mary founded

1696 Parliamentary Act establishes vice-admiralty courts to try violators; Board of Trade created by the Crown

1702–1713 Queen Anne's War

1704 *Boston News-Letter* begins publication

1729 North and South Carolina become separate, royal colonies

1733 Colony of Georgia founded

1739 George Whitefield first visits America

1740–1748 King George's War

1749–1752 Benjamin Franklin experiments with electricity

1751 Philadelphia Academy (later University of Pennsylvania) founded

1754 George Washington's clash with French soldiers signals start of French and Indian War

1763 Treaty of Paris; French Canada and Spanish Florida ceded to Great Britain

occasional item of copper), domesticated animals, or a written language, the Amerinds—or "savages" as the English chroniclers usually called them—lived in simple agricultural and hunting societies. With little contact and even less cohesion between the scores of identifiable tribal units, the American aborigines could offer no effective resistance to European attempts to settle along the eastern seaboard. Actually, the Indians at first saw no need to resist; the white man could give them valuable tools, weapons, ornaments, and information. Furthermore, land was incredibly plentiful. To both European and native it seemed inconceivable that enough colonists would ever arrive to make the million Indians north of the Rio Grande feel cramped for space. Early contacts were for the most part peaceful except where marred by explorers who blatantly carried off a few Indians to show as oddities in the courts of Europe. Eventually, however, many tribes came to fear and hate the white man, perhaps as much for his arrogant assumption of superiority as for his hunger for land.

During the sixteenth century Europeans accumulated information about North America and debated rival territorial claims. Spain, busy plundering the Indian civilizations south of the Rio Grande, rested its case on the explorations of Juan Ponce de León (1513), and Pánfilo de Narváez (1528) in Florida, Hernando de Soto and Vásquez de Coronado in the lower Mississippi Valley and New Mexico (1539–1542), and Juan Cabrillo and Bartolomé Ferrelo along the west coast of the continent. The papal bulls of 1493, which allotted all the New World west of Brazil to Ferdinand and Isabella, provided ecclesiastical endorsement. But Spain's claims meant little to her European rivals. Some found new reason to embarrass His Most Catholic Majesty after the Protestant Reformation added religious conflict to Europe's problems. England, relying on the discoveries of John Cabot in 1497, developed enthusiasm for New World possessions under Elizabeth I; at the same time the French and Dutch began to take notice of the huge land mass to the west. The North American continent slowly gained appeal as a source of raw materials, an area to settle surplus population, and a place to build outposts against Spanish power.

France seized an early lead in the contest for possession of the temperate zones of North America. In 1524 Giovanni Verrazano investigated almost the entire coast from Spanish Florida to Nova Scotia; ten years later Jacques Cartier explored the St. Lawrence River and planted a small colony on the site of present-day Quebec. Within less than a year, finding no immediate wealth and unnerved by the climate, these colonists sailed home. But French Basque fishermen made increasingly frequent voyages to northern waters, often camping for months on the shores of New England and Newfoundland. Finally, in 1608 the French, following up earlier explorations by Samuel de Champlain, secured a permanent foothold at Quebec.

The next year a Dutch expedition under Henry Hudson laid claim to the river that bears his name. Actual Dutch settlement began there in 1624 and soon expanded into the Delaware and Connecticut river valleys. By 1638 Sweden also had footholds on the Atlantic coast, principally on the Delaware.

Despite an almost complete absence from the American scene between the voyages of the Cabots in the 1490's and Martin Frobisher in 1576, England's commercial and political growth soon thrust her into the forefront of the colonial race. Prodded by propagandists such as the two Richard Hakluyts, seadogs of the mettle of Francis Drake, Humphrey Gilbert, and Walter Raleigh began to make a mockery of Spanish claims to North America. They explored the region at will and set up colonies at several locations along the coast, some within a few hundred miles of Spanish garrisons. In 1578 and 1583 Gilbert tried to settle Newfoundland, but the climate proved too formidable. Raleigh's attempts in the 1580's at Roanoke Island off the North Carolina coast failed for reasons still mysterious. England, it seemed, could not extend its power into the New World until the troubles with Spain subsided and stronger inducements for colonization appeared. Smashing the Spanish Armada in 1588 was but the first step.

It is ironic that the unimaginative Stuart monarch James I rather than the visionary Elizabeth succeeded in finally planting the British flag on American shores. The reasons lie not so much with the efficiency or generosity of the Stuarts as with the disruptions in English life that accompanied their erratic rule, and the civil and religious disturbances that plagued seventeenth-century England. The disruptive effects of the enclosure movement and the rapid growth of an urban proletariat caused thousands of Englishmen to despair of earning a decent livelihood at home. The growing Puritan effort to reform the Church of England created equally profound discontent, as did, later in the century, the political fragmentation accompanying the Civil War. England, it seemed to contemporaries, was overpopulated. America beckoned. In the first half of the seventeenth century, more than 60,000 Englishmen sought refuge in the New World.

Although England rapidly gained ascendancy over most of North America, her early attempts at settlement came close to failure. The first permanent success occurred in 1607 at Jamestown, not far from the earlier site of Roanoke. Three shiploads sent out in late 1606 by the London Company of Virginia—which had a royal charter to settle between the 34th and 41st parallels—barely survived the first winter: only 32 of the

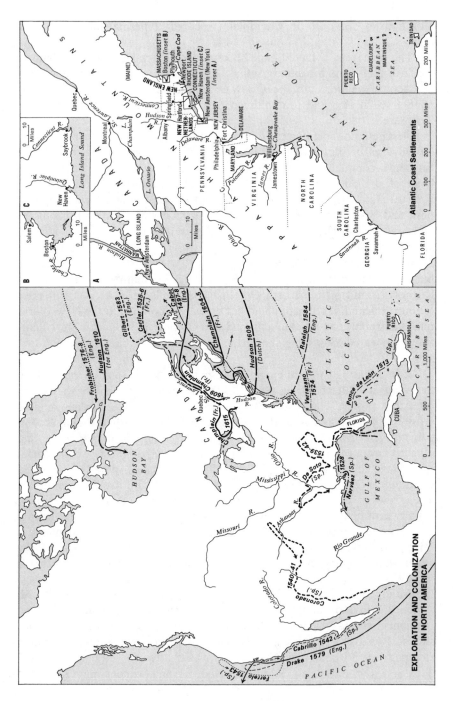

Atlantic Coast Settlements

EXPLORATION AND COLONIZATION
IN NORTH AMERICA

original 105 members of the all-male expedition were alive seven months later. The colonists suffered from disease, hostile natives, and their own incompetence; only when Captain John Smith, a member of the governing council but of relatively low social status among the gentlemen leaders, imposed near-dictatorial authority on the survivors did Jamestown's prospects improve. After Smith left Virginia in 1609 the colonists again faced possible extermination. Starvation in the winter of 1609–1610 drove one man to cannibalism, and by spring the majority were ready to forsake the experiment—especially since they had discovered neither gold nor a northwest passage. But the arrival of new settlers and supplies in 1610, the exportation of tobacco after 1612, and some major administrative changes soon ensured stability and prosperity. Significant too were the introduction in 1619 of representative government—important to Englishmen who contemplated migration to the New World—and the beginnings of Negro servitude—important, despite its inhumanity, to the economic future of North America.

Although Jamestown survived, the London Company did not. The costs of ships and supplies and manpower were high, returns on investment disappointingly low. Factional rifts within the London Company, and a frightful combination of Indian massacres and epidemics propelled the company into bankruptcy. In 1624 the crown revoked its charter. Henceforth Virginia was administered by a royal governor under the supervision of the imperial bureaucracy.

Despite the failure of private enterprise in Virginia, British colonization of North America continued to be largely a private affair. The role of the crown was essentially legal, issuing charters which granted to one or more individuals the right to settle and govern specified portions of the New World.* Included in each charter were a few limitations on the patentees' powers—customarily a reservation that their laws not conflict with the laws of England and that legislation be passed only with the consent of the freemen. Not specified was the definition of freeman or the extent to which local laws must conform to the spirit as well as the letter of English law.

These matters became important in the second major plantation in British America. The same charter that permitted the settlement in Jamestown had also created a Plymouth Company of Virginia with authority to settle in the area between the 38th and 45th parallels. The Plymouth Company's initial attempt was short-lived, and by the time settlement was again attempted in New England—as Europeans after 1614 began to call the northern part of British America—it was less as a commercial venture than as a religious hegira. At this point the issues of the rights of colonists

* Of course these charters did not bind either the aborigines or England's European rivals.

and their authority to restrict membership in their own communities became paramount.

Since the accession of James VI of Scotland to the throne of England in 1603, the Puritan movement for reform of the Church of England had made remarkable headway. Inspired by such men as William Ames, William Perkins, and John Preston, a growing number of Englishmen sought to "purify" the Anglican Church in the light of reforms carried out by John Calvin in Geneva and other Protestants on the Continent. But the times seemed to conspire against them. The accession in 1629 of William Laud to the See of London signaled increasing determination by orthodox Anglicans to ignore Puritan protests; depressions in 1619–1624 and 1629–1631 coincided too closely with widespread epidemics in 1624–1625 and 1631–1632; and the crown under James I and Charles I appeared increasingly arbitrary and callous. "This lande," observed John Winthrop in 1629, "growes wearye of her Inhabitants." For Winthrop and many other Puritans salvation lay in America: there they could set up a model church and state which by its very perfection would serve as example and inspiration to those who remained in England. The Bible would regain its divinely intended role, and an orderly society would observe God's will—both in the structure and spirit of its religious services and in the organization and behavior of its citizens.

Two practical considerations had to be met first: the acquisition of a desirable piece of land and the establishment of a political authority that would free the experiment from the baneful intrusion of Bishop Laud and other officials at home. Both conditions were fulfilled in 1629. In March of that year the Crown issued to a group of ninety noblemen and gentry, most of them Puritans, title to an extensive strip of land between the Merrimac and Charles rivers, previously controlled by the now defunct Plymouth Company. In August, twelve of the most prominent patentees agreed at Cambridge to move themselves and their families to the New World provided they could take their charter along and thus ensure control by resident directors—an opportunity made possible by the omission from the document of the usual stipulation that the annual meeting of the company's General Court must be in England. Armed with the charter, the company's stockholders and officers would be free to govern as they saw fit, protected by 3,000 miles of ocean from the prying eyes of William Laud and King Charles.

The Puritan leaders had good reason to believe that America would provide both isolation and a free rein. A decade earlier a radical sect of English Protestants, descriptively labeled Separatists, had taken up land immediately south of their own, at New Plymouth. These Pilgrims, as their historian and ofttime governor William Bradford called them, had moved earlier in the century from southeastern England to Leyden. There the Dutch had treated them well, but the Pilgrims' urge to remain English and their fear of a bleak economic future in Holland combined with the imminent resumption of war between the Netherlands and Spain to convince them that America offered a better haven.

From the time of their arrival at Cape Cod in the fall of 1620 the Pilgrims demonstrated that dissenters from the Church of England could live in America much as they pleased—although not without hardships and danger. The Pilgrims in their first year suffered almost as severely as had the settlers of Jamestown, for they encountered similar problems with disease, neighboring Indians, and an unfamiliar climate. The Plymouth settlers did not, however, risk defeating themselves through poor leadership or internal dissension. An agreement (the Mayflower Compact) signed by all heads of households and all free single men, vested authority in elected leaders. And more important, most of the substantial settlers were carrying out a mission on behalf of their brethren who remained for the time being in Holland. Two-thirds of the expedition who boarded their ship, the *Mayflower,* in London, may not have shared the religious convictions of the Separatists, but at least the "strangers" understood and accepted the purpose of the expedition. Under the benign leadership of William Bradford and William Brewster, the little colony at Plymouth slowly recovered from the losses of the first year and by 1630 boasted a population of about 400 fairly prosperous and contented souls. Their example boded well for the nonseparating Puritans of Massachusetts.

In the summer and fall of 1630 a score of ships carried more than 1,000 settlers to Massachusetts Bay. Within a few years English settlement—predominantly Puritan—had spread into the surrounding river valleys and the population had more than quadrupled. Before emigration was curtailed in the early 1640's by the outbreak of civil war in England, more than 20,000 Englishmen made the pilgrimage to New England. For the most part they came in families so that New England, unlike Virginia, rapidly acquired the demographic characteristics of the mother country. In many respects, however, New England was unique. Its relatively high level of education, its religious consensus on major issues if not on particulars, and its widespread prosperity marked the Puritan migration as the most successful effort in the first half of the seventeenth century to colonize the North American mainland.

Before England's civil war, the Interregnum, and the Restoration caused profound changes in the pattern of colonization, Massachusetts had evolved stable forms of civil and religious society. A two-house legislature had emerged by 1644, with a governor and deputy governor elected annually by the freemen. The freemen, in turn, had to be full members of the church, which admitted them in the belief that they were chosen by God for everlasting salvation. Thus the Bay Colony represented—outwardly at least—a true Bible Commonwealth, governed by men who tried to live in accordance with holy injunctions and to make sure that the ungodly did not undermine the experiment. During most of the 1630's and 1640's the governor was John Winthrop, a former attorney and lord of the Manor of Groton, who combined brilliantly the religious fervor of the Puritan movement with administrative talent and common sense. Largely as a result of his moderate leadership, Massachusetts survived internal dissensions and external threats, the former taking its most serious forms in the religious heterodoxies of Roger Williams and Anne Hutchinson, the latter appearing most critically in the efforts of some Englishmen to revoke the Bay Colony's charter.

In order to prevent what they feared would be the subversion of their "errand in the Wilderness," the Puritans banished Williams and Mrs. Hutchinson. They and their followers settled in lands to the south, where in 1637 a separate colony emerged under the awkward name of "Rhode Island and Providence Plantations." In one sense the colony was an off-shoot of Massachusetts, for most of its European inhabitants had originally migrated from England to the Bay Colony. They were, however, a dissident element, and their creation of a new colony was more a protest against the Puritan stronghold than an extension of it.

Not so Connecticut, which took root at about the same time as Rhode Island. Most of the early settlers in the Connecticut River valley were staunch Puritans, attracted by the fertile soil of the watershed and the network of streams that probed the interior and led to rich forests. During the mid-1630's several whole communities moved into Connecticut from Massachusetts; later migrants usually moved on to Connecticut after a brief sojourn in the Bay Colony, or sailed directly to Saybrook at the mouth of the river. A few years later, still another colony sprang up to the west of the Connecticut at the mouth of the Quinnipiac River. Under the leadership of Theophilus Eaton and the Reverend John Davenport, New Haven reflected Puritanism in its strictest form. However, New Haven never acquired a clear legal title, and by 1665 it had been absorbed into Connecticut.

Despite their loyalty to England, by the time of the civil war in the 1640's most Puritans who had settled in America were deeply rooted in their new homes. With the possible exception of Rhode Island, then plagued by dissension over political organization and land titles, the New England colonies were remarkably stable and prosperous. Connecticut, New Haven, and Plymouth all had representative governments, broad franchises (compared to England's), bustling trade with Europe and especially with the West Indies. More important, at least to the Puritan spokesmen, was the "New England Way" that had emerged. At bottom, the New England Way was English Independency. In its New World application, however, it evolved more rigid requirements for church membership and a more pervasive influence by the "visible saints," as the members of the New England churches called themselves. Throughout most of the seventeenth century they held a monopoly on the political franchise and on positions of prestige in New England.

One other major effort at settlement in British America succeeded before civil and religious strife descended on the home country. Roman Catholics, no less than Puritans, were unhappy with the Church of England and sought a means of promoting their faith without losing their freedom. In 1632, the Catholic George Calvert, a former secretary of state, received from Charles I a grant of land north of Virginia. George did not live to see his colony of Maryland established, but under the aegis of his eldest son Cecilius and the resident governorship of another son, Leonard, a settlement was established in 1633 at St. Mary's. In addition to the usual problems of creating a new society in the wilderness, from the beginning the colony at Maryland faced boundary disputes with neighboring Virginia and religious conflict between its Roman Catholic settlers and the more numerous Protestants. An Act of Toleration, passed in 1649 by the Maryland legislature at the suggestion of the proprietor, failed to ameliorate the antagonism, and by 1654 the act had been repealed and proscriptions again placed on papists. Partly as a side effect of the turmoil in England, Maryland after 1650 experienced friction between colonists and the proprietor. In addition the colonists suffered from continuing conflicts with Virginia and with Indians, and among themselves over theology and politics.

By 1650 the English wing of the Puritan movement had risen to power at home, decapitated Archbishop Laud and the king, and established a Puritan government under Oliver Cromwell. To some New Englanders it now seemed senseless to remain in the wilderness: the righteous now ruled in mother England and a man could be both patriotic and godly without self-exile. The result was intermittent migration from New England back to the homeland, a brief and curious break in the long history of the settlement of North America. In the end, the restoration of the Stuarts convinced many of the repatriots that New England had not been such a bad place after all, and they again took ship for the New World. But others, such as clergymen Hugh Peter, Thomas Welde, and Nathaniel Eaton, lived out their lives in the country of their birth. Meanwhile Virginians reacted very differently to the events in England. The rise of Puritan power at home appalled a colony that identified closely with the

Church of England and royal prerogative, and not until 1651, two years after the execution of the king, did Governor Berkeley submit to Cromwell's authority—then only in the face of a Parliamentary expedition. Most Virginians weathered the Commonwealth period in quiet anguish, covertly hoping for a revival of the Stuart monarchy. Neighboring Maryland, on the other hand, underwent a minor civil war of her own as Puritan, Catholic, and Anglican factions vied for supremacy.

The Restoration returned stability to most of British America and stirred new interest in settling the remaining unoccupied areas. Between Virginia and Spanish Florida lay several thousand square miles of territory, claimed by both Spain and England. In 1663 Charles II granted to eight proprietors all lands between the 31st and 38th parallels, from "sea to sea." Some settlement had already taken place in the scrub forests along the Virginia border, and the area soon became distinct, in social and ethnic composition as well as topographical features, from a second region of settlement farther south on the Ashley and Cooper rivers. The founding of Charleston in 1680 gave a cosmopolitan center to the latter section which quickly attracted large numbers of immigrants, especially from the West Indies. By the 1690's the area near Albemarle was known as North Carolina, although not until 1712 did it achieve a separate government. South Carolina in the meantime survived Indian wars and local rebellion. In neither region, however, could the proprietors, despite their legal ownership of the colony, resist the efforts of the settlers to break free from their paternalistic and exploitative hold. South Carolina ousted its last proprietary governor in 1719, and in 1729 both it and North Carolina became royal colonies.

A more successful effort to promote settlement under proprietary rule began north of Maryland in 1682. In that year William Penn gained title to a choice tract of land between New Jersey and Maryland, where he attempted a religious haven not unlike those of the Puritans and Catholics before him. Restoration England was more tolerant than Jacobean England, but there were limits, and the Quakers, who believed that God communicated with man through an "inner light" rather than through an established clergy, fell beyond them. By 1682 Penn had established Philadelphia as the nucleus of his "Holy Experiment" and had issued a Frame of Government which offered a tolerant and liberal administration. Quakers from both England and neighboring colonies made up the most influential groups of settlers, but Penn needed income and offered plots to all comers on attractive terms. Soon the fertile lands of the colony were filling with settlers of all faiths from England and the Continent, lured by promotional tracts and recruiting agents who made promises only slightly mixed with hyperbole.

The settlement of Pennsylvania under English auspices illustrates not only the ethnic mix that emerged in British America but as well the international rivalry that accompanied the European conquest of North America. Some of the land under Penn's jurisdiction had once belonged to the Dutch and even earlier to the Swedes. Indeed, Pennsylvania was the former Swedish outpost on the Delaware River, Fort Christina. For a time its settlers had been on friendly terms with the Dutch colony to the north, but in 1655 Governor Peter Stuyvesant of New Netherland took possession of New Sweden in the name of the States General. Although most of the settlers chose to remain where they were, they became politically subordinate to the Dutch colony on the Hudson.

The conquest of New Sweden marked the last act of expansion by the Dutch in North America. Their colonial enterprise had grown slowly from a few trading posts on the upper Hudson until it included footholds in present-day New Jersey, Delaware, and Connecticut. They suffered encroachments by the English on Long Island and the Connecticut Valley in the 1630's and 1640's, and less than ten years after taking over Fort Christina, Governor Stuyvesant had to surrender all the Dutch possessions to the English.

The conquest of New Netherland in 1664 brought England important but largely underveloped territory. The Dutch had not conceived New Netherland as a haven for religious outcasts or the poor, for the home country had few of either. To enterprising Hollanders, an outpost in North America should serve as part of the Dutch commercial empire; it held vast deposits of fur, fish, timber products, and potentially, food crops. Settlers would be welcome but were not at first deemed essential. They proved scarce, in fact, for Englishmen were reluctant to migrate to New Netherland where they would have to accept Dutch rule, and the patroon system of land distribution offered little to the aspiring yeoman. During the Dutch period, settlement was mostly confined to eastern Long Island, Manhattan, the Hudson Valley, and Albany, for the powerful Iroquois Confederacy of Indian tribes controlled upper New York, thus closing it to colonization. Along the Hudson River a few large patroonships, farmed by tenants, were established but the great age of settlement in New York came late in the eighteenth century, under English rule.

In the process of reassessing their domestic situation after the Restoration of 1660, British leaders also took a long look at the organization of Britain's overseas outposts. For the first time since Englishmen sailed to the New World, a serious attempt was made to integrate and systematize the empire. During the remainder of the Stuart regime and in the years immediately following the Glorious Revolution, the imperial government made important and for the most part well-intentioned efforts to recast British America into a more efficient and governable polity.

Two basic priorities appear to have guided royal policy toward the colonies between 1660 and 1700. First, and most pressing, was the need to make sure that activities of both the colonies and the mother country were coordinated for the benefit of the whole empire. Accordingly, between 1660 and 1696 Parliament passed a series of Navigation Acts designed to keep the carrying trade of the empire in British bottoms. Cargo between England and the colonies had to be in British built, owned, and manned vessels; and an ever lengthening list of "enumerated goods" could be shipped only to another colony or to England, regardless of their ultimate destination. The Crown appointed customs collectors to levy duties in colonial ports and established a complex system of bonds and officials to ensure compliance. In the eighteenth century Parliament passed additional trade restrictions aimed at curbing colonial manufacturing and at tightening further the imperial economic system.

England's second priority after 1660 was the need to end the proliferation of small colonies and to place all of them under royal control or at least under more restrictive charters than those enjoyed by the early proprietors and corporations. In one of his last important acts, Charles II created the Dominion of New England, a federation of the New England colonies, New York, and New Jersey. Such drastic consolidation required the revocation of several royal charters, including the Bay Colony's charter of 1629, but in the interests of imperial efficiency and discipline, this was done. The Dominion was overthrown by the Glorious Revolution, but William and Mary seized the opportunity presented by the confusion to continue, though less drastically, the trend toward tightening royal political control. When Massachusetts, without a charter since 1684, applied for a new one, the colony was not permitted to return to its former condition of semi-independence. The charter of 1691 provided for a royally appointed governor, and at the same time added Maine and Plymouth to the Bay Colony's holdings, thus accomplishing both consolidation and centralization. The proprietary colonies of Pennsylvania and Maryland were also put under royal control, although both regained their original charters after protracted negotiations.

By the end of the seventeenth century, the colonies of North America had advanced dramatically since the first precarious settlements at Quebec and Jamestown. In 1700 there were perhaps 275,000 inhabitants of European and African stock. Many of them were American born, for large families proved an asset rather than a liability in the spacious farmlands of North America, but throughout the colonial period the flow of Europeans and Africans to American shores outnumbered the natural increase. Between 1607 and 1700 perhaps 200,000 Europeans and 25,000 Africans made the long passage to America, most of them to the British colonies. British America attracted mainly Englishmen, although a few Frenchmen,

Italians, Swiss, Germans, Welshmen, and Scots went too. Settlers in New France were almost exclusively French.

Patterns of migration changed dramatically in the eighteenth century. Between 1700 and 1763, Britishers from Scotland, Wales, and Ireland arrived in ever increasing numbers, seeking the peace and prosperity denied them at home. Settlement in North America had now become feasible for the masses, not merely the most hardy and discontent. At the same time, deep distress in several European lands encouraged continental migration. Lured by the propaganda pamphlets and speeches of "Newlanders" or "crimps" sent by American proprietors and land developers, Germans, Scandinavians, Swiss, Belgians, and Frenchmen by the thousands signed terms of indenture in return for passage to America. Some turned back before reaching a port town; others rapidly became disillusioned with the New World and returned to their homelands. Most stayed, however, and they gave to North America a peculiarly international character. Estimates are at best educated guesses, but fragments of evidence suggest that in 1763 about 50 per cent of the population was English, 18 per cent Scotch and Scot-Irish, 18 per cent African, 6 per cent German, 3 per cent Dutch, and the rest French, Spanish, Swedish, and other European stocks. But already intermarriage was making America somewhat of a "melting pot."

Religious variety represented as important a dimension of migration as did the variety of ethnic strains. From the British Isles came Scotch Presbyterians (both from Scotland and from Ulster, Ireland), Anglicans, Puritans (who by the eighteenth century were more frequently known by their organizational preferences as Presbyterians and Congregationalists), Quakers, and a few Baptists and Roman Catholics. From France came some Catholics and many Huguenots. German groups included Lutherans, Moravians, Dunkards, Schwenkfelders, Mennonites, and Amish. Sephardic Jews migrated from Spain and Portugal. Religious variety in turn generated pressure for toleration, a condition reached in most British colonies before 1763. It was an imperfect toleration, however, as the established churches in many areas imposed political limitations and social stigma on other denominations. Roman Catholics in particular continued to suffer from legal restrictions on voting and officeholding; and as late as the 1760's an Anglican missionary was roundly abused by Protestant dissenters in the Carolina backcountry.

Unlike British America, French Canada did not become a refuge for religious dissenters. Strict laws limited emigration from France to those who were theologically and politically orthodox. French Huguenots, most of whom undoubtedly would have remained loyal to their mother country had they been allowed to settle in her colony, were forced to expatriate themselves to the British colonies or remain at home. Furthermore, few

Frenchmen of any religious persuasion were keen on moving to the cold climate and rocky soil of New France. Some, of course, did go, but never enough to make the French part of North America a major place of settlement for the many thousands of Europeans who migrated to the New World. And throughout the colonial period, settlers in New France found a comparatively rigid society, heavy with feudal vestiges and dominated by church and government officials whose decisions were often dictated by the home country.

Population figures reflected the effectiveness of England's colonizing policies and her growing international power. In 1625 there were perhaps 500 settlers in Canada, 200 in New Netherland, and 2,000 in the English colonies of Virginia and Plymouth. By 1650 the figures were 2,000, 5,000, and 100,000 respectively. Fifty years later the Dutch settlements had been absorbed into the English sphere; the inhabitants of the English colonies then totaled about a quarter of a million while New France had perhaps 20,000. At the time of England's conquest of Canada in 1763, the population of British America numbered nearly two and a quarter million, that of New France less than 100,000.

Not all of the disparity in population can be attributed to differences in policy or systems of passage. More important were contrasts in climate and soil and in the verdict of arms. Yet the very fact that Sweden, the Netherlands, and France were unable to expand their original footholds into the choicest regions, and that they eventually lost everything to Great Britain, stems in large part from their failure to attract enough immigrants to offer effective resistance against the relentless British expansion. Throughout the seventeenth and eighteenth centuries larger neighbors swallowed smaller. The Dutch took New Sweden in 1655, England absorbed New Netherland in 1664, and finally took New France and Spanish Florida in 1763. By the eve of the American Revolution only two European powers held territory on the North American mainland, England controlling all lands east of the Mississippi, Spain all to the west; and Spain could hardly be said to have settled her territory. In all of the trans-Mississippi north of the Rio Grande there were only a few hundred residents of Spanish origin, most of them clustered in Catholic missions. Patterns of population would soon dictate the termination of Spanish control as the United States expanded westward in the nineteenth century.

In the century and a half before the American Revolution, the powers of Europe engaged in intermittent warfare on the new continent. Most of the conflicts were offshoots of European wars, but from time to time the colonies themselves initiated clashes. Thus settlement of North America gave rise to new international hostilities at the same time it served as a battle ground for nations already at odds. This proved especially true in the late seventeenth and early eighteenth centuries as settlers from England and Spain in the southern part of the continent and France and England in the northern segment vied for territory, trade, and the allegiance of Indian tribes.

The Indians played an integral part in most intercolonial conflicts, often merging their own feuds with those of their white neighbors. As early as 1608 Samuel de Champlain allied himself with Canadian tribes against the Iroquois of New York; settlers in Virginia, Plymouth, and Connecticut also took part in battles that had begun as intertribal hostilities. Occasionally too there were bloody conflicts within a European colony between its white settlers and one or more tribes (as in Virginia in 1622 and 1644, New Netherland in the 1640's and 1660's, New England in 1675), and there might have been more had not the native population been relatively small, materially unsophisticated, and rent by deep intertribal hostilities. Several tribes did attempt to prevent the intruders from gaining prized land and trade advantages, but for every tribe or faction that stood to lose, another stood to gain—in allies, new trade, or the booty of war. Almost invariably therefore, Indians fought on both sides of New World conflicts. And almost invariably, too, the Indians lost more heavily in numbers and land than did the Europeans whenever the races clashed. That proved true when the conflicts focused clearly on friction between the two ethnic groups—as in New England's King Philip's War of 1675–76—or when ethnic conflict entered the struggle only tangentially, as in Virginia's contemporaneous Bacon's Rebellion.

Not all relations between white men and red involved bloodshed, but too often they did. The efforts to promote peaceful cooperation between the races by men of good will such as the Puritan missionary and linguist John Eliot, the Pennsylvania proprietor William Penn, and Jesuit missionaries like Isaac Jogues in upper New York and Canada often went for naught. But the most lethal of all aspects of interracial contacts was the impact of European diseases, especially smallpox, which struck heavily among the native population. Most of the tribes encountered by white men during the first century and a half of colonization either succumbed to disease or retreated inland. One of the lasting tragedies of European colonization was the inability of diverse racial groups to exploit their mutual needs rather than their potential frictions. In the end the less numerous and less sophisticated society crumbled before the aggressive expansion of history's largest migration.

Throughout the seventeenth and early eighteenth centuries migrants to North America usually sought land along the bays and river valleys where access to the interior and communication with Europe were relatively easy. The sites of earliest settlement were the St. Lawrence, Chesapeake, Delaware, Hudson, Connecticut, and Charles; later Cape Fear and Savannah became secondary centers. It was on the Savannah that Georgia, England's final American colony, was founded in the 1730's. From the valleys colonists pushed relentlessly inland in search of cheaper land and more abundant game. By 1763 the frontier of British settlement had reached the foothills of the Appalachians. In the plantation areas of the south, rivers continued to dominate the pattern of settlement; smaller waterways became choice sites after the larger ones had been preempted. Farther north the colonists soon moved away from river valleys into the hill country, where roads replaced rivers as the main channels of internal communication. After 1763 in the trans-Appalachian region, rivers would again become the principal routes of settlement.

Partly because of the need for mutual protection and assistance, but mostly because of habits deeply ingrained by European experience, settlers in British America clustered in small villages centered on a church building and a common grazing field. Regional patterns varied widely, for the migrants brought different modes of life with them, but the principal concern throughout most of the colonies was to blend the social and political advantages of closely placed homesteads with the economic benefits of privately tilled fields stretching out from the village on all sides. Gradually larger villages emerged along the coast to serve as focal points of trade and communications. New Amsterdam by 1660 contained 2,400 inhabitants and provided a link between the Hudson Valley holdings of the Dutch West India Company and the home country. Boston performed a similar role for Puritan New England. Later in the seventeenth century Philadelphia and Charleston emerged as important centers of population. Farther inland towns like Albany, Springfield, Williamsburg, and Hartford achieved regional importance. Meanwhile Quebec and Montreal in French Canada tied the interior of the upper continent to the St. Lawrence River.

The cities of North America served not only as important centers of trade and communication but also as seedbeds for the emerging culture of the New World. During the seventeenth century American literature and art were imitative. During the eighteenth century, however, they began to show distinctively American characteristics. Whereas the writings of seventeenth-century authors had been largely didactic—histories, sermons, political pamphlets—in the eighteenth century there emerged the first tentative signs of uniquely American expression in belles-lettres, poetry, and even in portraiture. *The American Magazine,* despite its brief career, serves as a sign of native literary gropings, while Peter Harrison's design for Newport's Redwood Library and the portraits of colonial gentlemen by John Singleton Copley and Benjamin West reveal promising beginnings in architecture and art. Still, the civilization of North America before 1763 remained heavily dependent on England. Migrants continued to think of their colonies as outposts of the British Empire. Except for customs and skills brought as cultural baggage from their homelands, little thought was given to artistic expression. The dawn of a creative American culture would have to await the Revolutionary era.

In political, religious, and economic life, too, the settlers of North America leaned heavily on previous experience. Anachronistic ideas and forms were often discarded; new practices frequently emerged to herald the coming of a new society. But the Old World pattern clung tenaciously.

Because the bulk of migrants to British America in the seventeenth century came from England, the political structure of the colonies assumed a strongly English flavor. Each colony, in fact, became a miniature of the mother country: a governor and council represented the executive authority, a two-house legislature (the upper house serving also as council) became a miniature Parliament, while town and country governments closely resembled the local governments of England. Similarly, a sequence of local and colony-wide courts provided judicial systems. But in neither legislative nor judicial matters did the colony have final say; the Privy Council in England reserved the right to disallow acts and decisions of the colonial governments. New France, by contrast, had no representative assembly and no formal institutions of local government. A governor and council, both appointed by the crown, ruled the French territories, aided by an intendant, who had wide fiscal, judicial, and administrative authority, and a bishop, who had broad control over religious matters.

British America also differed from the mother country and from New France in the extent of its political franchise. In most of the English colonies, as in England, an adult free male could vote if he held property above a specified minimum—usually land earning 40 shillings per annum. In America that was not a difficult minimum to meet, and perhaps as many as 75 per cent of adult freemen were eligible to vote for colonial legislators and officials, in two of the colonies even for the governor. In some colonies the franchise was even broader on the local level. There were, however, religious as well as property restrictions in many colonies, discriminating in most cases against non-Protestants but occasionally against radical Protestant sects as well. In America, as in Europe, a clean line between politics and religion was seldom discernible. Disputes between rival sects formed a major part of the social turmoil of the times.

During the seventeenth century religious conflict usually took isolated episodic forms—as for example the persecution of Quakers in New England, discrimination against Puritans in Virginia, and anti-Catholic measures in all colonies. Important as these episodes were to the individuals involved, they were infrequent, for each major religious group had one or more colonies in its control where its devotees could enjoy freedom from persecution, and incidentally make life uncomfortable for other sects. By the eighteenth century, however, the ethnic and denominational exclusiveness of the previous century had largely disappeared; now Anglicans and Presbyterians, and even Jews, rubbed shoulders in the major cities. Much of the old hostility had died out. Some of it was replaced, however, by bitter rivalry within denominations during the Great Awakening of 1730–1760. First in the middle colonies, then in New England and eventually in the South, waves of religious enthusiasm rolled over areas in which the fervor of the seventeenth century had grown stagnant. Before it ended, America's first revival had contributed importantly to the growth of colleges, the spread of egalitarian ideas, and the lessening of clerical influence. At the same time it had fragmented most of the larger denominations—especially the Congregationalists, Presbyterians, Baptists, and Dutch Reformed—into Old and New factions, while the Anglicans saw many of their followers lean toward Methodism. Only the Quakers, centered in Pennsylvania, and the Roman Catholics, predominantly in Canada and Maryland, escaped the divisive effects of the revival.

The Great Awakening served notice that the settlement of North America was no longer simply a transit of civilization from the Old World to the New. To be sure, the revival and its opposite but parallel movement, the Enlightenment, drew heavily on European influences. But the American experience also fed ideas and attitudes back to Europe, where, for example, the writings of the Congregational clergyman Jonathan Edwards received serious attention. Furthermore, the revival had been initiated largely by native Americans—Gilbert Tennent, Samuel Davies, John Davenport, and Edwards; it was only after they had prepared the ground that the greatest preacher of the Awakening, George Whitefield, could journey from England to spellbind vast audiences from Massachusetts to Georgia. Finally, the Awakening, with an important assist from the liberal ideas of the Enlightenment, helped pave the way for the disestablishment of religion. At the beginning of the eighteenth century only Rhode Island, New Jersey, Pennsylvania, and Delaware did not support the dominant church out of public taxes. By the 1760's a move to discontinue such support was under way in most colonies.

Another indication that European colonies in North America were groping toward maturity and perhaps independence could be found in their remarkable economic growth. During the seventeenth century the infant colonies often had struggled with varying success to find feasible modes of production and trade, and the way was marked by frequent commercial failures. But each gradually found economic stability and a measure of prosperity. Canada, despite the meagerness of its population, made healthy profits in furs, fish, and lumber products. New England followed much the same pattern, though it added a lively trade in livestock and rum. The colonies of the middle area specialized in grains and livestock. Maryland and Virginia tied themselves to tobacco, for which the market in Europe was extensive, although chronically depressed. North Carolina excelled in lumber products and livestock, while South Carolina raised large quantities of rice and indigo. Exports from the colonies never exceeded imports in value, largely because the needs of a frontier society for manufactured goods and finished products were insatiable. The colonies' potential for manufacturing increased steadily, but the mercantile laws of England and France sought to prevent the growth of industries that would compete with their own, and investment capital was lacking in the frontier society.

Equally inhibiting to the growth of American industry was the persistent shortage of labor. High wages kept profits low. Paradoxically, the labor shortage also gave rise to two of the most distinctive features of the settlement of North America: indentured servitude and Negro slavery. During the seventeenth century most colonizing companies and their political successors, the provincial governments, lured settlers by granting fifty acres of land to anyone who paid the passage of indigent men, women, and children. The migrant, in return, signed an agreement to serve a stipulated number of years to the investor or his assignee. This system provided much of the manpower of British America's first century. In the eighteenth century the lures were increased by the promise of land to the laborer himself rather than to the investor who paid his passage; the latter made his profit by selling the worker's indenture to an assignee for more than the cost of passage. In addition, indentured servants received on expiration of their terms certain clothes, tools, and sometimes cattle.

Negro slaves made the passage to America under far less favorable conditions. Packed into cramped and unhealthy slave ships and sold on delivery to the highest bidder, the Negroes—some coming directly from Africa, others by way of the West Indies—were an important element in the economy of the southern states by the late seventeenth century. Some of the early blacks were freed after a period of service, and there were scattered attempts to end the forced importation of labor, but the practice persisted, and with it arose a system of permanent, inheritable servitude that would blight North America for generations. By 1763 Negroes, the vast majority of them bound for life, constituted about 15 per cent of the population north of the Rio Grande.

Despite the presence of Negro and Indian minorities isolated from the white culture of British America, there emerged by the mid-eighteenth century a society distinctively American—in fact the degraded role of black men and red men was a mark of that society. Other characteristics, as noted by European observers, were the high level of education, prosperity, widespread political participation, ethnic and religious variety, and the absence of rigid class divisions. All of these features were relative, not absolute, but when taken together and blended with the New World's spacious geography and varied climate, many contemporaries predicted that British America—and perhaps Canada—would one day become independent. But such prospects seemed unlikely so long as the colonies depended on their mother countries for protection from rival empires. Then, primarily as a result of the prolonged contest between European nations for control of North America, that necessity suddenly changed.

From its earliest exploration, North America had served as an international battle ground as well as a land of peaceful settlement. Englishman and Spaniard clashed frequently along the southern borders, while to the north, French and British colonists seemed forever at each other's throats. As early as 1613 an English squadron attacked French posts; in 1689 France and England began a protracted series of battles which developed, in most instances, as offshoots of larger conflicts in Europe. As a result of King William's War (War of the League of Augsburg) from 1689 to 1713, Queen Anne's War (War of the Spanish Succession) from 1702 to 1713, King George's War (War of the Austrian Succession) in the 1740's, and finally the French and Indian War (Seven Years' War), France lost her hold on the mainland of North America. Britain's victories and the Peace of Paris of 1763 relegated French control to two small islands in the mouth of the St. Lawrence River and the Caribbean islands of Guadeloupe and Martinique; Spain, at the same time, ceded Florida to the English. Thus almost two centuries after Sir Humphrey Gilbert's attempts to plant English colonies in the New World, His Britannic Majesty could claim control of the entire North American continent east of the Mississippi, with a population of almost 3 million persons representing nearly every ethnic and religious group in Europe. But the very size and diversity of the mainland colonies, together with the fall of New France, set the stage for the disintegration of England's vast American empire.

For Further Reading

Boorstin, Daniel J., *The Americans: The Colonial Experience.*
Craven, Wesley Frank, *The Colonies in Transition, 1660–1713.*
Morison, Samuel Eliot (ed.), *The Parkman Reader: From the Works of Francis Parkman.*
Pomfret, John, *Founding the American Colonies, 1583–1660.*
Thwaites, Reuben Gold, *France in America, 1497–1763.*
Ver Steeg, Clarence, *The Formative Years, 1607–1763.*
Wright, Louis B., *The Cultural Life of the American Colonies 1607–1763.*

The Enlightenment

21   The Scientific Revolution

Human skills for obtaining food and shelter are not inherited biologically. They are fruits of more or less reliable knowledge concerning how various things in the environment behave. And like the knowledge on which they are based, they are transmitted to succeeding generations through socially instituted processes. Some knowledge of this sort, however primitive it may be, is clearly indispensable for human survival, and no society could exist which lacked it completely. Were every item of such knowledge counted as a scientific achievement, science would be coeval with the human race.

But such an undiscriminating use of the word "science" would be incongruous with the historical meanings of the word, and would, in particular, fail to identify what is distinctive of modern science. Albert Einstein once characterized Western science as made up out of two basic ingredients: deductively organized theories formulating, often in mathematical terms, general relations of dependence between types of events; and systematic experimentation to suggest and test the theories. However, science so understood is a relatively recent achievement. Logical proof and demonstrative mathematics were invented by the ancient Greeks, who were also the first to construct mathematical theories for various classes of phenomena. Moreover, while a tradition of experimental study, especially in the arts and crafts, can be traced back to Greek antiquity and even beyond, the systematic use of controlled experiments to assess the worth of theories did not take place until the late Renaissance.

In any event, an experimentally controlled mathematical science of nature, resembling in essentials the science of our own day, did not become firmly established as a continuing institution in Western society until the seventeenth and eighteenth centuries. The new findings and habits of mind that resulted from scientific inquiry during those years and the century preceding them—especially in astronomy, physics, and biology—marked a major turning point in human history. They undermined the medieval view

B.C.	4th cent.	Establishment of the two major philosophical schools of Greek antiquity by Plato (427–347 B.C.) and Aristotle (384–322 B.C.)
	3d cent.	Outstanding developments in mathematics, astronomy and physics, among others by Euclid of Alexandria (330–260 B.C.), Aristarchus of Samos (310–230 B.C.), Archimedes of Syracuse (287–212 B.C.), and Apollonius of Perga (c. 220 B.C.)
A.D.	2d cent.	The synthesis of Greek astronomical thought, presented in his *Almagest,* by Claudius Ptolemy of Alexandria (A.D. 127–151)
	8th–12th cents.	Development and spread of Arabic science and philosophy; eventually the transmission of Aristotelian thought to the West by Islamic scholars, in particular by Averroes (1126–1198)
	13th cent.	Assimilation of Aristotelian philosophy into Christian doctrine in the epochal writings of St. Thomas Aquinas (1225–1274)
	1543	Publication of *De Revolutionibus Orbium Coelestium* by Nicholas Copernicus (1473–1543), also of *Concerning the Fabric of the Human Body* by Andrea Vesalius (1514–1564)
	1600	Publication of *Concerning the Magnet* by William Gilbert (1540–1603)
	1603	Founding of the Accademia dei Lincei in Rome
	1605	Publication of *Advancement of Learning* by Francis Bacon (1561–1626)
	1609	Publication of *Astronomia Nova* by Johannes Kepler (1571–1630), containing his statement of the first two laws of planetary motion
	1610	Publication of *Sidereal Messenger* by Galileo Galilei (1564–1642), describing his telescopic observations of the heavens
	1619	Publication of Kepler's *Harmonia Mundi,* an-

nouncing his discovery of the third law of planetary motion

1628   Publication of *On the Motion of the Heart and Blood in Animals* by William Harvey (1578–1657)

1632   Publication of Galileo's *Two Chief Systems of the World*

1637   Publication of the *Discourse on Method* by René Descartes (1596–1650)

1638   Publication of Galileo's *Discourses and Demonstrations Concerning Two New Sciences*

1647   Revival of the ancient Epicurean atomic philosophy by Pierre Gassendi (1592–1655)

1657   Founding of the Accademia del Cimento in Florence

1660   Publication of *New Experiments Physico-Mechanical Touching the Spring of the Air* by Robert Boyle (1627–1691)

1662   Founding of the Royal Society of London

1666   Founding of the French Academy of Science

1676   Determination of the finite velocity of light by the Danish astronomer Olaus Roemer (1644–1710)

1677   Discovery with the microscope of the existence of male spermatozoa by Anton van Leeuwenhoek (1632–1723)

1678   A wave theory of light proposed by Christian Huygens (1629–1695), subsequently developed systematically in his *Treatise on Light* (1690)

1687   Publication of *Principia Mathematica Philosophiae Naturalis* by Isaac Newton (1642–1727)

1704   Publication of Newton's *Opticks,* some of whose basic ideas had been communicated to the Royal Society in 1672

1789   Publication of *Traité Elémentaire de Chimie* by Antoine Lavoisier (1743–1794)

of the world and man's place in it by making untenable the Aristotelian physics and cosmology on which that view was in large measure based; they challenged entrenched conceptions of human reason and of how the investigation of nature must be conducted; and they produced tools of intellectual and physical analysis that eventually transformed the human scene almost beyond recognition.

These revolutionary changes did not take place suddenly or appear from nowhere. They owed much not only to the scientific achievements of Greek civilizations in antiquity, but also to the contributions of Arabic, late medieval, and early Renaissance thinkers. The great treatises of Greek science were lost to Western students for many centuries, and it seems unlikely that had they been lost permanently natural science anything like our current one would have come into being. However, those treatises did become available to the West gradually, in large measure from Islamic sources. In consequence, the centers of learning that were established in various parts of Europe during the twelfth and thirteenth centuries were heavily influenced by Greco-Arabic views in natural philosophy. But by the close of the fifteenth century the best scholars at these and other universities—men such as Robert Grossetest, John Buridan, and Nicolas Oreseme—were not mere expository commentators on ancient scientific texts, but creative thinkers who anticipated mathematical and physical ideas that came to be employed fruitfully only a century or two later.

The revolution in men's conception of their world occurred most dramatically in astronomy and mechanics. But science includes much more than these disciplines, and the scientific developments that transformed the medieval outlook took place on a broad front. But since it would be impossible in brief space to describe all these developments, which included such important discoveries as the circulation of the blood by William Harvey (1578–1657), the existence of microscopic organisms by Anton van Leeuwenhoek (1632–1723), and the nature of chemical combustion by Antoine Lavoisier (1743–1794), it is with the emergence of modern astronomy and mechanics that the present chapter is mainly concerned.

The expanding commercial economies of the Renaissance generated problems—such as the need for improved methods in navigation or in civil and military engineering—adequate answers to which required a sound theory of motion. Stimulated by these problems, and inspired by the writings of Archimedes that became generally available in the sixteenth century, a number of thinkers sought to construct such a theory. Although it is generally agreed that it was Galileo Galilei (1564–1642) who laid the foundations of the modern science of mechanics, there is also no doubt that he was heavily indebted to the work of these predecessors.

Ptolemy's geocentric theory of the heavens was a scientific achievement of the first magnitude. It illustrated the power of mathematical analysis to account systematically for the bewilderingly complex apparent motions of celestial bodies, though on the assumption that their actual motions must have uniform speeds on circular orbits. The apparent motions of the planets do not conform to this requirement. Relative to the fixed stars, at certain times they seem to move forward rapidly, at other times to stand still, and at still other times to have a retrograde motion. To account for such anomalous planetary motions, Ptolemy introduced a number of ingenious mathematical constructions, among others the notion of epicyclic motion. According to this idea, a planet moves with uniform speed in a circle, but the center of this circle (the epicycle) may in turn be moving uniformly on the circumference of another circle (the deferent circle); thus the apparent oscillatory motion of a planet could be shown to result from a combination of such uniform circular motions.

The central ideas of the Ptolemaic theory were simple enough. However, agreement between those ideas and the known data on celestial motions could be obtained only by introducing many additional but arbitrary assumptions. For example, the number of epicycles required to account for the data had increased to 79 by the sixteenth century. Yet when Copernicus (1473–1543) developed his alternative theory, according to which the sun was at rest while the earth and the planets revolved around it, no new observations were available to him that challenged the Ptolemaic system but supported the heliocentric theory. Indeed, the observations at his disposal did not confirm some consequences implied by his theory, such as the conclusion that Venus ought to have phases or that there should be apparent shifts in the positions of the fixed stars. What Copernicus found unsatisfactory in the Ptolemaic system was the diversity of its supplementary assumptions, and the absence of any general principle which integrated them into a unified whole. He did not doubt that celestial motions must embody a simple, coherent order; and he believed his heliocentric theory to be true, because the logical structure of its ideas seemed to him to reflect that order.

De Revolutionibus Orbium Coelestium was published in 1543, when Copernicus was on his deathbed. For many years the book created little excitement, and was not felt to be a threat to the dominant scientific and religious conceptions of the world. Indeed, it was construed by many in consonance with the interpretation advanced in the preface, which was assumed to have been written by Copernicus though in fact it had been added by Osiander, his editor. On this interpretation, the heliocentric theory was not a new account of the actual physical organization of the heavens, but just a convenient device for simplifying astronomical calculations. Moreover, the Copernican hypothesis of a moving earth appeared to have consequences that were incompatible with what were generally regarded as the empirically well-supported principles of Aristotelian physics. Accordingly, until an alternative physical theory became available, and until fresh observational evidence was obtained confirming the heliocentric theory, men continued to accept the Ptolemaic conception of celestial motions. The Copernican notion that the earth is a moving planet was an important step in disproving the Aristotelian view that celestial and terrestrial objects and processes are utterly different in kind. But the successful undermining of this central thesis of medieval cosmology had to wait upon the work of Galileo, Kepler, and Newton.

The hold of this cosmology on men's minds was seriously weakened by Galileo's exploration of the skies, and by his vigorous defense of the Copernican theory. On learning that by combining two lenses a lensmaker in Holland was able to see remote objects more clearly, Galileo constructed a telescope with which he examined the heavens. His discoveries, published in his *Sidereal Messenger* in 1610, were astounding. He found that the moon's surface was not smooth but mountainous; that in agreement with Copernican theory Venus had phases; that the sun's face was blemished with moving dark spots, with the sun itself having a monthly axial rotation; and that Jupiter had four satellites revolving around it, thus providing a visible illustration of the Copernican conception of the solar system. These findings were a grave challenge to the established belief that unlike the earth celestial bodies suffer no alteration; and they made it difficult to construe the heliocentric theory as nothing more than a set of convenient rules for simplifying astronomical computations.

Moreover, Galileo also tried to construct a theory of mechanics that was fully compatible with, as Aristotelian physics was not, the assumption of a moving earth. In his great *Dialogue on the Two Chief Systems of the World, the Ptolemaic and the Copernican,* published in 1632, he showed that objections to this assumption, which were based on the supposed inconsistency between observed facts and consequences drawn from the assumption, were mistaken, since those consequences depended upon a false theory of motion. In developing the argument in the *Dialogue* Galileo complied formally with the injunction issued by the Church to discuss the heliocentric theory simply as a useful mathematical hypothesis. But his presentation of the issues was overwhelmingly favorable to the Copernican system as a physical theory of celestial motions, and no one was really in doubt about his convictions. He was compelled by the Inquisition to denounce the Copernican theory as heretical, and the *Dialogue* as well as the astronomical writings of Copernicus and Kepler were placed on the Index, where they remained until 1835.

A further major break with traditional assumptions about the constitution of the heavens was made by Johannes Kepler (1571–1630), who combined exceptional mathematical gifts and a meticulous respect for careful observations with a mystical Neoplatonic faith in the existence of a determinate mathematical order in nature. Kepler was an enthusiastic Copernican, in part because the heliocentric theory accorded with his own religious veneration of the sun. He found, however, that the positions of the planets, as observed with unprecedented precision by his one-time master Tycho Brahe (1546–1601), did not agree with their positions as calculated from the Copernican theory; and he devoted several decades of unflagging work to a search for the correct planetary orbits. After years of unsuccessful attempts to devise a combination of circular motions that would generate the observed planetary paths, the idea came to him that perhaps the planets move on ovals rather than on circles. Kepler had mastered the theory of conic sections which Apollonius developed in the third century B.C.; and he therefore tried to fit Brahe's data on the positions of the planet Mars to an elliptical orbit. This attempt eventually proved to be successful, and in 1609 he announced the great discovery known as Kepler's First Law, according to which the planets move on elliptic orbits with the sun at one focus. His Second Law of planetary motion, that the line from the sun to a planet sweeps out equal areas in equal times, was also discovered that year. His Third Law, on the relation between the time of one complete period of a planet and its average distance from the sun, was discovered ten years later.

Thus Kepler's Neoplatonic faith was confirmed. His three laws accounted for the apparent motions of the planets in a much simpler and more accurate manner than did the Copernican system, though at the cost of abandoning the assumption Copernicus (and indeed most of Kepler's own contemporaries) shared with ancient science that only uniform circular motion is appropriate for heavenly bodies. Kepler's labors thus helped forge a method of inquiry into nature that is characteristic of modern science—a method that combines the mathematical analysis of quantitatively specified properties with the scrupulous testing of the analysis by accurate observation.

However, as has already been noted, the conception of the earth as a rotating planet required the creation of a new dynamics (or theory of the conditions of motion) before that assumption could seem compatible with the supposed facts of common experience. The foundations of modern dynamical theory were laid by Galileo, though he built on the work of many previous thinkers, and are contained in his *Mathematical Discourses and Demonstrations Concerning Two New Sciences*—a book he completed after his banishment to a country estate by the Inquisition and published in

1638. The radical difference between Galileo's analysis of motion and Aristotle's is best seen in their accounts of bodies moving with uniform velocity (i.e., with constant speeds along straight lines). In Aristotle's view, a terrestrial body can remain in motion only if some force continues to act on it, but in Galileo's analysis, no force is needed to maintain the uniform velocity of a body. Accordingly, although in his discussion of such motion Galileo did not get the matter entirely right, he was in effect the discoverer of the principle of inertia, which Newton eventually stated as his first law of motion. More generally, Galileo's contributions to mechanics proved that terrestrial motions, and not only celestial ones, embody determinate orders of dependence which can be formulated quantitatively and explored mathematically.

Galileo supplied experimental support for some of his laws of mechanics. But experimental considerations played a subordinate role in his mechanical investigations. It would be an error to suppose that he thought scientific inquiry consists primarily in collecting observational and experimental data, or that laws of nature can be automatically extracted from them. He was convinced, as he once put it, that the characters of the language in which the book of nature is written are triangles, circles, and other mathematical figures; and he believed that to be scientifically significant "sensible experiments" must first be interpreted in terms of those characters. Moreover, he noted that laws hitherto not exemplified in experience may be discovered by deducing them from principles elicited in previous analyses of phenomena. Accordingly, while he apparently did not think that reason unaided by experience can certify the factual truth of a proposed law of nature, the function of experiment for him was to test such proposals or to persuade others of their truth.

Although Galileo envisaged the possibility of an all-embracing mathematical science of nature, the system of mechanics he actually constructed was only a partial realization of this possibility. Thus, his laws of mechanics did not account even for the planetary motions. Much more had to be done before the assumption that nature was to be understood as a mechanical order could completely replace the entrenched teleological accounts of events. One such task was the development of a philosophical basis for interpreting animate as well as inanimate processes in mechanical terms; another was the construction of a science of mechanics whose range of application included both terrestrial and celestial phenomena. The first task was in considerable measure the work of René Descartes (1596–1650), the second of Isaac Newton (1642–1727).

Descartes' philosophical views were closely related to his scientific work, especially to his important contributions to the development of analytic geometry, mechanics, and optics. He believed that fully certain knowledge is obtainable not only in arithmetic and geometry, but also in the study of nature, provided that we adopt in the latter the method of mathematics as he saw it. According to him, the certainty of mathematics flows from the certainty with which we can directly intuit the clear and distinct component ideas involved in those of number and figure, and then demonstrate further properties of extension that are not immediately evident. But he also maintained that the fundamental properties of bodies are their extensive ones, all others (such as weight, hardness, or color) being reducible to modes of extension, so that everything in the world, insofar as it is extended, is a proper subject for mathematical analysis. In consonance with this view, Descartes presented in outline a universal mechanics that attributed all changes in the motions of bodies to impacts between them. Except for God and the human soul, which he assumed to be unextended, all other existing things, whether animate or inanimate, were to be explained in such mechanical terms. For example, according to him the planets revolved around the sun because they were caught up in the vortex motions of a subtle matter pervading all space.

Descartes' formulation of the principle of inertia and his mechanical explanation of the refraction of light were direct sources of Newton's first two laws of motion. Moreover, his ideas on the foundations of science had a profound influence on the general climate of opinion during his own as well as later generations, and stimulated much research into the detailed mechanisms of nature. However, his proposed universal mechanics involved many speculative assumptions which turned out to be mistaken, nor did it provide adequate explanations for many phenomena of motion. It was the theory of mechanics developed with impressive mathematical rigor and detail by Newton in his *Principia Mathematica Philosophiae Naturalis* (published in 1687) that became the foundation and model for physical inquiry for more than two centuries. Newton's monumental achievement gave a unified explanation of the motions of bodies previously regarded as falling into disparate domains of existence; he presented an account of the system of the world so cogently reasoned that it replaced the traditional outlook on the nature of things.

The magnitude of Newton's accomplishments becomes evident from some examples. He completed Galileo's work on the construction of a science of motion by stating the general laws of dynamics; and he adopted the further assumption that every particle of matter attracts every other particle with a gravitational force whose intensity varies in a manner he specified. He then showed that from these assumptions it is possible to deduce improved versions of Galileo's laws concerning the acceleration of bodies falling toward the earth, as well as of Kepler's laws of planetary motion. He thereby produced compelling evidence for the universal scope of the principles of mechanics, and undermined once and for all the medieval belief that terrestrial and celestial motions conform to radically different laws. Those assumptions also enabled Newton to account for the behavior of the tides, the precession of the equinoxes, and much else. Moreover, in addition to the things he proved in the *Principia,* he made momentous contributions to physical optics and mathematics. To be sure, many questions about phenomena of motion were left unanswered, for the *Principia* deals mainly with the mechanics of systems of discrete particles; but the extension of Newtonian mechanics to the study of the behavior of fluids and other continuous media was successfully made in the eighteenth century. It is no wonder that Newton came to be widely regarded as the unequaled genius who discovered the ultimate principles of the world's invariable order.

Newton's views on how scientific inquiry should be conducted carried great weight, and influenced eighteenth-century investigations not only in physics but also in the psychological and social sciences. Like Descartes, he believed that the fundamental principles concerning the forces of nature must be formulated in mathematical terms, so that other laws about the phenomena of nature could then be systematically demonstrated. Unlike Descartes, however, he did not think that those principles can be asserted with self-evident certitude; he maintained that they are inductive conclusions drawn from properly analyzed experiments or observations. Newton articulated the complementary roles of mathematical reasoning and experiment in the study of nature, and so combined important components in the rationalist and empiricist philosophies of knowledge that went into the making of the new science.

As was noted earlier, the changes in astronomy and mechanics we have been recounting were only the most spectacular steps in the emergence of modern science; and during the three centuries we are considering, important advances were also made in other divisions of physics, in chemistry, and in the life sciences. Many of these inquiries were undertaken primarily to satisfy the desire to understand the nature of things, but many resulted in theoretical or experimental discoveries that contributed to the development of commerce, manufacture, and the military arts. Indeed, the chief value of the new science to some minds consisted in the greater control over nature it made possible, a view of the goal of scientific inquiry for which Francis Bacon (1561–1626) was an eloquent advocate long before the new science achieved its major triumphs. Although Bacon's ideas on how such inquiries ought to be conducted were quite inadequate, he saw the need for planned, cooperative effort if science was to yield increased human power over nature. The description in his *New Atlantis* of the House of Solomon, a projected center for experimental research, anticipated and influenced the institutionalization of scientific research as a profession.

It was not until the nineteenth century that the universities became the major centers of scientific research, and many contributors to the scientific revolution (such as Kepler and Descartes) had no university affiliations. On the other hand, by the end of the seventeenth century a number of societies for the experimental study of nature were formed in various countries. These societies provided opportunities for exchanging scientific ideas, engaging in experimental research, and witnessing experimental demonstrations, by making available to their members information and apparatus not generally obtainable otherwise. They frequently began as informal gatherings of experienced investigators of nature, amateurs of science, and even men whose concerns were primarily with the practical uses of scientific discoveries. Some societies had distinguished but relatively short careers, often terminating with the death of their financial patrons. This was the case with the Roman Accademia dei Lincei, which came into existence in 1603 and included Galileo as a member. Its energies declined after Galileo's Copernican views were condemned by the Church, and it came to an end in 1657. The Florentine Accademia del Cimento, founded in 1657 by disciples of Galileo, had an even briefer life, although in the ten years of its existence it made significant contributions to experimental knowledge of a variety of physical phenomena, and helped to improve a number of important instruments, such as the thermometer and barometer.

However, not all of these initially private scientific societies had such an ephemeral existence. Some of them were formally recognized by the state, though not always financially supported by it, and have continued to flourish. For example, the Royal Society of London for Promoting Natural Knowledge, incorporated by royal charter in 1662, grew out of weekly meetings of scientists and other interested persons that began to be held in 1645 in London. Its further growth brought innovations that reflected the increasingly professional and social character of the new science. Thus, although for many years there were no professional requirements for membership in the Society, even during its early years the experimental investigations in its own laboratory were the responsibility of the Curator of Experiments, a scientist of proved competence. Moreover, to keep the Society informed about scientific matters, its permanent secretary carried on a large correspondence with scholars at home and abroad. This task of disseminating scientific knowledge was made easier when the Society began in 1665 to publish its *Philosophical Transactions,* one of the earliest scientific journals. But the Baconian belief that scientific inquiry holds the promise of augmenting human power over nature was not confined to England. Officially approved scientific societies also appeared on the continent of Europe, although unlike the Royal Society they were created and financially supported entirely by the state. For example, professional qualifications for membership in the French Academy of Sciences, as well as the obligations and privileges of its members, were fully spelled out when it was established by Louis XIV in 1666. Many of the research centers that were eventually set up elsewhere in Europe resembled the French Academy in organization as well as in the regular publication of scientific periodicals.

This multiplication of scientific societies testified to a widely felt and growing need for institutional innovations essential for a flourishing science —for effective social mechanisms that would distribute the financial costs of experimental research; make possible the systematic exchange of ideas between investigators in different parts of the world or occupied with related problems; and develop common standards of workmanship in experimental as well as theoretical inquiry. Scientific societies provided such mechanisms, so that by the close of the eighteenth century scientific research as a recognized profession was firmly established.

For Further Reading

Burtt, E. A., *The Metaphysical Foundations of Modern Physical Science.*
Butterfield, Herbert, *The Origins of Modern Science.*
Kuhn, Thomas S., *The Copernican Revolution.*
Wolf, A., *A History of Science, Technology and Philosophy in the 16th and 17th Centuries.*

22   Society and Politics

It is from the new, radical opinions of the eighteenth century in western Europe—the so-called Enlightenment—that the two centuries following derived the notions of Individual Liberty, Political Rights, Equality, Democracy, and (to use the latest twentieth-century slogan) Participation. All these words point to large abstractions, and over the years they have been given varying embodiments in various national traditions and constitutions. To understand their meaning it is necessary to know how they emerged first as ideas, and then to trace their career, singly or in combination, to their present development.

On the continent of Europe, society in the eighteenth century can be

A.D. 1713–1715   Peace of Utrecht; death of Louis XIV; Vanbrugh's Blenheim Palace completed
      1721   Bach's Brandenburg Concertos completed; Montesquieu's *Persian Letters*
      1724   Fahrenheit's thermometer devised
      1734   Voltaire's *Philosophical Letters on the English*
      1748   Montesquieu's *Esprit des Lois*
      1750   The *Encyclopédie* begun; the Diplomatic Revolution
      1752   Franklin shows that lightning is electricity
   1756–1763   Seven Years' War
      1762   Rousseau's *Social Contract*
      1764   Beccaria's *On Crimes and Punishments*
   1765–1790   Enlightened despots in Austria, Germany, Spain, Portugal, and France
      1776   Adam Smith's *Wealth of Nations;* American Declaration of Independence
      1778   Beaumarchais' "private fleet" mustered in aid of rebelling Americans
      1783   Beaumarchais' *Marriage of Figaro*
   1787–1788   Assembly of Notables; censorship lifted; Sieyès' *What Is the Third Estate?*
      1789   Outbreak of revolution in France

described as made up of classes that bore the marks of their medieval creation. But these classes were losing or had lost their functions; some had acquired new functions; others were without any; at the edges of contact there was blurring. In France, England, Italy, the Netherlands, and parts of Germany and Spain, the serfdom of the Middle Ages had largely disappeared and the tillers of the soil formed an actually "free" peasantry, though it was still burdened by old levies and duties, strong reminders of serfdom. Above them was the artisan class, hand workers who were also "free"—except that the old system of guilds retained enough control to be an annoyance and a barrier to self-help. The lower middle class, consisting of small shopkeepers and modest professional men, similarly felt capable but shackled.

And so did the higher bourgeoisie, which theoretically led all commoners, that is, the lowest of the three "estates" or recognized conditions of men. For the middle and upper bourgeoisie actually manned the civil service and often ran the government. The nobles or highest class had largely given up the responsibilities that had once justified their preeminence. Particularly in France, they lived as courtiers in Paris and Versailles; only a few of their number served in war, government, or diplomacy. As for the clergy or second estate, most of their upper ranks were filled as sinecures by aristocratic younger sons, who imitated the conduct of their secular relatives. The pastoral work of the church was done by the poor parish priests, who led the same life as the peasants and small bourgeois to whom they ministered.

Education was in the hands of the clergy, as had been true since Charlemagne, and more especially since the sixteenth century, when the Jesuit order had begun to organize first-rate schools. The university too was church-dominated, regardless of the country or the church established in it. Yet nowhere was the clergy distinguished for great religious fervor; indeed, "enthusiasm" was a common term of reproach akin to "fanaticism." The church was political and orthodox rather than religious.

In France, there was another group, forming neither an estate nor an economic class, but rather a closely held profession: the "nobility of the robe," that is, the judges whose prosperity rested on the fees, fines, and gifts that they were entitled to collect in dealing out justice. Akin to this group in feeling and type of income were the holders of purchasable offices under the crown. Many bourgeois, large or small, invested their fortune— painfully acquired through perhaps two or three generations—in some office that carried a known revenue and prestige and entailed no work: the use of a deputy was lawful and expected.

To picture English society at the same time—say, in the year 1715—it is necessary to modify some details. For example, the English aristocracy and bourgeoisie intermarried a good deal more readily than did the French; and England had a sturdy gentry that lived on the land and thus maintained personal bonds with its own peasantry. Squire Western in *Tom Jones* is a good example of the class; his tastes and manners show that though part of the local ruling class, he is still very close to the soil.

It is sometimes said that another characteristic of English society was the willingness of noble lords to engage in trade, as the French aristocrats would not. This is inexact. Astute French nobles engaged in trade by proxy and thereby kept up their fortunes when the land which they neglected failed them—or they profited from both trade and agriculture when they chose able stewards in each activity. It was not so much fear of degradation as the pleasures of idleness that kept the French nobles out of trade, coupled with the love of prestige, which could be satisfied only by assiduous attendance at court. The court of Versailles was the center of glory for the nation, just as its great "suburb" Paris was the hub of Western civilization for all Europeans of wealth, title, or talent.

What we see with the advantage of hindsight, then, is a society whose formal organization no longer corresponds to its actual functions, ambitions, and needs, while its consciousness dwells on the fact of having attained one of the high moments of perfection in European civilization. Writing of the Age of Louis XIV, who died in 1715, Voltaire a quarter-century later cites it as one of the four great eras of Europe, on a par with fifth-century Athens.

The comparison is apt in one way at least: in each case the high achievement immediately precedes the fall. Many thinkers of the eighteenth century had presentiments of revolution ahead; and it is now obvious that these thinkers themselves contributed to the upheaval, for the most part without desiring it or knowing how they were hastening the day. Their ideas, their hopes, their apprehensions fitted themselves to the unstable structure and helped bring it down. One can argue endlessly about the "causes" of great events and deny or affirm that ideas—"mere ideas"—are among the causes. It is more profitable to think of *conditions*—and among them are states of mind. For history is made by men, that is, more or less conscious beings, who in the mass continue to follow their habits and opinions in great circumstances as in small.

The eighteenth century strikes the observer as an age of opinion, of reasoning, *par excellence,* and it is not surprising that it should be so. The discrepancy between form and function that we have noted was an incitement to thought. The simplest form of critical thought is comparison: *This* does not match *That.* From one such observation by an alert mind a whole theory of society can grow, and the presence of the fact will seem to prove the theory.

Another circumstance helped: the Treaty of Utrecht in 1713 having put an end to half a century of exhausting wars, the public mind was open to new excitements. During this time of peace, flecked only by skirmishes, that mind became truly cosmopolitan. The educated class (now reaching through all three "estates") adopted French as the common language, traveled incessantly, read the same books, enjoyed the same neoclassic and baroque styles of art and dress and life, and adopted the same thought clichés as these fell from the worktables of the numerous and openly admired philosophes. Even in far-off central and eastern Europe, the "correspondence" of the Baron Grimm, stationed in Paris, carried week after week the news, gossip, and revelations of the great Thought-factory.

What is more, these publicists (which is the closest rendering of philosophes) by no means agreed among themselves, nor did the conservative, traditional opposition leave them a clear field for their debates. Important consequences followed from these two facts: first the debates, from vehement to acrimonious, accustomed the public to an incessant battle of ideas about political and social views. It was no longer a religious sect or the followers of a duke who formed a compact phalanx battling with another, but the articulate supporters of doctrines dealing with state and society. Nothing on that scale or of this degree of explicitness had been unleashed in Europe since the Protestant Reformation, which is to say another era of revolution. And now the reading public was larger and the subject matter more transparent. The harsh discord which we find on every page of our large metropolitan dailies and which is the essence of liberal democracy is first manifested in the intellectual politics of the eighteenth century.

The second effect of this debate was to stiffen the resistance of the old order. Diverse parties closed ranks against the new enemy, and since churchmen were the main and best spokesmen for what was old and established, the battle came to be drawn between the Church buttressing the Monarchy on one side and the philosophes on the other. That is why Voltaire, alluding to the Church, made the motto of his party *Ecrasez l'infâme*—tread down the loathsome thing!

What were these new ideas, this new "light," which has given to the eighteenth century and its galaxy of great writers the names Enlightenment, Age of Reason, philosophes, Rationalists? These ideas, in the first place, were *critical* ideas, ideas that did not so much propose goals as raise questions, point to absurd impediments to good sense, ridicule established beliefs and institutions. Pamphlets or treatises or encyclopedia articles were aimed at showing that the accepted beliefs were contrary to experience, that the institutions did not work. Thus in that brief series of two- or three-page articles which Voltaire called a *Portable Dictionary of Philosophy,* he says under the heading "Equality": "What does one dog owe to another or one horse to some other horse? Nothing. No animal depends on his fellow. But man, having received from God the light we call reason, has with it made himself—what? A slave nearly everywhere. . . All men would necessarily be equal if they were free from needs. It is want that subjects one man to another—not that inequality is in itself an evil, but dependency is. It does not matter if someone is called Your Highness and somebody else His Holiness, but it is grievous to slave for the one or the other."

The technique of the passage is characteristic not only of Voltaire's voluminous writings but also of his fellow critics'. First the innocent question that simplifies a whole tangled issue—dog and horse compared to man. Then a quick "solution" of the puzzle why some men are free and powerful, others slaves. Finally, the irony of accepting the status quo: "Highness" and "Holiness" stand for the king and the pope. They must not be attacked. Let us advocate keeping the titles—what does it matter if the names entail no servitude? But obviously, with the servitude removed the titles lose all meaning. Thus, without seeming to do so, you have abolished king and pope.

Voltaire does not really go as far as his words imply. He winds up justifying the present order, though he has implanted the germ of a new one. "Each man," he says, "can within his heart believe himself entirely equal to all other men. This does not mean that the cook of a cardinal should order his master to prepare dinner for him, but the cook can say: 'I am a man like everybody else, born like him in tears just as he will die like me in anguish and be given the same rites. We both perform the same animal functions. If the Turks capture Rome and I become cardinal and my master a cook, I shall take him into my employ.' " Every word of this monologue is reasonable, but while waiting for the Turks to take Rome, the cook must do his duty, or all human society is perverted.

"As for other men, who are not cooks or cardinals . . . but who are annoyed at being treated with contempt or condescension and who see that their lordships have no greater mind, knowledge, or virtue than themselves . . . what should they do? Simply go away."

In that last suggestion lies the grievance of the eighteenth-century intellectual and high bourgeois: he is misused and mistreated. He wants a state in which the inherited pretensions of superiority will be ignored in favor of ability and hard work. Voltaire consents to maintain the trappings (Highness, Holiness), but for two reasons only: first, he knows that equality is an inner feeling which, once aroused, will spread by itself. (One proof is that twenty years later, in *The Marriage of Figaro,* Beaumarchais demonstrated with the aid of comic situations that the nobleman was useless for all the serious business of life and his valet all-important.) And second, Voltaire pays ironic respect to the heads of church and state so that the censorship will let him alone.

Censorship in eighteenth-century France (and elsewhere) was a peculiar institution. It was fitful, inefficient, but always a threat. Voltaire built himself a house at Ferney on the Swiss-French border so that no matter whom he offended he could claim that he belonged to the other jurisdiction. Exile, imprisonment, the burning of condemned books, and other means of persecution and obloquy were always available. Still, there were loopholes, such as pseudonyms, false place names on title pages, and the like. In France, moreover, the censorship was in the hands of noblemen sympathetic to the new ideas. But these friends could not always resist pressures from the church or the court. That is how the great *Encyclopedia* came to be censored, behind the editor's back and with the connivance of his publisher. The *Encyclopedia* nonetheless became an institution in itself, and it is instructive to sketch its history.

A French man of letters, Denis Diderot, was invited in 1747 to bring out, purely as a piece of elevated hackwork, a French edition of the English encyclopedia of Ephraim Chambers. Mulling over the plan, Diderot conceived the idea of using the proposed work to carry the new doctrines, to spread the light. Starting from a plan he devised with the mathematician D'Alembert, and working with undiscourageable energy for years on end, Diderot produced between 1750 and 1772 the tremendous storehouse of fact and propaganda that swept Europe and taught it what "reason," "rights," "authority," "government," "liberty," "equality," and related social principles are or should be. The work was subversive in its tendency, not in its advocacy: *it took for granted* toleration, the march of mind exemplified by science, and the good of the whole people. It was a true encyclopedia, not a collection of pamphlets.

The full title of the work is: *Encyclopédie, ou Dictionnaire raisonné des arts, des sciences et des métiers.* The last of the three subjects is not the least important. Diderot, the son of a cutler, was concerned with artisanship and mechanics, and many of his hours of labor were spent in shops, studying the devices which his engravers illustrated for the encyclopedia. The eleven volumes of plates were in themselves a revolutionary force, for they made public what had previously been kept secret by the guilds, and thus supported the philosophe doctrine that the dissemination of knowledge was the high road to emancipation.

Another aspect of the *Encyclopédie* is worth noting: Diderot could not have written all the articles, even if his time had not been filled with editorial work and political skirmishing. He relied on several scores of contributors, scattered over French-speaking Europe, most of them confirmed adherents of the new ideas. In other words, by the middle decades of the century, the principles of the Enlightenment were already well diffused among the kind of people who think and write. The *Encyclopédie* did spread the attitudes and arguments still further among a population that was steadily becoming more literate, but those volumes so eagerly subscribed for despite their high price did not create the demand for reform, they fed it.

How is this situation to be explained? Through several circumstances. One is that the visible enlightenment of that century had hidden roots in the preceding one. Behind the *Encyclopedia* of 1750, behind Voltaire's guerrilla tactics, behind the incessant appeal to reason, stands Pierre Bayle's *Critical and Historical Dictionary,* written (for safety) in Holland in the 1690's. And Bayle was not alone. All through the seventeenth century we find in France, England, Holland, and Italy writers who in one domain or another of intellect and belief question, criticize, compare, and condemn. The so-called libertines in France include Protestant and Catholic thinkers who doubted orthodoxy. Their influence is paralleled or seconded by: statisticians and political economists like William Petty in England; sensationalist philosophers like Gassendi and Hobbes; English empiricists going back to Bacon: all these prepare the ground for the rational and naturalistic (soon "scientific") view of all human experience. And that view is the intellectual prerequisite to reform. For reform (and later revolution) is the application of systematic thought to society.

When, therefore, the Continental Enlighteners invoke as their heroes and torchbearers Newton and Locke, they are putting forward the great summarizers of a long movement. Newton is the culmination of a hundred years of discovery, as is Locke, whose three years in France and five in Holland made him, consciously or not, a disciple of at least three generations of intellectual "libertines" concentrated in those countries.

This historical reminder is not intended to redistribute credit for initiating the Enlightenment. Men and achievements maintain their old worth. But it is needful to look at origins when one wants to assess justly the different roles played by the first groping explorers and the later proclaimers of the gathered truth.

Nor is this all that needs to be said about origins. The politics and social ferment of the Age of Reason are sure to be misunderstood by anyone who clings to the cliché of "an upsurge of the bourgeoisie against the nobility" as the main explanation of the popularity of the philosophes. The "enlightened" in mid-century Europe numbered as many aristocrats and crowned heads as well-to-do commoners. The "enlightened despots" in Prussia, Austria, Russia, and Portugal are there to show that no "class war" is involved, since the efforts at reform in those countries came from the top—the monarch—and it was the peasantry and hinterland nobility who generally resisted change.

In Austria, for example, the Emperor Joseph was a headlong, "theoretical" man who entertained very "bourgeois" ideas of order and business-like regularity. He saw the need of them after the defeat of his empire at the hands of Frederick the Great, and he recognized that a "modern" people cannot be governed by amateurs chosen as favorites by the head of the state. Nations need a trained bureaucracy, organized in clear orbits like the universe of Newton. Joseph's attempts at reform failed in ten years, but the upheaval they caused was like a foretaste of revolution—everything made new—while the methods he used foreshadowed the police-state totalitarianism of a day even later than that of the French Revolution.

Even the generality about nobles and peasants needs modification. As everybody knows, when Revolution came, its leaders and encouragers numbered many aristocrats and members of the clergy. "Reason" had done its work upon their minds. On the strength of their example it can be said that revolutions are mostly made by their victims. How account for this seeming paradox? One important consideration here is that for more than a century the French aristocracy had been restless under the emasculating power of the monarchy. Deprived of their ancestral role as governors and warriors, the nobles discussed reform. They too were rebels, but what they rebelled for was a restoration of an intermediate power—theirs—between the exclusive and centralizing monarchy and the Third Estate.

They listened, therefore, when the jurist Montesquieu, using England in idealizing fashion, described in his *Spirit of Law* the mixed or balanced constitution, under which a parliament composed of lords and commons legislates, and other bodies divide the executive and the judicial functions. But France had no such institutions to reclaim and modernize for a reform of the monarchy. So the theorists of aristocratic power (seventeenth-century nobles such as Saint-Simon and Boulainvilliers) argued for a return to the Middle Ages, when the king was merely the first among peers.

We have, therefore, the political spectacle of certain eighteenth-century monarchs (Joseph, Frederick the Great) allying themselves with the commoners in an effort to modernize the state; of certain nobles, opposed to the monarchy, adopting bourgeois ideas of reform in hopes of restoring aristocratic power; and of the monarchy resisting them, because aware that centralized government depends not on abstract ideas but on habitual consent. Meanwhile the peasantry, most conservative of classes, begins to overhear remarks that suggest the possibility of emancipation—from ancient dues, from exclusive taxation, from inability to enrich themselves through buying the land engrossed by the Church. But so far the peasantry remains unenlightened, unwilling to change its habits and beliefs, suspicious of whatever comes from above, afraid of the confusion inherent in reform.

Yet orderly patterns were not wanting. In the second half of the eighteenth century, several of the French law courts (*parlements*), manned by an enlightened nobility of the robe, made attempts at systematic change. The famous *parlement Maupeou* in Paris tried to play the role of benevolent despot; the *parlement* of Provence in the 1760's sketched out most of the solid reforms achieved in the first years of the Revolution of 1789. Shortly before that revolution, men such as Turgot and groups such as the Assembly of Notables struggled with the mounting difficulties and with one another, in a fog of misunderstanding and futility. Group interest *does* come into play in these various abortive attempts, but the prospect is not that of an oncoming war between an oppressed majority and a frivolous ruling class drinking champagne while the people starve. That is but the Hollywood version of the complicated story. The reality is one of confusion about goals and suspicion about motives, in a society full of intelligent perceptions, yet divided between those who saw hopeless disorder in the present and those who saw endless disorder in the future if the edifice was tampered with. As in all tragedies, both sides were right.

At this point it should be clear why the reformers could unite under the intellectual leadership of the philosophes: their doctrine was abstract, even though illustrated by concrete examples. With the abstractions we are familiar today, since many of them have with much travail been turned into working devices. But it is necessary to rehearse these principles in order to appreciate how easy, natural, rational they seemed to those who first heard them expounded.

What they saw was this: monarchy, the class system, and the established church forming a conglomerate of institutions and laws held together only by the force of habit and the self-interest of groups. The "constitution" was a historical product of long growth and relatively infrequent revision. Although France and Prussia had rather recently invented and put into practice the essentials of modern bureaucracy, they could only apply these rules of efficiency to a society that was the very antithesis of order and system. It was like trying to run a large corporation from an old castle built at different times on different levels linked by meandering corridors.

The appeal of the Enlightenment was that it undercut this "absurd" clutter by proposing the great simplicities. Just as the philosophes mocked at the Ptolemaic scheme's trying to cope with celestial movements by hooking orbits upon orbits, and said, "Follow Newton instead and all is clear," so in human affairs they said: "Begin with Locke and all follows." Locke (they thought) begins with the human mind as a blank tablet. Experience in the form of sensations imprints whatever knowledge the mind acquires. Hence the teaching of superstitions, pious falsehoods, incredible myths, and social prejudices turns men into the wicked and suffering creatures that we see. Teach the simple truth as science has begun to disclose it and you will make men free, equal, and happy. That simple truth derives from axioms within the mental reach of anyone—just listen! And Voltaire would proceed with his little lesson on equality, the dog and the horse, the cardinal and the cook. Or Diderot or Helvétius or Condillac or D'Alembert or Quesnay—all preeminent in the art of enlightening—would take up a similar and supplementary demonstration. Altogether it amounted to a geometry of man and society.

From sensation furnishing the mind, one went on to a consideration of Man—born free, obviously, then giving up a part of his freedom for the advantage of mutual protection in society; therefore retaining a number of inalienable rights: security for life and property; entitled to a voice in government and to the tolerance of his beliefs; deserving of education; permitted to speak and print his opinions unhindered; subjected to laws, but guaranteed that they will be the same for all and administered without regard to persons. Reason, in short, dictated the Bill of Rights very much as we know it in the United States Constitution and based it on what seemed like a scientific study of the human condition. Such principles must inevitably bring about the release from that servitude which Voltaire noted as prevailing all over the earth. For like the propositions of geometry which they resembled, these principles could not be contradicted by anyone capable of reasoning at all.

To be sure, the practical steps toward making these relationships actual among men might be difficult. There was so much hardened prejudice in every institution, so many follies to eradicate, faith in omnipotent churches and kings being the chief ones. And then vested interests stood in the way: there were two hundred different sets of custom law in France, two kinds of provinces, and three or four layers of local government. Sinecures were bought and sold; nearly the whole weight of taxation bore on the peasant. Inevitably, those exempt or privileged thanks to such inequities clung to their private advantage. And the upshot of such a crazy-quilt constitution was that while the country was growing more prosperous, the government was going bankrupt, and while its bourgeois bureaucracy was perfecting its methods, old rights and powers hampered every action.

It is here that the bourgeois outlook, the tradesman's eye for profit and loss, his need of clear and simple accounting—in a word, his business sense—gave impetus to the rationalist theory of society. In one of its manifestations, this theory proposed the first form of free trade and the single tax. The school of thinkers known as Physiocrats and of which

Quesnay, Turgot, and Du Pont de Nemours were the chief members, argued very simply (as always) that only those who worked on the land, farmers and miners, produced wealth. Everybody else lived off their output. It was absurd, therefore, to tax the successive steps of manufacture and distribution, or to tamper with the natural flow of goods, especially within one country. To do so only raised prices and impoverished everybody. As for international trade, the old export bounties and import duties, like the list of articles prohibited from coming or going—all these rules known collectively as the mercantilist system—were an anachronism born of the needs of war and the selfishness of merchant groups. Free trade would mean peace as well as the return of economics to the wise governance of nature itself.

Here were practical proposals indeed, proposals which it took the studious amplifications and modifications of Adam Smith in *The Wealth of Nations* (1776) to make first palatable, then popular, in the early nineteenth century.

A similar evolution was needed for the reform of the law, particularly the criminal law, upon which obviously the liberty of the citizen as well as his equality and dignity depend. The rousing call to reform in this domain was the famous work of Beccaria *On Crimes and Punishments*. Everything about this essay (it covers fewer than 100 small pages) is symptomatic of the age that gave it birth. The author was a timid Italian nobleman of twenty-six, still under the thumb of an authoritarian father, whom he resented to the point of referring to this oppression in this very essay. In Milan, Beccaria formed with a few other young intellectuals an "academy of fists" devoted to waging war on economic and official misgovernment and religious bigotry. They published a periodical and discussed likely topics for articles. With these friends Beccaria was no longer timid but impassioned and articulate; he often worked himself into spasms of indignation when the subject of judicial torture came up. He knew in fact little or nothing about the law and its administration. But his friends (mainly Pietro Verri) coaxed and coached him until he had set down in continuous, and sometimes incoherent, fashion his eloquent protest against the ill adjustment of punishment to crime.

The work was published in 1764, anonymously to avoid censorship and its penalties. But the authorities seemed indifferent, and within two years the "treatise" had aroused all Europe. Beccaria was invited to Paris, but when there fled the tributes, from shyness and inability to converse. The book remained a force: it helped Blackstone in his Commentaries and spurred Jeremy Bentham to take up arms against the English penal code in the early nineteenth century.

That thorough reform of all penal codes was urgent appeared in the eloquent but fruitless appeals by Voltaire in the Calas and La Barre cases, both travesties of justice and memorials to an age of barbarous punishments. In the American colonies, John Adams, then defending the British soldiers accused in the Boston massacre, was inspired by Beccaria's words to see himself as also "defending the rights of man and unconquerable truth."

It was Beccaria's concluding maxim that struck the chord of reason in all these enlightened minds: "In order that punishment not be invariably an act of violence committed by one or many against a citizen, it must be essentially public, prompt, necessary, the least possible in the given circumstances, proportionate to the crime, and in accordance with the law." To the modern mind this seems a commonplace. But when new it had to be argued. What is the reason behind this reasonableness? Beccaria makes it explicit, and thereby puts into words the most powerful principle of modern times, the notion namely that the ultimate criterion of lawmaking must be "the greatest happiness to be shared by the greatest number." This idea of course governs not merely law reform; it underlies as well all the other abstractions of the Enlightenment. One might sum up its goal as *happiness spread wide*. Or, as the American Declaration of Independence says in its preamble, the guaranty to mankind of life, liberty, and the pursuit of happiness. It is easy to understand why, for this purpose, men must be considered equal, not to say identical; and why also the meanings of law, government, society, and happiness itself must become secular and practical, not to say materialistic. For what makes men equal is their common needs, practical and material.

From these roots the liberal tradition, now so widely and variously attacked, has grown and borne fruit. One complaint today is that it has not been able to transcend the utilitarianism just mentioned; its political arithmetic cannot rise, apparently, above this common denominator and its material base. Yet during that first "century of reason," there was one man, a member of the enlightened phalanx, who, because he saw man's needs as going beyond the utilities, came to occupy a third position, equidistant from the orthodox and the philosophes. That man was Jean Jacques Rousseau. His genius no one could dispute from the start, and despite many vicissitudes he wound up as the most influential thinker of his time, eclipsing Voltaire with the young generation that was to witness the upheaval of 1789.

What Rousseau provided for his contemporaries was the satisfaction which all the geometrical reasoning, all the appeals to practicality, denied or overlooked. Like their kind in all ages, the men and women of the eighteenth century did not live by reason alone—they had feelings, passions, fears, and prejudices. Not even the philosophes could exist as mere intellects stuffed with axioms. This is evident (if proof were needed) in the readiness with which the best minds of the period were moved to tears and tenderness by the simplest appeal to sentiment—to friendship, parenthood, self-sacrifice, heroism: these words sufficed by themselves to agitate their hearts. Whether the stimulus was found in the novels of Samuel Richardson or in the plays of Denis Diderot and other writers of "bourgeois drama," the rationalist responded like a virtuous, palpitating soul, regardless of his behavior or belief in other situations.

Rousseau's singular art and wisdom was to connect this fount of feeling, the inner reality of living man, with the critical doctrines of reason and reform. When he broke with the philosophes he gave up also the elegant life of the salons—he had never thought as highly of "civilization" as they did, and he sought a mode of life in which honesty, sincerity, hard work, and the absence of personal display would establish *in fact* that equality, that simplicity, that virtue advocated *in words* by his former companions in social philosophy.

As a poor and vagrant orphan from Geneva, Rousseau had observed European society from all levels and all sides. He had been a novice in a religious house and a footman waiting at the tables of the great; he had been the secretary of an ambassador in Venice; the kept protégé of a provincial bluestocking and the lover of titled Parisian ladies; a successful composer feted at the opera, the famed winner of a literary prize, the friend of the encyclopedists, and a common man living in a dingy quarter by copying music. He was a botanist, a musician, a mathematician, and a master of language; and by and large he prided himself on none of these roles and experiences. He was solely interested in finding out what this "Man" was whom the entire age kept defining in absolute propositions and trying to improve out of all recognition.

For his part, Rousseau began by representing Man as he might be imagined in his primitive simplicity, before the advent of property and of law, and again as he saw him in his sophisticated depravity, ornamented with the arts and sciences. Then Rousseau depicted man as fathered by the child, that is, man made or corrupted by his education. Next Rousseau provided the youth with a mate and subjected him to the storms and temptations of love. In the course of this narrative (*The New Héloïse,* a novel), Rousseau showed what a decent life might be: gambling and drunkenness replaced by outdoor sports, mothers nursing their own children and men wearing their own hair; work and modest sociability in place of finery, affectation, intrigue, and the competition over symbols of status.

After this, Rousseau dealt with the theory of government, both in the well-known *Social Contract* of 1762 and in the equally important practical works on the governments of Poland and of Corsica. Finally, that which sealed his reputation with the future revolutionists, Rousseau wrote his *Confessions,* in which he tried to show what the stuff of life is, how it feels, and how thought and emotion form but a single energy that eludes all abstract formulas. Though Rousseau frequently argued with the skill and the weapons of a geometrician, his whole work was an assault on the abstractions of the age, which he considered too facile and hence surely false.

To this day Rousseau's intention and philosophy are matters of debate. Because he gave his century the emotional outlet that it lacked and was himself taken up by diverse parties, the clichés about his views stand in the way of what he plainly said. For example, he did not say "Back to Nature!" nor did he want men to return to innocent (or noble) savagery. He thought "nature" was difficult to discover and was a goal to be attained by effort. It lay ahead, not in the past. Much of what we do today, how we dress and talk and act in our present democratic love of the simple and casual, is Rousseau in action. Likewise our feeling for nature, our appetite for greenery and holidays in the woods, our need of an antidote to the city—all are emotions prophetically given worth and form for the first time in Rousseau's work.

Much space and many examples would be required to expound the system of ideas that made Rousseau an original and far-reaching influence. Let it be said dogmatically here that his political conclusions led him to advocate representative democracy as the best device for ensuring at once individual rights and the sovereignty of the people. What is of equal importance, he saw that *Man* is a convenient fiction: the earth is populated by *men*—different, only partly rational, and moved by habit and history as much as by articulate ends. Moreover, man is inescapably religious and lives by the moral sense as much as by calculations of utility and material advantage.

It was these beliefs of Rousseau's that alienated the philosophes: they saw their handiwork being undone by a sophist of incredible popularity. He seemed to be the savior of the European soul against *their* pernicious aridity: the reversal was intolerable—and unjust. For Voltaire and Diderot and their friends were by no means unaware of human irrationality—look at *Candide,* look at Diderot's wonderful dialogues about sex and dreams and the mystery of life. But these perceptions, thought the philosophe party, must be kept out of the limelight for the good of the cause.

Unquestionably Rousseau's works and fame were confusing the great issues and even the battle lines. Some enemies of light, monarchist and clerical writers, were admitting that although a confessed heretic, Rousseau had in him the root of morality and faith. Others felt that he understood human beings and the historical nature of institutions better than the Voltairian cynics and atheists with whom he had once consorted. This acknowledgment on the part of *l'infâme* was enough to confirm the enlightened in feeling that they had been betrayed by their most gifted recruit.

The significance of this conflict goes far beyond any party quarrel. It is fundamental to an understanding of the whole modern age. The nineteenth and twentieth centuries were to witness the working out of the reformist ideas of the Enlightenment, from the birth of the liberal, parliamentary world of yesterday to the exacerbated populism of today, democratic or totalitarian. And during this same era the turmoil of that birth, the instability of those politics, tended to show that the abstract, regular, and utilitarian model of society does not suit the wayward moral being that man is, diverse and irrational as he evidently remains in his impulses, traditions, and faiths.

For Further Reading

Voltaire, *The Man with Forty Shillings.*
Fielding, *Joseph Andrews.*
Diderot, *Rameau's Nephew* (J. Barzun trans.).
Montesquieu, *Persian Letters.*
Rousseau, *On the Government of Poland.*
Beccaria, *On Crimes and Punishments.*

23   Science Versus Theology

The history of Western thought since the eighteenth century has not borne out the familiar maxim that "a little science takes one away from God, but a great deal of science brings one back to Him." By the end of the nineteenth century, Friedrich Nietzsche felt entitled to state as a matter of observation that "God is dead"; and in the middle of the twentieth the same cry was repeated by many—characteristically—as if it were a new discovery. To retrace the decline and fall of theology and the rise of the secular outlook in which science and naturalistic presuppositions enjoy unbounded confidence is to explain the intellectual concerns and the moral anguish of ten generations. In this chapter the opening phase and main features of that decline will be retold.

Science and theology are rivals, because each professes to supply

A.D.   1687   Newton's *Principia Mathematica*
          1690   John Locke's *Essay Concerning Human Understand-
                 ing*
          1697   Bayle's *Dictionnaire historique et critique*
          1704   Death of John Locke
          1713   The bull *Unigenitus* and the war against the Jesuits
     1733–1734   Pope's *Essay on Man*
          1736   Butler's *Analogy of Religion*
          1741   Voltaire's *Mahomet* (on toleration) praised and re-
                 warded by the pope
          1747   La Mettrie's *Man a Machine*
          1748   Hume's *Essay on Miracles;* Treaty of Aix-la-Chapelle;
                 Montesquieu's *Esprit des Lois*
       1750 ff. Buffon's *Natural History* (evolutionary theory)
     1750–1772   Diderot and D'Alembert's *Encyclopédie*
          1751   Voltaire's *Age of Louis XIV*
          1756   Voltaire's *Essay on the Customs and Manners of
                 Nations*
       1760 ff. *Dictionnaire de Trévoux* (Jesuit response to *Ency-
                 clopédie*)
          1762   Rousseau's "Confession of Faith of a Priest from
                 Savoy"
     1764–1765   Voltaire's *Candide* and *Dictionnaire philosophique
                 portatif*
          1778   Mesmer and mesmerism; death of Rousseau
          1779   Hume's *Dialogues on Natural Religion* (posthumous)

mankind with a comprehensive account of the universe, including man and his deepest concerns. It is true that scientists often disclaim this large intention and assert that natural science (or, as it was called until about 1850, natural philosophy) deals only with inanimate things and is silent about the realm of consciousness which is man's. But this dividing line is not in fact respected. A science of living things and a science of man are goals actively pursued by the scientific mind from its earliest impulse toward universal knowledge; and so soon as "natural philosophy" boasts that its method holds a monopoly of tested, "objective" truth, it is inevitable that every great scientific advance should bring with it direct applications to man and society. At the least, "implications are drawn" in domains other than that of brute matter, which means supplanting the existing theological or philosophical teachings.

This is precisely what happened on a large scale under the impact of Newton's great synthesis of physics, optics, astronomy, and mathematics. As the fame of his *Principia Mathematica* (1687) spread throughout Europe and its leading ideas were popularized in numberless forms (there was even a French "Newton for Ladies"), the thoughtful, the curious, the ambitious, the anticlerical began to find in the new institution that we call modern science reasons for disputing or losing faith in Christendom's traditional and orthodox beliefs.

This is not to say that men of science and their admirers ceased to believe in God and the Bible. Newton himself was religious to the point of superstition; at the end of his days he spent more time studying and writing about the prophecies in the Book of Daniel than he did in charting the heavens. And to the present day it has been possible for some great scientists to retain a fervent faith in God and the Christian ethic. But that possibility depends on the willingness or the power to keep separate in the mind two sets of axioms and conclusions about reality.

What did Newton's scientific study of reality disclose to the men of the eighteenth century? It disclosed a machine. The system indeed is commonly known as "the Newtonian world machine." The meaning is obvious: by the law of gravitation every particle of matter attracts every other particle with a force proportional to the product of their masses and inversely proportional to the square of the distance between them. This force is the motor that keeps the machine going, for of itself matter is inert and motionless. The parts of the machine—and nothing exists outside it but space—consist of various aggregates of matter, from stones to stars. Their position, orbits, and destiny are determined inescapably by the nature of matter and the laws of motion, which in turn permit the mathematical expression of any given relationship. With the categories of matter, space, time, and motion anything perceptible to the senses as a body (or inferred, technically speaking, as "extension") can be fully "placed" and accounted for.

This full accounting obviously leaves no room for God or even mind. It is the distinguishing mark of early modern science that it excludes the observer—and of course the deity. For one thing the observer (or man's mind) is a variable, "subjective" element which cannot be taken as the cause of any event or brought into observation and calculation without rendering them uncertain. Since the world machine works by itself, the observer is necessarily outside. And so, for the same reason, is God. It may be that he has created matter and decreed its laws—indeed that would seem a likely explanation. But once his task has been accomplished, he by definition (and deference to Newton) stands outside his creation. Newton apparently believed that space was the *sensorium* of God, but the words have no imaginable meaning or much moral force. Unless God is inside the universe, steadily controlling its operation and using it as the theater of man's moral pilgrimage, there is no Providence. Revelation becomes an illusion, the law of the Prophets and the grace of the Gospels appear as man-made things. As for recorded miracles, they are but superstition. The very scheme of science, the logic of mathematics, rules out miracles from the outset.

Going through such reflections as these, the men of the late seventeenth and early eighteenth centuries arrived at two formulations to take care of their inherited beliefs at the same time as their glorious new science. The first came to be known by the suggestive name of "natural religion." Thinkers such as John Locke, Archbishop Tillotson, and Samuel Clarke took as their point of departure the unity of Reason and Truth. If reason leads to the truth of science, it leads to some matching truth of religion; there can be no different set of axioms and conclusions applicable to God and faith. Natural religion therefore denies and stands over against revealed religion. Far from being the fruit of an intuition or the outlet for an inborn emotion, religion in this new guise is a deductive science like mathematics. Natural religion forbids atheism and, just as compelling as natural science, commands the acceptance of every man able to use his reason. Its propositions are few and simple: since the universe is but a machine working according to law, it could not create itself. The beautifully made watch implies the watchmaker. So we infer a creator, who is God. His intellect must have been remarkably like Newton's, with the power of physical creation added. This is the point of Pope's intended epitaph for Newton:

> Nature and Nature's laws lay hid in night:
> God said, Let Newton be, and all was Light.

To which Warburton, Bishop of Gloucester and a man who considered himself devout, added the remark that "It had been better: 'and there was Light'—as more comformable to the *fact* and to the *allusion*. . . ." By these words he was making Newton, Pope, and himself coauthors of a new Book of Genesis. The pride of the Age of Reason dismisses—most politely —the old Book of Genesis for its inadequate physics.

Natural religion, then, posits a God, not of love, wrath, or justice, but of supreme artisanship. He was in fact variously known to the enlightened minds of the eighteenth century as the "Great Architect," the "Divine Watchmaker" (or Artificer), the "Supreme Mechanic"—no longer *our* Maker, but the maker of the stuff dealt with in the *Principia*.

From this tremendous reduction of the complex, encrusted, mysterious Christian theology to a single, simple Entity with Technological Leanings, the believers in natural religion came to be called Deists, that is, God-ists, partisans of a streamlined God who was the first practitioner of automation.

At the same time, the rational mind of the age retained a conviction that morality was both natural and necessary. But lacking a God who could open his mind to Moses and Jesus, how could this morality be made solid and universal? The Deists replied: "Look within yourselves and you will find conscience, the moral sense, which tells you about right and wrong and which you disregard at the cost of remorse." This inner light is universal: by it all men are brothers. Civilized society, moreover, relies on this moral sense to sustain peace and fair dealing, which can never be ensured by force or threats alone. As in Newton, reason unites with utility and the result is beautiful to behold.

But how did conscience come to be rooted in man? The answer is, once again, God; the moral sense is another of his discreet creations. The argument here is not from any supposedly mechanical nature of right and wrong, for temptation does not attract the sinner with a force inversely proportional to the square of the distance; it is much less predictable. No: the argument is from universality, which is the very mark and proof of reason. Locke, Voltaire, and their fellow Deists were sure that all religions rest on a common, identical moral sense, and that the differences among creeds are merely superstitious and irrelevant accretions—the inventions of crafty priests to secure themselves power and riches by deceiving the people and keeping them ignorant.

A third and final proposition of the new theology is also self-evident. The moral conscience which is implanted by God works by approving or disapproving a man's acts, and so does God. He holds in reserve ultimate rewards and punishments. Men's souls must therefore survive death to receive their deserts. How this occurs is not amenable to observation and is therefore not explained. On earth morality is strengthened by the expectation of this deduced but unprovable judgment, and at this point the scheme begins somewhat to resemble a *moral* machine akin to Nature's material one.

A moment's thought will show that Deism amounts to a compromise position. It embraces science without abandoning God. But side by side with Deism in the eighteenth century stood, on the one hand, the ranks of the orthodox and, on the other, the growing numbers of materialists and atheists. What could the orthodox theologians argue against the powerful certainty of Newtonian physics and mathematics? In Catholic countries, the principal argument was drawn from the manifest authority of the Roman Church: so great, prosperous, and long-lived an institution could not have been founded on an imposture. Millions of believers strengthened the testimony of the wise and the saintly all the way back to the Gospels and the Old Testament. The continuity and coherence of the tradition, coupled with its power to convince and coerce, proved that Deism was but one of many frivolous heresies, the speculation of a few abstract minds, without true moral feeling or divine grace, and certainly without wide popular support. If universal experience was to be appealed to and serve as proof, it should be the universal fact that unsophisticated men everywhere believed in the direct governance of the world by God, in the ordained function of the church as mediator between man and God, and in the reality of miracles. The Jesuit order, founded in the sixteenth century, and in most countries the controlling force in education, was also the leader in the polemic which went on during most of the century with the Deists and other religious radicals. It was the Jesuit writers who denounced the works of Voltaire and the French *Encyclopedia* and who called down censorship or exile on others whom they suspected of atheism.

But entrenched as was the old orthodoxy, the spread of "light" was swift, and wherever the natural philosophers had well-placed partisans even kings were dazzled. Thanks to the influence of the ruling favorite Pombal, the Jesuits were expelled from Portugal and its colonies in 1759. (Did the catastrophic Lisbon earthquake of 1755 discredit Providence? Many said so throughout Europe. Voltaire wrote a poem about it.) In France and Spain the Jesuits were suppressed in 1767. Aranda in Spain also persuaded Charles III to abolish the Inquisition. Frederick the Great in Prussia and Joseph II in Austria decreed religious toleration; in England and elsewhere trials for witchcraft declined or disappeared; and finally in 1773, the enlightened pope whom even Voltaire loved and praised, Benedict XIV, abolished the Jesuit order altogether. To be sure, there were behind these moves political reasons added to the philosophical, but the tolerance that led to suppression marks all the same the progress of un-belief.

Meanwhile in Protestant England, Christian theology was defended on the same rational ground as that on which it was attacked. The appeal was to logic in the first place, not authority or ancientness. The boldest attempt along this high line was that made by Joseph Butler in *The Analogy of Religion, Natural and Revealed, to the Constitution and Course of Nature,* which he published in 1736 and which earned him the Bishopric of Bristol the following year. The phrase "Butler's *Analogy*" became by itself the magic formula by which for seventy-five years believers who never read the book invoked what they took to be a conclusive refutation of Deism. Later, orthodox faith was transferred to a more recent work, "Paley's *Evidences*" (*of Christianity*).

In the span between them the conservative position relied on the state-ment that it was just as difficult to ground the truth of natural religion in pure reason as it was to accept revealed religion without reason. How could reason alone bring man to believe in the immortality of the soul, rewards and punishments, and the sway of absolute moral law under God? To pretend to demonstrate these as true was only to borrow fragments of the Christian tradition and cut them off from their original source and warrant, revelation. Butler points out that far from natural reason being able to establish the universality of the moral law, history shows that the pagans "fared ill" in the light of nature alone; their minds struggled with a chaos of contradictory precepts. Further, if we examine the modern natural religion we find revealed religion to be a "republication of it in all its purity," but with divine guarantees and definite commandments added. In other words, the Christian tradition is a unity, to be taken or left as a whole.

To the arguments put forward by such writers as John Toland, a disciple of Locke's, or even by churchmen such as Tillotson, that only those parts of Christianity that passed the test of reason deserved belief, Bishop Butler answered that the course of nature, the scene of God's moral order (which the Deists accepted), was just as mysterious and hard to make out as anything in revelation; or (again in other words) that religion was the domain of faith, not demonstration. In either view, the universe remains beyond man's comprehension, which is why man has and needs a religion.

At this point a thinking man is in effect given the choice whether he will choose religion or Deism as a matter of taste, and it is evident that Butler's argument for religion may well push the resolute mind to abandon both revealed and natural religion, to find ultimate reason in atheism and materialism. This was the path followed by many eighteenth-century thinkers. They became materialists and atheists from logic, with or without the addition of lip service to Christian doctrine for the sake of avoiding trouble with the authorities.

Such was the position reached by the Scottish historian and philosopher David Hume a dozen years after Butler's *Analogy*. In his *Essay on Miracles* of 1748, Hume shows how the test of reason serves a consistent mind. Believing in the Newtonian system (for how can mathematics lie?), disbelieving, therefore, in the possibility of supernatural events, what Hume must meet head on is the testimony of the intelligent and honest minds on whose report miracles are believed. To do so, Hume turns the tables on these witnesses with the all-embracing formula that "no testimony is sufficient to establish a miracle, unless the testimony be of such a kind that its falsehood would be more miraculous than the fact which it endeavors to establish."

The catch lies in the phrase "more miraculous," for surely there can be no degrees in miraculousness. The slightest deviation from the order of nature is just as supernatural as the largest. What Hume means, then, is that any apparent deviation from the natural should at once be investigated by the method of science in order to be disproved—or else fitted into the system of science, instead of being taken as the miraculous support of a "subjective" belief. The test of reason boils down to this: the concurrence of trained minds when they use mathematics to control attentive observation. Newton had meant very much the same thing when in differentiating his work from others', he said: "I don't make up hypotheses" (*Hypotheses non fingo*). He was not referring to hypotheses in the usual sense, but to his conviction that science dealt with unquestionable evidences "out there." The realities themselves disclosed their order and system to a competent mind without the aid of intuition and imagination. Obviously, there could be no "evidences of Christianity" in the same sense.

The certainty felt by all the enlightened in this power of things "out there" to project themselves correctly on man's mind like a sharp beam of light on a screen is what gives the answer to the question: How is it that there is no argument about true science? What is it that produces the remarkable concurrence in observation and reasoning, now that we have found the true method? The theory of mind—it would be called today the psychology—that goes with eighteenth-century science is that known as "empirical" or "associationist." It was developed in England by a series of philosophers who are accordingly known as the British Empiricists. Their work established side by side with Newton's world machine its equivalent, the human mind machine.

The principle of this psychology is not a discovery of the Enlightenment. Philosophers here and there through the ages had flirted with the attractive but dangerous *nihil in intellectu quod non prius in sensu*—noth-

ing is in the mind which is not first in the senses. The senses here mean
what we feel, touch, hear, smell, and see. They are at once the channels
through which experience imprints its multiple patterns on the plastic and
receptive mind of man, and the contents of that natural operation. From
the first minute of conscious life, the bombardment of sensations begins to
"make" the mind. The pictures on it correspond to "reality" which exists
"outside." It is these pictures which enable man not only to guide himself
in his workaday affairs, but also, ultimately, permit Newton to recapture
the mental operations of God when he was creating the heavens. For the
sensations necessarily come in a sequence which by "association" generates
true ideas.

From Hobbes to Locke and from Locke to Hume, Condillac, and
Hartley, this "sensationalist" and "associationist" explanation of the work-
ings of mind supplied the desired basis to a number of fundamental activities. If experience acting automatically on the mind reproduced reality
there, this was sufficient validation for the experimental method of science.
Only experience had authority, as Bacon had taught, and experiment was
simply a bit of contrived experience. This was looping the loop: all normal
minds receive the same impressions from the experiments of science because the source of these impressions is nothing but the consistent and
unified order of nature. Science is thus true because it gives a summary of
this natural order, and the summary is confirmed by the concurrence of
these normal minds.

This mechanical model of the mind had other implications, for both the
individual and society. It suggested first a far greater equality among minds
than had ever seemed likely before, since in this new psychology all minds
start equally blank. Upon these originally equal minds, accident and wicked
imposture (by kings, priests, and others) had worked quite arbitrarily, had
twisted or degraded them—which accounted for the diversity of customs
and rituals, the wars of religion, the superstitious fears of primitive man,
and indeed of "civilized" man too, when he was kept in ignorance as he was
in contemporary Europe.

This being so, it should be possible by the right education to maintain
the natural equality, or at least not utterly destroy it, and in time develop
reasonable men. Let the common experience of the young be abundant,
orderly, free from hobgoblins and old wives' tales, and the grown man will
be a reasoning creature, fully capable of understanding Newton, and rational also in the sense of self-controlled and law-abiding. Right education
supplementing a good environment will infallibly improve mankind. There
was the key to progress, progress indefinitely extendable and depending
only on the intelligent contriving of the right experiences, as in experimental science. Man's fate lay entirely in man's control.

Why, in these circumstances, was it said above that the root idea of the sensationalist psychology is dangerous? Its first proponents, of course, ran the risk of being burned as heretics who denied the existence of the soul. Later, as we have seen, the clumsy compromise of Deism took care of the theological objection, verbally at least, and fended off orthodox attacks. With the success of science as backing—almost as weapon—the empiricists of the eighteenth century need not fear the stake. But a far worse danger came from within rationalism itself. It took two forms—skepticism and thoroughgoing materialism—both of which led to the destruction not merely of the props supporting theology (as we have seen) but also of the props supporting science. Ultimately, rationalist analysis seemed to require giving up the vision of enlightened, progress-making man, and to replace it by the spectacle of a mindless universe in which automata (or at best animals) pursue mechanically a meaningless existence.

Both these outcomes of rationalist speculation were reached before the end of the Age of Reason, though their full impact over a wider public came only later. In the eighteenth century, skepticism and overt materialism created only ripples of disturbance; they did not dislodge the prevailing Deism of the advanced thinkers or the entrenched beliefs of the conservatives. The latter were learning to live at peace with the new doctrines, and toward the end of the century a placid, polished genius such as Edward Gibbon could, in his literary masterpiece on the decline and fall of Rome, devote two long ironic chapters to Christianity as the obscurantist creed that had helped to bring down the high civilization. To the author and his readers one implication was: We, thank God, have just got over the effects of this protracted error and our rationalist civilization is secure.

But the inner corrosive was already at work. As early as 1747, the French writer La Mettrie gained the ear of the public (incidentally convincing the new king of Prussia, Frederick the Great) by the theory summed up in the title of his book *L'Homme-Machine* (Man a Machine). La Mettrie was a physician and a follower of the great seventeenth-century mathematician and philosopher Descartes. In Descartes' system there are only two entities—mind (or soul), which emanates from God, and matter, which is mindless "extension." The point at which the two substances meet, said Descartes, is the will of man, which presumably moves him in his actions and leads his mind to know and experiment with matter. But Descartes found it unnecessary to use soul and will in accounting for the behavior of animals. These he declared to be automata, pure machines. Likewise, he believed that there was no need to invoke the Creator's continuous action to explain the present state of the universe. It could have reached this state from any given beginning by a mechanical evolution.

With these two premises, it was tempting (and not difficult) for La

Mettrie to take the next step and to picture man as also a purely material arrangement of bones, nerves, and other fibers—a machine. All one has to suppose is that the interplay of these elements produces the phenomenon of consciousness—the *illusion* of a mind (or soul) independent of the body. The proof of materialism lay in the fact that drugs, fever, and other physical influences on the body are immediately translated into changes of sensation, feeling, and ideas.

La Mettrie, whose first essay had been entitled *The Natural History of the Soul* (1745), went on to write *L'Homme Plante* (Man a Plant), in which he drew other analogies not essentially different from his mechanical ones. He had inklings of the evolution of plants and animals, like several of his contemporaries, notably the great Buffon. This sharp observer and master stylist included in his vast *Natural History* an explicit theory of evolution, based on the similarity of structure between whole groups of animals, including man, and suggestive of far-reaching conclusions. But with the characteristic irony which was the safeguard of the advanced thinker, he added: "One would believe all this if one did not know by revelation that the animals were created as separate species by the creator."

Among the consequences of materialism was the disestablishment of morality. La Mettrie advocated complete hedonism, or the undeviating pursuit of pleasure. For all these heresies he had to flee France and even Holland and take refuge in Berlin with his convert Frederick, who practiced what his guests preached, as more and more of the enlightened came to do. Voltaire, a Deist to his last breath, called La Mettrie "the King's Atheist-in-Ordinary." But quips and flights into exile did not end the matter. Committed to science and to reasoning, the century could not stop where Voltaire arbitrarily and inconsistently chose to: he was all for Light, but he confessed that he would not teach his philosophy to his servants for fear that loss of belief would emancipate them so far that they would steal his spoons.

The post-Voltairian world pursued a more rigorous line of thought. For one thing it took in the reports of the many explorers whom a scientific generation kept sending out to the South Seas, in the course of which a new continent (Australasia) and innumerable primitive tribes were discovered. The simple or strange habits of these peoples taught Europe a complete moral relativism: right behavior was what society decreed to be such. Whatever the code, it had grown up by chance, or had been suggested by "benevolent nature," as in the easy and agreeable sexual morals of Tahiti. And if harmless and pleasant there, why not in Europe?

In short, though the total hedonism of La Mettrie and his pupils was an extreme position, it might still show the right direction. The richer and greater mind of Denis Diderot, the master encyclopedist, frequently played with this subject and veered toward a materialism coupled with a Deist morality. What kept Diderot from adopting the voluptuary's creed was his strong sense of obligation to others; his understanding of the *social* machine, which requires brakes and levers; and his vivid awareness of mind as an irreducible element. Diderot may not have believed in God and immortality, but neither could he accept consciousness as an illusion—for if matter alone has real existence, sensation itself and ideas and emotions are deceptive appearances.

Less questioning and introspective, the Baron d'Holbach, another French philosophe and encyclopedist, disposed both of God and of any proof of his existence drawn from the harmonious design of the cosmos by denying that special harmony. "Matter acts because it exists and it exists in order to act." We know this from ordinary experience and we can go no further. Why or by what means matter acts is beyond us. The reason for the existence of matter is locked up within matter itself, and we should rather inquire (d'Holbach was a physicist) *how* it acts than waste time looking for an external cause, a first cause, or a preordained purpose or end. Harmony is a fiction because the "fixed sequence of necessary motions" is at times favorable to us and at times disastrous. Order is only the unvarying effect of identical causes; in a word, it is regularity without point or purpose.

Even in man's man-made order, the uniformity of cause and effect determines acts and consequences, a determinism which disposes once and for all of the deist "morality" implanted by God in the heart of man. One has only to compare what the theologies pretend and what experience shows. Here d'Holbach quotes Epicurus, who two thousand years earlier had said: "Either God wants to prevent evil and cannot; or can and does not want to." The choice is between a God who is powerless and one who is lacking in love and justice. But evils we suffer are quite compatible with blind matter, which does not know that it is inflicting evil or serving good: the knife does not know that it is cutting meat or committing murder.

Thus does rationalist logic, starting from Cartesian and Newtonian science, end in a cold gray world, strictly determined and not likely to favor the hopes of Progress. But one must interpose here that such atheism does not necessarily lead to the hedonism of La Mettrie, who thought of death as the curtain rung down on the last act of a farce. D'Holbach was by contrast a stoical moralist with lofty notions of honor and humanity. But just as one can be sardonic or sad at the godless, mindless, universe, depending on one's temperament, so one can reach that same vision of the cosmos by other means than the study of matter. Simple skepticism will suffice. One can get there by following Locke instead of Newton, the "new" psychology instead of the "new" physics.

This second path is the one that Hume took to arrive at his distrust of science and theology alike. In an *Essay on Providence and a Future State* (1748) and a long dialogue *On Natural Religion* published after his death in 1779, Hume pursued his method of asking, first, what grounds there were in experience for believing that the imperfect world we see is matched by a perfect one hereafter. On earth we see men treated not according to their deserts; what evidence is there that a just ruler will later correct these injustices? It is all "mere possibility and hypothesis." But observe: we do not even know and cannot reasonably infer the existence of a creator. The analogy with a watch takes us nowhere, for we have seen a watch being made, but we have no good reason to think that a universe is also and similarly "made." Discarding d'Holbach's analysis of order as simple regularity, Hume suggests that the order we find may be accidental; chaos would be equally natural. Besides, there is every reason to suppose the world finite. Why then expect a finite product to have an infinite cause? For all we know, its maker may have been a limited, fallible being like ourselves, or he may be dead, or he may have worked with one or more other gods of either sex, each or none of them concerned with good and evil.

Hume's last word of doubt on religion carries with it such a doubt about the mind of man that the certainty of science goes down in shipwreck too. In its ultimate phase in Hume, the psychology of sensation turns upon and destroys itself. For Hume's last word is that there is no warrant for believing in the existence of anything but the sensations that we receive. To be sure, they follow in fairly usual order; our habits make them seem real and regular, but they are after all nothing more than impressions. Objects we can never know directly; still less do we know directly the relation of cause and effect. What we take to be such is our habitual expectation that the impact of one billiard ball on another will be followed by the motion of that other. This habit is good enough for the business of daily life, but it does not bestow certainty on the system of causal connections we proudly call science. The Lockean mind, in short, fails to support a rational belief in either the natural religion of the Deists or the natural science of the Newtonians, whether they be materialists or not.

Of course, the practicing scientists went on with their work regardless: Priestley, Lavoisier, Cavendish, Volta, and Laplace discovered elements, laid down chemical laws, developed electricity, predicted celestial events by mathematical deduction—quite as if Hume had never doubted. In psychology, the world was startled by the "immaterial" effects of hypnosis produced by Franz Anton Mesmer (mesmerism) and was taken in by the magnificent sleight of hand of the impudent adventurer Alessandro di Cagliostro; all this regardless of the "proofs" that only matter existed and that superstition could not survive reason. The "associationists" went on refining, and certain physicians among them (Pierre Cabanis, Destutt de Tracy) became interested in the abnormal mind. Under the name of Ideologues, they opened up inquiries of great moment for the future, not only of science but of art.

In short, man's mind is unconquerable in the sense that arguments found definitive by one generation sound either silly or irrelevant to the next. Arrived at the point where there seemed to be nothing more to say—Hume having uttered the last word—a new surge of energy and speculation kept philosophy going and began the restoration of theology. The German professor of logic and metaphysics at Königsberg in Prussia, Immanuel Kant, did not think Hume either silly or irrelevant: he found him a stimulus; the impasse was—so to speak—a springboard. Kant accepted the failure of speculative reason to establish the truth of theology or any part of it—God, free will, or immortality. All these truths belong not to pure reason but to practical reason. It was in *The Critique of Pure Reason,* published in 1781, that by this distinction Kant opened the way out of skepticism, renewed the possibility of religion and moralism, and slipped a fresh foundation under the work of science. The revival of the constructive energies in all realms marks the period known as Romanticism, which ushers in the nineteenth century.

But Kant's saving formula owes its existence to something else than reflection on the difficulties Hume had advanced. Seventeen years before Hume's death and the publication of his testament of skepticism, Rousseau had inserted in his *Émile* or treatise on education a remarkable chapter on religion, which he entitled "The Confession of Faith of a Priest from Savoy." In sixty short pages Rousseau shifted the ground of discussion entirely away from physics and psychology and made the knowledge of God rest on man's religious impulse. The inner consciousness of morality and love of God is first a feeling, later *aided* by reason; it is not a product of cogitation. *All* thought is of this character: need, impulse, will, precede intellect and argument. Being primary and instinctive, the feelings cannot be explained away: subtlety does not remove hunger.

Rousseau's "Confession of Faith" nevertheless takes up all the current arguments for skepticism, materialism, and orthodox dogmatism in the best eighteenth-century rationalist manner. It shows their futility by arguing both their inconsistency and their abstraction: they are not "practical." A man may *say* some of the things the philosophers write, but a man does not *live* them. They are debating points, not animating convictions. Belief is a living thing.

Brilliant and compact, the priest's discourse to his pupil Émile passes from the reasonings to the revelations, and there Rousseau again takes the "practical" view that three-quarters of the human race have never heard of European theology, so that if there is but one God and he a just one, he must expect and receive from men a worship of another kind than that preached as essential, eternal, and exclusive in Christendom. And since, as everybody knows, even Christendom is rent by virulent disputes based on differences of ritual and revelation, there can be no greater illusion than the belief in this exclusive truth about the one God.

Rousseau, in short, first puts himself inside man as he is, then takes all men in their concrete diversity and asks himself what religion can embrace the inner and the outer realities. It is still a *natural* religion, but not a rationalist one. It is a reasoned faith, but at many points reason declares itself powerless to know. It is a religion that sanctions and supports moral action, but in deciding what is moral it relies on feeling rather than casuistry. In its simplicity and humility it is what we should call a democratic religion, not a sophisticated or learned one—the priest from Savoy is only a vicar, which means that he has not even a parish. But his mind does embrace the whole world, and when he asks himself where he has learned to worship the one true and universal God, he answers that it is not in books of theology or of enlightened philosophy, for he is "unable to believe that God commanded him under pain of hell to be a scholar." From those treatises of sterility he turned to the open book of Nature, in which all may read and from which all can teach themselves to serve and adore the Creator. No one can be excused from going to it, for Nature "speaks to all men a language intelligible to all minds."

In saying this, Rousseau may have been anticipating. His contemporaries and disciples were just beginning to look at Nature as he did, and to discover there a divine presence that raised echoes in the human heart. When thirty years after him a whole generation spontaneously came to share such emotions, a new age was at hand. The quarrel of science and theology was in abeyance, displaced by the vivid synthesis of art, religion, and individual consciousness that we call Romanticism.

For Further Reading

Berkeley, *Commonplace Book.*
Voltaire, *Poem on the Lisbon Earthquake.*
Hume, *Dialogues on Natural Religion.*
Pope, *Essay on Man.*
Diderot, *Dialogue on Bougainville's Voyage.*
Kant, *Prolegomena to Every Future Metaphysics.*

Europe: The Great Powers

24 Forming National States

It was a tribute to the effectiveness of their political institutions that in the 1640's France and Spain, despite the economic strains and the social unrest that their costly participation in the Thirty Years' War had produced, were still powerful nations, by far the most powerful in Europe. In France the Nu-Pied, or Barefoot, Revolt in Normandy (1639), in which thousands of peasants were joined by numbers of merchants and even by some local judges in resistance to high taxes in a period of poor harvest, could not shake the power of Richelieu. Spanish-controlled Portugal and Catalonia seethed with unrest, yet Prime Minister Olivares held them in check. Both powers sought by subversion to encourage rebellion among the other dissatisfied peoples, adding further to the internal unrest on both sides of the Pyrenees. At the same time they refused to invest any of their resources in measures that might ease the burden of their own unhappy subjects. To both victory in the war took precedence over all else. The common strategy was total offense—each would endure the risk of revolution rather than reduce the pressure on the enemy in any way. It was a policy of rule or ruin, and the fact that both monarchies survived this brutal policy explains why their governments were respected and admired by contemporary students of politics everywhere.

As early as 1463 the English legal theorist Sir John Fortescue had pointed to the French king's power to tax his people without their consent and to humble the proudest nobles of the realm as the hallmarks of absolute monarchy. At the end of the next century, after decades of debilitating war, the French crown under Henry IV and his minister Sully seemed by these standards more powerful than ever. This circumstance impressed every European politician enormously, which goes far to explain why the absolutist ideology flourished in the first half of the seventeenth century in almost every country of Europe. If only other rulers would copy the French

A.D.	1581	Proclamation of Dutch independence from Spain
	1594	Henry of Navarre crowned as Henry IV of France
	1603	Union of Scottish and English Crowns under the Stuart James I
	1611–1614	Rebellion of the French princes
	1624	Richelieu admitted to the Council of State
	1625	Hugo Grotius publishes *De Jure Belli et Pacis* (international law)
	1635	Founding of the French Academy, which establishes uniform grammar and usage for French language
	1636–1637	Peasant revolts in southern and western France
	1639	Nu-Pied, or Barefoot, Revolt in France
	1640	Revolts of the Catalans, Portuguese, Irish and Neapolitans
	1642	Outbreak of the civil war in England
	1648	Peace of Westphalia; sovereignty granted to the Swiss and Dutch states
	1648–1652	Civil war in France
	1649	Repression of the Irish by Cromwell
	1652	Anglo-Dutch War
	1653	Defeat of Brandenburg Estates
	1655–1660	Northern War; Brandenburg gains sovereignty of Prussia
	1660	Charles II issues the Declaration of Breda
	1661	Beginning of the "personal" reign of Louis XIV
	1663	Louis XIV occupies the Papal State of Avignon (Comtat Venaissin)
	1678	Elector of Brandenburg attempts to suppress Wendish speech
	1680–1683	Chambers of Reunion
	1685	Revocation of the Edict of Nantes

(and Spanish) model, they too could create powerful centralized states. In "mixed" monarchies where sovereigns depended upon representative bodies to raise money, the sovereign was, relatively speaking, poor and had little to offer those who served him. Thus, at least, it seemed to the ministers and bishops in the court of Charles I of England, to the courtiers and princes of Orange, and later to the noble followers of the Hohenzollerns in Prussia, of the Vasas in Sweden, and of the Romanovs of Russia. In all these countries the "ideal" of the absolute monarch was dangled temptingly before the noses of kings repeatedly over decades and centuries. Indeed the oppressive, blighting influence of the idea was not finally and totally eradicated from Europe until 1917.

Seventeenth- and eighteenth-century absolutism lacked, however, the cold, cruel power of twentieth-century totalitarianism. The ideology sanctioned the monarch's interference in every aspect of the national life. But most of the kings lacked both the temperament and the actual power to dominate their subjects totally or crush out racial and cultural minorities like a Hitler or a Mussolini or a Stalin. Haughty nobles posed a constant internal threat and formed the power center around which dissenters could rally. More basic, no absolute monarchy approached the modern totalitarian state in its degree of cultural and economic centralization. From southern Italy to Scandinavia, from Scotland to Auvergne, primitive semi-tribal social enclaves persisted unassimilated by the larger nations. Scottish kilts and the coifs of Brittany were superficial reflections of this insularity and diversity. Hundreds of dialects and equally numerous local semibarbaric religious cults sustained these pockets of the past in the midst of "modern" centralized states. Their existence seemed a constant threat to absolutism. This led, for example, statesmen as diverse as Cromwell and the Earl of Stratford to try to crush the Irish. Although most of these tribal-like subcultures were poor and primitive—inhabiting the poorest land and scraping a bare living from rocky soils or an unfriendly sea, ruled by feudal patriarchs—they somehow appeared to "civilized" European statesmen as ferocious beasts which must be subdued at all costs. Of course they stubbornly resisted surrendering their freedom or their ways of life, however mean. Bitter warfare resulted, warfare which the outlanders could never win. But rugged minorities could usually exact a terrible toll both physically and psychologically from their overlords. The screaming kilted Scotch highlanders terrified English troops. Well into the eighteenth century control of such tribal peoples sapped the resources of the powers, a drain similar to that exacted from the Roman Empire by the barbarians who ringed its perimeter in ancient times.

Moreover, even in France and Spain provincial loyalties remained strong even when unsustained by significant linguistic and cultural differences. Parish, village, county, and provincial council, diocesan and guild institutions, remained powerful centers of local life and government. Everywhere the landed gentry and the bourgeoisie drew upon economic power and local prestige to resist centralized authority. The great aristocratic families also employed these local loyalties in their larger struggles against absolute kings. Royal orders emanating from Paris, Madrid, London, or Vienna always met resistance, especially when they took the form of demands for money. When royal officials such as the intendants of France settled in the provinces, they tended soon to take on the ideological coloration of their surroundings and thus to defend the very local liberties they had been dispatched to destroy. This was especially true of ambitious officials drawn from the lower orders; they also proved particularly susceptible to the blandishments of the provincial ruling classes.

Everywhere in the provinces in rich Kent and Beauvais, as well as in poor Scotland and Brittany, subsistence agriculture was still the rule. Thus the poor classes lived under the constant threat of famine. After about 1620 the whole continent suffered from a food shortage as the population increased. Conditions were worse in some regions than in others, but the common result was political instability. During famines the upper classes tried to improve local controls to conserve scarce supplies; they dared not place their very survival in the hands of remote officials in the capitals. Inefficient and expensive means of transportation prevented the swift movement of food to stricken areas in any case. Therefore the most absolute kings met only frustration when they sought to break down regional economic barriers in the name of efficiency and centralization.

Coastal cities which profited from fishing and foreign trade opposed protective tariffs which interfered with their profit, whereas towns in the interior favored tariffs which were a source of income to officials and served to keep local food supplies in the area. Again local interests acted to hamper monarchical efforts to achieve uniformity and control. Even when the kings attempted to establish new manufactures in the towns, ostensibly to increase local resources as well as to make their kingdoms more independent of foreign supplies, the traditional guilds protested bitterly, arguing that the new businesses would stimulate competition and drive up wages. The mercantilistic dream of a self-sufficient, truly national economy dear to the hearts of the absolutists had no appeal to these local interests.

On the other hand, the nationalization of the culture of the upper classes proceeded swiftly. In France and Spain national courtly styles triumphed over the Italian fashions. Between about 1550 and 1680 provincials willingly aped the dress, speech, architecture, and diversions of the Escorial and Versailles. By way of contrast, however, the princes of Orange and the Stuart kings exercised no such dominance over the culture of the Netherlands or England. There national styles were chiefly fashioned by local institutions such as the universites and by the burghers of Amsterdam and the town oligarchs of London. Ambitious young men in these lands adopted the sober dress of scholars and merchants while the older generation clung to Elizabethan styles. In the Germanies the Viennese court styles were widely influential, but Protestant princes were oriented toward the Dutch, at least until the 1660's when the court manners and dress of the French "Sun King" Louis XIV slowly spread across the continent.

The printed word exerted an increasingly powerful impact. In states that succeeded in controlling the presses, most notably in Spain but also in eastern Europe, the monarchs maintained their grip on religious, social, and political thought. In most of northern Europe, however, the flood of printed matter prevented centralization and contributed to the breakdown of traditional values and institutions. Literacy was on the rise particularly in England, where groups that possessed power, the nobles, judges, and merchants, took a heated interest in books, pamphlets, and broadsides dealing with religious and political questions. But in Geneva as in Oxford, in Douai, Louvain, and in hundreds of Jesuit schools, young minds were taught to see Europe as divided by ideological and religious conflicts. Before the sixteenth century politics, foreign policy, and finance seemed beyond the scope of even educated nobles, merchants, and professional men; thereafter bewildered kings, cardinals, and their ministers of state found these classes clamoring for a voice in public affairs. The spread of printed matter aroused public opinion as parliaments ceased to be docile, and this explains why kings began to try to get along without them. One major aspect of absolute government was rule without estates.

The flood of printed matter seemed also to exacerbate the religious conflicts of the Thirty Years' War. Hundreds of pamphlets served to polarize opinions on theology, history, government, and morals, to say nothing of specific questions of foreign policy, taxation, and the like. How to deal with the resulting politicization of their subjects challenged the imagination of the monarchs. Although censorship had failed miserably against the Reformation, kings and bishops continued to try to stamp out ideas they considered subversive to the established order. But books could be easily transported across national boundaries, and secret presses were almost impossible to locate and destroy.

Some kings, James I of England for example, joined directly in this struggle to influence opinion by writing themselves; others hired propagandists to advance their cause and refute the arguments of their foes. Richelieu was a pioneer among the latter. From Paris poured a flood of print designed to influence French opinion. Théophraste Renaudot, editor

EUROPE IN 1660

Hapsburg possessions

Hohenzollern possessions

Holy Roman Empire boundary

of the influential *Gazette,* was in his pay, as were many intellectuals. Other national leaders, the Duke of Buckingham in England, Olivares in Spain, and Cardinal Mazarin in France, were less adept in the use of this tactic than the great Cardinal.

Nevertheless, by the 1640's rebellion was everywhere in the air. Heavy taxes and religious oppression lay at the root of the unrest along with famine and hard times. In the past such conditions had led the poor to focus their resentments upon local lords, but now the kings themselves stood in the path of the storm. Pamphlets and engravings of the period reveal the depth of popular resentment against royal tax collectors and other symbols of centralized authority.

The results of the upheavals of the 1640's varied from place to place, but in England and France, where absolute monarchs had suffered crushing defeats initially, stability could be restored only by reestablishing centralized royal power. The radicals, having broken the monarchical dominance, proved incapable of devising and maintaining responsible national governments without it. At the same time, European elites, the nobility, merchants, and gentry, did not really want to rule. Religious radicals had sought to legislate new Jerusalems or enforce the articles from the Council of Trent, while statesmen like Omer Talon in France, John Pym in England, or—somewhat later—the De Witt brothers in the Netherlands, could not create national policies that would transcend local interests, let alone establish a republic or mixed monarchy that could govern effectively. Their constitutionalist ideologies only led to more violence and social revolution. Thus even victory against absolute monarchy seemed to be to no avail. The Catalonian rebels chafed under the directives of their French liberators, until their contempt for the French soon equaled their contempt for the Castilians. Nor could the Anglo-Dutch wars of the 1650's, in which Protestants fought Protestants over trade and colonies, be explained by the dominant revolutionary ideologies of either country. Should not the Protestants be joined against Catholics? asked English and Dutch radicals. To his despair Cromwell was forced into a war with his religious allies.

Similarly, the Jesuits had never quite succeeded in portraying the Franco-Spanish war as a crusade against heresy, since both powers were Catholic. At every turn, as Cardinal Richelieu realized, these religious-political ideologies failed to explain either commercial rivalries or conflict between states. Thus the first ideologies to permeate European societies, dividing as they did Protestants from Catholics and constitutional monarchists from absolute monarchists, had to be rejected by statesmen. A new ideology would gradually replace them—it was political and economic in character and we call it mercantilism, or statism. From the mid-seventeenth century to the French Revolution late in the eighteenth, the idea that each state should seek its own economic independence by founding colonies and controlling large supplies of gold and silver shaped European politics and caused a series of imperial conflicts.

But if the revolutionary parties and programs were rejected, this in no way meant that powerful social groups wanted to return to the absolutism of the early seventeenth century. In his Declaration of Breda, Charles II of England made it clear that the restored Stuarts would rely on a "free Parliament" under the new order. When Mazarin returned to Paris after his expulsion during the Fronde, he accepted the fact that aristocratic privileges and the Parlement of Paris could no longer be ignored. The earlier type of absolutism survived only in a declining Spain, and there more in form than in substance. The revolutionary spirit of republican decentralization prevailed only in the Netherlands, long a haven of religious nonconformity and a monument to the commercial spirit. Spain and the Netherlands were in many ways the extremes of European social and political organization in the mid-seventeenth century. A prudish moral climate prevailed in both, despite their different political systems. Their differences but also their similarities survived in the work of the two great artistic geniuses of the era, Velázquez in Spain and Rembrandt in Holland—the royal decadence depicted by the one, the solid burgher substance of the other, and in both the mannered reality and humanity of the age.

For Further Reading

Aston, T., (ed.), *Crisis in Europe, 1560–1660.*
Clark, G. N., *The Seventeenth Century.*
Moote, A. L., *The Seventeenth Century.*

25   The Age of Louis XIV

To name an age after a man—any man—is, of course, to distort history. No human being, not even an Alexander or a Caesar, has ever shaped a whole society. Yet Louis XIV, who was certainly not an Alexander or a Caesar, during his incredibly long reign as king of France (1643–1715) affected the lives and thoughts of the peoples of Europe to such an extent that to name that time in his honor is only slightly an exaggeration. Because of what he did, peasants by the thousands exchanged their hoes and plows for the tools of war. To win his patronage, artists and writers adopted new styles and the children of noble families all over the continent bent with furrowed brow over grammar books to learn the new "universal" language. Like those who aped the great Sun King, those who most stubbornly resisted his influence—the English and Dutch for example—were themselves shaped by the mere act of resistance.

Louis, by establishing for France such a powerful political and cultural identity, awakened national feelings all over Europe. The totality of French achievements shook every other nation to the core. Where they were admired and adopted, as in Germany, they blended subtly with local tastes and habits; where they were hated and resisted the results, while different, were still profound and directly traceable to French influence. When Louis came to power European culture lacked a focus, a national center of

A.D.   1636   Corneille presents *Le Cid*
          1637   Descartes publishes the *Discourse on Method*
          1638   Birth of Louis XIV
          1642   Death of Richelieu
          1643   Death of Louis XIII; regency of Anne of Austria for
                 Louis XIV; Battle of Rocroi
     1648–1652   Civil Wars in France (the Frondes)
          1656   Creation of the General Hospital, Paris
          1660   Marriage of Louis XIV to Maria Theresa of Spain
          1661   Death of Cardinal Mazarin, beginning of the "per-
                 sonal" reign of Louis XIV
          1663   Le Nôtre designs the gardens of Versailles
          1664   Molière presents *Tartuffe;* the play is banned
          1664   Creation of the Compagnie des Indes
          1665   Bernini visits Paris
          1667   War of Devolution
          1670   Promulgation of a reformed criminal code for
                 France
          1670   Treaty of Dover
          1670   War with the Dutch; assassination of the De Witt
                 brothers
          1674   Invasion of the Franche Comté
          1679   First fortress built by Vauban
          1679   Bossuet publishes the *Politique tirée de l'Ecriture
                 Sainte*
          1679   La Fontaine publishes Books 7-11 of the *Fables*
          1683   Death of Colbert
          1685   Revocation of the Edict of Nantes
          1688   War of the League of Augsburg; the Glorious Revo-
                 lution in England; death of Frederick William the
                 Great Elector
          1691   Racine presents *Athalie*
          1697   Bayle publishes *Dictionnaire historique et critque*
          1700   Philip V proclaimed king of Spain
          1702   Death of William III
          1704   Battle of Blenheim
          1713   Peace of Utrecht
          1715   Death of Louis XIV

leadership. The decline of Spain, of the Holy Roman Empire, and of the papacy left the Catholic countries particularly without a focus. Italy was still rich and a center of culture and fine living, but politically unstable. Thus the monumental synthesis of military force and high culture that developed in France after about 1600 affected all Europe enormously.

France achieved political and social stability swiftly after the mid-seventeenth-century revolution, aided by a new professional army and a sound public administration guided by Cardinal Mazarin. In 1659 the long war with Spain was finally won and Spanish power pushed back once and for all behind the Pyrenees. Louis was the fortunate beneficiary of these developments; he had been only five when he inherited the crown in 1643. But from the very beginning of his reign his mother, Anne of Austria, along with Mazarin, taught him to believe that *he* ruled; he learned to act like a sovereign early, and by the time he actually could rule, he did so naturally, with total confidence. He was regal in every respect—in look and gesture as well as deed—the very epitome of the divine-right monarch. In addition, as the descendant of Clovis and Charlemagne, he even had a claim to the title of Holy Roman Emperor. When compared to the sorry Hapsburgs of his day—the ugly Leopold and the impotent Charles—or to a base-born pope, like Innocent XI, he seemed a true prince, one destined to conquer and to judge, to impose order on all Europe.

Louis in modern terms had charisma. But even if he had been a mediocre monarch like his father, France would have dominated Europe, partly because of the collapse of Spain, partly because of its effective government and army, and its culture and learning. This was the age of Descartes, Pascal, Corneille, Racine, Molière, La Fontaine, Bossuet, and many others whose work and thought shaped Western culture profoundly. At a time when convention demanded that artists and intellectuals, generals and statesmen, give praise to their monarch and credit him with their successes, the achievements of such men were bound to make even a third-rate ruler appear like a combination of Solomon and Marcus Aurelius.

Louis XIV first appeared on the European stage, after Mazarin's death in 1661, in the role of a militant bully—brash and offensive in his dealing with foreign heads of state. French diplomatic successes, however, resulted from the shrewd policies of Mazarin and then Lionne, who took advantage of the small German states which tried to use France against the Hapsburgs and found themselves French satellites. In Brandenburg-Prussia, however, the quiet but competent sovereign Frederick William the Great Elector, although beset by Swedish pressure from the north and the claims of Polish kings to the east, avoided commitments to France and concentrated on building up a small but sound professional army of 8,000 men, and on strengthening his internal control of his territory against the pretensions of the Junker families. The Austrian Hapsburg emperor Leopold would have liked to rekindle the religious wars but lacked both financial resources and freedom of action. The smoldering threat of revolution in Hungary and of Turkish invasion from the east held him back. Indeed, the possibility of a future war with France over the succession to the Spanish throne— Charles II of Spain had no heir—led Leopold to abandon all thought of another religious crusade. Later he would have to ally himself with the Protestant Dutch and English to stop the power of France.

In Spain, disorder and defeatism were the order of the day. Charles II was one of the most pathetic creatures ever to rule a great European state. Physically, mentally, and emotionally abnormal, he was impotent, plagued by superstitious fears, supernaturally devout. Spanish courtiers and statesmen could look forward to little but the dismemberment of the empire, but like the Austrian Hapsburgs they continued to dream of past glories and to pretend that they possessed far more power than they really had.

In England the restoration of the Stuart king Charles II in 1660 brought no end to constitutional and religious conflicts. Popular fear of absolute royal power and of plots real or imagined to restore "popery" served to check Charles's freedom of action in foreign affairs. Although he was the cleverest monarch in his line by far, the London merchants, accustomed since the English Revolution to influencing foreign policy, were less affected by the anti-Catholic hysteria; their interest in commerce had high priority. Charles dared not openly challenge the merchants, even going along with their desire for war with the Dutch. But eventually his fondness for Catholicism and absolutism and his need for money led him to a secret treaty (Dover, 1670) with Louis XIV and other devious tactics. He did not, however, dare to try to undo the result of the Puritan revolution.

Despite the backing of a Royalist Parliament, he could not keep the promises of the Declaration of Breda. Those Royalists who had lost their land in the 1640's could not be compensated without injury to those other Loyalists who had supported the restoration. Numbers of great families thus lost the economic basis of their social position and the Anglican Church suffered in a similar fashion.

Nor were the religious provisions of the Declaration fully honored. Parliament in a counterrevolutionary mood enacted the Clarendon Code, excluding non-Anglicans from public office. Although some Catholics and Dissenters made their peace with the established church, others went underground, adding to the conspiratorial climate of the times. Charles worked in various ways to control parliamentary elections, and this plus the pro-Catholic proclivities of his brother James, the heir to the throne, made Parliament increasingly refractory. On his deathbed Charles, keeping a promise made to Louis XIV, publicly declared himself Catholic. This contributed to the Sun King's illusion that he could restore unity to Western Christendom.

Only among the Dutch did republicanism and localism increase in strength in Europe after 1660. In the chaotic conditions that existed there in the seventeenth century, religious toleration had developed not out of conviction, but out of fear of violence and a passion for making money that had made the ruling oligarchs the richest merchants of Europe. Only when nationalist-oriented and protectionist groups in France and England won control of government policy in these powerful countries did Dutch economic power begin to decline. Despite their wealth, the Dutch were politically and religiously divided and militarily weak. Fearing that a large army would mean the rise of the House of Orange and therefore of monarchy, they ignored the dangers posed by English sea power and by the new armies of Louis XIV. While Mazarin lived, French policy was expressed in diplomacy rather than in war. But historic French territorial ambitions in the Netherlands and also in Italy did not die.

In 1666 Louis attacked the Spanish Netherlands, basing the invasion on his Hapsburg wife's claim to the area. The war quickly revealed the weakness of Spain and the strength of the new "model" French armies. The French war machine was closely controlled and well supplied. Instead of pillaging the countryside the armies were provisioned by bureaucrats called intendants who insisted that the generals follow orders from Paris and who commandeered supplies from local officials in an orderly manner. Louis himself accompanied his armies in the Netherlands, inspiring loyalty among the troops and the lesser officers but prudently leaving strategy and tactics to the professional soldiers. The era of the condottiere was over; no longer did generals as Wallenstein had in the Thirty Years' War pose a political threat to their governments. Condé and Turenne, generals famous throughout Europe, remained faithful servants to the Crown under the new system, and Louis, on the scene, could coordinate military and diplomatic policy efficiently. Thus the great problem of the Thirty Years' War was solved; war no longer served as a stepping stone to political power for generals and local aristocrats. Eventually the French system was imitated all over the continent. Armies were also growing larger; at the height of his power, Louis XIV had 400,000 men under arms, probably more than had ever been engaged at any one time by all the belligerents in the Thirty Years' War.

By the Treaty of Aix-la-Chapelle (1668) France gained part of the Netherlands from Spain. But this victory only inspired Louis and his ministers to play for larger stakes. Colbert had set high tariffs on imports into France, a direct blow at the commercial-minded Dutch. Louis, who

ENGLAND

ENGLISH CHANNEL

ENGLISH CHANNEL

Rhine R.

1668
1679
1668
1679
ARTOIS
1659
1659
1679
LUXEMBOURG
1659
SAARLAND
1684
Verdun• •Metz•
1648
Strasbourg
1684
ALSACE
1648

Seine R.
•Paris

FRANCE
Loire R.

Saône R.

FRANCHE COMPTÉ
1679

Garonne R.

Rhône R.

FRENCH ANNEXATIONS
BY TREATIES, TO 1684

ROUSSILLON
1659

MEDITERRANEAN
SEA

1648 Treaty of Westphalia
1659 Treaty of the Pyrenees
1668 Treaty of Aix-la-Chapelle
1679 Treaty of Nimwegen
1684 Treaty of Reumons and Truce of Ratisbon

SPAIN

0   50   100   150 Miles

viewed the Protestant republican merchants who controlled the Netherlands with contempt, proceeded to spin a web of treaties to isolate them.
For example, the secret Treaty of Dover with Charles II brought a promise
that Charles would remain neutral in a Franco-Dutch war. Under Colbert's
direction a powerful navy was also constructed, and in 1672 French troops
launched a massive assault. At first the Dutch with their army in disorder
were routed. The oligarchy fell, the brilliant De Witt brothers who had run
the government were assassinated, and the youthful Prince of Orange,
William III, took over control of the country. Then with the French about
to envelop Amsterdam, the Dutch opened the dikes, flooding a huge area
occupied by French troops and thus avoiding a total disaster. Nevertheless,

Louis continued the war, capturing Maastricht and Ghent and invading Alsace, the Franche Comté, and Germany. At the Peace of Nijmegen in 1678 he obtained sizable chunks of Spanish territory in northern Europe. The cost of these victories in money was high, however. And while Louis' desire to expand remained unsatisfied he was forced thereafter to rely more upon diplomatic means. He put great pressure on the territories of Strasbourg, Zweibrücken, and Luxembourg, basing his claims on various antiquated titles "sustained" by his own courts of law which forced these cities to acknowledge French suzerainty. Other European rulers, not daring to resist, contented themselves with writing petulant letters of protest to Versailles.

Only the Hapsburgs in Vienna had the power to challenge Louis' brutal aggressiveness, and Leopold, still concerned with his rebellious Hungarian subjects and with the Turks, dared not attack Louis XIV out of fear of a two-front war. Nevertheless war came, precipitated by the Turkish siege of Vienna in 1683.

Meanwhile, events in England had produced a coalition between the Dutch and the English. King James II, immediately after the death of his brother Charles II, attempted to rule as an absolute monarch. He ignored laws of Parliament and the courts, began to build a standing army, and showed his partiality to Catholicism by appointing leading Catholics to key government posts. Combined with Louis XIV's revocation of the Edict of Nantes in 1685, this convinced English Protestants that a horrendous papal plot was afoot to re-Catholicize England. In 1688 Protestant leaders turned to the Dutch stadtholder William of Orange for aid. William accepted the call and mounted an invasion. This was the bloodless Glorious Revolution. James fled, and William and his wife Mary became joint monarchs of England, not by divine right, although Mary as James's sister lent an aura of legitimacy to their rule, but by act of Parliament. William's power was limited by law, the fundamental liberties of Englishmen firmly guaranteed.

For his part, William gained the ships, soldiers, and money necessary to confront Louis. Swiftly putting down a French-supported Irish revolt, he turned to this task with a will. A Dutch English fleet smashed the French navy off La Hogue, and soon his combined army was masked behind the fortifications on the French border. Louis had foolishly assumed that William's invasion of England would produce a debilitating civil war. Now he miscalculated again, assuming he could crush the Protestant army easily. The war was, however, bloody, widespread, and long, lasting from 1688 to 1697. Once again the powers poured their wealth into sterile arms, crushing their subjects beneath heavy taxes. Crop failures heightened the suffering almost everywhere.

The Hapsburg Leopold joined the coalition against Louis, for after 1688 the Turkish pressure on his realm had lessened. Bitter, inconclusive fighting raged in the Rhineland. When the French failed to win a decisive victory, they resorted to a scorched-earth policy, seeking to insulate themselves against a counterattack by making the area so desolate that no army could cross it. But gradually the allies increased their pressure. By the late 1690's Louis' troops were everywhere on the defensive. King William, however, limited by his dependence upon Parliament for money, and willing to settle for containment rather than total victory, agreed to a peace in 1697, signed at Ryswick. The great Sun King surrendered some small bits of territory and, despite his monarchical and religious principles, officially recognized William as legitimate king of England. The threat of internal rebellion influenced his decision. "I sacrificed the advantages I had gained," he admitted, "[to] public tranquillity."

William had coolly abandoned his ally Leopold, who did not regain French-held imperial territory including the important city of Strasbourg. But although his armies continued to do well against the Turks, regaining (the Peace of Karlowitz, 1699) much of Hungary, Transylvania, and the Ukraine, he lacked the strength to fight France on his own. Nevertheless, the war had forced him to strengthen the administration of his ancient sprawling domain. Once again Hapsburg power in both eastern and western Europe was increasing.

In France, although half-surrounded by hostile powers, Louis ensconced in Versailles continued to rule with magnificent disregard of the changing times. For money he depended upon the sale of offices to the wealthy and the taille exacted from the peasantry. For policy he depended upon the game of dynastic politics and—he sincerely believed this—on God. To this amazing man, who had now ruled the most powerful nation in Europe for more than half a century, victory or defeat was God's reward or punishment. Other European rulers, and all but a few of their subjects, shared Louis' views. He sent thousands of men to their death and drove Protestant heretics from his realm to win the favor of the Lord, and it is an indication of the faith or the psychology of the age that the great majority of his subjects approved of his actions and of the motivation behind them. Indeed, in what is sometimes called the Age of Newton and Locke, it is likely that many English Tories also agreed with Louis. It was a time of change, of transition, in which old and new ideas existed side by side, sometimes in the same man. Newton, the discoverer of gravity, believed in miracles.

In such a time of change it is no wonder that the cultural monolith represented by the court of Versailles made an enormous impact on Europe. Love of elegant clothes, speech, and manners, along with a fondness for classical columns, formal gardens, and lofty sermons, united gentlemen and would-be gentlemen all over Europe in the admiration and envy of Versailles. Louis' personal charisma, sustained as it was by French culture, accounts for much of his political impact in Europe.

The patronage of the papal court had been the greatest in Europe until Louis enlarged both the Louvre and Versailles. The chief sculptor and architect of the age, Giovanni Bernini, was enticed to France to work for the Sun King. His visit marked a turning point in the cultural history of Europe, a shifting away from Italian dominance to French. With the help of the finest architects and designers of the age, the Sun King created a massive monument to himself and to the strength of the French monarchy, in the palace of Versailles, and with Italian help. At the court itself, with Molière and Racine furnishing the theatrical entertainment, Jean Baptiste Lully the music, with Nicolas Boileau, Jean de La Bruyère, and Jean de La Fontaine serving as satirists and critics, the French and the Europeans together witnessed a splendid spectacle. The spread of French among the educated nobles of Europe guaranteed a large and continuous international audience for the balls, hunts, and receptions of Versailles, with the principal actor himself serving as impresario.

But cultural influence alone did not decide the course of European power politics. Louis XIV had learned in the 1690's that he could not defeat all of Europe when every major power was allied against him. He therefore followed a more cautious policy. He compromised about the Spanish succession. He signed two treaties with the English which, had either gone into effect, would have partitioned the enormous Spanish empire to preserve the balance of power in Europe. But the Spanish grandees objected, and the superstitious Spanish king, Charles II, finally left his entire empire to Louis XIV's grandson. This put Louis in a difficult moral position. Should he profit from Charles's will or stand by his promise in the treaties? The fact that Spanish leaders were prepared to offer the whole empire to Leopold if Louis refused it helped him make up his mind. He accepted Charles's will and his grandson became king of Spain as Philip V. William III of England at first held his peace, for he had had enough of war and preferred to see a Bourbon on the Spanish throne to fighting still another world-wide war. But when Louis, sensing victory, boldly recognized the Stuart pretender as the legitimate heir to William III as king of England, Parliament and the English public cried out for war against France. This enabled William to win parliamentary support for raising the armies needed to fight France in the War of Spanish Succession, 1702–1714. Leopold, who did not have to concern himself much with public opinion and who was as convinced as Louis that God was on his side, in 1702 sent his best general, Eugene of Savoy, to attack French positions in

WAR OF THE SPANISH SUCCESSION

Grand Alliance
Franco-Spanish Coalition
× Battle

northern Italy. Eugene overran Spanish territories in Italy which the French could not defend, and then struck at France's satellites in Germany.

The war dragged on despite the deaths of both William (1702) and Leopold (1705). Eugene wielded great influence in the Hapsburg empire, and the great Marlborough backed by Parliament dominated English policy. When Louis organized an assault on Vienna, Marlborough and Eugene met his army at Blenheim in Bavaria. Although the French had taken a strong position, Marlborough launched a series of bloody frontal attacks, using his superior numbers recklessly until he had carried the day. What his critics called the "butcher's bill" was high, but Marlborough's victory was decisive. It was followed by further victories at Ramillies and

Oudenarde, after which the French armies ceased to be a threat to foreign nations.

This did not mean that France lay open to easy invasion. The great French military engineer, Marquis de Vauban, had fortified every strong point ingeniously; the war dragged on. Cost and casualties again mounted, with each side struggling to foment internal trouble in the other's domains.

During the bitter winter of 1708–1709, disastrous for harvests, France seemed on the brink of defeat, but Louis, truly by this time an institution in France, roused his people in defense of *la patrie*. A new army under General Villars met Marlborough at Malplaquet (1709). After a battle which left 40,000 dead or wounded, the allies held the field, but the French retreated in good order. The English public was now appalled by the heavy losses and tiny gains from the long war. Thus the result of more years of bloody destruction was another stalemate. Louis, publicly as haughty as ever, nevertheless made private overtures for peace. Marlborough fell from power, and new English leaders signed the Peace of Utrecht with France in 1713.

The treaty brought large colonial gains for England. The Dutch regained their fortifications along the French border, and the Austrian Hapsburgs got Naples, Sardinia, and Milan. Brandenburg-Prussia officially became a kingdom, and Savoy got control of Sicily. Louis XIV's grandson retained the throne and overseas empire of Spain. Although the Austrians were not a party to the Anglo-French negotiations, and bitterly opposed the placing of a Bourbon on the Spanish throne, they could make no military progress against the French armies and finally made peace. The balance of power had been restored, or better, the attempt to disrupt it had been tacitly abandoned. In effect, after Utrecht, the great powers gave up their attempts at continental expansion and thereafter for a long season, concentrated on building colonial empires and on expanding their commerce. In this sense, 1713 marked the end of the Age of Louis XIV. The sad and uncomprehending Sun King finally died in 1715.

For Further Reading

Ranum, O., *Paris in the Age of Absolutism.*
Rule, J. (ed.), *Louis XIV and the Craft of Kingship.*
Stoye, J., *Europe Unfolding, 1648–1688.*
Wolf, J. B., *Louis XIV.*

26   Europe in the Eighteenth Century

The philosophes of the eighteenth century were convinced that theirs was the age of enlightenment and progress *par excellence*. This view may seem naïve, even perverse, to one who knows the century well, but the philosophes, looking back on the disorders of the sixteenth and seventeenth centuries, were understandably impressed by the peace and political stability of their own times, by the slow but steady improvement of living conditions, and—at least in some of the countries of Europe—by significant increases in the personal liberties of individuals. Seventeenth-century thinkers had little reason to be optimistic, and their writings show that they were not. The writings of the philosophes of the eighteenth century reflect a new, hopeful world view. The philosophes, as Voltaire made so clear in *Candide,* were well aware that they were not living, despite Dr. Pangloss, in "the best of all possible worlds." They noted the injustices of European legal procedures, the poverty of the masses, the persistence of serfdom in eastern Europe and of slavery in the colonies of their own countries. They protested, sometimes despaired, over official censorship. They were worried by the sharp increase in Europe's population with its threat of famine. Nevertheless, and again Voltaire's view was typical, they believed that the Age of Louis XV, Frederick the Great, and Catherine the Great was a vast improvement over any period since the Renaissance, and in many respects they were right.

The eighteenth century, however, was also the time of the *ancien régime,* a time of bungling politicians, of nobles feeding off the labors of masses of peasants, of immorality and corruption among Europe's ruling elites. It is possible to see the French Revolution both as the final flowering of an age of liberal reform and as a cataclysm bringing just retribution to a century of stupidity, avarice, and corruption.

Progress or decline? The evidence points in both directions. After 1715 peace generally reigned and ideological and religious storms had subsided. Royal armies held rambunctious nobilities in check. Religious and political minorities were no longer subjected to mass persecution. Assassination ceased to be an acceptable device for settling political disagreements. Fewer witches and heretics were burned. Some leaders even began to think about improving the way government dealt with the poor, the sick, and the depraved, and even to see that the obtaining of abstract justice was a legitimate purpose of the state. In 1761 Jean Calas, a Huguenot merchant

A.D.   1709   Battle of Poltava (defeat of the Swedes by Russians under Peter the Great)

1714   George of Hanover becomes king of England

1720   Collapse of Law's Mississippi Scheme in France, and English South Sea Bubble

1721   Montesquieu publishes the *Persian Letters*

1721–1742   Administration of Sir Robert Walpole

1726   Cardinal Fleury becomes prime minister in France

1734   Voltaire publishes *Philosophical Letters on the English*

1736   John Wesley begins to establish Methodist Societies

1740   Frederick II of Prussia invades Silesia

1741   Empress Maria Theresa rallies Hungarian nobles to fight the Prussians

1745   Battle of Fontenoy

1747   Richardson publishes *Clarissa Harlowe*

1748   Treaty of Aix-la-Chapelle

1750   Death of Johann Sebastian Bach; Voltaire begins his visit at the court of Frederick the Great; Diderot and collaborators publish first volume of the *Encyclopédie*

1756   Outbreak of the Seven Years' War

1761   Resignation of William Pitt

1762   Catherine II becomes ruler of Russia; Rousseau publishes the *Social Contract*

1771   *Parlements* abolished in France by Louis XV

1773   Diderot visits Catherine the Great in Russia

1774   Louis XVI becomes king of France and recalls the *Parlements*

1778   France intervenes in the War of American Independence

1781   Joseph II promulgates the Edict of Tolerance

1783   Russia annexes the Crimea; Beaumarchais presents *Marriage of Figaro*

in Toulouse, was accused of murdering his son in order to prevent him from becoming a Catholic. He was convicted, tortured, and executed, all on the flimsiest of evidence. (The young man probably had committed suicide.) In earlier times such an incident would have passed unnoticed. But Voltaire seized upon the case, and soon a wave of protest swept across France; prominent men expressed outrage at the way the religious authorities had interfered in the trial and at the brutal conduct of the judges. Fair play and proper procedure were becoming important.

Religious passions clearly had cooled; the diplomats at Utrecht in 1713 grappled with questions of national interest and the balance of power, not with religious issues such as had dominated their negotiations at Westphalia which ended the Thirty Years' War. After 1715 no monarch tried seriously to impose religious unity on Europe. At every royal court churchmen were less influential than in earlier times and a freer intellectual climate flourished. Despite the work of the Counter Reformation in stimulating religious feeling and rebuilding church institutions, church power did not increase in the eighteenth century even in Catholic states. The eighteenth was a century of weak popes, declining monasteries, lazy bishops.

The decline of the importance of religion in political affairs had profound effects on the general public. No longer were merchants and peasants and judges asked to pay such high taxes and make other sacrifices in the name of a particular faith. As early as 1709, Louis XIV made his dramatic appeal to save the nation, not the Church, even though the enemies were Protestants. Political stability enabled leaders to conduct diplomacy without constant appeal for public loyalty and support. Indeed, in a paradoxical way, eighteenth-century Europeans, while more cosmopolitan, were also more isolationist than those of the seventeenth. Both the lower classes and the educated elite "disengaged" themselves from politics. Frederick the Great of Prussia (and he was not very different in this respect from most absolute monarchs) fantasized that he could even fight a war without his subjects knowing about it.

No eighteenth-century king could realize this "ideal," but peace and the decline of ideological politics created a kind of isolationism which permitted both profitable colonial expansion and an increased concern for internal problems. Probably this isolationism also explains the increasing concern of the educated elite for justice and sound finance. Even in England, where bitter memories of the seventeenth-century revolution combined with problems resulting from the succession of the very Germanic George I to produce a period of plotting and rebellion, the trend was toward stability. Gradually the Whig Sir Robert Walpole built a system of control that extended from the king's cabinet to the lowest levels of the local bureaucracy. Whig supremacy, as Walpole well knew, depended on peace and economy in government; he constantly slapped down members of his own party, chiefly London merchants, who favored a more aggressive foreign policy.

Low taxes appealed to the rural gentry, and England was still primarily an agricultural country. The gentry families that Fielding described so well in *Tom Jones* owned most of the arable land, dominated local government, sat in Parliament, held the chief places in the Anglican Church and in the army and navy. Within this group, Tory contested with Whig for office, but on underlying social and economic issues all were united. The lower classes —the farmers and artisans—accepted political impotence in exchange for prosperity and lower taxes. Prosperity and commercial growth in the age of Walpole combined after about 1740 with a rising population to lay the groundwork for the Industrial Revolution.

Walpole was a master politician, personally familiar with officials high and low all over the kingdom. He was convinced that all Englishmen wanted what he wanted: peace and profit. These he could give them, thanks to the general European stability of his time. The decline of the Dutch merchants opened up vast opportunities, particularly in the Baltic. At the same time the growth of the American colonies provided both raw materials and markets, and gave bankers valuable new investment opportunities. A succession of good harvests kept food prices at reasonable levels. England, as the eighteenth century wore on, became richer, more sure of itself, and more tolerant. It was an age when the aristocracy built enormous and elegant country houses, often with money gained by accepting a merchant's daughter into the family. Andrea Palladio, the great Italian architect of the sixteenth century, inspired the Duke of Burlington in the building of Chiswick House. The monumental classical style which the English now favored harmonized with the splendidly designed plaster ceilings of Adam, the Chippendale furniture, and Gainsborough portraits of beautiful women and children. Alexander Pope, Samuel Johnson, and James Boswell, along with the novelists Samuel Richardson and Henry Fielding, gave England a kind of literary dominance in Europe similar to the scientific dominance established by John Locke and Isaac Newton.

Not even the religious revival of the Methodist zealot John Wesley could shake English society. Wesley made converts by the thousands, for the Anglican clergy of the time was, by and large, lazy and out of touch with the people. Religious enthusiasm seemed to many Anglican leaders positively dangerous, an invitation to revolution. But Wesley was not a social reformer—piety, not "progress," was his objective. In a society in which the ability to read was still considered an enormous accomplishment and in which prosperity bred complacency among the middle classes, most persons were content to remain "in their place."

When war broke out again on the Continent in 1740, Frederick of Prussia invading Silesia, this basic conservatism enabled the brilliant political tactician William Pitt to thrust Walpole and his system aside. The French became involved in aimless campaigning against Frederick, and Pitt saw this as a chance, by joining in the conflict, to strike at the rich French overseas possessions. Using their powerful navy effectively, the British by 1763 had swallowed up nearly all of the French colonies in America and in India. English arms were less successful in the European phases of the wars of this period, but maintaining the status quo on the Continent adequately suited British purposes. But even successful wars cost money. Country gentlemen began to balk at high taxes, and this combined with the death of George II and the succession of his politically ambitious grandson George III led to the ending of the imperial wars.

In France, too, conflicts were more political than social or economic in this era. Religious disputes inherited from the seventeenth century continued, but did not seriously threaten the peace of the realm. Old landed families and judicial nobles had common interests, most notably the desire not to pay taxes, while the lower orders, politically impotent to begin with, benefited from the lowering of taxes after the Peace of Utrecht and from commercial and agricultural prosperity. Louis XV's chief minister, the aging Cardinal Fleury, held together a coalition of nobles and merchants behind a policy of making the main function of the state the providing of offices and pensions.

But Frederick of Prussia's invasion of Silesia made Fleury as obsolete as Walpole, and France produced no William Pitt, who saw the significance of colonies in buttressing the state. Belle-Isle, who took over the role of chief royal minister in France, saw Frederick's attack on Silesia as an opportunity to resume the ancient war of Bourbon against Hapsburg. Without forethought or planning, France allied itself with Prussia and invaded Hapsburg Germany.

Frederick, however, made peace with the Hapsburg ruler, Maria Theresa, leaving the French, deep in Germany, to face the Hapsburg armies alone. The result was disaster, exacerbated by heavy losses to the British on the seas and in the colonies. The war had been undertaken mindlessly and the results should have been predictable.

Louis replaced Belle-Isle with the hard-working and honest Machault, who attempted to place new taxes on all classes of French society to get government finances on a sound basis. This produced grave protests, and Louis dismissed Machault rather than face the storm. Royal power was declining, that of the nobility on the rise, a fact Louis finally recognized in 1764 when his parliamentary enemies voted to dissolve the Jesuit order in the realm. The king then roused himself to the defense of his authority. He

FINLAND
(to Russia)

NORWAY
(to Denmark)

SWEDEN

Stockholm

St. Petersburg

GULF OF FINLAND

RUSSIA

NORTH

SEA

BALTIC SEA

W. Dvina R.

Dnieper R.

DENMARK

EAST
PRUSSIA

POMERANIA

Vistula R.

HANOVER

HOLLAND

BRAN'DENBURG

Berlin

Warsaw

POLAND

CLEVES

Elbe

Oder

SAXONY

SILESIA

AUSTRIAN
NETHERLANDS

Rhine R.

BOHEMIA

Dniester R.

• Paris

BAVARIA

BREISGAU

Vienna

Buda • Pest

FRANCE

AUSTRIA

HUNGARY

SWITZERLAND

TYROL

STYRIA

Rhône R.

SAVOY

Milan

Po

VENETIA

Venice

CROATIA

Sava R.

Danube

R.

Genoa

ADRIATIC SEA

DALMATIA

OTTOMAN

TUSCANY

PAPAL
STATES

EMPIRE

CORSICA
(to Genoa)

Rome •

KINGDOM

Naples •

SARDINIA
(to Savoy)

OF THE

TWO

CENTRAL EUROPE, 1740

SICILIES

MEDITERRANEAN SEA

Hapsburg possessions

Hohenzollern possessions

Venetian possessions

Holy Roman Empire boundary

0   100   200   300 Miles

tried to reduce the power of Parliament, to regain control of the judiciary, to make the nobles pay taxes. But he died in 1774, and his successor, the desultory Louis XVI, was incapable of carrying on the fight. Probably he could not have won it even if he had been able, courageous, and intelligent (he was none of these), for even the professional classes and the artisans were siding with the nobles in the struggle against what seemed to them royal despotism. A curious alliance of limited democracy and high privilege was in the making in France, one that would lead to the great revolution. Louis XV and Louis XVI were both ineffectual and unwilling to turn over the machinery of state to able ministers. A Colbert or a Richelieu might have saved the Crown, but a strong hand would have made open enemies, and both kings wished, above all, to be loved. They purchased this love by surrendering power, and paid for it, in the end, with their patrimony, the throne of France. Ironically the peace that came to France after 1763 had much to do with the inability of the rulers to strengthen the monarchy. Arbitrary royal power and the heavy taxation needed to institute social and fiscal reform were hard to justify when no foreign threat existed. The effort to revive the famous *capitation,* or head tax, for example, did not succeed because no pressing wartime expenses had to be made. In France, at least (although not in Germany or in eastern Europe), the consequences of peace for absolute monarchy were fatal.

As with France, Frederick the Great's invasion of Silesia had profound effects on the central European states. What was surprising about Frederick's decision was not his objective but his method. Instead of seeking to build an alliance against the Hapsburgs, whose potential enemies were legion—Turks, Russians, and French—he struck directly and alone in a bold bid to make Prussia a great power. His success, and the means of achieving it, shaped the later history of Prussia and of the other German states.

War, especially the Seven Years' War of 1756–1763, compelled the raising of taxes and increased royal power. In state after state in the Germanies representative assemblies declined in influence to the advantage of royal authority. Even tiny Denmark became an absolute monarchy. Frederick I and Frederick the Great dominated the Prussian nobility, built large, well-trained armies, the best in Europe, and reduced the proud aristocrats to the status of bureaucrats in the service of their war machine. Prussia in 1750 resembled France in 1675, the heyday of the great Sun King. Territorial expansion, governmental efficiency, and a mercantilistic economy were common to both. Frederick the Great, however, was a different man from Louis XIV. He stifled initiative among his ministers and generals and developed among the Prussian hierarchy a blind, total obedience that persisted long after his death. In seventeenth-century

France, courtiers were obsequious but independent-minded; in eighteenth-century Germany they were merely obsequious, and if they incurred the royal disfavor they could be dismissed or even imprisoned by royal fiat. The almost military discipline of the Prussian bureaucracy made for efficiency; thus monarchical absolutism weighed more heavily by far on Prussian society than Louis XIV's absolutism had ever weighed on French society. Hundreds of inspectors checked up on royal officials and submitted confidential reports to Berlin; junior bureaucrats were encouraged to report on the failings of their superiors to the king himself. Overlapping jurisdictions and wasteful rivalries, so common to the French bureaucracy, were virtually nonexistent. The price of such efficiency, of course, was the stifling of initiative and the imposition upon society of a militaristic, almost Spartan type of government. Frenchmen had surmounted absolutism by finding ways around it, especially where taxes and the judicial process were concerned. Prussians merely submitted. The rapidity of unification and the emasculation of the nobility left Prussian society without any group strong enough to resist the Crown. Frederick was his own foreign minister, treasurer, tax expert, chief justice, minister of the interior, and commander in chief. No earlier sovereign anywhere in Europe so thoroughly dominated the machinery of government. He was Europe's closest approximation to an Oriental despot.

By contrast, the Hapsburg monarchy, having survived the "reforms" of the Emperor Leopold, slumbered in feudal confusion. Each principality preserved many of its distinctive institutions and had its own army and laws and its own special relationship to the Crown in Vienna. Patronage, especially that connected with the Church, remained the principal instrument of royal authority, and it was often limited by local tradition and by the influence of the pope in Rome.

When Maria Theresa went to war with Prussia over Silesia, she and her ministers finally acted to strengthen control, but they did not succeed in developing a centralized system comparable to Frederick's, or even to that in France. Provincial opposition to Vienna was too strong and too well organized. Maria Theresa's son and heir, Joseph II, attacked the privileges of his nobles and of the Church even more vigorously. He has often been judged the most enlightened of all emperors, but he was as willing to use force against these powerful interests as any contemporary ruler. He closed down the monasteries and freed the serfs, thus delighting European philosophes, but he did so as much for reasons of realpolitik as for liberal and enlightened reasons. And he sought avidly to extend his sway over the new territories: in this sense he was a traditional Hapsburg.

In Russia, the death of Peter the Great in 1725 brought an end to his frenetic efforts to create a modern state. His passing was greeted with relief and pleasure by his troubled people. The kind of "Westernization" he favored was expensive, and destructive to Russian traditions, and imposed without regard for the primitive state of the Russian economy. The country remained agricultural; serfdom was as entrenched as ever after Peter's death. Peter did succeed, however, in increasing Russia's military power and thus in extending its territory. After he defeated the Swedes at the Battle of Poltava in 1709 he controlled most of the eastern Baltic and he also extended Russian power in the area of the Black Sea. His immediate successors were weak and plagued by court intrigues, but held the state together, thanks to the army Peter had created. And when the more forceful Elizabeth took the throne in 1741, she was able to exert considerable weight in international affairs, thanks to this army, especially during the Seven Years' War.

In Russia, however, a strong state was maintained by building a powerful landowning and military class. Peter had built that state without yielding to these interests, but his successors gave them new privileges and power to hold their allegiance. Their gains were paid for by the virtual enslavement of the peasants, whose taxes and obligations to their lords were sharply increased. Catherine II, known as the Great, was great only because she was the darling of these military and landed powers. Her domestic policies were determined by their needs and interests. Catherine admired Voltaire, Diderot, and other philosophes, but she ruled Russia like a reactionary absolutist, never hesitating, for example, to suppress peasant uprisings brutally. The difference between her pronounced objectives as queen and her actions was monumental, probably because the former were based on her wish to ape western European rulers, the latter on the social and political realities of eastern Europe.

Whether any of these monarchs were really "enlightened" is an interesting question. If we focus on how they admired the philosophes and talked of "reform" based on the enlightenment principles of these intellectuals, they do indeed seem like enlightened despots. Frederick, Catherine, Joseph II, Louis XVI, knew many of the philosophes, read their works, entertained some of them at their courts. But hard evidence that the philosophes influenced any royal policy is extremely scarce, as many of the philosophes themselves admitted. The eighteenth-century monarchs employed a rhetoric different from the sovereigns of the seventeenth century, but beneath and behind the rhetoric they were still sovereigns. Voltaire supposedly had the ear of Frederick the Great, but Frederick behaved very similarly to Frederick William, the great elector. Diderot was a confidant of Catherine the Great, but her policies resemble closely those of the tyrannical czar Peter. The philosophes condemned expansionism and war; Frederick and Catherine practiced both.

The eighteenth century, writes the German historian Fritz Hartung, was "the final phase in the history of hierarchical feudal society which descended from the Middle Ages. Already it had begun to doubt the rightness of the inherited division into classes determined by birth, and in having a privileged nobility which stood in contrast to a less free middle class and an unfree peasantry . . . as Pirenne pointed out enlightened absolutism was really nothing new, but rather a new version of an old idea of the prince as father of his country." Hartung prefers to speak of absolutism rather than despotism, and in the sense that these kings were reluctant to violate established principles of legitimacy, they were perhaps not despots. But when Frederick the Great called himself the "first servant of the state" and repudiated the divine right of kings, he was not thinking of abjuring power.

As for the elite elements in European society, the landed gentlemen, merchants, bishops, judges, and the like, in the late eighteenth century they were more relaxed and secure than their predecessors before 1715. They were less afraid of hell, smallpox, and revolution. But they were perhaps more concerned for the safety of their investments. Most European governments were in a dreadful financial state in the 1770's. Then the American Revolution weakened the fiscal structure of Britain and France still further. Moreover, that revolt engaged the elites of both these countries profoundly. Liberal ideas, long discussed, suddenly seemed possible of achievement. After the American victory in the revolution, while Louis XVI's ministers in Versailles were congratulating themselves on the humbling of the mighty British Empire, the cafés of Paris hummed with idealistic talk of political reform, tempered by anxiety about the powerless state of the French treasury. In 1784 Immanuel Kant wrote, "When we ask, are we now living in an enlightened age? the answer is, no, but we are living in an age of enlightenment." The question, sure to be answered, was: Has there been progress *enough?*

For Further Reading

Anderson, M. S., *Europe in the Eighteenth Century, 1713–1789.*
Dorn, W., *Competition for Empire, 1740–1763.*
Gay, P., *Voltaire's Politics: The Poet as Realist.*
Palmer, R. R., *The Age of Democratic Revolution: A Political History of Europe and America, 1760–1800.*

Revolution in the Western World

27   The American Revolution

Inaugurating an era of world revolutions, the American Revolution had points of similarity with the revolutions that followed. First of all, it was an anticolonial war waged by a colonial people for their independence; in that respect it was the seedbed for all later anticolonial movements in Latin America, Asia, or Africa. Second, it was a revolt against monarchy which supplanted the royal system by a republic. This was true of all the major revolutions down to the overthrow of the czarist regime in Russia in 1917. Third, it was a civil war fought not between great sections of the country, as the American Civil War, but rather in each state, county, and village. Fourth, it resulted in the creation in America of a nation different both in origins and in character from the nations of the Old World, thus touching off an era of revolutionary nationalism that has not yet run its course. Finally, it marked the formulation of new principles governing the relation of men to government, which might be put under the rubric of constitutionalism.

In other respects the American Revolution differed from those that followed in its wake. It was a civil war without being a clear-cut class war. The Patriot cause found recruits in all classes and economic groups, but members of the very same groups were numbered among the Loyalists. Even many poor tenant farmers and frontiersmen remained loyal to Great Britain. The American Revolution stands in notable contradiction to the French Revolution in that the former was accomplished without the seizure of power by extremists, without resort to dictatorship, and without that violent reaction that has come to be known as the Thermidor. However, if the American Revolution was not a clear-cut class war it did involve far-reaching democratic reforms. Self-government was inaugurated, but also relatively democratic government; egalitarian principles proved central to the American revolutionary ideology.

1763 Treaty of Paris ending Seven Years' War; Proclamation of 1763, restricting trans-Appalachian settlement; Patrick Henry's arguments in the Parson's Cause

1764 Passage of the Sugar Act and Currency Acts

1765 Passage of the Stamp Act; Resolves of Virginia House of Burgesses denouncing Stamp Act; Stamp Act Congress meets in New York and adopts Declaration of Rights and Grievances

1766 Repeal of the Stamp Act accompanied by passage of Declaratory Act

1767 Passage of Townshend Acts; revival of nonimportation agreements; publication of first of John Dickinson's *Farmer's Letters*

1768 Massachusetts House of Representatives adopts Circular Letter

1770 Townshend duties repealed in large part except for duties on tea

1772 Burning of the *Gaspee;* Committees of Correspondence organized by Samuel Adams

1773 Passage of the Tea Act; Boston Tea Party

1774 Passage of the "Intolerable Acts," including the Quebec Act; First Continental Congress convenes at Philadelphia, defeats Galloway's Plan of Union; adopts Declaration and Resolves and Continental Association

1775 Battles of Lexington and Concord; Second Continental Congress names Washington commander of the Continental forces; Battle of Bunker Hill

1776 Publication of *Common Sense* by Thomas Paine; Declaration of Independence; Battles of Long Island and Trenton

1777 Battles of Princeton and Germantown; Burgoyne's surrender, Saratoga; Congress adopts Articles of Confederation

1778 Franco-American treaties of amity and commerce and of alliance with the United States

1779 Formal entry of Spain into the war against England

1780 Siege of Charleston and fall to the British; treason of Arnold

1781 Ratification of the Articles of Confederation; surrender of the British at Yorktown to combined Franco-American forces

1782 Fall of Lord North's ministry; signing of Preliminary Articles of Peace in Paris

1783 Signing of Definitive Treaty of Peace with Great Britain; British evacuate New York City

While the American Revolution increased in complexity as the war progressed, it originated as a protest against the subordination by the mother country of colonies inhabited by people of the same nationality as the homeland, and grown to a degree of maturity that could no longer accept a status of total subordination within the British Empire.

That colonial discontent had long been smoldering is obvious in retrospect, but it is equally obvious that the beginning of the sharp cleavage between the colonies and Great Britain can be traced only to the closing years of the French and Indian War, the colonial phase of the last of the world wars fought between England and France in the period between 1689 and 1763. By that concluding war England acquired from France not only Canada but all land lying between the Appalachians and the Mississippi, along with East and West Florida, which were ceded by Spain.

The peace settlement posed innumerable administrative and fiscal problems for the victors while removing the threat of invasion by a hostile power which had long contributed to reconciling the English colonies in America to rule by the mother country. Indeed, the proposals to resolve these new and enlarged administrative and fiscal problems carried over at the peace triggered the crisis between the colonies and the mother country. For example, the effort to prevent smuggling and illicit trade with the enemy in wartime precipitated a confrontation in 1761 over the issuance of general search warrants ("Writs of Assistance"), which the Massachusetts lawyer James Otis exploited to the full. The exercise by the British home authority of the right to disallow colonial laws and hear cases on appeal from colonial courts precipitated a similar crisis when Virginia sought to pay its clergy in overvalued currency. In the so-called Parson's Cause, young Patrick Henry, arguing the colony's case, gained instant notoriety by his daring attack on the royal authority. To compound its difficulties, the British government antagonized a motley collection of land speculators by issuing the Proclamation of 1763, temporarily reserving land west of the Appalachians as Indian hunting grounds.

To meet the enormous new fiscal problems inherited from the war the Grenville ministry in 1764 proposed a tariff on sugar, molasses, and rum imported into America from the foreign West Indies. It did so not with the intent of stopping this trade, for the unenforceable Molasses Act of 1733 had shown that to be impossible, but rather to raise revenue in America. The enforcement of the Sugar Act involved overhauling the entire customs machinery and the relentless prosecution of smugglers. In addition, the Stamp Act of 1765 levied a tax within the colonies by requiring that stamps be affixed to newspapers, pamphlets, legal documents, and other items. While the Sugar Act was unpopular among merchants, the Stamp Act aroused even wider condemnation, touching off a violent three-pronged attack—an ideological assault on the nature of the British Constitution, an economic boycott of British goods, and civil disorder and disobedience. An extralegal Stamp Act Congress meeting in New York City denied the right of the British Parliament to tax the colonies without representation. The scale of the Americans' resistance, notably their ability to retaliate economically, astonished the home authorities. After fierce debate the Stamp Act was repealed. Deferring to the ill-omened advice of William Pitt, Parliament attached to its repeal a Declaratory Act explicitly asserting its unbounded right to legislate for the colonies.

A provocative element in these colonial disputes was the presence of the British army in America with its headquarters first in New York and then, after 1768, in Boston. The ostensible ground for maintaining troops in America after the French and Indian War was to secure peace on the frontiers, but as long as the colonies were torn by civil disorders it was obvious to everybody that the troops would be held in a state of readiness at strategic seaboard locations. A number of clashes between colonists and Redcoats occurred, culminating, on March 5, 1770, in the so-called Boston Massacre.

Meantime, the various British ministries, after backpedaling on the taxation issue, tried once again to raise revenue in America through the Townshend Acts of 1767, which imposed duties on a long list of imports. Once again the home government miscalculated: the American response repeated the pattern which had been set during the Stamp Act crisis. And once again the home government backed down, leaving merely a tax on tea, to uphold the principle of the Declaratory Act. That tax was still on the books in 1773 when the ministry of Lord North, seeking to rescue the East India Company from financial straits, secured the passage of the Tea Act by which the company acquired a monopoly of the tea trade with America. The colonial response was the Boston Tea Party of December 16, 1773, and it was this defiant action which confirmed George III in his resolve to use force to reduce Massachusetts to submission. Meanwhile, Parliament passed a series of punitive measures, the "Intolerable Acts." The Boston port was closed until that town had paid for the destroyed tea cargo, and in various ways the self-government of Massachusetts was severely restricted. In addition the Quebec Act, passed at the same time, turned over to the Province of Canada the lands north and west of the Ohio River which the colonies had long claimed by charter right.

The Intolerable Acts confirmed the Patriots in their conviction that Parliament had no constitutional right to tax or legislate for the colonies, a line which was forcefully advanced in the year 1774 by such noteworthy revolutionary political figures as James Wilson of Pennsylvania, Thomas Jefferson of Virginia, young Alexander Hamilton of New York, and John

Adams of Massachusetts. Indeed, the Intolerable Acts accomplished what a decade of laborious agitation had failed to bring about—union among the Thirteen Colonies. On September 1, 1774, a Congress convened at Philadelphia. Quickly routing a strong conservative element, the radicals secured the adoption of a drastic boycott of British goods and a Declaration and Resolves setting forth the colonists' right to "life, liberty and property." Congress took measures to put the colonies in a posture of self-defense, and before adjourning agreed to meet again on May 10, 1775, if by that date American wrongs had not been redressed.

With Redcoats vigilant and Minutemen organizing, drilling, marching, and stockpiling arms in various colonies, a confrontation seemed inevitable. It came on April 19, 1775, when some advance British units, rounding up subversives and searching for arms and munitions, clashed with seventy armed Minutemen on the town common of Lexington, Massachusetts. Marching on to Concord, the Redcoats destroyed such military stores as they could find, but their return march to the protection of the coast became a frantic retreat, with soldiers running a gauntlet of fire from the roadside and suffering surprisingly heavy casualties.

From that date until July 4, 1776, the Americans fought a fairly large-scale military action without avowedly seeking independence. The largest of these actions took place in June, 1775, when the British managed to drive a heavily entrenched American force from Bunker Hill in Boston. The British at Bunker Hill won only a Pyrrhic victory, however, for they suffered enormous casualties, while the Patriots demonstrated that their soldiers were no mere rabble in arms but the core of a disciplined army.

It was at this strategic time that Congress designated George Washington to be commander in chief of the Continental army. An affluent Virginia planter, Washington had gained seasoning by his experience commanding his colony's militia during the French and Indian War; a dedicated patriot, he possessed qualities that inspired confidence and commanded respect. Daringly stripping Fort Ticonderoga, on Lake Champlain, of its cannon, and transporting them 300 miles to Boston, Washington was able to fortify Dorchester Heights and place the British fleet in Boston Harbor in an untenable position. Deprived of naval support, on March 17, 1776, the British Army evacuated the city, ending an eight-month siege.

In other ways, however, the Patriots fared poorly in the north. A daring campaign to capture Quebec and make Canada the fourteenth state collapsed after a costly frontal attack was repulsed on the night of December 31, 1775. In turn, the British failed to exploit their adversary's weakness on the northern frontier.

For fifteen months American and British troops fought without a formal declaration of war, but various events conspired to work against reconciliation. King George III refused to receive a so-called Olive Branch Petition drawn for Congress by John Dickinson. Confronted with a poor enlistment rate for an unpopular war, the British Ministry bolstered its army with German mercenaries, loosely called "Hessians" because of the large number purchased from the Landgrave of Hesse-Cassel. Also contributing to the irreversible trend toward independence was Tom Paine's *Common Sense,* published in January, 1776. This pamphlet was a sensational and persuasive attack both on monarchy as an institution and on the monarch, George III, as a person. Town after town pressed for a public declaration of independence, and colonial leaders responded to the groundswell. Finally, on June 7, 1776, Richard Henry Lee of Virginia proposed a resolution in Congress that the United Colonies "are, and of right ought to be, free and independent states." Congress named a committee of five— John Adams, Benjamin Franklin, Thomas Jefferson, Robert Livingston, and Roger Sherman—to prepare a declaration. Jefferson, then only thirty-three, was chosen by the committee to give literary expression to the arguments justifying the colonies in dissolving their political bonds with the mother country. Congress endorsed the Declaration on July 4, 1776, at which time it was signed by John Hancock as president of the Congress. Subsequently the fifty-five signers attached their names to what has become the official proclamation of American sovereignty, of the principle of government by consent, and of the ideal of equality.

Although the British outnumbered the Americans both on sea and on land, and had incomparably superior financial resources, the Americans had the advantages of fighting from much shorter interior lines of communication and of conducting a war on familiar soil. They had, however, one serious disadvantage which the British expected to exploit: the presence in the colonies of a very substantial element of Loyalists or Tories, who opposed independence. In addition, the British counted upon the backing of their Indian allies on the frontiers, who could be expected to consider the king their protector against the aggression of colonial settlers. Unfortunately from the British point of view, neither Loyalists nor Indians proved crucial factors in the conduct of the war, nor were they effectively utilized to crush colonial resistance. To a large extent, however, the British military operation was inspired by the Loyalist presence. Having in effect abandoned New England, the British government decided to carry the war to the middle states and the south, areas which they were confident would rally to the support of the Redcoats. Except for an unsuccessful attempt in the year 1776 to capture the southern port of Charleston, the British for the next few years largely confined their efforts to the middle states. Thereafter, the main theater of operations was in the south.

In the battle for New York the British won all the opening engagements. Admiral Lord Richard Howe and General William Howe, conducting a successful amphibious operation on Long Island in August, 1776, quickly routed the American defenders at Brooklyn Heights, but allowed Washington to withdraw his main army across the East River to Manhattan. New York City quickly fell, forcing Washington to pull back his forces into Westchester and, after an inconclusive stand at White Plains, to retreat across New Jersey. As the year 1776 was coming to an end and enlistment time was running out, Washington decided in desperation to strike a blow while he still had an army. He surprised the Hessians at Trenton and defeated the British in a night march to Princeton. His nine-day campaign rid all but easternmost New Jersey of Redcoats and gave sinking American morale an incomparable boost.

The Patriot victories at Trenton and Princeton did not break the hold of the British on the middle states. Under a plan drawn up by General John Burgoyne in February, 1777, the British hoped to isolate New England by a three-pronged attack, a main army moving southward down Lake Champlain and the upper Hudson River, a second force operating through the Mohawk Valley from Oswego, both to be reinforced by a strong contingent dispatched up the Hudson from Howe's New York City base. A wonderful plan on paper, everything went wrong with it in execution. Howe decided to attack Philadelphia in the impractical belief that he could take the seat of the Congress and return in time to execute his role in the Burgoyne plan. Burgoyne himself suffered a series of setbacks. His auxiliary force from Fort Oswego was repulsed by the Americans, a raiding party into Vermont was trounced there by General John Stark, whereas the overcautious Sir Henry Clinton in command of the New York garrison moved too late and with far too little to reach Burgoyne at Saratoga. There, blocked by the army of General Horatio Gates, Burgoyne surrendered his entire force, bringing the war in the north to an end. While Burgoyne's grand scheme was collapsing, Howe managed to take Philadelphia, repulsing Washington's main army at Germantown but failing to capture or destroy it. In May, 1778, however, Philadelphia had to be evacuated on news that a French naval expedition was headed for America.

The disastrous middle-states campaign was followed by a new southern campaign which had as its initial objectives Georgia and then South Carolina. In 1780 Charleston capitulated to British besiegers, and the Redcoats soon brought the rest of the state to heel. However, here too the tide turned. The Patriots completely enveloped the Tory forces at King's Mountain, a short distance from the boundary line between North and South Carolina, thereby ridding North Carolina of Tory influence. This victory coincided with the appointment to the southern Patriot command of General Nathanael Greene. He dispatched General Dan Morgan to reduce the

British outpost in western South Carolina while he himself went to bolster the partisan forces led by Francis Marion and Thomas Sumter, then operating in the north-central part of the state. Morgan crushed the British at Cowpens in January, 1781, while in March of the same year Greene clashed at Guilford Courthouse with the forces of Lord Cornwallis. Cornwallis kept the field but at the expense of one-fourth of his army.

Disillusioned with his campaign in the lower south, Cornwallis moved his army into Virginia and, bowing to orders from Sir Henry Clinton, took his troops to Yorktown, which he heavily fortified. But reinforced by a French army under the Comte de Rochambeau, Washington eluded the British defenders of New York and moved down to Virginia, where he laid siege to Yorktown. When the British naval forces sailed to the Chesapeake to rescue Cornwallis they found French Admiral De Grasse, with a fleet he had brought up from the West Indies, barring the way. On October 19, 1781, Cornwallis' troops surrendered. Although a few scattered engagements took place thereafter, and the war continued at sea, to all intents and purposes the battle was transferred to the peace table.

The American Revolution posed novel issues in diplomacy. A cluster of colonies which had defied their monarch sought recognition as independent states from other nations which were ruled by monarchs and supported the principle of kingly authority. In addition to seeking recognition, the insurgent Americans counted on obtaining financial and military assistance from England's traditional enemies. In November, 1775, Congress had set up a five-man Committee of Secret Correspondence to make contact with "friends" abroad. The first prospective friend was France. Still nursing her wounds from the Seven Years' War, France had most at stake in the weakening of British power. In various underground operations, Silas Deane of Connecticut, joined shortly thereafter by Benjamin Franklin and Arthur Lee, secured French aid—military supplies and equipment, clothing, blankets, and above all cash. The kings of France and Spain secretly put up 2,000,000 livres to subsidize a private company to carry on these operations. In addition, the American commissioners recruited many French and European officers including the Marquis de Lafayette. Ultimately the triumvirate of quarreling commissioners was supplanted by a single man, the internationally renowned Benjamin Franklin. Franklin used his unique talents as a propagandist to win friends for America abroad.

The alliance with France, however, came not as a result of American pressure but as a consequence of the American victory at Saratoga. Fearful that the British government was about to come to terms with the Americans, the French entered into a treaty of amity and commerce and a treaty of alliance with the United States on February 6, 1778. The treaty bound both parties not to make a separate treaty with a common enemy without the consent of the other. In the spring of 1779 Spain came into the war on the side of France when England refused to cede Gibraltar. But Spain made it clear that she was not fighting for the independence of the United States. Finally the United Provinces (the Netherlands), which had provided the United States with an immense quantity of military stores, was dragged into the conflict late in 1780 when England declared war against the Dutch. By that date the American Revolution had become a world war, waged not only in continental North America but at Gibraltar, in the English Channel, in India, and off the African coast, and fought for national objectives quite different and distinct from American independence.

Both sides were war-weary by 1780, and looked hopefully to foreign mediation. Austria and Russia proposed to force a truce upon all the parties and impose a settlement based on the military status quo. Had their diplomacy succeeded, Maine, New York City, and most of the Carolinas and Georgia would have remained part of the British Empire and a united nation might never have been achieved. However, the news of Yorktown put an end to these complicated backstairs intrigues and hardened the move in England for a quick peace. On March 4, 1782, the House of Commons resolved to consider as enemy of king and country all those who should further attempt to carry on the war. Two weeks later Lord North's ministry resigned. The new government was first headed by the Marquess of Rockingham and after his death, on July 1, by Lord Shelburne. Congress named as its peace commissioners Benjamin Franklin, who had been in France for the greater part of the war, John Jay of New York, who had attempted unsuccessfully to secure recognition of the United States from Spain, John Adams, who had negotiated a loan from the Dutch, and Henry Laurens of South Carolina, who had been captured by the British on the high seas and was released only in time to sign the preliminary treaty. By that treaty of November 30, 1782, confirmed by the definitive treaty of September 3, 1783, the United States secured recognition of its independence, its claims to the Mississippi as its western boundary, and fishing rights off Newfoundland and Nova Scotia.

As a war for independence or an anticolonial revolution, the American Revolution came officially to an end with the signing and ratification of the definitive peace. But as a movement of internal political and social reform the years of the Revolution marked merely the beginning of a long period of innovation. A new constitutional system was established based on the principle of consent of the governed. All the states with the exception of Connecticut and Rhode Island, which were satisfied with their liberal colonial charters, adopted constitutions which attested this principle. Indeed, Massachusetts went one step further when it submitted its constitutional draft to the people for ratification. Although they drew heavily on the colonial charters, the state constitutions reflected revolutionary experience in several of their aspects. The powers of the governor were diminished, the powers of the legislature enhanced. And the incorporation into the Virginia Constitution of 1776 of a Bill of Rights which also served as the model for most of the constitutions that followed, as well as the first Ten Amendments to the federal Constitution, proved to be pathbreaking.

The social and economic changes inspired by the American Revolution were less revolutionary but important. Thus, Tory estates were confiscated not to create a peasant freeholding class (a very broad class of freeholders already existed) but to punish Loyalists and to raise funds desperately needed for the war effort. Although much of the land eventually came into the hands of former tenants and small farmers, the initial purchases were often made by wealthy speculators. Some of the states canceled the debts owing to Tory and British merchants, and in Virginia, where the indebtedness of tobacco planters to British businessmen was massive, the struggle took on the character of a class conflict of creditor versus debtor.

One of the major areas of revolutionary reform was that of property law. Entail (in effect, an inheritable life estate) and primogeniture (exclusive inheritance of the first-born male heir) were abolished. It has been argued that the egalitarian effects of these reforms did not amount to much, since most southern planters made ample provisions for younger children in their wills, and legal devices already existed for breaking entail. Yet to a legal reformer like Thomas Jefferson the revision of the property laws was central to the reform of a society whose egalitarianism was based on land. In other areas such as the disestablishment of the Church of England, the extension of religious tolerance, and the reform of the criminal law, the Revolution can be shown to have created a climate which encouraged reform and innovation.

Slavery, on the other hand, was an institution that was substantially untouched in the great slave states by the Revolution. Though the war triggered a movement in the northern states to abolish slavery, none of the southern states, where most of the slaves were, acted against the institution. Some southerners, like Washington, George Mason, Jefferson, and Henry Laurens, explicitly avowed their opposition to the institution and their determination to bring it to an end, but the climate of opinion was not congenial to so radical a reform.

What gave to the American Revolution its durable qualities were the principles upon which it rested as enunciated in the Declaration of Independence. These served as a standard for defining a free society. Admittedly, the phrase "all men are created equal" did not accurately describe the America of 1776, where half a million persons lived in slavery. But as

Abraham Lincoln, speaking of Jefferson's generation in 1857, put it:
"They meant to set up a standard maxim for free society, which should
be . . . constantly looked to, constantly labored for, and even though
never perfectly attained, constantly approximated, and thereby constantly
spreading and deepening its influence and augmenting the happiness and
value of life to all people of all colors everywhere."

For Further Reading

Becker, Carl L., *The Declaration of Independence.*
Jameson, J. F., *The American Revolution Considered as a Social Movement.*
Morgan, E. S. and H. M., *The Stamp Act Crisis.*
Morris, Richard B., *The American Revolution Reconsidered.*
————, *The Peacemakers: The Great Powers and American Independence.*
Peckham, Howard H., *The War for Independence.*

28   The French Revolution

Louis XVI began his momentous reign in 1774. The time was critical
because France's enemy Britain was having serious difficulties with the
American colonies. With a view to hurting the British and undoing some of
the damage the French had suffered from their defeat in the Seven Years'
War, Louis' government gave substantial financial assistance to the Americans. This French aid enabled the Americans to win their war of independence, but it complicated the already baffling difficulties of Louis' government. For although France was a rich country, the French government
was repeatedly on the brink of bankruptcy because those with the capacity
to pay taxes failed to bear their share of the burden. In addition, as
scholars have emphasized recently, the growth rate of the French economy
left much to be desired, and this further complicated the difficulties of the
monarchy.

Year after year Louis sought advice from experts about the financial
woes of his government, but to act on that advice invariably meant that
some privileged group would lose some of its traditional exemptions. By
1787 the financial situation had become desperate, and so in the very year
that the Philadelphia Convention met to draw up the American Constitution, Louis XVI summoned 140 leaders of the French aristocracy, both lay
and ecclesiastical, to an Assembly of Notables, requesting that they con-

A.D. 1789 Meeting of the Estates General; conversion of Estates General into National Assembly; fall of the Bastille; Decrees Abolishing the Feudal System

1790 Civil Constitution of the Clergy

1791 King forgiven after attempt to flee from France; Legislative Assembly convenes

1792 Beginning of war with Austria and Prussia; manifesto of the Duke of Brunswick; abolition of the Monarchy and establishment of the Republic

1793 Execution of Louis XVI; arrest of the leaders of the Girondins

1793–1794 The Reign of Terror

1794 Elimination of the Hébertists; elimination of the Dantonists; fall of the Robespierrists

1794–1795 The Thermidorian reaction

1795 Constitution establishing the Directory; dissolution of the Convention

1795–1799 The Directory

1796–1797 Italian campaign of Napoleon Bonaparte

1799 Overthrow of the Directory and establishment of the Napoleonic Consulate

---

sent to abandon some of their traditional fiscal privileges. Instead of cooperating with the monarchy to which they owed their special status, these notables hid behind a host of legalisms and insisted that they had no right to do what their king wished them to do. They urged the summoning of the old parliamentary assembly, the Estates General, last convened in 1614, arguing that it alone could legally deal with the fiscal crisis.

Thus the very aristocrats who benefited most from the old regime were the first to undermine it. They took advantage of the plight of their king to reassert their own authority and to reverse the whole trend of modern French history in the direction of strong centralized monarchy. Although aristocrats and their apologists everywhere like Edmund Burke and Friedrich von Gentz were soon eager to forget what they had done, the fact remains that they started resistance to the Crown—the Great French Revolution began as an aristocratic revolt. In 1787 French nobles were

still fighting the memory of Richelieu, Mazarin, and Louis XIV. Dissatisfied with government of the people, by the king, for the aristocracy, they
sought government of the people, by the aristocracy, for the aristocracy.
The instrument of revolt would be the Estates General, they thought, for
aristocrats, after all, controlled the first estate (the clergy) and the second
estate (the nobility). Since voting, they expected, would take place by
order, the two upper estates could always outvote the third, which represented the commoners.

After the dissolution of the Assembly of Notables, the king was subjected to enormous pressures to convene the Estates General. From almost
everywhere in his realm and from all sections of society came petitions
begging him to resurrect the old institution. Louis XVI, a good-natured,
kind-hearted nonentity who wished to be the ruler of a happy people, at
last consented. Once he did so, however, new pressures confronted him.
For aristocrats, whether laymen or ecclesiastics, insisted that the old
system of voting by order continue. Otherwise they would speedily lose
control of the course of events. But articulate commoners, and some of
their radical allies in the privileged estates, wanted the third estate to have
what came to be called double representation—some 600 representatives
for the third estate as opposed to about 300 representatives each for the
clergy and the nobility. The king at last yielded, but he refused to act on
the critical request of spokesmen for the third estate that voting be by head
in an Estates General whose three orders sat and voted as a single body
and which the third estate could therefore easily control.

When the Estates General met in May, 1789, the king insisted that it
had one purpose: to solve the financial problems of the government. But
few of his subjects shared his view. On the one hand, there were the nobles,
still eager to carry through their aristocratic revolt. On the other hand,
there were those members of the third estate who argued that their task
was really to draw up a written constitution for a modern France. After
weeks of delay, confusion, and frustration, three momentous events occurred. On June 17 the members of the third estate proclaimed themselves
a National Constituent Assembly and urged the members of the other
orders to sit with them—an unmistakable revolutionary step. Three days
later, on June 20, came the Tennis Court Oath: members of the newly
proclaimed Assembly swore that they would not disband until France had
a written constitution "established and consolidated upon firm foundations." A week later, on June 27, Louis XVI ordered the members of the
first and second estates to sit and vote with the third estate in a single body,
in effect legalizing the extralegal actions of the third estate. Voting by head
in the National Constituent Assembly meant the end of the aristocratic
revolution and the beginning of the antiaristocratic revolution.

The best-known event in the history of the Revolution, the fall of the Bastille on July 14, 1789, was important in its own time not as an attack on a symbol of royal tyranny but as a step to save the National Constituent Assembly. Troop movements in the neighborhood of Paris as well as the dismissal of the popular minister Jacques Necker gave rise to suspicions that the king had changed his mind about the concessions he had made in June and that he would now use force to get rid of the Assembly. Parisian sans-culottes—mostly small shopkeepers and artisans—moved on the Bastille to find arms and ammunition with which to defend the Assembly against the king's evil designs. Taking the Bastille was no great military feat, but it was a critical event because it demonstrated that ordinary people in Paris were determined that the Assembly should not be disbanded until it had finished its work. The British ambassador did not exaggerate greatly when he noted that after the fall of the Bastille "we may consider France as a free Country, the King a very limited Monarch, and the Nobility as reduced to a level with the rest of the Nation."

Beginning in the summer of 1789, the National Assembly undertook some momentous changes in the interests of liberty, equality, and fraternity, changes that would have reverberations not only in France, but in the rest of Europe and the world. These changes were above all antiaristocratic—designed, in other words, to deprive the higher orders of the special privileges they had long enjoyed in French society. At the same time, these reforms reflected the needs of other social groups—notably the peasants and the urban middle classes.

The first important reform of the Assembly, passed early in August, 1789, was the series of "Decrees Abolishing the Feudal System," which entirely did away with certain kinds of manorial obligations that peasants owed to their landlords and guaranteed that other manorial obligations would also be abolished after suitable compensation had been made to landlords. In keeping, however, with the opening words of the Decrees —"The National Assembly abolishes the feudal regime entirely . . ."— peasants assumed that the abolition was total, immediate, and without compensation, and so they became in many cases loyal supporters of the Assembly. Although the Decrees were important for peasants above all, they also contained provisions that made them meaningful to middle-class, that is, business and professional, people as well. They wiped out special tax privileges and the privileges of geographical districts, and they opened all offices to all citizens "without distinction of birth."

The next important revolutionary change made by the Assembly—and the document by which French Revolutionary ideas were transmitted to other countries—was the Declaration of the Rights of Man and the Citizen (late August, 1789). It contained a moving preamble that attributed public misfortunes solely to ignorance, forgetfulness, and contempt for the rights of man. To prevent these hateful forces from operating in the future, the National Assembly spelled out the basic human rights and duties—freedom of speech, press, and assembly, freedom of religion, equality of all people before the law, the obligation of all people to pay taxes in keeping with their means, rights of private property, and rights to justice on the basis of due process of law.

The third key reform of the Assembly was the Constitution, completed in 1791. It provided for a limited monarchy run by property owners. It divided the French into active and passive citizens according to the tax burden they bore. Active citizens—about three-quarters of the adult males —could vote and hold office; passive citizens could not. The Constitution further provided for a one-house legislature, the Legislative Assembly, which for all practical purposes would rule France. The king would have a suspensive veto—he could delay but not thwart the enactment of laws.

The fourth major reform of the National Assembly was the Civil Constitution of the Clergy. This had nothing to do with doctrinal matters but concentrated on the reorganization of the episcopal structure and the status of clergymen as civilians. Since the National Assembly had taken over church lands and issued bonds, certificates, and paper money (*assignats*) with those lands as security, it now assumed the obligation of paying clergymen's salaries. In return, the Civil Constitution required that the clergy be elected and that they take an oath of loyalty "to be faithful to the nation, to the law, and to the King, and to maintain with all [their] power the Constitution decreed by the National Assembly and accepted by the King."

Not surprisingly, Pope Pius VI condemned the Civil Constitution of the Clergy, and not surprisingly Louis XVI, as a good Roman Catholic, was deeply moved by the papal action. In addition, Louis opposed the measures that limited his authority and left him only "a vain semblance of monarchy." In despair, he and the royal family tried to flee from France in June, 1791, but their flight was hopelessly mismanaged, and they were caught some 150 miles from Paris in Varennes, near the German border.

The embarrassment of the members of the National Constituent Assembly was immense. Having worked for many months to reshape French government and society in an antiaristocratic mold and having drawn up the measures that embodied their view of the right kind of limited monarchy, they were now faced with a king who would not serve. Thus the summer of 1791 saw a great debate in the Assembly between those who said that the king should be forgiven if he would promise to conduct himself as a proper constitutional monarch, and those who insisted that the king was untrustworthy and that the establishment of a republic was there-

fore necessary. It was the flight to Varennes that created the French republican movement as a significant political force.

Since most members of the Assembly thought republicanism both an
alien and a dangerous doctrine, the group that favored the continuation of
the monarchy won a temporary victory: so the Assembly finally put the
Constitution of 1791 into effect. Elections were held, and the active citizens of France chose the members of what was to be known as the Legislative Assembly. Convened in October, 1791, this Assembly was faced
with one problem that overshadowed all others. Within a few months of its
meeting, war broke out between Austria and Prussia on one side and
France on the other—a war that began as an attempt to take advantage of
France's weakness but a war that became increasingly complicated as it
dragged on for almost a quarter of a century. The Assembly, therefore, had
one responsibility: to save France from the allies. The Prussians and
Austrians considered the time to be ideal not merely to stop the Revolution
but to reverse some of the defeats they had suffered at the hands of the
French in previous wars. Within France itself two groups were especially
eager for war: some republicans in the Legislative Assembly who were
convinced that the king could not be trusted and who saw in the war a
device by which to get rid of the monarchy and at the same time to bolster
the French economy; and the king's court group, which worked on the
assumption that the war could only benefit the Crown: if the king led
France to victory, then his prestige would mount appreciably. If France
lost, the allies would undoubtedly restore his authority.

In the early stages of the war, things went badly for the French. French
troops broke and fled; inevitably rumors spread about treason in high
places. Hence French aristocratic refugees, fearing for Louis' safety, prevailed on the Duke of Brunswick, the commander in chief of the Prussian
and Austrian forces, to issue an incredible manifesto: he warned that if any
harm was done to Louis and the royal family, Paris would be totally
destroyed. The impact of this warning was profound. Within France itself
the manifesto was speedily and understandably interpreted to mean that
the king was really on the side of the enemy (which documents discovered
later would prove him to be), and panic encouraged some ugly episodes of
violence, including Louis' confinement. The experiment in limited constitutional monarchy had failed, a casualty above all of the war and the fears
it inspired. New elections and a new constitution were necessary. The
manifesto which was to protect Louis XVI served instead to undermine his
position and usher in the democratic phase of the Revolution.

In the late summer of 1792, a new legislative and constitution-making
body—the Convention—was chosen by universal manhood suffrage,
though many of those eligible to vote did not do so. It met in September,

and its first important act was to proclaim the formal end of the monarchy and the establishment of the French Republic. Hardly did it convene when word arrived of the Battle of Valmy, an engagement from which the Prussians withdrew because of a heavy fog and which the French claimed as a victory. It was an auspicious beginning. The Republic and victory, it seemed, went hand in hand. Yet in the whole history of politics it would be hard to find a government which faced so many difficulties simultaneously as the Convention. It had to cope with a foreign war, a civil war between republicans and royalists, and a virtual civil war among republican factions.

The foreign war became more menacing especially after the British joined the allies early in 1793, for the British brought into play both their navy and what was called, after the younger William Pitt, "Pitt's gold." To many well-informed contemporaries it was only a question of time before the French would be defeated, the Republic overthrown, and the monarchy restored. That this did not happen was due above all to the lack of unity among the allies. Indeed, Prussia and Austria were busy with the partitioning of Poland in 1793 and 1795 when they should have been concentrating on the defeat of France, and so it turned out that Poland helped to save the French Republic.

But it was not the suffering of Poland alone. The morale of French troops in the face of dangers to their country was high. The Republic's use of "propaganda decrees," which assured foreign peoples that France would support their attempts to overthrow their decadent monarchies, was ingenious. And the *levée en masse*—a universal conscription of people and resources—gave all sections of the population a sense of participation in their country and their war. In the words of one of the most famous Republican decrees: "The young men shall go to battle; the married men shall forge arms and transport provisions; the women shall make tents and clothes, and shall serve in the hospitals; the children shall turn old linen into lint; the old men shall repair to the public places, to stimulate the courage of the warriors and preach the unity of the Republic and hatred of kings." At all events, the fears that arose because of the foreign war throw much light on what happened to the French Republic in its early years. The Reign of Terror, with its guillotining of suspects and traitors, is unthinkable except in the context of the war.

At the same time that the republicans were fighting the Austrians, Prussians, and British, they also had to fight those of their countrymen who remained loyal to the monarchy. This struggle became more intense after the execution of Louis XVI in January, 1793, for "a multitude of crimes." The British in particular tried to work with and finance French royalists. Indeed, like the foreign war, the civil war between royalists and republicans helped to inspire the fear and panic that made for the Reign of Terror.

Foreign war and civil war were alarming enough, but to make matters worse the Convention was torn by a frightening factionalism. Between September, 1792, and June, 1793, the chief contending factions were the Montagnards and the Girondins. The Montagnards, or men of the mountain, derived their name from their seats in the highest part of the hall in which the Convention met. The Girondins derived their name from the Gironde, the region of France whose chief town was Bordeaux, since some of their leaders came from that area. They were also known as the Brissotins, after their leader Jacques Pierre Brissot de Warville. Both Girondins and Montagnards were not well organized and disciplined political parties, but loose coalitions of groups and individuals. Both were dedicated revolutionists and republicans, but the Girondins regarded the establishment of the Republic as the virtual end of the revolution, tended to be wary of government intervention in social and economic life, and stood for the rights of localities as against the power of the central government. The Montagnards, on the other hand, despite variations within their ranks, inclined to view the establishment of the Republic as the real beginning of the revolution. Lacking the Girondins' fear of state intervention in social and economic life, they saw further reforms as necessary. In fact, they looked at government as a positive force to protect the poor who could not otherwise hold their own in a competitive society. They sought to create an egalitarian society of small producers, both rural and urban, among whom democracy could thrive.

The victory of the Montagnards over the Girondins came in June, 1793, and it had much to do with the discrediting of two of the most important leaders of the Girondins, General Charles François Dumouriez and Brissot. Dumouriez's desertion to the side of the enemy and Brissot's involvement in financial scandal made it possible for the Montagnards to eliminate the Girondins from any significant role in the Convention. Nevertheless, this was not the end of republican infighting. During the Reign of Terror, the year of Montagnard ascendancy in the Convention (June, 1793–July, 1794), the Montagnards themselves broke up into warring factions: Hébertists, Dantonists, Robespierrists. The leaders of the Hébertists, or Ultrarevolutionaries, staunch advocates of popular radicalism and the de-Christianization of France, were executed in March, 1794, because their fellow Montagnards feared that they were doing untold damage to the Republic by their extremism and particularly their anti-Catholic outbursts —their attacks on nuns and priests and their burning of churches. The leaders of the Dantonists, or Citra-revolutionaries, were executed in April, 1794, in part for their involvement in some ugly bribery scandals—with Danton himself unable to explain how he came to be rich—in part for their power. And even the Thermidorians, who successfully conspired to overthrow Robespierre and his allies in July, 1794, had no intention of ending the terror. They simply wished to eliminate Robespierre and his cohorts before they were eliminated by them, for the Robespierrists set and demanded hopelessly high standards of morality and virtue, both public and private, and they tended to see betrayers of the Revolution everywhere.

Yet, despite all the difficulties the Convention had to deal with—factionalism, civil war with royalists, and foreign war—the republicans carried through important reforms. They committed themselves to a democratic regime in the Constitution of 1793, accepting universal manhood suffrage, the principle of representation in relation to population, and guarantees of civil liberties. They wiped out all remaining manorial obligations without compensation for landlords. They introduced compulsory rationing, passed "maximum laws" fixing prices and wages in a period of wartime shortages, and made profiteering a capital crime—all measures explicitly designed to help the poor to compete for goods with the rich. And while the republicans believed that in principle private property is sacred they also believed that this principle applied only to loyal citizens. Traitors, on the other hand, ceased to be citizens. They had no property rights, and their property should be distributed among the poor and the landless in their neighborhoods. In the words of the short-lived Ventôse decrees of 1794: "All the communes of the Republic shall draft statements of the indigent patriots within their confines, giving name, age, occupation, and the number and age of their children. . . . [The Government] shall make a report on the means of indemnifying all the unfortunates with the property of enemies of the Revolution. . . ."

Yet the most revealing measures enacted by the republicans were not so much political and economic as social and cultural. Believing in human dignity, equality, and fraternity, the republicans tried to make these beliefs part of the fabric of French life. In the eloquent words of one of their decrees:

The French nation, oppressed, degraded during many centuries by the most insolent despotism, has finally awakened to a consciousness of its rights and of the power to which its destinies summon it. . . . It wishes its regeneration to be complete, in order that its years of liberty and glory may betoken still more by their duration in the history of peoples than its years of slavery and humiliation in the history of kings.

In this spirit the republicans abolished slavery in the French colonies as well as imprisonment for debt. They proclaimed their faith in free public education. They discouraged the use of aristocratic words like Madame (my lady) and Monsieur (my sir) and replaced them with Citoyenne and Citoyen. They changed royalist names like Louis to good republican names like Benjamin (Franklin) and George (Washington). They reworked the calendar to get rid of its heritage of unreason, superstition, and tyranny. Thus November, the "ninth" month which was really the eleventh month, became Brumaire (the foggy month); and July (*juillet*) and August (*août*), named after those despots Julius and Augustus Caesar, no longer were permitted to disgrace the French calendar. Indeed, the republicans made clear their sense of their own importance in the sweep of human history by proclaiming the founding of the Republic on September 22, 1792, as the first day of the first month of the Year I. Ushering in a new age, they rid themselves of the old calendar that embodied so much inhumanity of man to man. And all this they did even as they fought a foreign war, even as they fought a civil war, and even as they fought among themselves.

The Montagnards, who overthrew Robespierre in Thermidor, 1794 (July, the hot month), did not intend to end the terror. Nonetheless, the aftermath of the fall of the Robespierrists saw an unanticipated revulsion against terrorism among members of the Convention. In part this was simply a moral outburst against some of the injustices done against some innocent, or relatively innocent, people in 1793–1794. Even more important, it was a reflection of the growing confidence that France could wage a successful war against its foreign enemies without recourse to terrorism at home. At all events, the period of the Thermidorian reaction (1794–1795) saw the decline of much of the panic and fervor of the previous year. It also saw the undoing of the most important reforms of the Montagnards, so that their permanent legacy became mainly ideological. The democratic Constitution of 1793 was replaced with the Constitution of 1795, which provided for a relatively conservative republic dominated by middle-class voters and officeholders. Furthermore, the Convention ended much of the Montagnards' interventionist legislation like rationing and price controls as well as the measures providing for the redistribution of land among the landless. On the other hand, the Thermidorians did important constructive work in the sphere of education. Indeed, some of the educational reforms for which Napoleon has been given credit were, in fact, the work of the Thermidorians, who sought to create an elite to meet their bureaucratic needs.

The Constitution of 1795 provided that France should be ruled by a two-house legislature and five executives known as Directors, and so this government (1795–1799) has been known in history as the Directory. It had some impressive achievements to its credit. Above all, it did magnificently from a military point of view, chalking up some momentous victories and carrying the war actively to foreign soil. And, despite efforts to dislodge it, the Directory survived year after year—longer than any previous revolutionary assembly. For all that, the Directory did not fare well in history, and has not fared well in history books. It was looked upon as a corrupt regime in its own time, and once General Napoleon Bonaparte overthrew it in 1799 his propaganda machine made it seem much more corrupt and immoral than it had really been. Otherwise, after all, he would have been hard pressed to justify overthrowing it. In part, too, however, the bad reputation of the Directory has been due to its unfortunate location in time. It ruled during the period of letdown between the two most dramatic periods of the Revolution—the age of the Montagnards and the age of Bonaparte. It was, in short, a fine period to precede but especially to follow. As Bonaparte bluntly put it, "On my return to Paris I found division among all authorities, and agreement upon only one point, namely, that the Constitution was half destroyed and was unable to save liberty."

For Further Reading

Cobban, Alfred, *A History of Modern France,* Vol. I.
Hampson, Norman, *A Social History of the French Revolution.*
Kaplow, Jeffry (ed.), *New Perspectives on the French Revolution.*
Rudé, George, *Revolutionary Europe, 1783–1815.*

Index

Abbas I, Shah, 132
Abdul-Hamid II, Sultan, 139
Accademia dei Lincei, 211
Accademia del Cimento, 211
Adam, Robert and James, 263
Adams, John, 224, 273–275, 278
Adda River, 14
Adrianople, *see* Andrinople
Afghanistan, 146
Afghans, 152
Africa: Portuguese exploration and trade, 142–144; slave trade, 144–145
Africa, North, pirates, 68
Age of Reason, *see* Enlightenment
Agra, 146; Taj Mahal, 150
Ahmed I, Sultan, 132
Ahmed III, Sultan, 135
Aix-la-Chapelle, Treaty of (1668), 253
Akbar, Mughal Emperor, 146, 148
Akkoyunlu, 127
Alba (Alva), Fernando Alvarez de Toledo, Duke of, 70
Albania, 137
Albany, N.Y., 191, 196
Albert of Hohenzollern, 56
Alberti, Leon Battista, 15, 25, 26, 28; and perspective, 32, 34
Alboquerque, Alfonso d', 142
Alembert, Jean Le Rond d', 218, 222
Alexandria, 8
Alfonso, King of Naples, 28
Algeria (Algiers), 128
Allegory, 6
Alsace, 110, 255
Amazon River, 166
America: agriculture, beginning of, 167; American spirit, 178; discovery, 118, 142; exploration, 143–144; Treaty of Tordesillas (1494), Spain and Portugal, 118, 143; *see also* Latin America; North America
American colonies, 183–200; British policies on, 191–192, 272–273; charters, 185, 192; Continental Congress, 274; culture, 196; economic conditions, 198–199; ethnic strains in, 192–193; European wars in, 194, 200; first, 183,

185–187; local government, 197; migration to, 192–194; population growth, 192, 194; religious variety, 188–190, 193, 197–198; representative government, 185, 187–188, 197; towns and cities, 196; voting requirements, 197
American Magazine, 196
American Revolution, 270–280; causes of, 272–274; character of, 270; chronology, 271; effects of, 278–279; French alliance, 277–278, 280; French reaction to, 269; French Revolution and, 270; international aspects, 278; Loyalists (Tories), 270, 275, 276, 279; peace negotiations, 278
Ames, William, 186
Amish, 193
Amsterdam, 79; trade, 120–122
Anabaptists, 46–48, 53, 54, 58
Anatolia, Ottoman Turks in, 124, 127, 135, 136
Andes, ancient civilizations, 167–171
Andrinople (Adrianople), 127; Treaty of (1829), 138
Anglican Church, 58, 97, 100–101, 252, 263; in American colonies, 190, 193, 198, 279; Catholics and, 189; Puritans and, 183, 186–187
Angola, 144
Anjou, Duke of, 78
Ankara, Battle of, 127
Anne, Queen of Great Britain, 102
Anne of Austria, Queen of France, 251
Antwerp, 78, 120
Apollonius of Perga, 207
Appalachian Mountains, 196, 272
Arabs as traders, 153
Aragon, 70; revolt (1591), 71
Aranda, Conde de, 232
Archimedes, 204
Architecture: English, 263; Gothic, 86; Mughal, 150
Ariosto, Lodovico, 3; *Orlando Furioso,* 14
Aristocracy: English gentry, 93, 214–215; in France, 214–215, 281–282; in Italy,